Aristotle

on

**Dramatic Musical Composition**

# Aristotle on Dramatic Musical Composition

The Real Role of Literature, Catharsis, Music and Dance in the Poetics

Second Edition

Volume 2

**Gregory L. Scott**

ExistencePS Press
New York, NY

Second Edition

Volume 2

Paperback

Copyright © 2018

Gregory L Scott

All rights reserved.

New York, NY
United States of America

ISBN-13: 978-0-9997049-4-3

Library of Congress Control Number (LCCN):

2018930827

# Contents

| | |
|---|---|
| **VOLUME TWO** | 347 |
| | |
| **UNIT 2: CATHARSIS, PITY AND FEAR IN THE *DRAMATICS*** | 349 |
| | |
| **Preface to Chapter 5** | 351 |
| | |
| **Chapter 5: Purging the *Poetics*** | 353 |
| Section 1: Aristotle's theory of definition and the *Poetics* | 354 |
| Section 2: 'Clarification' and definitional procedure | 358 |
| Section 3: The solution using necessary and sufficient conditions | 361 |
| Section 4: Petruševski's solution, its problems, and an alternative | 366 |
| | |
| **Postscript to Chapter 5** | 377 |
| | |
| **Chapter 6: Additional Reasons Why Catharsis, Pity and Fear Cannot be Authentic in the Definition of Tragedy, including a Reply to Halliwell** | 379 |
| Pakaluk | 383 |
| Destrée | 384 |
| Halliwell | 393 |
| Two Final Moves | 440 |
| | |
| **UNIT 3: THE REAL GOAL OF TRAGEDY AND COMEDY** | 457 |
| | |
| **Chapter 7: The Real Goal of Tragedy and Aristotle's Response without Catharsis to Plato's Attack on Tragedy and Comedy** | 459 |
| Section 1: The Goals of Tragedy | 459 |
| Section 2: Aristotle's Response to Plato | 471 |
| Section 2a: How Aristotle Agrees—and Disagrees—with Plato on Tragedy | 471 |
| Section 2b: Aristotle's Defense of Comedy against Plato | 484 |
| | |
| **Chapter 8: The Real Role of Catharsis and the Importance of Comedy** | 491 |
| Conclusion of Units 2 and 3 | 500 |

# Unit 4: The *Dramatics* and Its New Future — 503

## Chapter 9: The Future of the *Dramatics* — 505

Section 1: Why Aristotle's *Dramatics* Directly Applies Nowadays Only to Musicals — 505
Section 2: The Dangers, and Rewards, of Extending the *Dramatics* to Literature or Other Arts — 508
Concluding Remarks — 511
Final Postscript: New Dance-Related Scholarship — 520

## Appendix — 523

A History of the Two Fundamental Misconceptions — 523
The *Dramatics* from 322 BCE to the 11th Century CE — 524
Avicenna (980–1037) — 529
Averroes (1126–1198) — 533
The Transition to the Renaissance — 540
Francesco Robortello (1516–1567) — 544
Julius Caesar Scaliger (1484–1558) — 548
Ludovico Castelvetro (1505–1571) — 551
Summary of the Italian Commentators and Additional Considerations — 553
The 17th and Early 18th Centuries — 558
Claude-François Menestrier (1631–1705) — 561
André Dacier (1651–1722) — 566
Lope de Vega (1562–1635) and Thomas Rymer (1643–1713) — 570
Later 18th, and 19th, Century Views — 574
Carlo Blasis (1795-1878) — 577
Jacob Bernays (1824-1881) — 580
20th-Century Views — 586
More on the History of the *Dramatics* as Literary Theory — 586
The Exceptional, "Wide" Interpretation of the *Dramatics* — 590
20th Century Criticisms of Aristotle — 593
Summary of the First Misconception: Literature versus Drama — 598
Summary of the Second Misconception: Catharsis in *Dramatics* 6 — 600

## Bibliography — 603

## Index — 623

# Aristotle on Dramatic Musical Composition

## The Real Role of Literature, Catharsis, Music and Dance in the Poetics

Second Edition

Volume 2

# VOLUME TWO

*Aristotle on Dramatic Musical Composition*

# UNIT 2: CATHARSIS, PITY AND FEAR IN THE *DRAMATICS*

*Aristotle on Dramatic Musical Composition*

# Preface to Chapter 5

As mentioned in the Introduction of Volume 1, the issue of *katharsis* is independent of the matters discussed in Unit 1 (that is, Chapters 1-4) and would be relevant whether tragedy is conceived as a species of literature or as a species of dramatic musical theater. However, if tragedy has music, then musical *katharsis* becomes more relevant, if also more complicated because of the parallel possibility of *katharsis* as a result of staged plot or as a result of purely literary fiction. In any event, *katharsis* is given as the only goal in the manuscripts in the definition in *Dramatics* 6. One might read the upcoming arguments, then, separately from those in Volume 1. Indeed, I expect some readers of this book to skip immediately to this Unit in order to ascertain why I think *katharsis* is inauthentic in the definition, given how famous—or infamous—*katharsis* has been in Western literary and dramatic theory since the Renaissance. The misconception that the *Poetics* is about literary theory was entirely new with my Ph.D. dissertation in 1992 and is still known by hardly anyone except perhaps a few dozen or few hundred specialists in the world. For these reasons, and for some additional ones, I reproduce here in Chapter 5 my "Purging the *Poetics*" (2003) that some have considered to be too incredible to be true and others refreshingly groundbreaking. It was the first publication to claim that the *whole* clause involving *katharsis*, pity, and fear in the definition is inauthentic even though I followed Petruševski on the matter of *katharsis* itself.

I fully realize that by including this article, I am slightly repeating one topic. That is, I present again in the upcoming Section 1 ("Aristotle's theory of definition and the *Poetics*") the biological division given in detail in Chapter 2 in Volume 1. However, this will be necessary for those who skipped Unit 1. Those who read that Unit can do their own skipping and continue onto Section 2 ("'Clarification' and definitional procedure") unless they wish a quick review. Nevertheless, they should also read the one-page preface before Section 1.

"Purging the *Poetics*," which is to say Chapter 5 *per se*, begins with the history of *katharsis* at the middle of the twentieth century, when its meaning as "purification" or "purgation" had long been rejected by a large part of the profession (and the history of this topic in the Appendix finishes at this moment). Before starting Chapter 5, though, and to save the reader from reading the Appendix first in order to cover the reasons for those rejections, let us review them now very briefly.

As has often been conveyed in others' work, although not always in the same place:
- Purgation as the goal of all tragedy would treat the audience as unduly pathological;[488]

---

[488] Heath confirms this, but he argues further that, regarding *Dramatics* 13 and 26, tragedy is, for in-

- The goal of *mousikē* or "music" (as aural tones or as the Greek sense "music and dance"), and by extension of other arts, is best seen in the *Politics* VIII 3 and 5 as "intellectual enjoyment," which has no end beyond itself, whereas *katharsis* in the *Politics* VIII 7 does have a further end, to bring relief;[489]
- Pity and fear, which are to be purged, are sometimes good emotions for Aristotle (as explained more throughout this Unit), and therefore should not be purged;
- Given his ethical and psychological theory, it makes no sense for Aristotle to say the two emotions become "purified," which is arguably a "category mistake." Moreover, leaving this matter aside, why would "pure pity" or "pure fear" be desirable? Even granting that pure fear was desirable, if one had pure fear, how could one mix it with (pure or impure) pity? The fear would no longer be pure, it seems; conversely, with pure pity.
- A metaphorical account is not allowed in a definition for Aristotle, according to his own strictures, and "purification" and "purgation" are metaphorical;
- Finally, if the two emotions are too strong and are to be purged *mildly* in order to achieve moderation, as so many commentators have believed (note especially Averroes in the Appendix), Aristotle needs to include "moderation" in the definition *as the goal*, either in lieu of or in addition to *katharsis*, given his principles of definition in the *Topics*.

Let us now proceed with the article from 2003 and examine more deeply the option that *katharsis* means "clarification." Then we continue to my final objective, showing why it was impossible for even a moderately skilled philosopher much less a brilliant one like Aristotle to have written the whole clause with *katharsis* in *Dramatics* 6.

---

stance, better than epic because of the better type of audience that prefers it, which Heath says would rule out catharsis (*op. cit.*, 1996, pp. xl-xli). For reasons we have seen already, however, and for more we see below, tragedy is better explicitly because, e.g., of the better pleasures compared to epic. It is Plato who uses the better type of audience, the wiser, older men, to say that *epic* is best. Thus, I think Heath gets the right conclusion for the wrong reasons. Aristotle raises in Chapter 26 as a hypothetical the claim that the less vulgar art (epic) appeals to the better audience, in laying out the antagonist's position, but he never states that *the better audience is the cause of tragedy getting ranked above epic*, and he rebuts the antagonist's arguments for reasons I gave in Chapter 2.

489   As noted, L. Spengel relied on this insight to refute Bernays even by the late 1800's (Smerdel, *op. cit.*, 1937, p. 39).

# Chapter 5: Purging the *Poetics*[490]

> We say that the catharsis was, for Aristotle, the Final Cause of tragedy, and that the Final Cause was so fundamental to his analytical system that we need feel no surprise if it is incorporated without warning in his Definition. I myself used to say this to pupils, year by year, until the thought occurred with more and more insistence: If it was so fundamental, why did Aristotle allude to it only in this oblique way, and then never refer to it again? (H. D. F. Kitto)[491]

ARISTOTLE says in *Poetics* 6: "Tragedy is a representation of an action that...is serious and complete... through pity and fear accomplishing the *katharsis* of such emotions." With respect to the translation of *katharsis* there, Alfred Gudeman in 1934[492] indicated that previous solutions, notably "purgation" and "purification," were unfeasible. Whether or not because of his work, Anglo-American scholars subsequently attempted new tacks, and a number of them, such as Gerald Else, Leon Golden and Martha Nussbaum, championed '(intellectual) clarification' as the translation, making it the leading contender of the last thirty years. One advantage of this reading, which its proponents stress, is that *katharsis* is then prefigured in the first five chapters. The prefiguring seems required because when Aristotle starts compiling the essential conditions of tragedy he states that the definition—literally, the 'limit of the essence' (*horon tēs ousias*)—follows from what has been said (1449B23), and neither 'purgation' nor 'purification' could satisfy this requirement because neither notion occurs before chapter 6.

Gudeman's view definitely influenced M. D. Petruševski, albeit in a different manner. In what was then Yugoslavia, he published an article in 1954 in which he argues, on the basis both of various lacunae or inconsistencies in the *Poetics* and of passages from Strabo and Plutarch, that Aristotle never wrote the famous words *pathēmatōn katharsin* ('the *katharsis* of ... emotions') in the definition of tragedy. Instead, Petruševski contends, the original words were *pragmatōn sustasin* ('the arrangement of ... incidents'), which were corrupted and then changed by a subsequent restorer to

---

490     [Originally printed (2003) by, and reprinted with the permission of, *Oxford Studies in Ancient Philosophy*. - GLS] I wish to thank Alexander Nehamas, John Brown, Nick Pappas, and Robert Crease for either commenting on previous versions of this paper or setting up sessions at which they were discussed. Also, I extend not only my gratitude to Julius Moravcsik for inviting me to the Stanford seminar on the *Poetics* in 1997, but my appreciation to the members, especially Richard McKirahan and Giovanni Ferrari, for at least listening to my forceful views. Finally, without Paul Woodruff's encouragement, this article might never have made it to publication.

491     H. D. F. Kitto, 'Catharsis', in L. Wallach (ed.), *The Classical Tradition* (Ithaca, NY, 1966), 133–47 at 136.

492     *Aristoteles: Peri Poietikes* (Berlin, 1934).

*mathēmatōn katharsin* ('the *katharsis* of ... learnings'), the words we actually have in our oldest manuscript, Parisinus 1741.[493] On the surface, Petruševski's resulting contention that the definition should in effect read 'tragedy is a representation of a serious and complete action...the arrangement of such incidents [that make up the action] ending in pity and fear' renders completely irrelevant the question of translating *katharsis*, until now perhaps the most basic perennial unresolved problem of the *Poetics*, gives much more coherence and unity to the definition and to the rest of the treatise, and dissolves a host of other problems. In 1969 one Portuguese scholar, António Freire, accepted this solution,[494] and in 1973 Teddy Brunius, after stating that he was inclined to believe Petruševski's conjecture, quipped with a touch of resigned irony that it 'is almost too elegant and too reasonable to be accepted at once'.[495] However, rather than gaining more acceptance, Petruševski's solution has virtually disappeared from the scholarly landscape, and in this article I shall argue that a favourable reception for it, or better yet, for something close to it, is long overdue.

## Section 1: Aristotle's theory of definition and the *Poetics*

Independently of Petruševski's arguments, in an earlier work I analysed in detail the definition of tragedy *vis-à-vis* Aristotle's general theories of definition.[496] My purpose was not to resolve the problem of *katharsis* but to demonstrate why, for instance, music and dance, together with language, are not only included in the definition of tragedy but always maintained in the *Poetics* by Aristotle as essential conditions of tragedy, a view that counters the prevailing habit of treating Aristotelian tragedy as a merely literary art form. Much of the following simply repeats that analysis pertaining to definition, which, as we shall see, has important ramifications for other parts of the definition, such as *katharsis*.

Before taking up the analysis, it is worth mentioning that many other commentators have already recognized the link between the definition of tragedy in chapter 6 and the divisions in chapters 1–5 that prepare the way for it, and they have also explored to some extent the manner in which the treatment adheres to Aristotle's theories of definition as found in his logical or scientific treatises. For instance, Margaret Battin remarks that the account of tragedy provides the only example in the Aristotelian

---

[493] That the manuscript is the oldest is confirmed by E. Lobel, *The Greek Manuscripts of Aristotle's* Poetics (Oxford, 1933), 6.

[494] 'A catarse trágica em Aristóteles', *Euphrosyne*, 3 (1969), 31–45.

[495] 'Catharsis', in P. Wiener (ed.), *Dictionary of the History of Ideas*, vol. i (New York, 1973), 264–70 at 270.

[496] G. Scott, 'The *Poetics* of Performance: The Necessity of Spectacle, Music, and Dance in Aristotelian Tragedy' ['Performance'], in S. Kemal and I. Gaskell (eds.), *Performance and Authenticity in the Arts* (Cambridge, 1999), 15–48.

treatises of the procedure that for Aristotle is crucial in generating scientific knowledge.[497] However, notwithstanding that some of these commentators recognize that the missing division for *katharsis* generates a serious problem for Aristotle, their attempted solutions to this problem, when proffered, have been very unsatisfactory, as a look at the final definition itself and the preliminary divisions themselves begins to reveal. Aristotle says:

> Let us now discuss tragedy, taking up its definition, which results from what has been said. Tragedy is a representation of an action that, having a certain magnitude, is serious and complete; in 'sweetened' language, each kind brought in separately in the parts of the work; in the manner of drama, not narrative; through pity and fear accomplishing the *katharsis* of such emotions [*di' eleou kai phobou perainousa tēn tōn toioutōn pathēmatōn katharsin*].

In Aristotle's words—or at least according to the generally accepted sense of the awkward Greek phrase in the manuscripts[498]—the definition has been assembled 'from what has been said'. This is often taken to refer to Aristotle's use of Platonic dichotomous diaeresis, which is the method employed when commencing from one and only one super-genus and terminating once the sought-after kind has been reached (see Figure 1).[499]

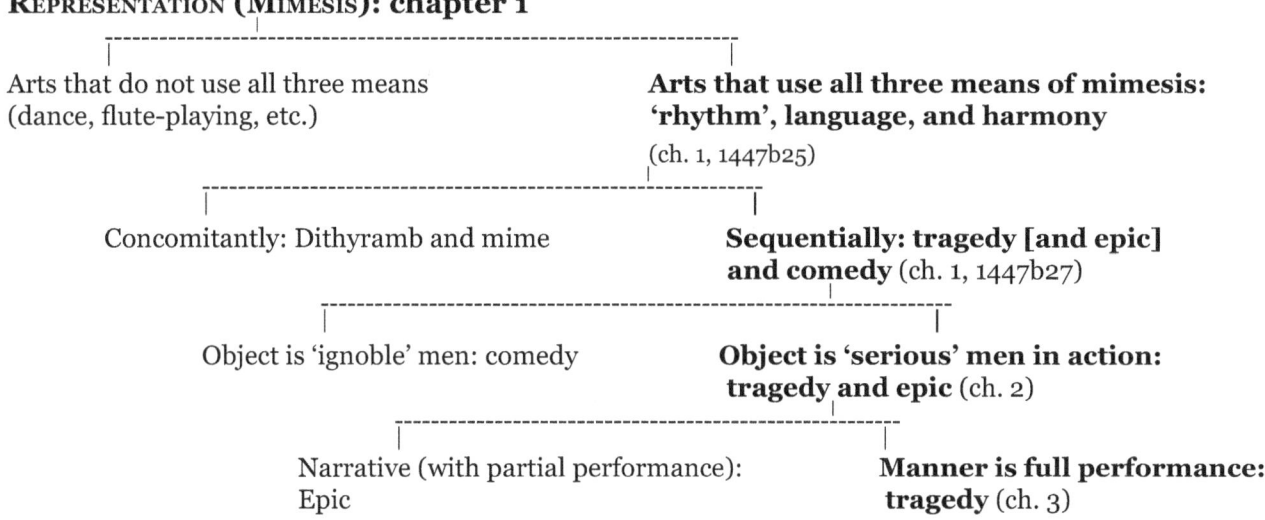

**FIG. 1. The dichotomous diaeresis (following Bywater)**

As one can easily determine from the figure, each right-hand condition gets included in the definition

---

497    M. P. Battin, 'Aristotle's Definition of Tragedy in the *Poetics*' ['Definition'], pts. 1–2, *Journal of Aesthetic and Art Criticism*, 33 (1974), 155–170; *Ibid.* (1975), 293–302 at 155.

498    D. W. Lucas discusses the problems with the Greek in *op. cit.*, 1968, p. 96. However one construes the passage, it is clear from the definition that its parts, except for the *katharsis* clause, come from previous mini-divisions (Scott, 'Performance', 20–3).

499    Thus e.g. I. Bywater, *Aristotle on the Art of Poetry* (Oxford, 1909), 98. Battin presents a slightly different diaeresis ('Definition', 298), but Bywater's divisions form the basis of it.

in chapter 6, although, as we shall see later in detail, Aristotle compresses 'rhythm',[500] language, and harmony into 'sweetened language'. However, these conditions from chapters 1–3 are incomplete: two conditions in the final definition, 'having a certain magnitude' and 'complete', are obtained from chapters 4 and 5 (1449a5, 15, 19, b11). Moreover, as indicated already, the term *katharsis* has no previous mention, much less a previous division, which, if Aristotle is indeed utilizing diaeresis, throws into doubt either the legitimacy of the term or that of the definition as a whole. This is because he says in *Posterior Analytics* 2. 13 that one should, when defining by division, admit only crucial elements, arrange them in the right order, and not omit any (97a22 ff.). Because he also insists in *Metaphysics* Z 12 that each differentia should stem correctly from any previous differentia,[501] the legitimacy of the definition of tragedy is also compromised because the final ordering of the parts is different from what is mandated by the preliminary divisions: the first 'cut' in chapter 1 concerns the means of mimesis—'rhythm', language, and harmony—but these means appear in the final definition *after* the object of mimesis, viz. a representation of good men in action, which itself had not been introduced until chapter 2.

However, we need not presume that Aristotle uses dichotomous division to define tragedy (nor need we even grant that he exploits any method articulated elsewhere, although the assumption that he is using one, *or a combination*, of his own methods is at least initially fair and will prove illuminating). Else believes[502] that Aristotle might instead be applying a second kind of definition, as found in his biological treatises, e.g. in *Parts of Animals* 1. 3. On this approach, one first makes a series of separate mini-divisions that need not have a common super-genus and then collects the final differentiae. The order of the final collection appears unimportant as long as all of the differentiae are collected. Yet even if Else is right on this point, as he might well be, *katharsis* has not been introduced in the

---

500   The word 'rhythm' (*rhuthmos*) is given in quotation marks because I argue ('Performance', 23–4) that it must mean something like 'ordered (body) movement', as it does explicitly for Plato at *Laws* 2, 665a, and because some translators render it as 'dance': see e.g. D. A. Russell and M. Winterbottom, *Ancient Literary Criticism* (Oxford, 1972), 91; also A. Bongiorno, *Castelvetro on the Art of Poetry: An Abridged Translation of Lodovico Castelvetro's* Poetica d'Aristotele vulgarizzata et sposta (Binghamton, NY, 1984), 55. The most common, innocuous transliteration as 'rhythm' and the more abstract 'temporal ordering' are actually deceptive, in spite of the fact that *rhuthmos* comes right after a remark about music in chapter 1, a remark that also involves the word *rhuthmos*. However, musicians 'moved in an ordered fashion' in order to play or 'danced' while playing (see e.g. *Poet.* 26, 1461a30 and 1462a7). Indeed, for Aristotle an extremely powerful case can be made that music is only possible given ordered body movement (note, for instance, *Poet.* 20, 1456b31 ff., and how spoken—and by implication, sung—syllables are formed by different conformations of the mouth).

501   1038a25–35. Without taking account of the *Posterior Analytics* and *Metaphysics* Z 12, Battin says, 'the order of the differentiae is slightly changed, but this of course has no effect upon the accuracy of the definition' ('Definition', 295). She may be right, for reasons I offer later, but then these reasons take us away from the kind of definition she assumes Aristotle is using.

502   G. Else, *Aristotle's* Poetics: The Argument [*Argument*] (Cambridge, Mass., 1963), 16.

first five chapters of the *Poetics*. Aristotle's account, therefore, of 'the limit of the essence' of tragedy cannot be legitimate on either of his two 'scientific' types of definition.

Many scholars, including James Hutton, seem not to recognize this problem fully.[503] Else, of course, notes the omission but apparently does not think a solution is needed, because he never discusses the issue.[504] Battin recognizes the problem but without any supporting argument says, 'the fact that he [Aristotle] was willing ... to spoil an otherwise perfectly straightforward and rigorous definition to include the notion of *katharsis* suggests that he accorded it more than ordinary importance, and surely considered it a central feature of tragedy'.[505] However, showing in one respect a greater appreciation of Aristotle's general concern for consistency, and as hinted at already, proponents of the clarification view argue that the mention of (pleasure in) learning in chapter 4 provides the necessary antecedent to the occurrence of *katharsis* in chapter 6. The following investigation will disclose, though, why their solution misses the mark.[506]

---

503  Hutton does recognize very well the connection of the general theory of definition in the *Posterior Analytics* to the *Poetics*, but seems to want to explain away the elements that actually come from chapters 4 and 5 and ignores the germane problem of *katharsis* (*Aristotle's* Poetics [*Poetics*] (New York, 1982), 9–13).

504  Else, *Argument*, 221–32, 439 ff. He interprets *ek tōn eirēmenōn ton ginomenon horon tēs ousias* as referring to a process of becoming: '[Let us talk about tragedy] picking out from what has been said the definition of its essence as it was (which was, which we saw in process of) becoming' (222). Yet he still says that the 'items in the definition ... are in fact taken both from the systematic chapters 1–3 and from the "history" [of chapters 4–5]' (*ibid.*). Even if the definition is in the process of 'becoming', this may only mean that Aristotle is finished with the preliminary divisions and is now ready to collect the final characteristics. It need not mean that an unmentioned condition is being imported spontaneously into the final definition. I might add that it is obvious from the rest of chapter 6 that Aristotle, once he begins explaining the terms of the definition, has finished the formal account of the definition itself.

505  'Definition', 301.

506  J. Lear, 'Katharsis', *Phronesis*, 33/3 (1988), 297–326, repr. in A. O. Rorty (ed.), *Essays on Aristotle's Poetics* [*Essays*] (Princeton, 1992), 315–40 at 318–326, offers very persuasive reasons, usually different from those I advance, why *katharsis* cannot mean 'clarification' in the *Poetics*. L. Golden attempts to rebut those criticisms in *Aristotle on Tragic and Comic Mimesis* [*Tragic Mimesis*] (Atlanta, 1992). A. D. Nuttall, *Why Does Tragedy Give Pleasure?* [*Tragedy*] (Oxford, 1996), to some extent accepts Lear's arguments, addresses (11–14) the view of M. Nussbaum ('Tragedy and Self-Sufficiency', in Rorty, *Essays*, 261–90), and, without grappling with any of the rigorous arguments *against* the purgation theory, adds: 'the case meanwhile for the full, medical sense, "purgation", remains strong. The parallel in the *Politics* is decisive' (15). The purgation theory, however, is actually still utterly weak, as has been established by many scholars (e.g. Lear, 'Katharsis'; A. Nehamas, 'Pity and Fear in the *Rhetoric* and the *Poetics*' ['Pity and Fear'], in Rorty, *Essays*, 291–314; and F. Sparshott, 'The Riddle of Catharsis', in E. Cook *et al.* (eds.), *Centre and Labyrinth: Essays in Honour of Northrop Frye* (Toronto, 1983), 14–37), and Nuttall never addresses their criticisms, nor does he seem to recognize the problems pertaining to definition and to the *Posterior Analytics* that are central to this paper.

## Section 2: 'Clarification' and definitional procedure

First, some more background. The translation of *katharsis* as 'purgation' or 'purification' is typically based on *Politics* 8. 7, in which Aristotle distinguishes five goals of music—education, *katharsis*, enjoyment, recreation, and relaxation—and in which he says he will explain *katharsis* further in a treatise on poetry. In that chapter, *katharsis* is intimately connected with the states of pity, fear, and 'ecstasy' (1342a6 ff.). Similarly, *katharsis* in the definition of tragedy is intimately connected with pity and fear: it arises *through* (*dia*) them. However, because of contradictions with other, core Aristotelian doctrines, plus, again, the fact that neither notion occurs before chapter 6, 'purgation' or 'purification' cannot be a legitimate translation. Accordingly, 'clarification' is proposed as the alternative rendering for the *Poetics*, a reading which is inspired both by Plato's occasional, and undeniable, use of the term to mean a cognitive process that involves a transition from a less wise to a wiser state and by the following claims:

(i) Because Aristotle is only or chiefly concerned with educational goals in the *Politics*, a subject that has its own first principles, *katharsis* has a different meaning there from the one it bears in the *Poetics*.[507]

(ii) Aristotle emphasizes learning throughout his own works,[508] along with (the pleasure of) learning in *Poetics* 4. Assuming that clarification is a part of, or synonymous with, learning, this provides one of the retrospective links that Aristotle's theory of definition requires for the term *katharsis*.

(iii) Aristotle also states in *Poetics* 14 and 26 that pleasure is the goal of poets, which seems to provide a second, supporting link between the final cause of tragedy, *katharsis* as clarification (or learning), and the 'pleasure of learning' in chapter 4.

As we shall see, however, even though we can readily accept the first part of (ii) with the caution that Aristotle never ranks learning over an overall happiness that itself includes pleasure (see *Nicomachean Ethics* 10), neither the rest of (ii) nor (iii) can be plausibly maintained, which, in spite of the many fascinating issues pertaining to the *Politics*, renders (i) immaterial.[509]

---

507  Golden, *Tragic Mimesis*, 7–11.

508  *Metaphysics* A 1; *Poetics* 4; *Politics* 8. 7, esp. 1342a15–16.

509  The relation of the *Poetics* to the *Politics* is extremely complex and would take a book to discuss. A few basic points, though, can be presented here as prima facie evidence that there are crucial consistencies between the treatises and that merely asserting that the two works have different first principles is not enough to establish the views of Golden *et al*. First, clarificationists speak simply of different first principles without, surprisingly, presenting their nature precisely. What, though, are they for Aristotle? The question is vexing, and we can readily admit that there are some differences in the goals of the two treatises (an emphasis on education being a concern in certain chapters of the *Politics*). However, clearly there are similarities, too. For instance, both treatises strive to reach truth. More importantly in the current context, both share the same goal pertaining to the art forms that each treats: Aristotle emphasizes enjoyment as the primary end of music in the *Politics*, and pleasure as the end of poetry in the *Poetics*. I shall examine in the body of this paper the goal of pleasure; suf-

## Chapter 5: "Purging the *Poetics*"

Let us, then, examine whether *katharsis* as 'clarification' has been reasonably anticipated in a preliminary division before chapter 6.

Clarificationists assert, as noted, that the 'cut' takes place with the phrase 'pleasure in learning' in chapter 4. However, as Lear has aptly remarked,[510] pleasure in learning is given explicitly at the beginning of that chapter only as one of the origins of poetry in general, not as any goal of tragedy. In support of Lear it should be added that Aristotle states in chapter 4 with respect to the visual arts that one can take pleasure in the colours or in the technical skill if one does not know the object of a representation (1448b18). One implication of this, clearly, is that we need not learn anything from visual art and that no clarification is crucial—the pleasure will be sufficient in and of itself. It follows both that pleasure in the mere technical skill, or in the analogous formal properties, of tragic drama will be sufficient at times as an end and that clarification is not always required.

Another reason why 'pleasure in learning' does not provide the relevant preliminary cut for *katharsis* stems from the fact that the other terms in the definition of tragedy are pellucidly identical to their corresponding ones in the previous divisions, with one seeming exception, 'sweetened language'. Obviously realizing that he has introduced a fresh term, though, Aristotle immediately says in the sentence after the definition (1449b28) that sweetened language means 'that which involves "rhythm"

---

fice it to say here that *diagōgē*, translated usually as 'enjoyment' or 'leisure' but by Golden as 'intellectual enjoyment' *(Tragic Mimesis,* 13), is given by Aristotle in the *Politics* as the primary goal of music, for which the pertinent examples are listed with no ambiguity in 8. 3 and 5: being delighted by a bard and listening to the voice of a minstrel (1338a21–32; 1339b17–40). Aristotle denies, furthermore, that *diagōgē* always includes acquisition of knowledge (especially 1338a11 ff.) and says that learning is associated with pain (1339b29). Besides, just as pleasure for him is part of the best life *(NE* 7. 11–14 and bk. 10; *Pol.* 8. 3 and 5, esp. 1338a6 and 1339b25 ff.), so enjoyment or leisure is the first principle of political life *(Pol.* 1337b31 ff.). Finally, and most importantly perhaps, he emphasizes in *Pol.* 8. 3 (1338b2) that noble men should not always be concerned for things, including music, that have utility. This repeats his principle from the *Nicomachean Ethics* that the most virtuous man 'will possess beautiful and profitless things rather than profitable and useful ones; for this is more proper to a character that suffices to itself' (4. 3, 1125b12–13, trans. W. D. Ross). Thus, in *diagōgē* the experience is an end in and of itself, with no utility, whereas learning (including clarification) and *katharsis* (as used in the *Politics)* have knowledge and health as their respective ends.

    Other scholars have long noted parts of this. For instance, Hutton correctly stresses in numerous places that 'pleasure (which need not be mindless) is the only external purpose for poetry that the *Poetics* recognizes' *(Poetics,* 11; also 8–9, 14, 18–19), and further states that 'for both Plato and Aristotle...poetry...is distinguished from rhetoric by its form of imitation and by the fact that its sole aim is to give pleasure' (22). G. M. A. Grube also notes that Aristotle perpetuates the Homeric tradition, which itself holds that art is primarily or solely for pleasure *(The Greek and Roman Critics,* Toronto: Univ. of Toronto Pr., 1965, p. 3). In short: assuming that enjoyment and pleasure are at least functionally equivalent, Aristotle consistently maintains the purpose of two fine arts across treatises, something to which clarificationists pay too little heed.

510    'Katharsis', 321–2.

and harmony, i.e. choral composition [*legō de hēdusmenon men logon ton echonta ruthmon kai harmonian kai melos*]'. 'Rhythm' and harmony, I have shown, are used just as Plato explicitly uses the two terms in *Laws* 2 (665 a), as 'ordered body movement' and 'ordered voice' (see n. 10 [= footnote 500 in this reprint]), and had been listed in chapter 1 along with language as the means of mimesis that are necessary to tragedy (1447b25). As I demonstrate further,[511] *kai melos* should not be translated in the usual way—as 'and song'—but rather as something like 'that is, choral composition', and this whole 'sweetened language' is an essential ingredient of tragedy. In any event, no matter how one wishes to treat *melos* here, clearly Aristotle is concerned with explicating 'sweetened language', the only term in the definition (apart from the *katharsis* clause) that was not used in exactly the same way in a preliminary mini-division.

Accepting the clarification view, therefore, entails accepting that Aristotle very oddly changes his behaviour, from repeating straightforwardly *all* of the previous differentiae to presenting utterly without warning the phrase 'pleasure in learning' from chapter 4 in a new and completely strange form, as '*katharsis* (through pity and fear)'. The oddness of this move cannot be overemphasized. Not only were 'pity' and 'fear' themselves never introduced before chapter 6, but on reflection it is rather stunning to think that Aristotle would expect (intellectual) clarification to come *through pity and fear*. A clarificationist might be bold enough to accept this position,[512] and perhaps even to take advantage of the *mathēmatōn katharsin* in our oldest manuscript so that the *katharsis* phrase reads 'through pity and fear accomplishing the clarifications of such learnings'; but even if they can cleverly defend this idea (and, for instance, explain how pity and fear can be learnings), they will shortly flounder, I contend, on two indubitable Aristotelian texts, namely, the rest of chapter 6 and the whole of chapter 4. Regarding chapter 6: to rephrase Kitto's point that opened this paper, even if we assume that *katharsis* means 'clarification', Aristotle subsequently spends many paragraphs in chapter 6 discussing all of the other essential conditions (of which more in the next section) and many chapters examining secondary issues, but not a single sentence in the whole treatise referring to the crucial clarification. Moreover, the discussion of learning in chapter 4 revolves around the recognition of an object and around youngsters copying their elders. Even allowing that *catharsis* means clarification, Aristotle should then have said in the definition in chapter 6 that the clarification results *through the recognition of a mimetic original* or something similar, not through pity and fear. Finally, with respect to (iii) above, namely, to the supposed link between *katharsis* and the (pleasure of) learning in chapter 4 via the goal of pleasure in chapter 14: the pleasure noted in chapters 14 and 26 that tragedians are

---

511 'Performance', 29–31.

512 Nussbaum differs from Golden on this point, believing that clarification can actually come through pity and fear in a relevant way for Aristotle ('Tragedy and Self-Sufficiency', 281–2). See Nuttall, *Tragedy*, 12–13, for some counter-arguments. More crucially, though, in the context at hand, Nussbaum has not addressed the problem of pity and fear missing from all previous divisions.

supposed to strive for is, as we shall see shortly, never restricted to learning. In fact, as Aristotle's comparison of the pleasure of tragedy and epic in chapter 26 will also reveal shortly, that pleasure is clearly *not* one of learning, which undercuts any remaining argument that links *katharsis* of chapter 6 to learning in chapter 4.

Given all of the above, it is extremely implausible that *catharsis* could mean 'clarification' in *Poetics* 6. Chapter 4 in no way provides a cut for the *katharsis* clause; the clause has consequently not been derived from any previous division, and Aristotle's definition remains in dire jeopardy.

### Section 3: The solution using necessary and sufficient conditions

One way of resolving the problem of how *katharsis* surfaces magically in the definition is to imagine that Aristotle employs a third kind of definition that is briefly described in the *Posterior Analytics*. This kind consists of laying down necessary and sufficient conditions, stresses finding the combination of features that gets the extension of a term right, and contains no requirement that initial divisions be presented before a summation takes place (2.13, 96a24–b24). On this scenario, Aristotle could have included the *catharsis* clause in the definition of tragedy, no matter what *katharsis* means, without employing previous corresponding mini-divisions. Indeed, he could have included the clause even if he wishes, as he seemingly does, to rely on mini-divisions for all of the other final differentiae, because the third type of definition does not forbid the use of mini-divisions—it simply does not *require* them. Alternatively, if, as is often supposed, the *Poetics* is a series of lecture notes, he could have added the *katharsis* clause some years after a first redaction. Perhaps he had come to realize the greater benefits of the third type of definition while also realizing that the other terms in the definition would have fortuitously resulted anyway from that third type. Lastly, perhaps Aristotle utilizes no recognized methodology in spite of surface appearances and merely includes *katharsis*, intuitively and correctly.

Do any of these solutions, however, really withstand examination? First, if Aristotle included the *katharsis* clause in his initial draft, why did he incorporate the prefatory phrase indicating that the definition 'results from what has already been said', when in fact nothing had been said about *katharsis*? If he added the *katharsis* clause in a later redaction, why keep the prefatory phrase, when it could easily have been deleted without impairing the sense of the passage? More importantly, granting for the sake of argument that he lazily kept the prefatory phrase—or following Dupont-Roc and Lallot, who think that *katharsis* stems from chapter 4 and who read *apolabontes* rather than *analabontes* in the prefatory phrase[513] and thus interpret it to mean 'starting from what has already been said'—why

---

513   R. Dupont-Roc and J. Lallot, *Aristote: La Poétique* (Paris, 1980), 186–90.

does Aristotle not give *any* explanation of *katharsis* in the rest of the treatise? The term itself is only introduced a second and last time in chapter 17, when Aristotle indicates how a playwright should sketch the outline of a plot and then fill in the details. Offering the drama of Orestes as an illustration, Aristotle recounts that the protagonist is captured because of his madness and saved by means of the purificatory rite (*dia tēs katharseōs*); but this sense of *katharsis* as purification is, everyone now agrees, something not all tragedies are intended by Aristotle to have and is not directly connected to the definition.

The subsequent omission of any relevant occurrence of *katharsis*—or of any proper synonym that conveys clarification—in the *Poetics* is especially troubling with respect to the rest of chapter 6. The *raison d'être* of this chapter is obviously to explain further the elements in the definition, which get reformulated as six necessary conditions—plot, character, 'thought', language, music, and spectacle— and *each and every one* except those in the *catharsis* clause is covered in significant detail there and at some length in subsequent parts of the treatise. Even music and spectacle are treated with some concern in chapter 6 (and then in chapters 12,[514] 18, 24, and 26), although Aristotle prefers to leave a fuller discussion of these two elements to other treatises or to other thinkers. Hence, even granting that Aristotle himself wrote the *katharsis* clause in a later redaction, we might well ask why he did not add any relevant explanation in chapter 6, if only a brief note that he would discuss *katharsis* later.

It has been said that *katharsis* supplies the final cause of tragedy, that the other elements in the definition are formal or material causes, and that if Aristotle only desires to explicate these latter types of causes in chapter 6, he has good reason not to mention *katharsis*.[515] However, this reply ignores the fact that there he does briefly mention the function of tragedy (1450a31) and also the effects of tragedy, including, for instance, that of spectacle (1450a16–20). Much more tellingly, he says in chapter 6 that 'the plot is the end and purpose of the tragedy, and the end is everywhere the chief thing' (1450a22 ff.). It is the plot, therefore, and not *katharsis* that is the end of tragedy, and for him not to add a qualifying remark at this point would be a lapse of immense proportions were *catharsis* indeed the final cause.

Other chapters in the *Poetics* dealing with the function of tragedy also exhibit a disregard for *katharsis*—again, were it really part of his definition. In chapter 14, when analysing the best plots, Aristotle declares that we should not seek from tragedy every kind of pleasure but the one proper to it, and that the poet should use representation to produce the pleasure (*hēdonē*) from pity and fear (1453b10–14). *Katharsis* is never even alluded to here, although some apparently think—for reasons,

---

514  This corrects "Ch 14" in the original article.
515  I owe this to Walter Watson.

however, that will not withstand scrutiny—that pleasure and *katharsis* are being used co-referentially by Aristotle.[516] What chapter 14 actually and simply shows is that for Aristotle the psychological end of at least some kinds of tragedy (as we shall see later, those with the best plots) is to give a kind of pleasure that also involves a kind of pain, viz. pity or fear or both, analogous, we might say, in simplistic culinary terms to eating bittersweet chocolate. It is the kind of mixed pleasure and pain that Plato notes in the *Philebus*, for which tragedy and comedy are cited as examples, and which has nothing to do with *katharsis*.[517]

Another discussion from which the term *katharsis* is conspicuously absent occurs in chapter 26, when Aristotle ranks tragedy above epic. On all of the traditional readings, *katharsis*, whether it means purgation, purification, or clarification, is somehow supposed to make the audience better. When we remember that both epic and tragedy for Plato can be harmful art forms because of their content, and that epic can corrupt as easily as tragedy *(Republic* 3), we cannot help noticing that generating *katharsis* would be a prominent advantage of tragedy. It is very surprising, then, that Aristotle does not utilize *katharsis* to help accord tragedy favoured status. Rather, the only advantages he lists are that tragedy (i) is more compressed and thus gives a more intense experience than epic because the

---

516   For example, Elizabeth Belfiore claims: 'When Aristotle writes in *Poetics* 6 that "tragedy is imitation... accomplishing...katharsis", he is using "katharsis" where he uses "pleasure" elsewhere, to refer to the *telos* and *ergon* of tragedy' *(Tragic Pleasures: Aristotle on Plot and Emotion* [*Tragic Pleasures*] (Princeton, 1992), 259). However, two considerations obviate the co-referentiality of pleasure with *katharsis*.

First, pleasure is not referring to the *telos* ('end') and *ergon* ('work' or 'function') of tragedy—it *is* the end of tragedy (or, given our realization earlier that plot is the explicit artistic end, is at least the psychological end). If Belfiore means they both refer to the same psychological phenomenon, then we need only go to *Pol.* 8. 7, 1342a15–16, where Aristotle highlights the pleasure associated with *katharsis* but differentiates the two terms: the pleasure follows afterwards when one's unpleasant emotions are purged, and is clearly different from the purging itself. Belfiore might reply that this passage is irrelevant, because she says, 'I agree with Golden that *katharsis* should be connected, in particular, with the discussion of learning in *Po.* 4' *(Tragic Pleasures*, 258). However, even then other passages from the *Politics* throw a shadow on her view: Aristotle says unambiguously that learning—and by implication clarification—is associated with pain (1339a29), which means, in spite of his focus on the pleasure of learning in *Poetics* 4, that the issue of identifying clarification with pleasure, or using them as co-referential terms, is not a simple matter and cannot merely be asserted.

Second, as we saw earlier, Aristotle takes pains to use the same terms in the definition as in the previous mini-divisions. Given that he has the standard word for pleasure, *hēdonē*, in his vocabulary, a word that had already been incorporated in chapter 4 (1448B18), it is remarkable that he would instead use *katharsis* in chapter 6 as a co-referring term. In fact, that he would have explained *katharsis* in chapter 6, had he used it in an unusual way, is suggested by his concern to explain the new term 'sweetened' in the definition, as noted before.

517   At *Phileb.* 48 a Plato says that 'the audience at tragedy and comedy feel pleasure and weep at once', and at 50 b he reports that 'pleasure is mixed with pain in lamentations, tragedy, and comedy'. For more on pleasure and two kinds of pain—pity and fear—in Aristotle, see E. Belfiore, 'Pleasure, Tragedy and Aristotelian Psychology', *Classical Quarterly*, NS 35 (1985), 349–61. She gives an illuminating account that, in her own words, 'has the advantage of not depending on a particular view of *catharsis*' (349).

concentrated pleasure is better than the diluted one; (ii) has equal vividness in reading as in representation; (iii) can use not only the metres that epic employs but others as well; and (iv) includes all the elements that epic has plus music and spectacle, which give the most palpable pleasures (1462a15–17). One ramification and one question arise immediately from this comparison. The ramification is that the pleasure with which Aristotle is concerned is obviously not one of clarification or of learning. The question is: why does he stress pleasure and not invoke *katharsis* (as clarification or as anything else) at this opportune moment? The answer cannot be that epic, like the ecstatic melodies discussed in *Politics* 8. 7, also gives a *katharsis*, and that the common denominator thereby cancels the benefit of tragedy. The reason for this is that *katharsis* is not included at all in the entire account of epic.

It has been suggested both that *katharsis* should be the goal of that art form for Aristotle, whether he has said it or not, and that *katharsis* plays a central part in his defence of poetry in general. With respect to this dual claim we may admit all of the following: when defining epic, he says that its plots should be constructed dramatically, about a single whole action with a beginning, middle, and end, all of which is said about tragedy (1459a17 ff.); in chapter 24 he indicates that epic has reversals, recognitions, and sufferings, which are the factors cited in chapter 18 that help the dramatist accomplish the tragic effect; and in chapter 14 Aristotle asserts not only that pity and fear in tragedy can be produced without spectacle but that the poet places more reliance on the plot for the effect, so that in merely hearing the story a spectator will react accordingly, all of which obviously could apply to epic. Consequently, because for Aristotle epic and tragedy can in many ways be alike with respect to at least the story-making, the epic poet arguably should be able to produce some sort of *katharsis*. Plato implies as much himself in the *Ion*, for in this dialogue the epic rhapsode who is the title character maintains that he goes out of his senses when interpreting Homer and that, as a result, the audience weeps and casts terrible glances, apparently experiencing both pity and fear (535d). Hence, whether or not Plato recognized the entailments of this statement, an easy potential for *katharsis* in epic would seemingly exist for Aristotle.[518]

Apparently for reasons like these, some commentators state that epic has *katharsis*, or at least pity and fear, as a goal. For instance, Hutton says that the *Poetics* ends 'with a comparison of tragedy and epic in order to show that the common function (the stirring of pity and fear) is best performed by tragedy' (*Poetics*, 6). Kenneth Telford affirms that 'as chapter 26 states, tragedy and epic have the same function—namely the catharsis of pity and fear',[519] and Stephen White contends that tragedy's

---

[518] Stephen Halliwell says, 'epic *katharsis* ought to be entailed by Ar.'s own comparison between tragedy and epic at 59b7–15; it was widely accepted in the Renaissance (though often for the wrong reasons), and has been in modern times by e.g. Rostagni' (1986, p. 200, ftnote 43). Unfortunately, however, Halliwell does not explore the issue further.

[519] K. Telford, *Aristotle's* Poetics (Chicago, 1961), 74.

'distinctive pleasure ... which it shares only with epic, turns on the fear and pity we feel as we follow a play's action'.[520] Yet none of these authors cites any precise passage, and, contrary to their explicit claims, absolutely no Aristotelian passage in the whole corpus or especially in the account of epic states that the function of this art form is either to stir pity and fear or, more crucially, to provide *katharsis*. In fact, given that Aristotle states in the definition of epic that its goal is 'to produce its proper pleasure [*hēdonē*]' (ch. 23, 1459a17ff.), and given that he could easily have added *katharsis*, pity, or fear to that definition even after a first redaction, we must assume that for him none of these conditions was essential to that art form.

It is possible, of course, that the end of both tragedy and epic was discussed in a lost portion of the *Poetics* and that Aristotle identified pleasure with *katharsis*. However, given the distinction between *katharsis* and pleasure in *Politics* 8. 7, against this possibility stands the equally strong or even stronger alternative that he actually separated the two phenomena much more widely than is usually supposed, and thus nothing can be gained in this context by appealing to mere possibility.

To recapitulate: with *katharsis* (no matter what it reasonably means) included in the definition of tragedy, the subsequent discussions in chapters 6, 14, and 26 of the end or function of tragedy generate either great tension or outright contradiction. With *catharsis* omitted, the end of tragedy is either the plot, as stated in chapter 6, or pleasure, as stated in chapters 14 and 26 (or both if plot is taken to be the artistic, and pleasure the psychological, end).[521] The *Poetics* consequently becomes much more consistent. Moreover, given that enjoyment is the best goal of music in the *Politics* (see n. 19 [= footnote 509 here]) and pleasure the goal of tragedy in the *Poetics*, Aristotle's general aesthetic theory also coheres much more neatly.

In the light of the above, appealing to a third kind of definition that primarily employs necessary and sufficient conditions or supposing that Aristotle merely intuits the conditions of tragedy does not lessen his problems. Rather, he is actually left in a deeper quagmire than is usually thought if *katharsis* is kept in the definition. That quagmire, however, is so obvious and suffocating that a thinker as astute as he cannot, in my opinion, be reasonably supposed to have fallen—indeed, to have dived—into it. Thus, something like the proposal of Petruševski to emend the two words *pathēmatōn katharsin* appears to be a better solution, one I now address.

---

520   S.A. White, 'Aristotle's Favorite Tragedies', in Rorty, *Essays*, 221–40 at 228–9.
521   I owe the internal/external distinction to Walter Watson (private correspondence).

## Section 4: Petruševski's solution, its problems, and an alternative

To summarize Petruševski's views:[522] he does not choose his emendation lightly nor does he invoke it to circumvent finding the correct translation of *katharsis*. Rather, he argues that it is forced upon him by some of Aristotle's own doctrines. According to Petruševski, the definition of tragedy with *katharsis* is very obscure and involves a phrase—*pathēmatōn katharsin*—that is found nowhere else in the entire ancient Greek corpus. Moreover, the definition as it stands, he says, not only employs *tōn toioutōn* ('such') and *pathēmatōn* ('sufferings' or 'experiences') in unusual senses in lieu of *toutōn* ('these') and *pathōn* ('sufferings' or 'experiences'), but uses *katharsis* and *peranousa* ('finishing' or 'ending') metaphorically. Both of these practices, however, contravene the *Topics*, e.g. 6, 139b30, which forbids metaphorical definitional terms.[523] Substituting *pragmatōn sustasin* for *pathēmatōn katharsin* allows us, Petruševski adds, to take *peranousa* literally, as 'finishing'. He concludes that 'the definition becomes indeed clear and complete, because it now contains the essential part of tragedy, determining the latter as a representation of a sad and terrible action that ends in fear and pity'.[524] *Pragmatōn sustasin* gets repeated, he easily and correctly enumerates, at a number of places in the rest of chapter 6 and later in the *Poetics*,[525] which entails that Aristotle explains the two terms, just as he explains all of the other essential conditions. Lastly, Petruševski argues, the text could originally have contained a different reading, because Strabo and Plutarch claim that Aristotle's library was not only hidden underground to save it from the Attalid kings but damaged by moisture and moths and then restored two centuries later by Apellicon of Teos, a bibliophile rather than a philosopher, who himself was responsible for many errors in the restored manuscripts.[526] Again, for Petruševski the

---

522 M. D. Petruševksi, '*Pathēmatōn Katharsin* ou bien *Pragmatōn Systasin?*' ['*Pathēmatōn Katharsin*'], *Živa antika/Antiquité vivante* (Skopje) (1954), 209–50 (in Macedonian and French). Another work of his, which I have been unable to consult, is *La Définition de la tragédie chez Aristote et la catharsis* (L'Annuaire de la Faculté de Philosophie de l'Université de Skopje, 1; Skopje, 1948) (in Macedonian, with summaries in French and Russian).

523 This is why, when speaking of the definition, Kenneth Bennett is too permissive in saying that 'catharsis...may well be used in a special metaphorical manner' ('The Purging of Catharsis', *British Journal of Aesthetics*, 21/3 [1981], 204–13 at 205).

524 '...la définition devient tout à fait claire et complète, car elle contient maintenant la partie essentielle de la tragédie déterminant celle-ci comme imitation d'une action triste et terrible qui se termine par crainte et pitié' ('*Pathēmatōn Katharsin*', 238).

525 Petruševksi, '*Pathēmatōn Katharsin*', 245–50, has the exhaustive list. Some of those places are ch. 6, 1450a16–17, 24–6, 33; 1450b1, 3–4; ch. 7, 1450b23 ff.; and ch. 8, 1451a33–5.

526 Petruševksi, '*Pathēmatōn Katharsin*', 242–4; he argues (240, 244) that Strabo's and Plutarch's reports are reliable. Ingemar Düring contends that 'except for a few dialogues and the *Protrepticus*, copies of Aristotle's writings were rare and no Corpus existed until after Andronicus' (*Aristotle in the Ancient Biographical Tradition* (Göteborg Universitets Årsskrift, 63/2; Göteborg, 1957), 462), and F. H. Sandbach accepts that the Aristotelian corpus was not well known in the 3rd cent. BC, a view also attributed by Sandbach to Paul Moraux and Fritz Wehrli (*Aristotle and the Stoics* (Cambridge Philological Society suppl. 10; Cambridge, 1985), 16–17).

definition of tragedy becomes something like 'a representation of a serious and complete action ... the arrangement of such incidents ending in pity and fear'. As I suggested above, this reading appears to sweep away many of the aforementioned difficulties and brings Aristotle almost all the way to safety. Nevertheless, two fatal problems still exist. First, as noted already, 'pity' and 'fear' are nowhere found in chapters 1–5. Petruševski himself says, in the extensive French précis that accompanies his primary Macedonian text,[527] that the elements in the definition except for *katharsis* exist before the definition or in the commentary thereafter. This reflects what he says in the Macedonian, namely:

> The meaning and content of the words pity and fear, even though they are not discussed before the definition, cannot be unfamiliar. Everyone knows what fear and pity are. And what kind of an explanation should a person expect from Aristotle before the definition? These are not unfamiliar words or terms, nor any sort of technical term... Why should Aristotle explain the words fear and pity, whose meaning is known to everyone, before the definition? ... We cannot agree with A. Smerdel that Aristotle had to explain before the definition all of the words in the definition (pp. 213–14, trans. George Mitrevski).[528]

This passage, however, ignores Aristotle's own words, and the rules of definition that Petruševski himself had taken such pains to elaborate, which seem to require that the elements come only from what has been said *before*. We might grant for the sake of argument that a subsequent discussion of a term could justify its inclusion in the definition, or we might agree that definition by necessary and sufficient conditions or by mere intuition is utilized. Still, Petruševski has no explanation for why pity and fear are never mentioned again in chapter 6 even though Aristotle obviously wishes to examine each and every part of the definition in some detail. With respect to Anton Smerdel, who was also influenced by Gudeman: obviously he pinpointed the general problem I am highlighting, and is, to my knowledge, the first (and only) person to report in writing the difficulty posed by including pity and fear in the definition. What his precise complaints and resolutions were, I cannot say, because his dissertation is cited as 'Skopje, 1937' and it has been impossible for me to locate a copy.[529] In any event, Petruševski's reply to him is entirely unconvincing, for if 'familiarity' were sufficient as a criterion for a term to be omitted before the final definition—the implication of Petruševski's remark—most, if not all, of the terms in the definition ('good men', 'serious', 'mimesis', etc.) would also have been omitted in chapters 1–5 because they, too, would certainly have been 'familiar' to the reader. On top of this is

---

Janko adds: 'There is as yet no solid evidence that Philodemus, or indeed anybody until later antiquity, knew the *Poetics*' ('Philodemus' *On Poems* and Aristotle's *On Poets*' ['Philodemus'], *Cronache ercolanesi*, 21 (1991), 5–64 at 64).

527   '*Pathēmatōn Katharsin*', 240.

528   Private correspondence. Mitrevski is a professor of foreign languages, specializing in Macedonian, at Auburn University.

529   Petruševksi, loc. cit. To facilitate efforts by others to track down the text, I note the title of Smerdel's work: *The Catharsis of Aristotle* (diss. Skopje, 1937) (in Serbo-Croatian, with a summary in German).

a related consideration: immediately after the definition in chapter 6 (1449b35–6), Aristotle actually indicates that there is a term that is too familiar to need explaining, but the term is neither 'pity' nor 'fear', but *melopoiia*, the making of the *melos* (the 'rhythm' and harmony that we discussed earlier). Yet Aristotle's concern to identify which term is so familiar as not to require explanation would have led him to note both pity and fear along with *melopoiia*, were Petruševski correct.

Finally, with respect to Petruševski's own translation of the definition, not all tragedies end in pity and fear for Aristotle, even if those emotions are always occasioned earlier in a tragedy (and even this may not be necessary on Aristotle's theory, as we shall discover shortly). This is abundantly transparent from chapter 14, where Aristotle ranks the best plots, citing some that end happily—and not *Oedipus Rex*—as the most admirable: the *Cresphontes*, *Iphigenia in Tauris*, and *Helle* (1454a4–9). Petruševski's solution, then, ingenious and correct as it is in some respects, cannot be quite right. Rather, it seems that the only course open, perhaps following Smerdel (depending on what he concluded), is to athetize the whole *katharsis* clause. I now defend this option, for, although the price of athetesis is admittedly extremely high and tolerated only as a truly last resort, in this case keeping the clause appears to exact even greater, astronomical costs, as the foregoing has revealed to some extent and as the following will demonstrate further. I start with issues pertaining primarily to *katharsis* before finishing with pity and fear.

Regarding the manuscript tradition, if the whole clause ('through pity and fear accomplishing the *katharsis* of such emotions', or however one chooses to read it) were excised or bracketed as spurious, the syntax of the remaining definition would remain perfectly viable. The current penultimate phrase can function properly as the ultimate one and none of the six necessary elements of tragedy developed by Aristotle in the rest of chapter 6 is affected in any way. Indeed, it now becomes perfectly clear why Aristotle never discusses the phenomena of *katharsis*, pity, and fear in that chapter even though he wishes to discuss all of the other essential conditions of tragedy. In addition, no worry arises because of the famous passage in the *Politics* mentioned earlier that points to a fuller discussion of *katharsis* 'in the writings on poetry' (*en tois peri poiētikēs*, 1341b39–40). Given that neither a discussion of *catharsis* nor any hint of such a discussion exists in our text called the *Poetics*, even in places where we would very much expect it, it is unlikely that Aristotle was referring in the *Politics* to the work we have, especially to a chapter in which the term *katharsis* is unexpectedly introduced, never to be mentioned again. Rather, it is much more plausible that Aristotle was referring in the *Politics* to a poetics on dramatic comedy, for the following reason. Two other phrases exist in the *Rhetoric* that exactly duplicate the expression in the *Politics*. Aristotle says: 'we have discussed the ludicrous separately in the *Poetics*' (1. 11, 1372a1) and 'jests have been classified in the *Poetics*' (3. 18, 1419b5). The Greek in both places is the same and matches the *Politics*: *en tois peri poiētikēs*. Consequently, because, for instance, jests are hardly mentioned, much less classified, in our *Poetics*, *catharsis* was probably discussed in the supposedly lost second book of our treatise or perhaps in one of the (comic) poetics that Diogenes Laertius attributes to Aristotle.[530] Aristotle indeed may have accepted comic but not tragic *katharsis* as the goal of a whole dramatic genre, or—what is more likely, I imagine, with regard to comedy—may have accepted *katharsis* as the psychological goal merely of some comic subspecies, perhaps a 'comedy of suffering'.[531] But whatever Aristotle's view may have been about the psychological goal of comedy or of its subspecies, the only point that I wish to propose now, given the identical phrases of the *Rhetoric* and the *Politics*, is that it is much more likely that *catharsis* was discussed in a text dealing with comedy. The *Politics* passage, therefore, is no evidence that the term *katharsis* should be in our *Poetics* 6.

Similarly, no contradiction with any other Aristotelian text ensues as a result of athetizing the *katharsis* clause, simply because there is none that addresses the relevant chapters of the *Poetics*. What, though, about the initial reports that Aristotle uses *katharsis*, which stem from the Neoplatonists?

The first writers to report Aristotle employing *katharsis* appear to be Proclus in the fifth century AD and Olympiodorus in the sixth.[532] Neither author, however, cites any relevant passages from the *Poetics*, and indeed, as Janko observes,[533] Proclus indicates that he is referring to Aristotle's early *On Poets*. In any case, no matter which text Proclus is referring to, it does not seem that he could have been describing Aristotle's mature views, as represented, say, in the *Nicomachean Ethics* or in the *Poetics*. Proclus believes that Aristotle had grounds for complaint against Plato because, in Proclus' opinion, 'it is possible to satisfy the emotions in due measure, and, by satisfying them, to keep them tractable for education, by treating the ache in them'.[534] However, *Politics* 7.17 and 8.7 strongly suggest that education should be completed, at least in the relevant ways, before one is allowed to see comedy and tragedy.[535] Also, as is evident from *Nicomachean Ethics* 2 and 3, Aristotle does not think

---

530  Diogenes is a notoriously unreliable scholar, but perhaps we can trust a mere enumeration from him. For reasons why the *Tractatus Coisilianus* may be the supposedly lost book on comedy, see R. Janko, *Aristotle on Comedy* [*Comedy*] (Berkeley, 1984).

531  For more on comedy, and Aristotle's identification of 'old' genres with 'absurd' (and 'new' with 'serious'), see Janko, *Comedy*, 41, 86–7.

532  The passages are conveniently located in R. Janko, *Aristotle:* Poetics [*Poetics*] (Indianapolis, 1987), 59–61. As Janko reports further, Iamblichus in the 3rd and 4th cents. AD presents a doctrine that some have thought to be Aristotelian, because of similar concepts. However, Janko acknowledges (186) that Iamblichus never mentions Aristotle.

533  *Poetics*, 186.

534  Proclus, *In Remp.* i. 42 Kroll, trans. Janko, *Poetics*, 60.

535  *Politics* 7. 17 indicates that legislators should only allow the youth to be spectators of comedy when they are old enough to drink strong wine at the public table, and that education will have fortified them against the

that emotions like fear are made tractable for educational purposes by having an ache treated or by satisfying them. Rather, it is habituation involving a rational component or following a rational set of guidelines that allows one to develop proper emotions,[536] and one learns to handle fear by learning how to handle fearful circumstances. Finally, whether one can even change one's emotional habits as an adult is a very debatable question on Aristotle's theory (see *NE* 3.5, 1114a3–22), and besides, sometimes not only is fear properly felt but there may be good reason *not* to rid oneself of it *(NE* 3.6 and 7). In short, nothing in the Aristotelian treatises indicates that a *katharsis* of, or through, the emotions is part of correct ethical training, nor does any passage suggest that pity or fear is an inherently bad emotion, to be removed at all times.

While on the topics of the transmission of the *Poetics* and of the doxographical belief that Aristotle relies on *katharsis* as the goal of tragedy, we might again well recall Janko. He argues that a work of the Epicurean Philodemus probably refers to an Aristotelian aesthetic doctrine that itself includes *katharsis*. However, on Janko's own account the doctrine does not come from the *Poetics* but rather from the early *On Poets*.[537] Inclusion in that treatise, though, guarantees nothing about the *Poetics*, and to assume that Aristotle maintains an unchanging aesthetic theory throughout his career would ignore the strong possibility of development in his philosophical life, which Werner Jaeger first plausibly sketched.[538] Thus, there seems to be no good reason to think that the Neoplatonists were referring to the *Poetics* when they tied Aristotle to *katharsis*. Even if they were, coming over six centuries after Aristotle and three hundred years after Strabo and Plutarch, they might have read a manuscript that already contained an interpolated phrase. Janko's work on Philodemus is also very important for showing just why someone might have interpolated *katharsis* in chapter 6: knowing that Aristotle himself embraced the phenomenon in *On Poets*, a reader may have either inserted the words into the text in order to rectify what appeared to him to be an omission on Aristotle's part or else added them as a marginal gloss, one which—as frequently happens—was later mistakenly copied into the text. I do not wish to insist on this last point, though, for there are many reasons why insertions have made

---

harmful influences of such events (1336b19 ff.). 'Such events' may be referring only to comedy (or to comedy and wine-drinking) but probably also includes tragedy, given the discussion in the subsequent passage of Theodorus, whom Aristotle explicitly calls a tragic actor (1336b29). At any rate, whatever the scope of 'such events', if education can protect youths against comedy, it stands to reason that, at least for Aristotle, it can protect them against tragedy too. Tragedy deals with good men in action *(Poetics* 2), whereas comedy deals with ignoble ones. Therefore, if the youth are already educated in the important ways so that comedy would not harm them, drama in general, including tragedy, would also not harm them and should presumably not be designed to provide them with a redundant, unnecessary educational experience.

536     Nehamas, 'Pity and Fear', 296–7.
537     Janko, 'Philodemus', 49–50, 63.
538     *Aristotle: Fundamentals of the History of his Development*, trans. R. Robinson, 2nd edn. (Oxford, 1948), from *Aristoteles: Grundlegung einer Geschichte seiner Entwicklung* (Berlin, 1923).

## Chapter 5: "Purging the *Poetics*"

their way into the Aristotelian corpus, and it is beyond the scope of this paper to delve into the issue.

To summarize the arguments of this section: neither any grammatical reason nor textual ground pertaining to references from other Aristotelian texts nor ancient doxography weighs perceptibly against the athetesis of the *katharsis* clause. This leaves only considerations internal to the *Poetics* itself as potential spoilers. I present now what appear to be the only two criticisms with strength, which pertain to the removal of pity and fear from that clause, because no good reason seems to exist for keeping the term *katharsis* itself in the definition of tragedy (which means that something like Petruševski's solution would be right, were my own to fail).[539]

In omitting the entire *katharsis* clause, the first criticism runs, we omit a mention of pity and fear, which are in fact closely tied to other parts of the treatise, and which can reasonably be considered essential to Aristotle's understanding of tragedy. The second criticism is that the focus on pity and fear in chapter 9, 1452a2–3, appears to be a reference back to the definition, which means that pity and fear were indeed included in chapter 6 because this is the only previous occurrence of the two terms. The difficulty with the first criticism is that a handful of other very important aspects of tragedy—pleasure, recognition, reversal, denouement, etc.—are also properly considered 'essential to Aristotle's understanding of tragedy' and yet are not found in the definition. Pity and fear, then, could be easily

---

539 A number of criticisms have come to me in conversation or in private correspondence in the four years leading up to this version. Two of them are as follows: (i) Aristotle mentions 'painfully' in chapter 4 at 1448b10, when discussing the pleasure that men can paradoxically experience while viewing an image of a despicable wild animal or of a corpse. Thus, he anticipates pity and fear before chapter 6 because these two emotions themselves, everyone agrees, have pain as their common denominator. (ii) Aristotle defines comedy as lacking in painful and destructive elements (1449a35) while also telling us that it follows a developmental path different from that of tragedy. Consequently, whatever comedy does not have—painful and destructive elements like pity and fear—tragedy has.

Regarding (i): to mention a genus, 'painfully', in a division and then to include in the final summation only a species, viz. pity or fear (or both), blatantly violates Aristotle's procedural rules of definition. (We might as well say no more than 'limbs' in a preliminary diaeresis for a definition of an animal, and then state 'three-toed' or 'two-handed' or 'hundred-legged' when collecting results.) Also, the pain mentioned in chapter 4 relates not to pity and fear but to images that are most despicable (*atimotatōn*).

Regarding (ii): the lack of painful and destructive elements is explicitly a contrast, rather, to the painfully vicious, personal attacks that were endemic to invective, before it started focusing on universals and became comedy proper (1448b27–1449a6; 1449a32–7). Further, because epic also followed a different path from comedy (chapter 4), the lack of painful and destructive elements in comedy might also be a contrast to characteristics in Homeric *epic* representations—e.g. impiety, lack of self-control that weakens character, and profit in injustice—which Plato had vilified at the beginning of *Republic* 3 because those epic characteristics are, on his own view, destructive. On the reasoning of the present objection, pity and fear should be in the definition of epic, because it also follows a different developmental path from comedy (and yet those two emotions are clearly not in epic's definition).

removed from chapter 6 without distorting Aristotle's understanding, as long as the later passages are kept (and I *strongly* emphasize that they should be kept). Pity and fear can be 'essential to Aristotle's understanding of tragedy' without being 'essential to tragedy'. Moreover, for pity and fear to be essential to tragedy and to be kept in the definition, all legitimately Aristotelian tragedies would have to involve the two emotions in some appropriate way. Yet, for the following reasons, tragedies exist or could exist which do not contain them.

The first reason—which seems to carry the battle all by itself—is that, as underscored already, pity and fear are never raised either in the first five chapters of the *Poetics* or in chapter 6 (apart, naturally, from the dubious occurrence in the definition of tragedy). In other words, the kinds of emotion that a tragedian must consider crucial are never restricted in those chapters, which set the basis for the whole definition of tragedy. Admittedly, in chapter 19 Aristotle discusses one of the six necessary elements of tragedy, 'thought' (*dianoia*), and associates it partially with pity and fear. However, that association is merely a list of the emotions 'thought' can manifest: 'such as pity, fear, anger, and the like' (*hoion eleon ē phobon ē orgēn kai hosa toiauta*, 1456b1). Aristotle does not say that the 'thought' must always at least manifest pity and fear, and clearly 'anger and the like' are emotions that a dramatist can be suitably concerned with.[540] In short, for the first six chapters, tragedy simply covers any drama that represents good men, has a certain magnitude, etc., and is never restricted to actions that convey (or cause) pity and fear. This is how Plato at least sometimes uses the term 'tragedy', and Aristotle follows suit.[541]

---

540 This means that a play similar to *Philoctetes* but only with themes of revenge, loyalty, and deception, and with anger or other emotions produced by the appropriate 'thoughts' but excluding pity and fear in any real measure, with a proper plot, focusing on good men, and with the remaining four necessary elements of chapter 6 (1450A8)—character, language, music, and spectacle—would be a tragedy on Aristotle's view (although admittedly not the best kind). This strikes me as eminently plausible, because otherwise, Aristotle would be abrogating his own essential conditions.

541 At *Laws* 7, 817b, 'tragedy' is a very broad term, being simply contrasted with comedy and only meaning serious drama dealing with noble or good people. Nothing disastrous need be implied, as Susan Sauvé Meyer asserts when discussing Plato's passage: 'Here "tragedy" is used as an honorific label, and the essential feature of the "tragic" is the "portrayal of the finest and best life" (*mimēsis tou kallistou kai aristou biou*, 817b4). According to this conception of "tragedy," the tragic imitates the best life, in contrast with comedy, which imitates low life. So understood, labelling something as "tragic" does not imply that it is regrettable. (There is nothing particularly tragic about tragedy in this sense.) Such connotations do accompany the Aristotelian analysis of tragedy as involving disaster and reversal, but this does not seem to be Plato's conception—witness his description of Homer as a tragedian in *Republic* X (605c)' ('Pessimism and Postponement: Comments on André Laks "Postponing the *Laws*"', unpublished conference presentation, Princeton University Colloquium, Dec. 1996). With one caveat resulting from my earlier analyses, I am fully in accord with Sauvé Meyer: the Aristotelian analysis involving disaster and reversal, though, pertains only to the best tragedy. If the opposite were the case, Aristotle would have established it in *Poetics* 1–6, when describing the differences between tragedy and the other genres.

## Chapter 5: "Purging the *Poetics*"

The second reason why pity and fear need not be in every tragedy stems from the opening statement of the whole treatise. Aristotle says he will discuss plots 'and how they should cohere if the composition is to turn out well' (*kai pōs dei sunistasthai tous muthous ei mellei kalōs hexein hē poiēsis*, 1447a9–10). In chapter 7 he explicitly begins to concern himself with the general issue of the best plots—the first six chapters being primarily descriptive, historical, definitory, and loosely taxonomical—and this concern for evaluation continues through chapter 14. In chapter 13 he covers the different patterns of change that one can find in tragedy, from fortune to misfortune or vice versa, and by good or bad men. Three of the four resulting possible patterns are neither pitiable nor fearful and thus, he says, not proper structures for the best tragedy. The 'best' here is crucial. As White insightfully says of Aristotle: 'his claim is not that no tragedies were or could be built on any of these patterns, but only that "the finest tragedies" avoid them'.[542] Aristotle implies, then, that there could be tragedies without pity and fear, although not the finest ones, and not the ones poets should strive to create.

The suggestion that there could be second-rate tragedies without pity and fear is, I believe, strengthened later in chapter 13 and in chapter 14, and leads to some ambiguous passages and complex arguments, but we can cut to the chase, as it were. The most severe objection to athetizing pity and fear from the definition in chapter 6 arises from chapters 9 (1452a2), 11 (1452b1), 13 (1452b31), and 14 (1453b10), where Aristotle appears to say that tragedy is considered a representation of pitiable and fearful events. On the surface, these statements clearly imply that pity and fear should be in the definition of tragedy. However, except for chapter 19, when, as just noted, Aristotle includes pity and fear in a list of the emotions associated with 'thought', each and every occurrence of pity and fear in the *Poetics* arises in the chapters just highlighted, falling within the section discussing how to write plots well. Take the instance from chapter 13, 1452b31: 'the construction of the finest tragedy should be ... complex, and ... represent terrifying and pitiable events (for this is particular to representation of this sort)' (trans. Janko). Commentators have taken 'this sort' to refer merely to 'tragedy', but the real reference, I submit, is the fuller phrase 'the finest tragedy'. The other three occurrences are very similar. The first mention of pity and fear in chapter 9 is embedded in a paragraph dealing explicitly with finer plots. The second in chapter 11 falls within a passage examining the finest discoveries and

---

It is also noteworthy that Lillian Lawler, in her very rigorous study of dance in ancient Greek theatre, indicates that the term 'tragedy' was used equally broadly, or even more broadly, at times. While speaking of late writers and lexicographers of antiquity, she says: 'Philoxenus the dithyrambist, for example, is called *tragikos* by a scholiast on Aristophanes' *Plutus* (290). By some late authors the word seems to be used literally, as coming from *tragos*, "goat", and referring to the dances of the satyr play; we may instance *Etymologicum Magnum* 764, s.v. "tragoedia", where tragedy and the satyr play are obviously confused, and where the choruses are said at times to imitate the *schēmata* of goats. Many modern scholars think that in the lexicographers the word *tragikos* means merely "pertaining to the drama"' (*The Dance of the Ancient Greek Theatre* (Iowa City, 1964), 34).

542 'Aristotle's Favorite Tragedies', 229.

reversals, which themselves are required for complex plots (themselves required for the best kind of tragedy). The final statement is contained in chapter 14, which along with chapter 13 is universally acknowledged to be discussing the best categories of plot. There is thus no contradiction between a definition of tragedy without the terms pity and fear and the later statements from chapters 9, 11, 13, and 14: pity and fear are not essential to tragedies in general, as defined in chapters 1–6, but only to the paradigmatic ones as examined in chapters 7–14. Aristotle is not implying, from chapter 9 onwards, that every tragedy has to have the two emotions—rather, he is simply holding that the best tragedies should have them.[543]

This suffices for the first criticism. Regarding the second, pertaining to the mention of pity and fear in chapter 9 that ostensibly refers back to the only previous use of the terms in chapter 6: Aristotle says that 'the representation is not only of a complete action but of things that are fearful and pitiable' (*ou monon teleias esti praxeōs hē mimesis kai phoberōn kai eleeinōn*, 1452a2–3). This might indeed be taken at first glance to refer to the definition, because in chapter 6 the action was said to be complete. However, Aristotle does not say in chapter 9 'as was said in the definition' or 'as said before', an expression he often uses when repeating himself, or anything similar. Furthermore, a few sentences later he speaks of plot, which also stems from the definition, stating that some are simple while others are complex (1452a10). According to the reasoning of the present objection, 'simple' and 'complex' should therefore also be in the definition, which is patently absurd. A better rationale, then, for the first authentic mention of pity and fear in the treatise, in chapter 9, is this: Aristotle, with the remark that the representation is not only complete but fearful and pitiable, is restricting tragedy to a narrower conception than had obtained in chapters 1–6 *just because* pity and fear had originally been excluded from the definition and just because he now wants to focus on that narrower conception. The reason, as emphasized earlier, is that he wishes in this section to examine the best sorts of tragic

---

543   Having noted all of this, we can easily handle another objection to the removal of pity and fear from chapter 6, viz. that we have reason to believe that those emotions were already well established as the quintessential tragic ones before Aristotle's time. Passages of both Plato and Gorgias can be adduced to support this objection, and Hutton (*Poetics*, 8–9; 19–20) and Nehamas ('Pity and Fear', 305, 313) have discussed the history to some extent. Gorgias considers poetry, for example, to be imitation or deception, states that poetry makes the deceiver more just than the non-deceiver and the deceived more wise than the non-deceived, thinks that the aim of poetry is pleasure, and emphasizes the effects of pity and fear. However, in reply to this objection, Hutton also indicates (*loc. cit.*) that, even though Plato may use 'tragedy' in the Gorgian sense, it appears he does so for the sake of argument. Furthermore, in my view, anyone who argues that Aristotle slavishly embraces the Gorgian tradition and takes pity and fear to be essential conditions of tragedy is saddled with the problem of explaining why he then omits the accompanying goal of pleasure as a companion essential condition, one that would have to be likewise included in the definition of tragedy—in lieu of *katharsis*!—and not only stated in chapters 14 and 26. Lastly, my view that, for Aristotle, pity and fear are required for the best plots and that pleasure is indeed the aim of tragedians in one way slightly modifies but arguably furthers the Gorgian tradition, so the objection dissolves.

Chapter 5: "Purging the *Poetics*"

plot, and pity and fear are for him crucial for these sorts. An analogy would be Aristotle defining men as two-legged, rational animals, and then, when switching to a discussion of the best men, requiring additionally that they study philosophy or practise ethical conduct.[544]

This finishes the defence of the proposed athetesis against the two criticisms. More evidence could now be stacked on the offensive side to boost the point advanced before, that the lack of any other mention of pity and fear either before chapter 6 or in the discussion of all of the essential conditions of tragedy in chapter 6 itself counts heavily against Aristotle having actually included the two words in the definition of tragedy. One point will suffice, pertaining to the absence of such ostensibly essential conditions in chapters 15–26. As we have seen to some extent already in the discussion of *katharsis*, nothing in chapters 24–6, where Aristotle compares and ranks epic and tragedy, shows any concern whatsoever with pity and fear, which is as troubling an omission as the one pertaining to the omission of *katharsis* in those chapters.

Balancing, therefore, all of the considerations above, pity and fear can hardly be considered essential to all Aristotelian tragedies even if these two emotions are necessary to the best sort. Consequently, they cannot reasonably be in the definition of tragedy, and, I maintain, the athetesis can stand. In fact, considering the host of tensions, inconsistencies, and outright contradictions that result from keeping in the definition any of the three problematic terms—pity, fear, and *katharsis*—and considering further the failure of generations of classical scholars to devise a persuasive solution to the meaning of *katharsis* and of Petruševski to address the very serious problems pertaining to pity and fear, arguably the fuller athetesis should stand. Aristotle did not 'spoil', to recall Battin's words, 'an otherwise perfectly straightforward and rigorous definition' in order to underscore the centrality of *katharsis* (or of pity and fear, which she completely ignores). Someone else—perhaps knowing that *katharsis* was embraced in the earlier *On Poets* or believing that Aristotle needed a 'better' goal than

---

[544] All of this may mean that Aristotle relies on his opening statement of the whole treatise (that he will discuss how the plots are best done) in order to prepare the audience for the switch in perspective from tragedy in general to the best tragedy that includes pity and fear. Yet, it may also mean that he merely abides by a linguistic practice that he recognizes twice in *Metaphysics* Δ 12: 'sometimes we say of those who can merely walk or speak, but not well or not as they intend, that they cannot speak or walk' (1019A24–6) and 'we say one lyre can speak, and another cannot speak at all, if it has not a good tone' (1019b13–15, both translations by W. D. Ross). In the case of tragedy, the kind that is not being done well is for the moment being conveniently 'denied', just as poor or mediocre (but real) walking is sometimes 'denied' as walking. In any event, leaving aside this rhetorical practice, without pity and fear in chapter 6, the text either makes a less than ideal transition in chapter 9 (relying on the treatise's first sentence) or switches without warning the notion of tragedy,—clearly a possibility if, as many have argued, the *Poetics* is a compilation of different, but related, works. Yet either disjunct is surely less repugnant than to suppose that Aristotle is ignoring his own strictures of definition (and if transitions are at stake now, the unexpected introduction of pity and fear in chapter 6 is an overtly appalling one).

pleasure to justify tragedy—mistakenly added the *katharsis* clause and sent hordes of later, well-intentioned scholars on a quest for their own Holy Grail.

In closing, I wish to focus on an aspect of the *Poetics* that might be surprising given my former conclusions: *katharsis* may well be for Aristotle the final cause of 'tragedy of suffering', one of the four subspecies of tragedy mentioned in chapter 18 (the other three being complex tragedy, tragedy of character, and simple or spectacular tragedy).[545] I say this without prejudice to the main thesis of this essay, viz. that *katharsis*, pity, and fear cannot be included as essential conditions of the entire species. However, I refrain from exploring further here the topic of a 'tragedy of suffering', because Aristotle says so little about the four subspecies in our surviving texts. Thus, I am by no means totally negating the previous discussions of *katharsis*, as it might be argued Petruševski does, and in this respect I am ironically less radical than he. Indeed, those previous discussions of catharsis might prove very helpful in establishing how the proper psychological effect might have been sought by Aristotle in one (but perhaps no more than one) subcategory of tragedy and quite possibly in at least some subcategory of comedy, or might reveal his beliefs from his early Academic days, when he wrote *On Poets*. The paradoxical value of this paper, then, is that attention might be diverted hereafter to those much more promising areas, how comedy and perhaps merely one subspecies of tragedy might have *katharsis* and what Aristotle's dramatic theory would have been in his earlier days. In any event, let this suffice. The exegetical epic of trying to wedge the *katharsis* clause consistently into the *Poetics* in general and chapter 6 in particular can be brought to its own, proper denouement. The whole clause should be purged—or at least bracketed as spurious—which would not only help purify the definition of tragedy but also clarify Aristotle's aesthetics.

---

545    The four subspecies of tragedy are given at 1455b32–1456a3. The text is corrupt and a favourite correction, *opsis* (spectacle), is not definite. The other option, *haplē* (simple), which many (including myself) prefer, results because Aristotle says in chapter 24 (1459b9) that there are four kinds of epic, as of tragedy, and he lists them as simple, complex, of character, and of suffering (*haplē ē peplegmenēn ē ēthikēn ē pathētikēn*). The last three terms match exactly the uncorrupted ones for tragedy. See D.W. Lucas, *Poetics*, 184–8, for an extensive discussion of the whole issue. I assume for the purposes of this paper that the four subspecies exhaust the tragic species, although there is a possibility, if our *Poetics* is a conflation of related texts, that tragedy in chapter 18 is restricted and is narrower than the broad genus of chapter 6.

Chapter 5: "Purging the *Poetics*"

## Postscript to Chapter 5

The expression of gratitude to the Stanford seminar at the very beginning in "Purging the *Poetics*" was elliptical for the sake of brevity and meant "my forceful (i.e., *passionately put*) views." In retrospect, I am sure some readers of that article took "my forceful views" to be an expression of arrogance, hence my correction now. Also, those views were simply comments at the seminar and were not a formal presentation. They were obviously not very "forceful" in the sense of being compelling, given, e.g., McKirahan's publication of 2010, which repeated the views I cautioned against in the seminar and which I addressed above in the mini-appendix to Chapter 2 (McKirahan himself presented his theory in Stanford apparently for the first time).

As I discuss more in Chapter 6, Tarán and Gutas have shown very recently with even more evidence that *pathēmatōn* in manuscript B coincides with the Syriac-Arabic manuscript that is arguably older than manuscript A (and its *mathēmatōn*). Thus, even though Lobel is correct in saying that manuscript A is the oldest Greek manuscript, *pathēmatōn* itself may truly be older as a word in a previous manuscript. However, as was discussed in great detail in Chapter 2 of Volume 1, although important from a paleographical perspective, this has no impact on my thesis, which pertains primarily to philosophical consistency and plausibility. Even Tarán admits that the source of all the existing manuscripts probably came about 700 years after Aristotle, which allows for more than a few opportunities for interpolations and corruptions, to put it mildly.

The most important correction: I said in "Purging" that "[Aristotle] in this section [Chapter 13] wishes to examine the best sorts of tragic plot, and *pity and fear are for him crucial for these sorts*." I made other statements that indicated pity and fear were only in the best plots *in general* for Aristotle. These italicized claims were, I believe, my only significant mistake in this article. I was still unclear in 2003 on the relation of Chapters 13 and 14, and so accepted for the sake of argument that the plots with pity and fear, like *Oedipus*, are the best plots for Aristotle, which has been almost a truism for specialists and educated non-specialists for centuries. In Chapter 6 below, though, I demonstrate conclusively that many—indeed most—other tragic plot-types, and even the best plots of Chapter 14, have no relevant pity and fear for Aristotle. I should emphasize now, then, that pity and fear are in the best plot-types *of Chapter 13*—and *only* of Chapter 13 (and the beginning of Chapter 14).[546] I do

---

546 Pity and fear are part of the discussion of the beginning of Chapter 14 but then are dropped when Aristotle begins discussing the ranking of four plot-types from the middle of Chapter 14 onwards, with a certain type of happily-ending play like *Cresphontes* being ranked explicitly over the type of play that must include *Oedipus*. I draw out the ramifications of this to some extent in Chapter 6 below, but more fully in my *Aristotle's Favorite Tragedy: Oedipus or Cresphontes?* (2nd edition, 2018), which itself also shows why *Cresphontes* is better than

not mean that pity and fear are mentioned just in Chapters 13 and 14. Indeed, they first appear (authentically) in Chapters 9 and 11. My claim is that even in those earlier chapters Aristotle presupposes the subtype of tragedy that he focusses on in Chapter 13, the kind of tragedy that has pity and fear in virtue of the *subtype* it is.

In short, I misleadingly suggested in "Purging" that the introduction of pity and fear results because Aristotle wishes to focus on the best plots of *all* tragedy. Instead, as I explain rigorously in detail in the next chapter, the introduction of pity and fear in the middle chapters of the treatise results only because Aristotle wishes: (i) to focus on a specific sub-type of tragedy (probably one of the sub-types, or a combination of sub-types, given in Chapter 18), *and* (ii) in Chapter 13 he also explicitly focuses on the best plots of *that* sub-type. As we will see, of the nine plot-types of tragedy discussed in Chapters 13 and 14, Aristotle expressly says that four do not have pity and fear (or at least that have no pity, which entails *a fortiori* that they cannot have *both* pity *and* fear). Furthermore, we can easily deduce that four other plot-types in those two chapters do not have at least any relevant pity, given how Aristotle explains that emotion in Chapter 13.

Finally, in 2003, I accepted that the four sub-types of tragedy matched the four sub-types of epic, with "simple" being the fourth one (involving the corrupted word in Chapter 18). I am not convinced, though, that this is necessarily correct, and believe that Janko's position, in which the fourth sub-type of tragedy is "of spectacle," may be equally plausible. In his interpretation, it is a coincidence that both art forms have four sub-types. However, no major thesis in this book depends on this issue, and I leave it for future scholarship to settle.

---

*Oedipus*. I do not cover this final topic here, given how long this book is already.

# Chapter 6: Additional Reasons Why Catharsis, Pity and Fear Cannot be Authentic in the Definition of Tragedy, including a Reply to Halliwell

Let us take stock of where we are concerning the second alleged misconception of Aristotle's treatise and the history since 2003, when the article reproduced in Chapter 5 was published. The shortest summary is that some scholars have accepted part of that article, notably that *katharsis* is or probably is impossible in *Dramatics* 6, whereas some have defended the authenticity of the manuscripts. Even some of the scholars, though, who have accepted my view about *katharsis* being interpolated, or who now want to ignore it when understanding the *Dramatics*,[547] are still leery of getting rid of pity and fear in the definition, because those emotions are spoken of throughout Chapters 13 and 14. Thus, the focus of this chapter is not only to provide the much more rigorous, indeed, I believe, insuperable reasons why pity and fear are likewise not authentic in the definition but to refute the only three scholars who to my knowledge have published criticisms of my 2003 article. By the end of this chapter, the *katharsis* clause I believe will be utterly, stone-cold dead, with no chance of being brought back from Hades, like Euripides at the end of the *Frogs*.

Before, though, getting to the rebuttals and the crucial section about pity and fear, let us first cover some of the developments since 2003. As noted, in 2007 Claudio William Veloso, a Brazilian-Italian-French scholar, advanced my position in some ways, also in *Oxford Studies for Ancient Philosophy*. He corrected, for instance, one part of the pity and fear argument, while providing different grounds stemming from the *Politics* to claim also that the whole *katharsis* clause, and not just the single word *katharsis*, was mistakenly interpolated by a later editor.[548] Veloso correctly argues for the importance of *diagoge*—"intellectual enjoyment"—in the *Politics* for tragedy, and develops his views thoroughly in a new book *Pourquoi la Poétique d'Aristote? DIAGOGE [Why the Poetics of Aristotle? Intellectual Enjoyment]* (August 2018, Vrin). Suffice it to say here that one of the authentic goals of "music" I mentioned in Chapter 4 concerning the *Politics* and that I discuss in detail in Chapter 7 as "delight" coincides exactly with Veloso's main conclusion, even if we sometimes have different interpretations of minor points.[549] However, it would extend inordinately this already lengthy book

---

547  As we see elsewhere, Woodruff says: "Whether or not the katharsis phrase is an interpolation, it is not woven into the fabric of the book, *and we had best set it to one side* as we work to understand the text of the Poetics." (*op. cit.*, 2009, p. 622). Yet he also says "*But we have seen that tragedy must select those actions that have the power to arouse pity and fear. So action serves the arousal of emotion, and therefore it is not at the top of the hierarchy of aims in tragedy* [my italics] (*op. cit.*, pp. 612-3).

548  Veloso, *op. cit.*, 2007.

549  This coincides with Smerdel's view, which Veloso knew nothing of, and which, again, I myself only discovered in autumn 2014. Smerdel says (*op. cit.*, 1937) "Pleasure is the aim of tragic drama" (p. 25, transl. Milivoj Vodopija, orally) and notes that the cognitive delight of the free man is the goal of art and is crucial to

even to summarize the parts of his comprehensive work that I have read in draft, and thus I refer the interested reader (of French) to it.

When a draft of my "Purging the *Poetics*" was finished for the most part around 2001, I had exhausted the obvious ways of trying to find Anton Smerdel's work, on which Petruševski had based his own bold conjecture that Aristotle had not written *katharsis* in the definition of tragedy. I assumed that Smerdel's work from Skopje was lost forever, in part because a Macedonian scholar had not been successful in finding it for me. However, while writing the antepenultimate draft of the first edition of this book, and in wanting to add more on Smerdel's biography, I discovered in 2014 on the Web that his book was available at the University of Zagreb, and that he was Croatian rather than Macedonian. I therefore hastened to Zagreb in the autumn of the same year and had the book translated. While at it, I had Petruševski's Macedonian text also translated, because before I had only worked from its French *précis* that Petruševski himself had written as a summary, which although extensive was still a *précis*. Recall from Chapter 5 above that he accepted Smerdel's (and Gudeman's) view that a solution to the meaning of catharsis in *Dramatics* 6 was impossible and he advanced their position by arguing that the word *katharsis* had to have been wrongly interpolated. I should add here the few additional points I discovered in getting those works translated before continuing with the replies to the three disbelieving scholars who have published critiques of my "Purging the *Poetics*" and who continue to advocate the authenticity of *katharsis*.

As partially covered above in Chapter 5: In some ways following at least two renowned German scholars, Ulrich von Wilamowitz (1848–1931) and Alfred Gudeman (1862-1942),[550] Smerdel in 1937 deeply questioned the reasonableness of the word *katharsis*, pointing out that inclusion of the word in the definition abrogated Aristotle's own rules of definition in both the *Topics* and *Posterior Analytics*.[551] Smerdel did not think "modern hermeneutical" methods would ever allow us to resolve the meaning of the word, given the centuries of conflicting opinions on the topic, and, in effect, recommended against continuing to try to untie this particular Gordian knot.[552] Smerdel had also been

---

happiness. This goal of delight is given by Aristotle in *Politics* VIII 5 and in the *Nicomachean Ethics* 1099b18 (pp. 28-9). Smerdel follows Spengel in this regard, as noted earlier.

550 Gudeman was actually born in America and studied at Columbia University before going to Germany. He perished in the concentration camp Theresienstadt.

551 Smerdel, *op. cit.*, 1937, esp. pp. 35-9 and 63-8. Petruševski himself says (p. 237) that the "wise German scholar, the author of the excellent edition of the *Poetics*, Alfred Gudeman (*Aristoteles PERI POIETIKES* [1934]), after long continual years studying the problem, arrived at a negative conclusion [on p. 171], namely, that it would never be solved [my transl.]" Tarán and Gutas moderate the praise of Gudeman by pointing out a number of problems with Gudeman's scholarship (*op. cit.*, pp. 70-1), but their criticisms have no bearing on the matter at hand.

552 All of this seems to have helped put Petruševksi on his own path, given his summary of Smerdel's book.

influenced by Heinrich Otte,[553] who is to my knowledge the first to propose that the word alongside *katharsis* was not *pathēmatōn* but rather *pragmatōn* ("actions" or "events") although Otte himself seemingly did not question the word *katharsis*. Rather, again, the first well-known, published argument claiming the inauthenticity of *katharsis* in *Dramatics* 6 is by Petruševski. Petruševski also recounts that because of the conflicting interpretations of *katharsis* and the resulting problems for the definition of tragedy, von Wilamowitz declared that it was a shame that the definition of tragedy had not remained as unknown in modern times as it had been in ancient times![554] After this witty, but half-serious, remark, and taking Otte's and Smerdel's position further, Petruševski finally cut this particular Gordian knot—actually, only half of it—because he still kept pity and fear in the clause. As we saw above in Chapter 5, he denied that Aristotle wrote *katharsis pathēmatōn*, in part because the phrase never appears in the first five chapters, as Smerdel had highlighted. Rather, the original words for Petruševski were instead *sustasin pragmatōn* ("the arrangement of actions," namely plot). What I did not mention in my "Purging," but alluded to in Unit 1, is another of Petruševski's insights: Plato himself had equated, in effect, the making of tragedy in the *Phaedrus* with *pragmatōn rhēseis* ("dramatic speeches" or "speeches of actions") at 268c-d. Aristotle, according to Petruševski, is thereby implicitly criticizing Plato and indicating with the similar phrase *sustasin pragmatōn* what the true nature of tragedy is.[555] Petruševski did not recognize how Aristotle's overall blueprint for the *Dramatics* also follows the *Phaedrus*, as discussed in Chapter 2, which makes Petruševski's own insight about *pragmatōn rhēseis* even more compelling.

This completes the overall picture of Smerdel and Petruševski and their major contributions to the issue at hand. Minor points will be added as appropriate.

Let us turn now to the three printed critiques[556] of my article from 2003, which defend the *katharsis* clause: A few paragraphs against me by an American professor, Michael Pakaluk;[557] a slightly longer

---

553   Heinrich Otte, *Kennt Aristoteles die sogenannte tragische Katharsis?* (Berlin: Weidmann) 1912.

554   Petruševski, *op. cit.*, 1954, p. 237. Clearly, this was said half, but only half, in jest.

555   Petruševksi, *op. cit.*, 1954, pp. 242 and 244. Still, Petruševksi, like all other ancient Greek scholars to my knowledge until my work in the 1990's, maintains the literary view of tragedy in the *Poetics*.

556   I leave aside an article by William Marx, "La véritable catharsis aristotélicienne. Pour une lecture philologique et physiologique de la *Poétique*," *Poétique* 166 (2011), p. 131-54, in which he calls me and Veloso "terrorists" (p. 132) because we dare argue for the athetesis of the catharsis clause. Marx appears to use the publications of the "terrorists" only as a pretext to help publish and advertise a work that, as far as I can tell, was finished before he ever heard of us, because he never touches my own arguments. Hence, there is no reason in this book to discuss him.

557   Pakaluk's argument is part of a review of the entire edition in which my article appears: "David Sedley, ed., *Oxford Studies in Ancient Philosophy* (Oxford University Press, Oxford) Volume XXV, Winter 2003." The review can be found at http://bmcr.brynmawr.edu/2006/2006-06-18.html or in *Bryn Mawr Classical Re-*

treatment against both me and Veloso by the Belgian ancient specialist, Pierre Destrée;[558] and a very fine-grained, five-page reply by the specialist who advocated the "imaginary" view of performance that I examined in depth in Chapter 3, the renowned scholar of the *Dramatics*, Stephen Halliwell, in a section in *Between Ecstasy and Truth*[559] entitled "Appendix: Is the Catharsis Clause in the *Poetics* an Interpolation?". Halliwell's defense is without a doubt the most rigorous critique, and one that defends the *katharsis*, pity and fear clause at the highest scholarly level, also against both me and Veloso. My purpose now is to refute these three scholars in order to demonstrate, as noted, that *katharsis* in the definition of tragedy is indefensible, whether or not the profession as a whole has recognized it yet. The further arguments about pity and fear occur in my reply to Halliwell. I trust that the length of these rebuttals are apropos, for if the critics, especially Halliwell, are decisively answered, the exegetical epic of how, for example, to resolve the meaning of *katharsis* in *Dramatics* 6 should be forever settled, at least for any reader not committed at any and all costs to the traditional position. By "traditional position" here in Unit 2, I mean very precisely that the word *katharsis*, however it is construed, is authentic in Chapter 6. Obviously, if *katharsis* is not authentic, there is no reason to answer the question about its meaning *there*, even if the issue of how Aristotle used the concept in other treatises or other periods of his life is still very much an open and important issue. To my knowledge, none of the other "doubters" (of the legitimacy of *katharsis*)—for example, Smerdel, Petruševski, Freire, Brunius, Veloso, and Rashed—ever deny that Aristotle authentically uses the term in the *Politics*, especially given that he was close to Plato, who himself uses *katharsis* frequently across his educational, epistemic, artistic, and ontological theories.[560] Nor do I deny catharsis apart from Chapter 6.

---

*view* 2006.06.18.

558   Pierre Destrée, "La purgation des interprétations : conditions et enjeux de la catharsis poétique chez Aristote," in *Littérature et thérapeutique des passions. La catharsis en question*, ed. J.-C. Darmon (Paris: Hermann) 2011, pp. 13-35.

559   Halliwell, *op. cit.*, 2011.

560   At *Sophist* 230b-d, Plato says that *katharsis* is the separating of the bad from the good so that the good parts are left in a better state. Hence, regarding the acquisition of knowledge on the part of a student, "refutation (*ton elenchon lekteon*) is the greatest of the purifications (*katharseon*)." That is, the student will be left more purified, with a more appropriate modesty in regards to learning, when his conceit is purged. Plato also states at *Phaedo* 69b-c that the moral ideal is the *katharsis* of the emotions and in his political treatises (*Laws* V 735bff; *Republic* II 385c and X 607a) that the *polis* may be cleansed by its rulers. By dispensing with evil influence and bad composers through either exile or death, the rulers purify the state (*katharmous poleos*). The cognate *katharon*—"pure"—also enters in Plato's related ontological theory in the *Symposium*, when he claims that the form of Beauty is pure. By implication, any instantiations of artistic beauties would be sullied. That beauty is at least one of the ends of art for Plato can be seen at *Republic* III and X—403c; 595c; 600e—and *Laws* VII 816d, and, by the way, for Aristotle in *Dramatics* 7. In perhaps the most relevant case for this book, in the *Laws* (VII 790d) the Athenian says that song and dance in religious rituals can provide beneficial psychological relief from fear (and we have seen that Aristotle suggests the same in *Politics* VIII 7, when he speaks of the catharsis resulting from the sacred "melodies" and when he speaks of a fuller explanation of catharsis *en tois peri poiētikēs*). Indubitably, then, catharsis is pervasive throughout Plato's philosophy.

Chapter 6: Pity and Fear in the Definition of Tragedy

## Pakaluk

Given that Pakaluk's critique of my interpretation amounts to two short paragraphs (after a first paragraph that significantly misrepresents my position) and given that Halliwell presents similar arguments, but much more rigorously and with a finer-grained examination of the Greek text, I focus here only on what is distinctive to Pakaluk. He indicates that two definitions in the *Nicomachean Ethics*—one on happiness (*eudaimonia*) and the other on the courageous man—also show Aristotle importing essential conditions at the very end without antecedent mention, which supposedly justifies Aristotle doing it in the definition of tragedy. However, this distorts Aristotle's views in the different cases.[561] With regards to the first definition in the *Nicomachean Ethics,* Pakaluk omits that Aristotle explicitly states "*but we must add* in a complete life" (my italics) when he gives the final condition of "in a complete life," thereby warning the reader explicitly that he is adding a condition. Moreover, Aristotle never says in the *Nicomachean Ethics* that he is developing his definitions based on what was said before, as he does in the *Dramatics*. Nor does he seem to make a series of divisions and then collect them, as he does in the *Dramatics (*although what Pakaluk calls a "patiently developed previous discussion" might seem to function like biological definition, which itself, as we saw above, requires that elements in the previous "divisions" be collected into the definition). The biological definition, then, arguably does not have an exact parallel in *Nicomachean Ethics*—demonstrating that Aristotle was much more concerned in the *Dramatics* with signaling the collection of all the previous conditions of tragedy than he was in the *Nicomachean Ethics*.[562] More crucially, the "final conditions" given by Pakaluk in the two examples from the *Nicomachean Ethics* are indeed mentioned or discussed *after* the definition: *kalon* or its synonyms many times for the word that is introduced at the last moment for the courageous man, and a "long life" at, for example, 100a5, when Aristotle discusses Priam. To

---

Let me add the voice of Francis Sparshott on this topic: "On the issue of the moral 'health' of people in general, Aristotle was more of a Platonist than is commonly allowed" (Francis Sparshott, "The Riddle of Catharsis," *Centre and Labyrinth: Essays in Honour of Northrop Frye*, eds. Eleanor Cook *et al*, Toronto: Univ. of Toronto Pr., 1983, p. 35, note 29). For transparency, I should add that Sparshott was the supervisor of my Ph.D. dissertation.

Finally, it should be noted that Plato was following a long tradition. As E.R. Dodds notes in speaking of catharsis in Empedocles: "The notion of catharsis was no novelty... it was a major pre-occupation of religious minds throughout the Archaic Age" (*op. cit.,* 1951, pp. 153-4).

561 Veloso says tersely (albeit correctly) in his own article of 2007 (pp. 271-2) in reply to Pakaluk that the cases are different, but Veloso relies on us reading the texts to see the obvious dissimilarities, and thus I supplement his reply.

562 I should add now that Aristotle is well known for signaling that he will discuss an issue later or in another treatise and it is utterly incongruous that he would indicate the definition of tragedy comes from what had been said already and then in no way signal that he is both adding a new word and also ignoring such an important essential condition in the whole treatise. As we saw, when he has very little to say of one of the "merely" necessary conditions, *dianoia* (reasoning or thought), the third highest in the ranking of the six necessary elements, he gives the reason why in Chapter 19: It is because the notion is discussed already in the *Rhetoric*.

the contrary, *katharsis* is *never* discussed subsequently after the definition in the *Dramatics*. The "spontaneously inserted" conditions in *Nicomachean Ethics* are then indeed legitimate, but the condition of *katharsis* not.

In any event, in 2003 I granted (but merely for the sake of argument) that the lack of any antecedent mention of *katharsis*, pity and fear in the definition when all the other conditions are discussed in some detail in those chapters probably does not suffice to carry my conclusions for traditionalists. Yet Pakaluk never addresses the problems resulting from Aristotle ignoring *katharsis* in the rest of the whole treatise, especially given, e.g., the inconsistency of Aristotle giving a different end of tragedy, plot, in Chapter 6 (at 1450a22), a mere few sentences after the definition of tragedy. Besides, as someone who relies on the *Nicomachean Ethics* to illustrate Aristotle's doctrines, he should then also explain why Aristotle did not give, as the function of tragedy, "to moderate pity and fear" instead of "to cathart them." As he should well know, pity and fear are appropriate emotions to have at times according to the *Nicomachean Ethics*[563] and, by implication, individuals should in many circumstances *not* cathart them, at least in the sense of purging them (and the sense of purifying or clarifying them has been shown many times even before my article by other scholars to be extremely implausible, given Aristotle's other texts[564]). Finally, as we saw above, Battin, after a rigorous examination of how Aristotle uses his own rules of definition to arrive at the definition of tragedy, claims that the exposition of tragedy provides the *only* example in the Aristotelian treatises of the procedure that for him is crucial in generating scientific knowledge.[565] Thus, to use Pakaluk's terminology, the definition of tragedy is "aberrant," but in an admirable way.

### Destrée

In his article, Destrée specifies as one of his goals rebutting the two articles by myself and Veloso from *OSAP* noted above, even though he graciously admits that the thesis in my work is defended by an "inexorable logic"[566] while Veloso's is also "very logical."[567] Let us now turn to his only three arguments regarding my own article. The first relies on Aristotle explaining verbally in lecture the omissions and

---

563  *Nicomachean Ethics* II 6, 1106b13ff; III 5, 1114a26-7

564  Scott, 2003, pp. 239-43.

565  Battin, *op. cit.*, 1975, p. 301.

566  *Op. cit.*, 2011, p. 16, my translation, as are the other passages from his work.

567  Pp. 13-4. Destrée unsurprisingly believes that the problem of catharsis has never been solved, and he says his second goal is to give two constraints according to which any new interpretation of catharsis must be successful. Those constraints, he adds, would take into account Plato's own use of catharsis and the requirement that drama better the lives of men, namely, an "ethical" approach (even though the attitude of Lessing and others to turn drama into moral education is too strict), and to deny for the goal of tragedy the purely aesthetical and medical senses of the word.

inconsistencies in the text; the second treats *dunamis* as the equivalent of *katharsis* of tragedy; and the third considers *katharsis* to be a political aspect that need not enter into the aesthetical *Dramatics*. I leave aside his arguments insofar as they deal with Veloso's different grounds, otherwise this chapter would get too extended.[568]

*1. The "Principle of Oral Addition"*

Destrée says that not having *katharsis* mentioned before the definition of tragedy—despite Aristotle's explicit claim that he is defining tragedy by taking up the preceding discussion—is not problematic because Aristotle could clarify his position in lecturing. In short, Destrée upholds what I call the "Principle of Oral Addition." However, in and of itself the Principle is itself extremely problematic. It could destroy the possibility of much rigorous ancient Greek scholarship because advocating the Principle cuts both ways. I—or anyone else—can also claim "explanation during lecture" to explain away any written point that is problematic for our views. Indeed, as I describe fully concerning Halliwell later, when I suggest as I did in 2003 that Aristotle introduces a narrow sense of tragedy in *Dramatics* 9 related to pity and fear virtually out of nowhere (assuming the inauthenticity of the *katharsis*, pity, and fear clause), I myself can appeal to the Principle. I can easily justify the narrower scope by saying Aristotle explained the narrowing during the lecture. This is not to deny Destrée's claim completely, but the Principle of Oral Addition must be used very sparingly, and with extremely compelling reasons. In any event, it is better to postpone this discussion until we discuss Halliwell, who also appeals to the Principle.

Also, we need not believe that Aristotle's text was written only as notes for a lecture, although they might have been that too. Much of the *Dramatics* seems to have been composed to stand on its own, one reason following: As we saw, Aristotle says that the definition arises from what was said before, which he could have mentioned more easily in lecture. Additionally, he proceeds just a couple of sentences later to note that *melopoiia* is understood by everyone, which is why, he says, he need not add any more explanation. Why would Aristotle write such a comment if he had been content to explain ideas or terms during lecture? There would be no need for him to waste ink and papyrus on the point about the well-understood meaning of *melopoiia* if he were orally to cover gaps. Appealing to the Principle is doubly absurd in this context because there is then no reason for other crucial elements to be explained in writing. Why illuminate the plot or anything else with a detailed manuscript, if he planned to explain crucial *and well-known* elements orally in lecture? Finally, even Petruševski had tried to explain away pity and fear not being in Chapters 1 through 5 because they were so well understood as not to require earlier introduction—yet Aristotle then explains them in Chapter 13, all of which counts against both Petruševski's claim and the Principle of Oral Addition.

---

568   Moreover, Veloso in *Pourquoi la Poétique d'Aristote? DIAGOGE, op. cit.*, replies to Destrée himself.

Consider also Destrée's claim that "From a point of view strictly philological and historical, our text has nothing suspect." Clearly, this is wrong insofar as Destrée suggests that no specialist has doubted the word *katharsis*. Not only about ten scholars reported in this work have published either denials or doubts, but, e.g., Brunius lists other German scholars who have been baffled at how and why Aristotle included *katharsis* in Chapter 6.[569] Moreover, the historical *reputation* of Aristotle and all of his other manuscripts, I would argue, heavily outweighs the dubiousness of one phrase. Aristotle is not a first-year undergraduate student in business ethics, being forced to take philosophy because of school requirements. He is one of the greatest philosophers of all time. For him, then, to include a condition in a definition, which all Aristotelians know gives the essential conditions and the substance of something, and for him to leave the condition completely undeveloped in the rest of the treatise, is too shocking a procedure for such a rigorous thinker. In other words, one should trust his reputation or—to rephrase the matter even regarding *texts*—his other twenty-five chapters (indeed, the rest of Chapter 6 also), given how extensive they are, rather than one word that is utterly inconsistent with those twenty-six chapters. In short, Destrée, like Tarán and Gutas, still has not understood that this matter is not as much a philological matter as a philosophical one, nor does he seem to recognize the desperation that traditionalists must be in when they start relying on the Principle of Oral Addition. Given all of the above, that Principle seems much more radical, to use Destrée's own term, than a single proposed athetesis that is grounded on Aristotle's explicit writing itself, namely, the whole text of the *Dramatics*, and, as we shall see further below, the *Politics* VIII 7. Naturally, athetesis is to be used only as an absolutely last resort in ancient scholarship, unless one should *never* allow athetesis, but I have yet to find a scholar who would take such an extreme position. I have already shown how my reading staves off other recommended excisions by Else, D.W. Lucas and Whallen.

Destrée also says: "I strongly doubt that a proposition so radical [as Scott and Veloso's claim that the word catharsis was interpolated mistakenly] can really gain the favor of specialists." Yet, the citations throughout this paper show that the favor has been happening, and probably started happening, long ago, perhaps with von Wilamowitz if not before. Putting an end to a tradition that is over 450 years old, though, and that in some ways goes back to Avicenna, is like stopping a cruise ship. It does not happen quickly.[570] As I discovered while finishing the last draft of the first edition of this book, apart

---

569     I should mention also that H. D. F. Kitto expresses his doubt and bewilderment on this issue, too, in "Catharsis" in *The Classical Tradition*, ed. L. Wallach (Ithaca: Cornell University Press) 1966, p. 136.

570     To add another voice that I only recently discovered, showing some "favor," George Boys-Stones, Professor of Ancient Philosophy at Durham University (U.K.), writes: "My favourite articles in *Oxford Studies in Ancient Philosophy* this year are two in volume XXV: one by Gregory Scott, who cuts one Gordian knot of Aristotelian scholarship by athetizing the clause that introduces *catharsis* into Aristotle's definition in the *Poetics*..." ("Subject Reviews," *Greece & Rome*, Vol. 52, No. 1, The Classical Association: www.classicalassociation.org). Moreover, although it is not publicly confirmable (unless one contacts his daughter Pumpkin Sparshott in Scar-

## Chapter 6: Pity and Fear in the Definition of Tragedy

from the other scholars or doubters summarized before, Marwan Rashed, who receives a postscript at the end of this chapter, also now writes that *katharsis* is not possible in the definition. Besides, specialists like Woodruff have also published that we should in effect ignore *katharsis* while trying to understand the *Dramatics*, as footnoted above. For convenience, I should repeat here what he states, in the context of him suggesting that my answer is one (if only one) of the possible solutions that interpreters focusing on *katharsis* in the *Dramatics* should consider:

> One condition we could safely omit, with no cost to our understanding of the argument of the *Poetics*, is the requirement that a good tragedy must achieve *katharsis*. That is because this condition does no work in the argument; it does not support any of Aristotle's judgments about how tragedy should be made.[571]

> ... Whether or not the katharsis phrase is an interpolation, it is not woven into the fabric of the book, *and we had best set it to one side* [my italics] as we work to understand the text of the *Poetics*. (Halliwell 2002 does just that, p. 206, with n. 7).[572]

To return to Destrée and the "favor of specialists": Within ten years of my publication from 2003, there have been more professional ancient Greek philosophers, including specialists in the *Dramatics*, suggesting that I might be correct than those following Petruševski in fifty-five years. However, the more important question arguably is how many specialists will continue to follow the traditional view, once these rebuttals of Pakaluk, Destrée himself and Halliwell become known. At any rate, these points about head-counting are just an *ad hominem* argument against Destrée's own *ad ho-*

---

borough, ONT, Canada, who has a photograph of the letter), I note also my supervisor Francis Sparshott, who changed his view from the time he published on the topic of catharsis: "I certainly agree that the catharsis clause can't possibly form part of a definition of tragedy." [private correspondence, Jan. 10, 2004].

571   Paul Woodruff, *op. cit.*, 2009, p. 614.

572   *Op. cit.*, p. 622. The reference to Halliwell is to Stephen Halliwell, *The Aesthetics of Mimesis: Ancient Texts and Modern Problems* (Princeton: Princeton University Press) 2002. Halliwell, who has perhaps questioned catharsis as profoundly as it probably could be challenged on traditional approaches (short of advocating bracketing it as spurious in *Dramatics* 6), states his increasingly skeptical position on catharsis in the book that Woodruff cites, also noting that Pier Luigi Donini ["La Tragedia, Senza la catarsi," *Phronesis*, (1):26-41 (1998)] denies "that Aristotle takes catharsis to be the essential function of tragedy." Halliwell indicates that he has had misgivings since at least his much earlier *Aristotle's Poetics* (Chapel Hill: Univ. of North Carolina Press, 1986, pp. 184-201), where he is one of the scholars who recognize, e.g., the severe problems endemic in relating catharsis in *Politics* VIII 7 to tragedy. Suffice it to say that, subject to the revisions I argue for in this paper, I sympathize with much of those pages on catharsis, and strongly recommend them to anyone interested in this whole topic; see also, though, Veloso, *op. cit.*, p. 267, on both Halliwell and Donini concerning the related matters. However, Halliwell still defends the authenticity of *katharsis* in *Dramatics* 6, as we see in great detail below.

Woodruff also says: "Gregory Scott argues that the phrase about katharsis may not belong in the text at all, and urges that it should be purged from the text" (*op. cit.*, p. 622). For the sake of non-specialists, let me add that this means bracketing the words as spurious, not deleting them entirely from the Greek version included as part of a translation/commentary. Given the 1000-year history of the commentaries, future scholars will want to know where the *katharsis*, pity, and fear clause was included in extant manuscripts.

*minem.* Truth for Aristotelians is not a matter of counting heads, as it might be for the pragmatist Charles Peirce. The best explanation will be that which corresponds to reality, or, as Aristotle himself puts it when he defines truth, "to say of what is that it is."

## 2. *Katharsis* as *dunamis*

To his credit, Destrée does not rely only on the Principle of Oral Addition but goes further than Pakaluk and takes a stab at the paradox mentioned above: Why does *katharsis* never get discussed, *or even mentioned again in the relevant sense*, in the *Dramatics,* given that it is important enough to be the only explicit goal of tragedy in the definition? Rarely do other scholars tackle this critical problem rigorously.[573] Usually, at best, they only offer arguments, if even that, as to why Aristotle could have added the goal of tragedy to the definition unexpectedly at the last moment (as Pakaluk in effect did), about as shocking an omission as I have ever seen in Aristotelian scholarship. An equivalent would be finding in the definition of *eudaimonia* ("happiness") in *Nicomachean Ethics* 1 10 a clause "eating well-marinated octopus once a week," without any discussion *or even relevant mention* in the whole treatise of octopi, either before or after the mention of octopus in something so important for Aristotle as the definition. In other words, accepting that a term in a definition can appear "out of the air" (as both Pakaluk and Destrée believe) or arguing that the definition of tragedy was augmented after the first version by Aristotle during a re-editing process, which Else infamously proposed, barely begins to address the real problem, namely, the absence of *katharsis* in the later parts of the *Dramatics*. What could be a good reason for Aristotle to not develop *katharsis* as an essential condition, especially when he develops *all* of the other conditions and especially when, for instance, the end of tragedy is explicitly discussed (as it is in *Dramatics* 6, 14 and 26)? Later I discuss this more concerning Halliwell and Bernays.

To return, though, to Destrée: Commendably, in my opinion, he indicates (p. 19) that any view purporting to use *katharsis* purposely and solely as a "subtext" to explain Aristotle's silence is unsatis-

---

[573] Heath tries to solve the problem of catharsis in *Dramatics* 6 with a complex set of reasons, saying his own:

> conclusion runs counter to the widespread assumption that the reference to *catharsis* in the definition of tragedy in chapter 6 is meant to state the 'final cause' of tragedy—that is, the end or purpose for the sake of which tragedy exists... On the interpretation I have outlined, then, *catharsis* is not the function of tragedy, but a beneficial effect which tragedy has on some members of the audience (*op. cit.*, 1996, pp. xli-xlii).

Unfortunately, his view in no way handles the problems noted throughout this book, e.g., why, given his own explanation, is the term not even used in the many places after the definition where one would expect it? His view is also fraught with unique problems. For example, why would Aristotle state what is merely a beneficial effect, or side-effect, in the definition and *not* the function of tragedy? He would be introducing an accidental consideration in the essential conditions, which completely goes against his own principles of definition.

factory. However, he then says (p. 20) that Aristotle's silence regarding *katharsis* in the treatise is perfectly understandable, in part because in the very first paragraph of the treatise Aristotle says that he will explore the *dunamis* (power or potential) of the art forms. Since Destrée adds nothing more on this point, the implication presumably is that *katharsis* is, or includes, the *dunamis* of tragedy, or vice versa, which is to say, that anytime Aristotle writes *dunamis*, he suggests *katharsis* and thus need not mention it overtly.

I now identify the problems with these claims. First, we will recall that Aristotle says in the opening sentence "Our topic is poetry in itself and its kinds, and what potential (*dunamis*) *each* has [my italics]." "Each kind" presumably includes tragedy, comedy, and epic, the three and only three (major) kinds examined in depth in the treatise, given the analysis above in Chapter 2 (and I discuss the sub-kinds of tragedy soon). How Aristotle can indicate here that he will explore the *dunamis* of each of the forms, and then, if *dunamis* means or implies *katharsis*, never explore it in any relevant way other than mentioning it once in Chapter 6 is baffling, especially given that much is said, e.g., about the proper *pleasure* of epic. Perhaps, though, Destrée would claim that when Aristotle uses *dunamis* he only implies *katharsis* as part of the power or potential. However, this is contra-indicated by all of the texts, with one possible exception: Almost immediately in Chapter 1, as we saw, Aristotle mentions the *dunamis* that attends the playing of the oboe and kithara in combination with dancing. Yet it is absurd to think that all such playing implies *katharsis*, for these instruments could be apropos in many scenarios and many types of music. The oboe (*aulos*) was specifically associated with *katharsis* in *Politics* VIII 6, we saw above in Chapter 4, but not the *kithara*. Also, Aristotle mentions in Chapter 6 the *dunamis* of the *melopoiia*—typically translated, I indicated above, as the making of the melody but instead in my view as the making of the "choral composition" (*choreia*), namely, music-dance—which Aristotle says is so plain as to need no explanation. Again, it would be stunning if *katharsis* was being always implied, given the wide variety of melodies or music-dance that was, and could be, created and experienced in the orchestral arts. Aristotle uses the term *dunamis* yet another time in Chapter 6 when he speaks of the similar potential (*dunamis*) of verse and prose (1450b13-15). This occurence in no way can mean *katharsis* (although perhaps Destrée would say *dunamis* switches within Chapter 6 to a different meaning). Another time that Aristotle introduces *dunamis* is at the end of Chapter 6, while speaking of spectacle:

> Spectacle (*opsis*) is something enthralling, but is very artless and *least* particular to the art of musical drama composition, because the *potential* (*dunamis*) of tragedy exists even without a competition and [its] actors; besides, the designer's art is *more* essential for the accomplishment of spectacular effects than is the dramatist's (my translation and italics, following Janko, 1450b18-20).

As seen in my Chapter 2, this sentence comes in a passage in which Aristotle ranks spectacle last, but still within the necessary elements. Perhaps *dunamis* could indeed suggest *katharsis* here as a part of a "tragic effect," but if catharsis were the important potential of tragedy, it is strange that Aristotle would be so oblique.[574] That is because the potential of tragedy seems to be the totality of the partial potentials of the various necessary elements (including ones just mentioned beforehand in *Dramatics* 6). The next and final noteworthy occurrence of the *dunamis* of tragedy pertains to its plot. In *Dramatics* 9, at 1451b38-39, Aristotle compares episodic plots with simple plots, and, as we saw, says that dramatists compose episodic ones to accommodate actors during the competitions, extending the plot "beyond its potential (*dunamis*)." Whatever this means—and I noted before one option—it hardly seems to imply *katharsis*. What could "extending a plot beyond its *katharsis*" even mean?

Finally, even granting that somehow Destrée could handle the above objections and still claim *dunamis* implies *katharsis* (or vice-versa), another puzzle arises that is an extension of the one I mentioned at the end of Unit 1. Why and how does Aristotle apply *katharsis* to musical arts, given his discussion of *katharsis* in *Politics* VIII 7 and given the passages about music in the *Dramatics*, rather than to what is usually conceived to be one of the poetic arts, namely, tragedy? On Destrée's approach, there would seemingly be at least two types of *katharsis* or a doubly-intense *katharsis* or conflicting types of *katharsis* in tragedy, which does not bode well for tragedies, especially after Agathon. That is, those tragedies, according to *Dramatics* 18, often have musical interludes that have nothing to do with the plot, so any cathartic musical effect may have no impact on the *plot's* cathartic effect or may be misaligned with it or may thwart the plot's *katharsis*. This may be possible, but why would Aristotle never even broach any of these issues, were *katharsis* so crucial to tragedy? Finally, according to even some commentators writing before me, including, e.g., Hutton, the *dunamis* of tragedy is (only) given explicitly as pleasure throughout the *Dramatics*.[575]

While on the topic of pleasure: How Destrée would establish in the future (because he does not do it in his article) any necessary *and relevant* connection between pleasure and *katharsis*—if his cryptic statements are somehow implying that linkage—is also utterly baffling. To reiterate what was stressed before, the *Politics* VIII 7 (1342a11-16) makes a connection during a discussion of musical modes between *katharsis* as purgation and a *resulting* pleasure for some, mostly pathological individuals (and then in a milder way to all people) for some types of "music" that audiences might experience. However, even were this linkage to be always holding, it would mean that pleasure is the goal of tragedy, and it, rather than the intermediary *katharsis*, should have been included as the final goal

---

[574] Also, Aristotle says in Chapter 14 that the pity and fear can come through the spectacle, which surely means a catharsis of pity and fear can also come through spectacle, were the catharsis clause authentic. Yet Aristotle does not care to explain any of this or even remark on it.

[575] For more on Hutton's view, see his excellent *op. cit.*, 1982, p. 85, or the summary in Scott, 2003, p. 240. As noted in Chapter 2, he is the scholar who to my knowledge best addressed the paradoxes of the origin of tragedy at the beginning of *Dramatics* 4 before my fundamental changes opened new options.

Chapter 6: Pity and Fear in the Definition of Tragedy

in the definition of tragedy, according to the *Topics*, where Aristotle discusses definition:

> Certainly it is what is best or final that should be stated, e.g., that desire is not for the pleasant but for pleasure; for this is our purpose in choosing what is pleasant (Book 6, 8.146b10-13)[576]...

> It might be said that it is possible for what is desirable in itself to be desirable because of something else as well; but still to define what is desirable in itself in such a way is none the less wrong; for what is best in anything is especially part of its substance, and it is better for a thing to be desirable in itself than to be desirable because of something else, so that the definition ought rather to have indicated this (Book 6, 12.149b33-49).

Highlighting that pleasure is not for the pleasant but vice versa, Aristotle surely would know that *katharsis* is for the sake of pleasure (or for health or relief) *and not vice versa*. He in effect says as much at *Politics* VIII 7, 1342a16, in the passage in which relief and pleasure come *through katharsis* for the relevant type of "musical" performance. Thus, to include the means to the end in the definition of tragedy, *katharsis*, rather than the desirable end itself, pleasure (*hēdonē*), ignores his own strictures in the *Topics* and also jars with what he explicitly says in Chapter 14, that the dramatist should produce the proper *pleasure* from pity and fear (1453b12-13). A traditionalist might claim that Chapter 14 is elliptical for "the dramatist should produce the proper pleasure from (the catharsis resulting from) pity and fear." However, given the assumed connection of catharsis with pity and fear, it would have been easier for Aristotle to say (were he concerned with brevity), "the proper pleasure *from catharsis*." For all these reasons, then, neither *dunamis* nor pleasure can be a substitute for an explicit discussion of *katharsis*.

*3. Catharsis is a political concept in an "aesthetically-motivated" treatise*
Let us switch now to Destrée's final claim that *katharsis* is only political and thus there is no reason for it to be discussed in the *Dramatics*, which is aesthetical. If this were true, why does Aristotle even bother including *katharsis* in the first place as the goal in the definition of tragedy, especially since *Politics* VIII 7 emphasizes that *katharsis* is but one goal of "music" and that the other goals like intellectual enjoyment, education, or amusement/relaxation should be aimed for also? If Aristotle thought *katharsis* was important enough to include in the definition of tragedy, he would presumably also have discussed it in some detail later in the *Dramatics*, just as he discusses every other part of the definition, whether in Chapter 6 or later. Optionally, as he is wont to do, he would have noted

---

[576] Tr. W.A. Pickard-Cambridge, as are other passages from the *Topics* unless noted (*The Complete Works of Aristotle*, Vol. 1, ed. J. Barnes, *op. cit.*) *Katharsis* also seems to contradict other sections of the *Topics*. The definiens (including catharsis) should be more primary and clearer than the definiendum (tragedy) itself, according to *Topics* 6.141a26-27. The definition with catharsis becomes unnecessarily complex, allowing a disputant to upend it easier (6.139b13ff; 7.153b34ff; 155a4ff). Similarly, 6.139b12-15 bans obscure language, yet the obscurity of catharsis has been amply demonstrated by over 450 hundred years of failed exegesis or by a millennium if one counts Avicenna and Averroes.

that he discusses *katharsis* in another treatise and is therefore omitting the discussion—as he does for *dianoia* in Chapter 19. Again, recall his statement in VIII 7 that *katharsis* is *explained* (and not merely mentioned) in a treatise on composition (*en tois peri poiētikēs*). At any rate, we should not accept Destrée's suggestion that there are no political considerations in the *Dramatics*. For example, in Chapter 25, at 1460b13-15, Aristotle talks about the difference between political and artistic principles: "there is not the same [standard of] correctness in the art of civic life as in that of *poiētikēs* ("dramatic musical composition"), nor is there in any other art as in that of *poiētikēs*" (my transl., following Janko, 140b13-15). Why does he not add here, then, if he has no political concerns in the treatise, that this difference is why he is omitting the expected discussion of katharsis?

At any rate, there are many motivations in the *Dramatics* other than civic life that would compel either a discussion or at least some mentions of *katharsis* on Aristotle's part during and after Chapter 6. For example, the concern with *katharsis* would have been triggered equally well by relevant psychological or ethical concerns, or even defensive, critical ones, especially if, as so many scholars think, Aristotle wants to defend tragedy against Plato's well-known attack on both it and comedy.[577] For example, Chapter 15 is devoted to ethical concerns in tragedy, and how goodness in character is right behind plot in importance. Why no mention of how catharsis is important here? Moreover, in *Dramatics* 13, as we saw briefly in Chapter 5 above, Aristotle adds that a good man must not be seen going from happiness to misery, because this would not be pitiful or fearful but rather odious or shocking *(miaron)*. *Miaros/miaron* has the general meaning of defiled by blood, polluted, and, in moral terms, brutal, coarse and shocking, according to Liddell and Scott. I will follow some who translate it as "shocking," but the overall coloring implying brutality or odiousness might well be kept in mind. Likewise, a bad man must not be seen going from misery to happiness, nor even an extremely bad man going from happiness to misery. These, Aristotle says, don't fulfill the prerequisites to cause pity and fear, nor, he adds, are they morally satisfying. I discuss for other reasons shortly the ramifications of these three tragic plots having no pity and fear, but the crucial question for the moment is: Why would Aristotle be concerned with pity and fear in Chapter 13, but not *katharsis*, especially when *katharsis* is associated in the definition with those two emotions, a point that Petruševski himself strongly emphasized?[578] Hence, even granting that the *Dramatics* is an "aesthetical" treatise, whatever Destrée would mean precisely by "aesthetical," without question Aristotle has many non-political reasons, including psychological, ethical and artistic ones, for discussing *katharsis* further. He should have been discussing it were it legitimate in Chapter 6. All of this, then, suffices for the reply to Destrée.

---

577 As suggested, I have a more complex view of Aristotle's relation to Plato than thinking that the student hoisted his mentor on his mentor's own petard with the doctrine of catharsis, all of which is addressed in Chapter 7 below.

578 *Op. cit.*, 1954, p. 241.

## Chapter 6: Pity and Fear in the Definition of Tragedy

Let us now turn to Halliwell, and his arguments against my "Purging," again itself reproduced above.

### Halliwell

My three major claims in "Purging" are:

- Neither *katharsis*, pity nor fear is mentioned in *Dramatics* 1-5 even though Aristotle proceeds with biological definition, with every element except *katharsis*, pity, and fear introduced before *Dramatics* 6,—yet it is crucial in this type of definition that antecedent differentiae are introduced and collected;
- Even ignoring the issue of biological definition, there is no subsequent discussion of *katharsis*, pity and fear in *Dramatics* 6-7 when *all* of the other essential conditions get developed into six necessary conditions, as we saw in detail in Chapters 2 and 3;
- Nor is there even a mention of *katharsis* in the rest of the treatise (apart from the second and final, irrelevant use in *Dramatics* 17), including those passages in which the goal of tragedy and epic is discussed, whereas all of the other elements in the (extended) definition are treated at length or explicitly postponed.

Halliwell replies with greater or lesser rigor to all of these points, and adds a fourth set of arguments, about a missing reference by Aristotle if *katharsis* in *Dramatics* 6 is removed, which I had not discussed in my article and which I explain more fully at the end. Let us now examine Halliwell's four sets of individual critiques precisely as he gives them:

> (S[1]) Aristotle's statement that the definition of tragedy arises or emerges from what has preceded does not entail that everything in it has been previously mentioned: the idea of 'wholeness' or 'completeness' of action has not been adduced prior to this (Scott wrongly suggests otherwise), nor indeed has the concept of (an) 'action' qua unified structure of events, as opposed to the more general notion of 'people in action' (ch. 2 etc.).[579]

In reply: First, notice that, to his credit, Halliwell does not quibble about "wholeness" (*teleias*) being missing in Chapters 1 through 5. Rather what is instead missing for him is "*the idea* of 'wholeness' or 'completeness' [my italics]," which is how *teleias* is normally (and correctly) translated. If he quibbled, he would be right, but then he would be immediately open to the parry that neither does the exact word *hedusmenō* ("embellished" or "sweetened") appear in Chapters 1 through 5, when it also is in the definition of tragedy as *hedusmenō logos* ("embellished speech"). Yet, as I explained,[580] obviously to Halliwell's satisfaction, "embellished" is derived as an idea from the preceding chapters, and no scholar has ever questioned its legitimacy. The proof, as we saw in Chapter 2, is that in the first sentence immediately after the dubious *katharsis* clause Aristotle explicitly states that he means by *hedusmenō* the music (*harmonia*) and dance (*rhuthmos*) that accompany the language, all of which

---

579  *Op. cit.*, 2011, p. 261-3, as are Halliwell's other three quotations given below, S[2]–S[4].
580  2003, p. 241.

are the three means of mimesis that indubitably come from *Dramatics* 1.[581] I now show that there are at least three possibilities according to which *teleias*, like *hedusmenō*, is a substitute for an idea broached in *Dramatics* 4 or 5, after a preliminary remark. Only one of these possibilities has to hold for the biological definition to be "protected," that is, to be shown in *all* respects to emanate "from what has been said" (leaving aside, naturally, the spurious *katharsis* clause).

The preliminary remark is this: *Teleias* is tightly coupled with magnitude (*megethos*) in the definition in Chapter 6 and then in the expanded explanation in *Dramatics* 7. For instance, at 6.1450b24-26, Aristotle says: "We have laid down that tragedy is the representation of a complete (*teleias*), i.e., whole action which has some magnitude (*megethos*) (for there can be a whole with no magnitude[582]). A whole is that which has a beginning, a middle and a conclusion."[583] He then adds that, if the magnitude is too large, the whole cannot be perceived or easily remembered, as in the case with a huge animal a thousand miles long (7.1451a1-6), the assumption being that you are right next to the animal. (If you were in outer space, you could perhaps see it as a whole, but Aristotle did not have satellites to cause him to consider sensibly such an option.) The same applies to epic poets who put too many events or plots in their works, or to historians, who themselves present many events happening at the same time, often with no connection between the events in a period of time (23.1459a20-29). Only a whole action has perceivable causal relationships between its events (7.1451a17-29; 23.1459a17-29). Yet, *megethos* is explicitly introduced in *Dramatics* 4 and 5, once when Aristotle mentions the mag-

---

581    For those who may have skipped Unit 1, I continue translating *harmonia kai rhuthmos* as "music (or tune) and dance" for the reasons given amply in Chapter 2.

582    This is a surprising claim, given that wholes for Aristotle usually have parts, as shown by the immediately following statement that a whole has a beginning, middle, and end. One cannot have parts of zero. Probably, though, this a rhetorical comment, and Aristotle only means by "no magnitude" such insignificant size that for all practical purposes is of no magnitude. This is suggested by his following remarks about animals so tiny as to be imperceptible. More on parts in a moment regarding McKirahan's views.

Another possible explanation was brought to my attention by Silvia Carli, a professor and specialist in Aristotle at Skidmore College. In discussing pleasure in *Nichomachean Ethics* X 4, Aristotle says:

> We have discussed movement with precision in another work, but it seems that it is not complete at any and every time, but that the many movements are incomplete and different in kind, since the whence and whither give them their form. **But of pleasure the form is complete at any and every time.** Plainly, then, pleasure and movement must be different from each other, and pleasure must be one of the things that are whole and complete. This would seem to be the case, too, from the fact that it is not possible to move otherwise than in time, but it *is* possible to be pleased; **for that which takes place in a moment is a whole** [his italics, but my bolding; 1174b2-8] (tr. by W.D. Ross and revised by J.O. Urmson, in Barnes, *The Complete Works of Aristotle, op. cit.*).

Thus, Aristotle might be making in the *Dramatics* a point about "whole" in general, and the immediately following claim about the beginning, middle, and end is elliptical for "the (relevant) whole (pertaining to tragedy) has a beginning, middle, and end."

583    Thus, something with only, for example, a beginning but no end is not a whole; cf. 1450b28f-33.

## Chapter 6: Pity and Fear in the Definition of Tragedy

nitude *(megethos)* of tragedy starting small with trivial plots and laughable diction before becoming grand (1449a19) and then again when he speaks of the length *(mēkei)* of tragedy versus epic (1449b11-15).

With this in mind, let us now examine the three possibilities for how the idea of *teleias* (completeness or wholeness) was suggested or actually given before *Dramatics* 6, to fill in what I ostensibly had omitted in "Purging" in 2003.[584]

*Option 1*: Aristotle compares epic with tragedy in *Dramatics* 5 and says that epic is unbounded *(aoristos)* in time whereas tragedy is limited. Tragedy is presumably thus bounded, which is to say, complete or whole. As Aristotle adds specifically, tragedy takes "one revolution of the sun or a little more" (1449b12ff). This is the option that Else notes, who says: "*Teleias* was ... at best implied in the 'norm of length' passage, 5.49b12-14."[585] Nevertheless, implication is good enough, as the case of *hedusmenō* shows, as long as the expanded discussion in the definition further establishes the legitimacy of the term, as it does for both *hedusmenō* and *teleias*. As part of that expanded explanation in *Dramatics* 7, Aristotle emphasizes that an animal too tiny or too large would cause its "unity and wholeness [to] vanish" from observation (7.1451a2). He follows this immediately by saying that just like animals, plots should have a "length that is easily memorable" (1451a6). Memory is the equivalent of observation for him here, and the "one revolution of the sun" in *Dramatics* 5 anticipates this topic. The one revolution suggests the proper "whole" or completeness, namely, a length that can be remembered or observed."[586]

---

584     I say "ostensibly" because I had mentioned some of the possible passages for this at p. 21 in "The *Poetics* of Performance," *op. cit.*, 1999, a publication which Halliwell cites without any significant comment, and which I had explicitly relied on for *OSAP* 2003.

585     *The Argument, op. cit.,* p. 223.

586     AnonC objects to this claim by saying that the "1000-mile animal is mentioned in the discussion of magnitude—introduced at 1450b34-6 as a factor different from completeness *(ou monon...alla kai megethos hyparchein me to tuchon)*. One of the disadvantages of exceeding the proper magnitude is that the completeness can no longer be observed (1450b39-51a2): but completeness on a scale that exceeds the limits of human observation is not incompleteness."

    I agree that completeness and magnitude, although "tightly coupled" in my terminology in Aristotle's discussion in Chapters 6-7, are in some ways distinct considerations. Still, that they are connected for him, and that a definite magnitude implies for Aristotle a definite size and thus a whole, is all I need for my position. Moreover, I never claimed, nor do I claim, that a 1000-mile animal is incomplete. Instead it (or the equivalent 1000 hours or days of drama) is not complete for tragedy for Aristotle *in the proper way, that is, in having the proper magnitude.* Try to imagine and keep in mind a drama as a whole that lasts 1000 hours, especially when, for example, Edgar Allan Poe claimed that an audience has an attention span of about an hour.

Smerdel also places the antecedent of *teleias* in *Dramatics* 5.[587] McKirahan does the same, for more detailed reasons than Smerdel, while also demonstrating how the definition of tragedy arises from the first five chapters, saying, "So I take it that Chapter 5, with its discussion of the length of a tragedy implicitly introduces the notion of parts."[588] Parts are necessarily connected to something whole or complete for Aristotle, as McKirahan argues briefly (and properly in my view). In short, no requirement exists for Aristotle's theory of definition that he has to explain in *full* detail all or even many of the important aspects of a differentia that he is introducing *before* collecting it into the definition. Indeed, the brief introduction of the core concepts is why he expands the definition in *Dramatics* 6 and 7, to develop the concepts that were merely introduced or very briefly explained previously.

An objection to all of this, perhaps, is that being bounded does not entail (in and of itself) being complete or whole. That is, my view runs the risk of ignoring the requirement of a causal connection that a single whole action is supposed to have because Aristotle precisely contrasts whole and complete actions with historical compilations (Chapter 23, 1559a18-24). However, bounding does indeed make something "whole" in and of itself, although this may not entail a *single* whole action. Single and whole can be different for Aristotle, which is one reason, I gather, he explicitly adds in the discussion of epic that it is "single" (*mian*) in addition to "whole and complete" (1459a19). Proof, though, that merely bounding something does make it whole, which is my sole concern for the moment, comes from the *Physics*: "... *what has nothing outside it is complete and whole ... as a whole man or box ... Nothing is complete which has no end and the end is a limit* [my italics]."[589] Hence, a section of time can be whole merely because of its being bounded. A "day" is complete for Aristotle because the boundaries are, say, 12:01 a.m. and midnight. This is why when Aristotle describes history in Chapter 23, he says, not that history is always unbounded, but that it describes all, or many, of the actions that happen randomly *within a certain time*, and this is what makes history different from "poetic composition" (which gives at least apparent causal connections to the events making up the plot). History for Aristotle can, and usually does, deal with a whole and complete period: a day or week or month or decade. It is not the lack of boundedness that is problematic in this context for history; it is the lack of clear causal connections between the incidents, some of which are merely "coincident" in time.

*Option 2*: D.W. Lucas examines "action," as used by Aristotle in the *Dramatics* and the ethical works. As Lucas says:

> It ["action"] means, not any random act like opening one's mouth or crossing the street, but an action initiated with a view to an end and carried on in pursuit of it; it can thus

---

587   *Op. cit.*, pp. 67 and 73.
588   McKirahan, *op. cit.*, 2010, p. 100.
589   *Physics* III 6, 206b34-207a14.

## Chapter 6: Pity and Fear in the Definition of Tragedy

include a whole complex of subordinate actions... Since *praxis* [in the definition] refers to an action begun for a purpose and carried on until it is realized or until the activity thus initiated terminates, it is implied that it is a complete whole *teleias*.[590]

Thus "wholeness" (or "complete") is implied in the fundamental concept "action" that is used throughout Chapters 1 through 5, and Aristotle is making explicit the aspect of wholeness in the expanded definition. It might be objected that in this case, the phrase "complete action" imports a redundancy into the definition, which is forbidden by the *Topics*. In other words, if Aristotle thought it necessary to specify completeness, this shows that he did not regard it as automatically implied by "action." Yet in reply to this objection, we can rely on Battin, who, as alluded to above, published before both McKirahan and myself a rigorous examination of Aristotle's definitory theory and how it gets applied to the definition of tragedy:

> Being complete or unified and having a length are inseparable from imitating action, and the mention in the formal definition that the actions imitated are complete and of some length is just an expanded way of saying that they are actions. This expansion of the predicate "of action" does not violate Aristotle's injunction against redundancy, we may suppose on the basis of a similar case he argues at *Topics* 140b33-141a2, because while the same concept is "uttered twice" in describing something, it is *predicated* of its subject only once [her own italics].[591]

*Option 3*: If neither of the previous options is acceptable to Halliwell, the following appears unassailable on his own grounds, according to which commentators can appeal to missing texts or, like Destrée, to oral explanation during a lecture, of which more later when Halliwell himself explicitly advocates this type of oral explanation. It is extremely probable that we are missing at least a few words and even a few sentences, if not more, in *Dramatics* 4 or 5, and perhaps "completeness" was included there. Take one very plausible location: At 1449a16, an account of Thespis (who started the practice of making one person the first "actor" to offset the chorus, engendering the term "thespian") is missing. The reason is that, in its current form, *Dramatics* 4 mentions tragedy beginning with the leaders of the dithyramb at 1449a11, but then jumps immediately to Aeschylus introducing the practice of increasing the actors from one to two. Yet, according to the Greek rhetorician Themistius (fourth century CE), Aristotle said that tragedy was entirely choral until Thespis introduced the prologue and the internal speeches:

> As Themistius says in *Oration* 26 (*On Speaking*), 316A-D: "Do we not pay attention to Aristotle, <when he says> that at first the chorus entered and sang to the god, Thespis invented a prologue and speech, Aeschylus (invented) actors and a stage..."[592]

---

590  D.W. Lucas, *op. cit.*, p. 96

591  *Op. cit.*, 1975, p. 297.

592  Richard Janko, *Philodemus: the Aesthetic Works. Vol. I/3: Philodemus, On Poems Books 3–4, with the Fragments of Aristotle, On Poets* (Oxford: Oxford University Press) 2011, p. 434-5. As Janko adds recently in

Aristotle, then, may well have written some sentences in *Dramatics* 4 not only speaking of Thespis introducing (himself as) the first actor but also introducing the notion of the "completeness" or "wholeness" of the more mature plays as they become "grand." Hence, if Halliwell permits traditionalists, as he does, to argue their case on the basis of lost passages, then in fairness he must allow me (and Veloso and the other "doubters") the same latitude. In our case, it is just a sentence or three on "wholeness" that might be lost, which is extremely plausible because of Aristotle returning to the concept *in great detail* in Chapters 6 and 7 and because of Themistius. By contrast, in order to cover all the problems with authenticating *katharsis*, Halliwell must argue that at least two sections are lost, one in *Dramatics* 1 through 5 and another, very large one after the definition of tragedy, probably the equivalent of a modern-day chapter of the *Dramatics,* given Halliwell's own appeal to *Politics* VIII 7 and its *explanation* of *katharsis* in a treatment of composition. Two large lost sections are much, much less likely.[593]

There is a fourth solution, although it does not require that *teleias* has an antecedent. Let us say Halliwell rejects all three options above, for whatever reason, perhaps dropping the privilege of appealing to missing texts, which will severely impact his other arguments. Historically, the fact that *katharsis* appears out of the blue, as it were, in the definition has only caused a handful of scholars over five centuries, and just starting in the last seventy years, to worry deeply enough to print their doubts that Aristotle wrote *katharsis*. If, however, anything is evident in the *Dramatics,* it is that *katharsis* is never mentioned before Chapter 6. Why then would the appearance of *teleias*, supposedly also out of the blue for Halliwell, be of concern for him, given that Aristotle spends much of Chapters 6 and 7 dis-

---

discussing Tarán and Gutas: "We may note that the Arabic testimonia that Themistius somewhere discussed the *Poetics* ... are confirmed by Elias and Olympiodorus" (*Book Reviews, op. cit.*, p. 4 of the web version).

593  AnonC says "It's not clear to me what reason we have to suppose that [there are sentences missing in Chapter 4 or 5] other than the failure to mention completeness—which is completely circular. As an *ad hominem* response to Halliwell's willingness to 'appeal to missing texts or to oral explanation', this is defensible. But as an argument *ad rem*, it is worthless—and highly dangerous: it is a doomsday weapon, making the text arbitrarily malleable."

In reply: First, in chronological order and to name only the most recent, Battin, I and McKirahan have shown that at least seven of the eight conditions for tragedy are antecedent to the definition (leaving aside the catharsis clause). Battin and McKirihan also believe the eighth, "whole" or "complete," is at least entailed by, or suggested in, Chapters 1-5. (I give the numbering of the eight conditions on the next page.) Why would Aristotle follow biological definition for seven of the conditions and not the eighth? Moreover, again, Themistius gives an account of Aristotle speaking of Thespis at least introducing a prologue and speech. Where if not before Aeschylus introducing two actors in Chapter 4 would this missing sentence have been originally written? Thus, my approach is far from being circular. Appealing to missing texts as a *matter of habit* is, of course, dangerous, which I explained myself above vis-à-vis "The Principle of Oral Addition," but not in a case like this, with ample motivation and ancient evidence. In any event, this appeal is only my third solution, and arguably not even needed, because one of the first two suffices.

cussing it in the expanded discussion of the essential conditions of tragedy? Even granting, therefore, to Halliwell that Aristotle abrogates *slightly* his biological approach to definition, something easy to do if at the last moment Aristotle realized he had omitted a condition when the manuscript for the first five chapters was finished (he had no word processor to redo those chapters easily), indubitably Aristotle wants *teleias* in the definition. It would be then entirely *inconsistent* for him to introduce *katharsis* out of the blue also in the definition, and then *not* to expand it. Thus, whether or not Aristotle follows biological definition, *teleias* is warranted but *katharsis* not.

In summary, either Halliwell should reject both "embellished" and "whole," which means he removes the crucial explanation of "embellished (speech)" that no other scholar has ever rejected, or he should accept both, given that Aristotle treats them similarly.

Halliwell's final complaint in this context—that **"the concept of (an) 'action' qua unified structure of events, as opposed to the more general notion of 'people in action'"** is not found in *Dramatics* 1 through 5—can now be shown to defy relevance. I never claimed that "unified *structure of events*" was in *Dramatics* 1 through 5, *nor do I need to*. Indeed, just the opposite: This formulation—"an action qua unified structure of events"—is not part of the essential conditions that result from the collection of the antecedent differentiae, as we saw in great detail in Chapters 2 and 3 and as was explained in my "The *Poetics* of Performance" (1999), which Halliwell cites without addressing. Rather, the formulation is brought in explicitly by Aristotle to expand "(serious and complete) action" during the derivation of the six necessary elements in *Dramatics* 6. Again, essential and ("merely") necessary conditions are different for Aristotle. The relevant phrase in the definition presenting the eight[594] legitimate, *essential* conditions *per se* is (to continue to use Janko's rendition, with my numbering): "Tragedy is a [**1**] representation of a [**2**] serious, [**3**] complete [**4**] action which has [**5**] magnitude, in [**6**] embellished speech, with each of its elements [used] [**7**] separately in the [various] parts [of the play]; [represented] [**8**] by people acting and not by narration [my italics]." Thus, only "(the more general notion) of 'people in action'"—to repeat Halliwell's words—needs to have been introduced in Chapters 1-5, as the notion indubitably was, especially in *Dramatics* 2.

In summary, all of the essential conditions are given antecedently to the definition *per se*, including but not limited to *praxeos* ("action") and *spoudaias* ("serious") in *Dramatics* 1 and 2 respectively (1447a28; 1448a1-2), and the rest in *Dramatics* 3-5. The sole seeming exceptions, *teleias* and *hedusmenō*, may not have been entirely obvious initially but, I trust, have now been amply justified. Finally,

---

594   If one breaks up "embellished speech" into the three parts that Aristotle uses subsequently, then the definition has ten elements, but this means that at least nine of the ten were introduced, even if *teleias* is denied a previous introduction.

Halliwell does not report that a number of scholars—Else, Battin, McKirahan, and I—have examined Aristotle's theories of definition and demonstrated that Aristotle uses "biological division" to define tragedy, although the four of us have slight differences of interpretation in this respect and grave differences concerning the legitimacy of catharsis, pity, and fear. For Halliwell, then, to assert that "Aristotle's statement that the definition of tragedy arises or emerges from what has preceded does not entail that everything in it has been previously mentioned" is false (leaving aside, of course, the dubious *katharsis* clause). This should be even more obvious now, with the problem of *teleias* resolved. We recall that Battin herself very briefly and cleverly grappled with the resulting problem of the omission of *katharsis*, saying without any supporting argument:

> ... the fact that he [Aristotle] was willing ... *to spoil an otherwise perfectly straightforward and rigorous definition* to include the notion of *katharsis* suggests that he accorded it more than ordinary importance, and surely considered it a central feature of tragedy" [my italics].[595]

As I argued before,[596] the better conclusion is that some later editor spoiled a "perfectly straightforward and rigorous definition." Even more hurtful to Battin's claim is that she never discusses the extreme problems resulting from *katharsis* being absent in the relevant sense from the whole treatise, either pre- or post-definition. Nevertheless, the crucial consideration now vis-à-vis Halliwell is that having seven of the eight essential conditions being clearly introduced beforehand (leaving aside the *katharsis* clause), with the eighth, *teleias*, handled above, means that everything in the definition except for *katharsis*, pity and fear truly has been previously mentioned in Chapters 1 through 5, at least as an idea.

While on this whole topic: What I find puzzling is how impressively rigorous McKirahan also is in trying to apply Aristotle's theories of definition to the definition of tragedy, but how unconcerned he is with the *katharsis* clause, when there is no preliminary "division" of *katharsis* (or of pity and fear). The only relevant comment he makes in his entire article is:

> The definition is based on what is said in the previous chapters, as Aristotle points out in introducing the definition: "Let us speak of tragedy, taking up the definition of its essence from what has been said" (1449b22-4). This is true for almost all the elements of the definition, the only exceptions being pity, fear, and catharsis.[597]

Unlike Battin, who at least tried to explain away the inclusion of *katharsis* with a clever remark,

---

[595] *Op. cit.*, 1975, p. 301

[596] 2003, p. 238ff.

[597] *Op. cit.*, 2010, p. 86. My guess is that McKirihan, like other very good scholars, does his best to protect the manuscript at any cost. Unfortunately, the unreasonable cost of one word (or phrase) has almost bankrupted the whole, or at least important parts of the, treatise for a number of famous dramatists, including Scaliger, Corneille, and Racine, as we see in the Appendix.

Chapter 6: Pity and Fear in the Definition of Tragedy

McKirahan stays remarkably silent on the whole issue of *katharsis*, pity, and fear, and on why *katharsis* is never discussed afterward. Although the problems of *katharsis* may have been outside the scope of his essay, he does not even say that. However, as is confirmed now even more with the explanations above and below, we see additional reasons why *katharsis* stands out like a sore—indeed mangled and bloody—thumb in the definition and why those terms cannot be legitimate. Assuming at least *katharsis* is athetized, though, and this is the point I am leading to now, all of this ironically helps *confirm* Else's, McKirahan's and Battin's own fundamental arguments about Aristotle's theory of definition as applied to the *Dramatics*.

Halliwell continues to his second group of criticisms:

> (S²) The absence of any further explanation of catharsis in the *Poetics* is certainly a prima-facie puzzle, but since *Pol.* 8.7, 1341b39-40...suggests that a concept of catharsis does belong somewhere in Aristotle's theory of poetry, we need not resort to the drastic hypothesis of an interpolation to account for this absence. **It is more plausible to suppose that the explanation was supplied in *On Poets* and then cited orally in the lectures on which the *Poetics* is based**. (Many have supposed, alternatively, that catharsis could have been explained in the lost second book of the *Poetics* itself, in the discussion of comedy. Scott himself, 252-3, is inclined to accept this, though he converts it into the wildly improbable thesis that **Aristotle may have believed in comic but *not* tragic catharsis**.) Another possibility, assumed by Bernays among others and less extreme than positing an interpolation in the definition, is to suppose that **an explanation of catharsis has dropped out of the text somewhere later in chapter 6** [my bolding, but his italics].

Halliwell's first point is that the *prima facie* puzzle of why *katharsis* is never discussed during the extension of the definition *per se* and then in the rest of the chapters is resolvable if we assume that *katharsis* was explained in *On Poets* and then orally explicated in the *Dramatics*—the Principle of Oral Addition. However, to invoke the example from before: To assert that Aristotle wrote *katharsis* with the expectation of explaining it orally would be the equivalent of claiming that he could write "eating octopus once a week" in the definition of *eudaimonia* with no other occurrence of octopus in the *Nicomachean Ethics* (except for a second and last irrelevant usage, such as a picture of an octopus on a shield) and then expecting Aristotle to explain all the related points in the *Nicomachean Ethics* in lecture. This is surely appealing too egregiously to the Principle of Oral Addition. Why this is doubly unbelievable in the context of the *Dramatics* follows. Regarding the remarks about *Politics* VIII 7 and *On Poets*, I accepted, and still accept, that "somewhere in Aristotle's theory of poetry" (with the correct interpretation, though, of *poiēsis*) *katharsis* is explained.[598] The question is where. I emphasized in 2003 that the editor who had the confidence to interpolate *katharsis* in Chapter 6 probably felt VIII 7 helped justify his action. I also claimed, and still claim, that an explanation of *katharsis* in *On*

---

[598] Cf., e.g., Scott 2003, pp. 261-2.

*Poets* might have been used to justify the wrongful interpolation and so am in accord with Halliwell on this point. However, to reiterate the inconsistency noted about only caring to explain orally one crucial concept while developing the other crucial concepts in writing, it is implausible that Aristotle would have left remarks about *katharsis* out of the *Dramatics* at the very places it is relevant (like the goal of tragedy in both Chapters 6 and Chapter 14) had he intended it to be crucial to all tragedies, *especially—and this is the new point—since everyone agrees* On Poets *was written earlier.*

That is, there is an additional absurdity to appealing to oral explanation if *On Poets* is brought in as evidence. Halliwell's suggestion that an important concept is explained orally only makes sense when an author accepted the concept (or changed his theory) after the ink was dry on the manuscript (or was writing notes with no more room on the papyrus). It is utterly implausible that a crucial concept, one which had been used already by Aristotle in earlier work (that is, *On Poets*), would not have been written immediately into the later text, whether or not papyrus or word processors were used. Consider the locations that oral explanation would be needed, had Aristotle really believed *katharsis* was crucial to all tragedies and had chosen truly to write the word in the definition: During the definition, when he explains why he is adding *katharsis* without preamble, unlike the other terms; in the middle of Chapter 6, when, as we saw above, plot rather than *katharsis*, is said to be the end of tragedy; at the end of Chapter 6, when all of the other essential conditions have been expanded and discussed and Aristotle needs to explain why he chooses to ignore *katharsis* completely; in Chapter 13, when pity and fear are explained and yet *katharsis* is not, despite all three concepts being connected in the extant definition; in Chapter 14, when it is pleasure that is said to be the goal of tragedians through pity and fear; and at a *variety* of locations in Chapters 23 through 26, when Aristotle discusses the proper pleasures and goals of epic and of tragedy, which we should examine now.

Epic often had or caused, pity and fear—think of the deaths of the heroes at Troy, the trials and tribulations of Odysseus and his companions, and his long-enduring wife Penelope. Indeed, Marina McCoy has recently reminded us of a paradigm of pity, the scene of Priam begging Achilles for Hector's body in Achilles' own tent, with all the grown warriors—friends and enemies—crying and lamenting.[599] Aristotle also states that, like tragedy, epic "in fact needs reversals, recognitions and suffering" (24.1459b11). Furthermore, in Chapter 23, in loosely defining epic, Aristotle says *"just as in tragedies,* [the epic poet] should construct plots that are dramatic (i.e. [plots] about a single whole action that is complete, with a beginning, middle [parts] and end), so that it will produce *the pleasure particular to it, as a single whole animal does"* (my italics, 1459a18-22). This completely omits *katharsis*. Yet the definition of epic recalls not only the "whole animal" discussion in *Dramat-*

---

[599] Marina McCoy, *Wounded Heroes: Vulnerability as a Virtue in Greek Tragedy and Philosophy* (Oxford: Oxford University Press, 2013).

*ics* 6 and 7, which we just covered, but the beginning, middle, and end that helped explain the length and completeness of tragedy.[600] Surely, then, the definitions of tragedy and epic are similar, albeit of course not identical, and it is remarkable that *katharsis* is not the goal, were it truly legitimate for tragedy. Another reason for this is that, as noted much earlier, epic is said at 24.1459b10-12 to have everything that tragedy does except orchestral art and spectacle. Aristotle's statement has been typically construed to mean that epic has no music whatsoever, but this does not follow. To repeat what I have asserted a few times: Epic does not have the full orchestral performance but may still involve a chanting or singing. Presumably, then, the end of both arts would likewise be similar, if not identical in every respect. Moreover, in Chapter 26, as we saw once before, Aristotle indicates while ranking epic and tragedy against each other that epic has the parts that tragedy does (except for music, dancing and spectacle, which give tragedy *not inconsiderable pleasure* [*hēdonē*], 1459b10 & 1462a15-17), and he adds:

> So if tragedy is superior in all these ways, **and also in [achieving] the function of art (for tragedy and epic should produce not a random pleasure [*hēdonēn*], but the one we have mentioned**), it is obvious that it will be superior to epic as it achieves its end more than epic does (1462b12-15) [my bolding].

The typical traditional reaction to these points by commentators has been to try to force pleasure to be identical or synonymous with *katharsis* (or elliptical for "pleasure via *katharsis*"). However, we saw already evidence before why this cannot be true, given, e.g., the *Topics* and *Politics* VIII 7. Also, pleasure in Chapter 26 is much more likely to be the pleasure that Aristotle calls pleasure itself in the other parts of the *Dramatics*, pleasure in mimesis and pleasure of "recognitions and reversals," the latter of which he explicitly says are also necessary in epic (Chapter 24, 1459b11). Also, pleasure is the primary goal of tragedy in the commonsensical Greek view according to Callicles in Plato's *Gorgias* (502a), notwithstanding that the character Socrates there argues against it, and if any thinker is "commonsensical" among philosophers, while being as profound as any other throughout history, it is Aristotle.[601]

---

600 For more illuminating insights on animals in the *Poetics*, even though he follows the traditional approach toward catharsis, cf. Gallop, *op. cit.*, 1990.

601 This is why those who cite (Aristotle's) *katharsis* rather than Callicles' pleasure as the primary reason the ancient Greeks went to the theater have been paying attention to the wrong passages (or have been misinformed by scholars they trusted regarding the *Dramatics*). Ben Brantley, normally one of the best New York Times drama critics, if not the best, writes very recently, while starting his review of Arthur Miller's *A View from the Bridge*: "This must be what Greek tragedy once felt like, when people went to the theater in search of catharsis" ("Bearing Witness to Pain of Fate," 11/13/2015, p. C1, *NY Times*). As an aside, I should mention that the only tragedy in this production in my view was Ivo van Hove's direction, which involved music sometimes played that drowned out the voices on stage, on which also sat audience members. One wonders if van Hove read about the music drowning out the words in ancient dithyramb and decided to experiment with the technique or if the producers were so desperate for money that they needed to add seats wherever possible. In any event, my wife and I both walked away from the performance very disappointed, especially given other produc-

In any event, it is not necessary here to handle possible objections to these points or explain more why pleasure can or cannot be synonymous with, or imply, *katharsis*. I cover this matter thoroughly in Chapter 7. The crucial point for the moment is that the outright claims about epic (and tragedy) having pleasure as the goal generate extreme tension with *katharsis* as the (sole) goal of tragedy. Moreover, as I queried once, if *katharsis* is vital for "tragic poetry," why not for every other artistic genre involving language? Given *Politics* VIII 7 and the discussion there of *katharsis* concerning certain "musical"[602] performances, why is *katharsis* not vital for any other art form mentioned in the Aristotelian corpus that could involve "serious men"? Halliwell would have to expect Aristotle—again, and again, and again, and again, and again, and again—to explain orally in all of these locations why the focus is not on *katharsis* but pleasure. In short, then, the need for the Principle of Oral Addition becomes so massive were *katharsis* authentically in Chapter 6 that it becomes more preposterous to believe that Aristotle followed that Principle than to question that he had written *katharsis*.[603]

In summary, Halliwell's proposal that Aristotle explained *katharsis* orally is too implausible, when Aristotle could have just written the word *katharsis* instead in the various places, especially given how well known that concept was to him already from *On Poets*. Furthermore, if one appeals to oral explanation, then it is just as likely—*indeed the omission of katharsis anywhere else in the treatise in*

---

tions of the drama I have seen over decades.

602   As we saw amply in Chapters 1-2, *mousikē* there means what it does in the *Politics* VIII 7, explained as "music (or tune/song) and dance."

603   AnonC remarks: (i) "Aristotle explicitly says that one should not seek *just any* pleasure from tragedy, but the pleasure that belongs to it (1453b10-11). So a definition that referred to pleasure without further specification would be defective: it would be satisfied by plays that produced pleasures that do not belong to tragedy… [Also] (ii) What is the pleasure that comes from pity and fear? One possibility is that it is the pleasure associated with catharsis (according to *Pol* 8.7); in that case, it would make no sense to say 'pleasure *rather than* catharsis'"

These remarks, however, do not impact my rejoinder to Halliwell (and perhaps they were not intended to). Concerning (i): AnonC gives no example of which plays would satisfy all the conditions with mere pleasure and yet not be tragedy. For instance, comedy would not be representing admirable men, so even if the pleasure resulting is generically the same, the type is ruled out already. Moreover, I explain more soon that Chapters 13 and 14 are in the context of *both* a narrower conception of tragedy (perhaps one or two of the four sub-types of Chapter 18, even if intermingled) *and* what makes the best tragedies rather than in the context of the general conception of tragedy from Chapters 1-8. Yet it still may be that for tragedies in general, whether they are the best or merely middling, pleasure is sufficient as a *general* goal. In any event, even if "proper pleasure" should be therefore in the definition instead of "pleasure," *a fortiori* pleasure rather than catharsis should be there, which is exactly my rejoinder against Halliwell. Finally, concerning (ii): being merely associated with pleasure does not allow catharsis to be substituted for the final goal, as we saw in the *Topics*. Nor does *adding* pleasure to the definition remove the problems of this paper if *katharsis* remains; anyone adding the word "pleasure" to the definition is changing the manuscript as much as I propose by athetizing *katharsis*, while *still* not resolving the paradoxes of the absence of catharsis in the other places!

## Chapter 6: Pity and Fear in the Definition of Tragedy

*the relevant areas makes it much more likely*—that in oral lecture Aristotle stated that he no longer held *katharsis* to be important, as he once held in *On Poets*. Thus, appealing to "added oral explanation" post-definition is even less useful for Halliwell than it was for Destrée pre-definition.

To switch now to Halliwell's hypothesis that Aristotle explains *katharsis* in the lost second book on comedy: Indeed, I gave the evidence from the *Rhetoric* to show that this is one strong possibility, and Halliwell gives no reason to question that evidence. However, I never said what the content of Aristotle's explanation was and to what it applied. I only said, for instance, as we saw in Chapter 5:

> Aristotle indeed may have accepted comic but not tragic *katharsis* as the goal of a whole dramatic genre, or—*what is more likely, I imagine, with regard to comedy*—may have accepted *katharsis* as the psychological goal merely of some comic sub-species, perhaps a 'comedy of suffering'... [my italics for the moment]

I explicitly stressed later that a sub-species (but only a sub-species) *of tragedy* might have had *katharsis also* as its goal.[604] (*Katharsis,* like pleasure, may have different types, I should now add, and it is puzzling that Halliwell did not consider this option when he had recognized it in a previous publication.[605]) Nevertheless, and this is something Halliwell completely ignores, an explanation in a lost part on comedy presumably means *katharsis* was at least *more* relevant to comedy than to tragedy.[606] I stated that *secondarily or peripherally* perhaps *katharsis* was applied to tragedy, and indeed even might be the goal of some (but only some) sub-categories of tragedy for Aristotle in his mature theory of the *Dramatics*. Moreover, I only claimed that the absence of *any* discussion whatsoever in the extant sections on tragedy, or even any mention of the term at the places Aristotle should have used it, shows that it cannot be essential to the *whole* dramatic genre for the Northern Greek. Therefore, it cannot be in the definition of tragedy. Besides, that my view about *katharsis* in comedy is hardly "wildly improbable," to repeat Halliwell's phrase—or that the Neo-Platonic commentators were as wild as I am—is shown in part by the following statements. As Janko translates, relating the passages to Aristotle's "dialogue against Plato," namely, *On Poets*, which Halliwell himself of course just appealed to:

> ... by observing others' emotions *in both comedy* and tragedy, we can check our own emotions, make them more moderate and purify them (Iamblichus, *On the Mysteries* I 11).

---

604  *Op. cit.*, 2003, p. 252-3 and 261.

605  Halliwell, *op. cit.*, 1986, p. 191; he also discusses (in footnote 33) previous scholars like Bywater also recognizing (very astutely in my view, of course) the possibility of different kinds of catharsis.

606  Halliwell may be relying on his earlier work, e.g., 1986 (*op. cit.*) where he says "If we discard, as I am inclined to do, the common but implausible hypothesis that the promised discussion of *katharsis* [in *Pol* VIII 7] was contained in the lost section on comedy..." (p. 31). Yet, Halliwell seems to suggest later that there *should* be a comic catharsis, saying "The decisive consideration, I believe, is that the Platonic charge (esp. *Rep.* 388e-9a, 606a-d) calls for comic just as much as for tragic *katharsis, and this is corroborated in the neo-platonic evidence...*" (my italics, p. 275, ft. 33). Hence, I am utterly baffled as to where Halliwell stands on comic catharsis.

[and from Proclus:]

Why does he [i.e. Plato] not accept tragedy *and the comic art in particular,* when these conduce to the expiation of the emotions? (*Commentary on Plato's "Republic"* I, p. 42)...

It has been objected that tragedy *and comedy* are expelled [from Plato's *Republic*] illogically, if by means of these [kinds of poetry] it is possible to satisfy the emotions in due measure, and, by satisfying them, to keep them tractable for education... Anyway, it was this that gave Aristotle, and the defenders of these [kinds of] poetry *in his dialogue against Plato,* most of the grounds for their accusations [against him] [my italics throughout].[607]

Thus, either Iamblichus, Proclus and I myself all wildly conjecture about *katharsis* in comedy for Aristotle, or, if Halliwell interprets me as saying that only comedy could have given *katharsis* for Aristotle, then he did not read my article carefully enough. Dacier also believed Aristotle explained *katharsis* in the lost material on comedy [see the Appendix], and Halliwell admits that "Many have supposed, alternatively, that catharsis could have been explained in the lost second book."[608] Until Halliwell gives a (relatively convincing) argument why my interpretation of comedy is wildly speculative—for instance, why the nature of comedy is such that Aristotle would not have dared apply *katharsis* primarily to it, especially since *katharsis* may well have been explained in the lost second book on comedy or a section on comedy in *On Poets*—nothing else need be added here on this particular point. If and when Halliwell gives that argument, though, he should also explain in the name of rigor why Aristotle would take a concept being developed in the second lost book on comedy and apply it back to tragedy (and presumably also to epic) in an *extensive or fundamental* way. This is because Halliwell's claim jars stridently with what Aristotle says in the final sentence of Chapter 26—which is of course the end of the extant treatise—when the Greek indicates that the discussion of tragedy and epic is finished: "So regarding tragedy and epic ... *their kinds and their parts ... and what are the causes of doing well* ... and regarding questions raised ... *let this account suffice* [my italics]."[609] I myself have no doubt that *incidental* remarks on tragedy could have been made in the section on

---

607 Janko, *op. cit.*, 1987, pp. 59-60. One might be tempted to think that the "comic art in particular" is being referred to, in the first passage of Proclus. However, the scope of the Greek, unless I am missing an obscure usage, is seemingly to both tragedy and comedy: *ti dêpote malista tên tragôdian kai tên kômikên ou paradechetai (sc. Platôn), kai tauta suntelousas pros aphosiôsin tôn pathôn...*

608 Halliwell, *op. cit.*, 2011. One of those who placed the explanation of catharsis in the treatment of comedy is W. D. Ross (1877-1971), perhaps the most prestigious British translator and commentator of Aristotle's works in the last 150 years. Ross asserts in a long unavailable little paperback:

> Tragedy and epic are the only forms of poetry of which much is said in the *Poetics*. There is a chapter on the history of comedy, and its nature seems to have been discussed in the missing second book. The chief other matter contained in that book was the full account of *katharsis* which we should give so much to have; comedy was probably described as effecting a purgation of the tendency to laughter, as tragedy does of pity and fear (W. D. Ross, *Aristotle: A complete exposition of his works & thought*, New York: Meridian Books, Inc., 1959) p. 280.

609 1462b16ff.

comedy, which would be consistent with this last statement of Aristotle's, but I contend that it is too dismissive of Aristotle's clear concerns in the extant *Dramatics* to think that extensive or fundamental aspects of *tragedy* would be given fresh in any lost section on *comedy*.[610]

Let us now examine Halliwell's third and last point in his second set of criticisms, to wit:

> Another possibility, assumed by Bernays among others and less extreme than positing an interpolation in the definition, is to suppose that an explanation of catharsis has dropped out of the text somewhere later in chapter 6.

First, Bernays did not assume the explanation "dropped out." As will be shown in detail in the Appendix, he shockingly claimed that an "anthologist" intentionally excised the explanation, which, to put it bluntly, is utterly absurd. Bernays, at least on one interpretation of his work, even claims the anthologist went through and cut out other, multiple passages on catharsis, namely, all other expected occurrences of the word in the rest of the book, where the end of tragedy is discussed, were catharsis genuinely the goal of tragedy. Petruševski argues against the view that a lacuna exists in Chapter 6 and against the possibility that the explanation of catharsis could have happened there, claiming too that it is more natural and logical that the explanation of catharsis occurred in Chapter 13, when Aristotle explains pity and fear.[611] However, as noted, the modern Macedonian also claims that even this chapter has no evidence of a lacuna and seems complete. I should add, *pace* Petruševski, that pity and fear should have also been explained in Chapters 6 and 7, given that Aristotle explained all of the other elements in the definition there. Aristotle would have warned us if he postpones their relevant discussions. At any rate, I address pity and fear soon. To return to catharsis: Arguing for a lacuna anywhere in the *Dramatics* to justify the absence of the *explanation* of catharsis is only half the battle that traditionalists must fight. Even granting to them that a lacuna exists somewhere and that the lost, extensive passage occurred in that location, they still must reconcile the extreme inconsistencies with Aristotle not including catharsis as the goal of tragedy in Chapters 6, 14 and 23-26, as detailed above, an arguably impossible task.

---

610   When I refer to the *Poetics/Dramatics* I mean Chapters 1-26, although I fall on the side of those who agree that Aristotle also wrote a further section on comedy, including perhaps some parts of the *Tractatus Coisilianus*. Whether I favor the position, or any part of the position, championed by Janko and Walter Watson that the *Tractatus* is wholly (or almost wholly) authentic, is another topic outside the scope of this book. Although I would probably argue that only the classification of jests is authentic, it would not be fair to them merely to make such an assertion, without covering rigorously their arguments. Whether or not they are right, in Chapter 8 I argue emphatically for the importance of comedy and comic catharsis for Aristotle, based on texts other than the *Tractatus*.

611   *Op. cit.*, 1954, p. 241. I slightly disagree with Petruševksi on this particular point: Had *katharsis* truly been written by Aristotle we would have an explanation or postponement in Chapter 6 *and more* on catharsis not only in Chapters 13-14 but in the other places it logically is needed, as described above. Petruševksi suggests an explanation in Chapter 13 would have been sufficient but that is not the case.

The claim of Aristotle using Oral Addition post-definition, then, on the part of Halliwell seems not only utterly arbitrary (similar to the pre-definition case above concerning Destrée) but merely convenient or a desperate last resort. Halliwell thereby in effect claims that my positing the interpolation of *katharsis* is more extreme than Bernays's positing a whole *purposefully* excised explanation of *katharsis* in *Dramatics* 6 (*along with* the excisions of the other locations that neither Bernays nor Halliwell consider)! Halliwell's view itself, then, seems very unprincipled and implausible. Given that for him and Bernays (and all others including myself), Aristotle promises in *Politics* VIII 7 a *(moderate if not full) explanation* in a different text, and given that my view applies to just one word or a tiny phase, not even a whole sentence, I would claim the reverse of Halliwell, namely, that his and Bernays's stance is much more extreme. On my side, it is a picayune but wrongful interpolation, with an editor probably taking Aristotle's earlier work (the *On Poets* and *Politics* VIII 8) as grounds for the interpolation. On Halliwell's and Bernays's side, it is a large amount of text lost *and purposefully deleted*, with, worse, no substantiation in the whole rest of the treatise, along with very jarring and numerous inconsistencies generated whenever the goal or end of tragedy is discussed.

Moreover, if, as mentioned, Halliwell permits those like Bernays to posit the excision of major sections of the text to explain *katharsis*, then he presumably should permit the "doubters" equal privilege. That is, Halliwell should consider much more seriously the reasonable possibility that the original goal—assuming Aristotle wrote a tiny phrase—in the definition of tragedy was corrupted before copies were made (perhaps following Strabo's or Plutarch's account of the burial and corruption of Aristotle's library[612]). It would have been very easy for the "(alleged) primary manuscript" then to be

---

612   For a discussion of Strabo on this point along with Plutarch, who confirms Strabo in some ways, and the related issues of the transmission of the Aristotelian texts into Roman times, see Natali, *op. cit.*, 2013, pp. 102-4. Natali mentions Jonathan Barnes's discussion of the editorial history of Aristotle's works until the 1st century BCE, and says:
> He [Barnes] rightly thinks that Athenaeus's version of the story about the destiny of Aristotle's library is not compatible with the version of Strabo; but he [Barnes] prefers Strabo's account, notwithstanding the many impossibilities it contains, because he thinks that Strabo derives from Posidonius and that Posidonius wrote the truth... [Nevertheless] Barnes rightly contradicts the main point of Strabo's testimony, that copies of Aristotle's treatises were not available in the Hellenistic period before the time of Sulla (pp. 148-149).

Note first that all of this means the library could have been hidden underground, with some copies circulating publicly. Moreover, Barnes in his own in-depth article does not state in any way whatsoever (nor does he even try to argue) that *every* manuscript had a copy, and Barnes's conclusions are entirely compatible with the position that only some texts were considered significant enough to copy. Nothing, then, that Natali says or that, e.g., Barnes gives in his own article adds anything conclusively new to the issues of this book and of the catharsis clause, although I would argue that Barnes gives slightly more weight to the view that the *Dramatics* could have been changed. Indeed, if anything, he gives evidence to question the authenticity of almost any extant Aristotelian phrase that sets up inconsistencies with other well established Aristotelian theory:
> We possess several thousand pages of ancient commentary on Aristotle's works, many of them

given the extant interpolation by someone not prudent enough to recognize the inconsistencies noted above. However, that so many scholars over at least 450 years have accepted the plausibility of the word *katharsis* shows that the interpolation, although wrong on rigorous reflection, was not downright idiotic, and, again, would have been very easy to make. This takes us now to Halliwell's third set of relevant criticisms, which pertain to pity and fear.

That set is the only published critique to my knowledge of my arguments from 2003 against the authenticity of both pity and fear in the definition of tragedy. Again, my arguments are *fundamentally* driven by three of the four tragic plot-types in Aristotle's examination in Chapter 13 having no pity and fear *in his own words.* (As we saw before, Aristotle says that the virtuous man incurring misfortune has no pity and fear; likewise the villain going from misfortune to fortune; or a thoroughly villainous man going from fortune to misfortune.) Thus, as I suggested in 2003, the two emotions cannot be essential conditions for all tragedies, and thus cannot be in the definition.[613] In effect, including pity and fear in the definition is too restrictive and is like including "blond-haired," "excellent in geometry" or "living virtuously and wisely" in the definition of man for Aristotle. Let us now consider Halliwell's objections to my claims regarding pity and fear before I deliver additional support

---

written by serious scholars (Alexander, Ammonius, Simplicius). The commentators frequently refer to variant readings, and are acutely aware that different manuscripts present different texts. So far as I know, *in none of these textual discussions is there any reference to a 'canonical' edition of the Aristotelian works, or any hint that one particular manuscript tradition might be better than another*" [my italics] (*Philosophia Togata II: Plato and Aristotle in Rome*, ed. by Jonathan Barnes and Miriam Griffin, Oxford: Clarendon Press, 1997, p. 29).

To me this suggests that anytime we read a word or phrase that blatantly contradicts solid Aristotelian doctrine, as the catharsis clause does, we have grounds to question the text, no matter how "canonical" that text has become *subsequently*. Thus, neither Natali, Barnes nor any other authors cited add any weight as far as I can tell to the view that *Dramatics* 6 was entirely authentic and that *Dramatics* 6 could not have been changed from its original form. One theoretical possibility, as alluded to before, which Else advocated, is that Aristotle started to add catharsis on a revision, but stopped immediately after the definition in Chapter 6, as soon as he started. This implies that before finishing the other changes needed to make this concept applicable to the rest of the treatise, he got interrupted with other writing or travels and then never returned to the task before dying, or something of the sort. Yet, again, even this is highly improbable for reasons given above, but which I repeat: Since Aristotle, it is widely agreed, used catharsis in *On Poets,* he could not in all practicality have first written the *later Poetics* while forgetting about it. Recently Janko added the following about Strabo:

Tarán's discussion of the Hellenistic transmission of Aristotle's books does not sufficiently allow for the probability that Apellicon acquired only Aristotle's autograph MSS; the fact that copies of his esoteric works circulated at Alexandria and elsewhere need not disprove Strabo's remarkable story of the survival of Aristotle's books, *a story now supported by the recovery of the Arabic translation of Andronicus' list of his works* [my italics]. (*Book Reviews, op. cit.*, p. 5. My page number is to the version on the web.)

613    *Op. cit.*, 2003, p. 258.

for those claims.⁶¹⁴ However, Halliwell only addresses part of the arguments, and not even the most important ones, in his critique. That is, none of his remarks address the crucial ramifications arising from three of the four plot types *not* having pity and fear! The only reply that he gives to my points about pity and fear is this:

> (S³) Scott fails to deal satisfactorily with passages in the *Poetics* which suggest that pity and fear are essential to tragedy. Two passages in particular deal a fatal blow to his attempt to remove pity and fear (as well as catharsis) from the definition of tragedy. The first is 9.1452a1-3, 'given that [tragic] mimesis is not only of a complete action but also of fearful and pitiable matters', which has all the appearances of a reference back to the definition of the genre. Scott tries to sidestep this inference by claiming (259-60) that Aristotle is here introducing a 'narrower conception' of tragedy than he has so far used, 'since he wishes in this section to examine the best sorts of tragic plot' and it is the latter alone, Scott maintains, that pity and fear are relevant. But 1452a1-3 is patently making a general (if normative) claim about tragedy, and the transition to explicit discussion of the 'best sorts' of tragedy takes place not in chapter 9 but at the start of chapter 13. It is here that the second passage occurs which undermines Scott's position. When Aristotle says at 13.1452b31-3 that the plot-structure of the finest tragedy 'should be complex not simple, as well as representing fearful and pitiful events (for this is the special property of such mimesis)', Scott's attempt (258) to restrict the parenthesis not to tragedy *per se* but to the finest tragedy is logically flawed: it would make the parenthesis, which purports to give a *reason*, into a mere duplication of the statement it is meant to support. Comparison with 11.1452b1 underlines this point."⁶¹⁵

There are three passages under dispute then, which I address, starting with the very last one, the passage in Chapter 11, where Aristotle is discussing recognition and reversal and speaking of the play *Oedipus*. Halliwell translates the passage there, at 1452b1, including the important word *hupokeitai*, as "... such a combination of recognition and reversal will produce pity or fear (and it is events of this kind that tragedy, *on our definition*, is a mimesis of), since both affliction *and prosperity* will hinge on such circumstances" [my italics].⁶¹⁶ Yet *hupokeitai* is more just "hypothesizing" or "assuming" (cf. Liddell and Scott). To my knowledge, it does not mean "definition" *per se*. I discuss in detail shortly *Oedipus*, pity, and fear, and the oddity of pity and fear being mentioned when "prosperity" (which we will see Halliwell understands means a fortunate ending to a play) is said to "hinge on such circumstances." That is, Chapter 11 will be shown to be part of a narrower discussion of the sub-types of tragedy (and not to a narrowed discussion, or at least the most narrowed discussion, of the best plots for *all* tragedy, as I badly suggested in 2003). I only mention for the moment another translation by

---

614   Again, as noted, Veloso replies to Halliwell in his forthcoming book, *Pourquoi la Poétique d'Aristote? DIAGOGE*. I should note that those arguments are independent of my thesis, despite Veloso ultimately having the same conclusion as I regarding the (in)authenticity of the catharsis clause in *Dramatics 6*.

615   *Op. cit.*, 2011, p. 262.

616   Stephen Halliwell, *The Poetics of Aristotle: Translation and Commentary* (Chapel Hill: Univ. of North Carolina Press) 1987, p. 43.

## Chapter 6: Pity and Fear in the Definition of Tragedy

a third party, Janko, who also accepts the traditional view: "... such a recognition and reversal will contain pity or terror (tragedy is *considered* to be a representation of actions of this sort), and in addition misfortune and good fortune will come about in the case of such events [my italics]." In brief, one option, given that the quantification of a simple sentence can be ambiguous for Aristotle, is that the Northern Greek only means "(*some*) tragedy is considered to be ... of this sort." Another option is that the word "now" was added in lecture—Halliwell's Principle of Oral Addition—and Aristotle says "tragedy is (now) considered to have pity and fear," to delimit his scope. All of this allows Chapter 11 to be entirely consistent with the definition of tragedy *without* the catharsis, pity and fear clause. For Halliwell to deny this option, he either has to give up Oral Addition or show why verbal comments on Aristotle's part make more sense on his reading than the oral comments on my reading. Indeed, the narrowing that I suggest will be supported in the upcoming arguments.

Neither of the two passages in Chapters 9 and 13 that Halliwell claims deal a fatal blow to my stance impacts the most crucial problem of three different tragic plot types being explicitly said by Aristotle not to have pity and fear. Therefore, I concede the two passages for the sake of the more important arguments, despite the following considerations. The beginning of the "transition to explicit discussion," to use Halliwell's own words, of the best plots seems not to be, as he stresses, in *Dramatics* 13, but rather in the middle of Chapter 9, *before* the first mention of pity and fear. Aristotle says there in Chapter 9, "among simple plots and actions, episodic [tragedies] are the *worst*" [my italics] (1451b33)—and best and worst appear to be flip sides of the same coin. Moreover, Aristotle adds later *and still in Chapter 9* that plots with events that do not appear random are necessarily finer (*kallious*) (1452a10). Also, the "transition to explicit discussion of the 'best sorts' of tragedy" arguably continues not, as Halliwell says, in Chapter 13 but in Chapter 10, when Aristotle begins explaining complex plots in contrast to simple ones, because complex plots become a condition of the finest tragedy.[617] Again, however, this matter of the "transition" is completely irrelevant for the issue at hand. We can give Halliwell now an even stronger argument against me if my article is interpreted as concluding that pity and fear are only in the best plots for tragedy *in general*—and I acknowledge that I unfortunately gave that impression in 2003—as opposed to being in the best plots *of a sub-type of tragedy*. According to Aristotle at the beginning of Chapter 14 (1453b1), pity and fear can also be given with mere

---

617 "Paul Feyerabend is one of the greatest philosophers of science of the 20th century" according to Amazon.com. Yet in his new *The Tyranny of Science* (first published in Italian as *Ambiguitá e armonia: lezioni trentine*, Gius. Laterza e Figli, 1996, and then in English by Polity Press, Cambridge, MA, 2011), Feyerabend says "According to Aristotle, Corneille or Lessing a tragedy must have a simple plot and it must contain conflict..." However, anyone who recalls Chapter 13, 1452b31-32, will know that Aristotle says "the construction of the finest tragedy should be not simple but complex..." So Feyerabend is blatantly wrong if Aristotle is necessarily included in his claim (Feyeraband's disjunction of theorists leaves the matter indeterminable for me). That is, if he means by his claim "According to Aristotle, Corneille *and* Lessing...," then he blatantly misrepresents the matter for Aristotle.

spectacle and simple plots, which themselves are second-rate, as everyone acknowledges. Hence, it would be short-sighted for anyone, including myself, to imply both (i) that pity and fear are *always* in the best tragedies and *only* in those tragedies, and (ii) that this reason *by itself* is sufficient to reconcile the athetesis of pity and fear in Chapter 6 with the importance of pity and fear in the middle chapters. The more crucial point is whether Aristotle could be working with, as I put it in 2003, a "narrower conception of tragedy" in the middle chapters when he establishes the best plot-types in Chapter 13. In no way does Halliwell address this issue, as I explain now in addressing the rest of his third criticism.

Concerning Halliwell's next and last passage in his (S³), and whether the parenthetical reference of pity and fear being a special property of "such mimesis" refers to tragedy or to the best tragedy: Halliwell criticizes my interpretation on the grounds it becomes a mere duplication. However, it may well be that Aristotle intends to emphasize the restricted notion of tragedy with which he is now working in Chapter 13—a sub-type that itself requires pity and fear. Thus, he duplicates for the sake of emphasis. On this hypothesis, starting with Chapter 9 Aristotle in oral lecture (or in lost texts) switched to a narrower notion of tragedy that requires pity and fear (and I speak more of the sub-types of tragedy as described in Chapter 18 in a moment). Thus, even if Halliwell is right and even if pity and fear are the special properties of "such mimesis" *as tragedy* (rather than as the *best tragedy [of a certain sub-type]*), then, because tragedy *ex hypothesi* starting with Chapter 9 is restricted to a sub-type that involves pity and fear, the result is still the same as far as my arguments go. *Halliwell needs to argue why Aristotle in lecture could not have narrowed after Chapter 8 the sense of tragedy orally.* Again, though, since none of these issues impact the much more important topic of this book, I leave them now aside. I voice them primarily to illustrate that even Halliwell, who gives the most detailed and rigorous critique of my arguments, expends all of his effort regarding pity and fear on secondary points, and leaves aside the crucial problem above of the three tragic plot types in Chapter 13 not having pity and fear.

He does, however, give a related, and final, argument on the topic of pity and fear in Chapter 13, about Aristotle saying there that a plot with a thoroughly (*sphodra*) villainous character going from good to bad fortune also has no pity and fear. Aristotle implies that a not thoroughly villainous character, namely, only a moderately villainous one, could trigger some pity and fear when going from good to bad fortune, perhaps a tragedy along the lines of Shakespeare's *Richard III*.[618] Otherwise, there is no

---

618    Notice I only say "*along the lines* of...Richard III." Aristotle is not recounting only a history of plays, although as an empiricist he definitely points to a variety of tragedies. He also presents philosophical dramatic theory that should and would apply to drama that gets created a day, month, year, ten years, two hundred years, or a thousand years after his treatise, as long as human nature stayed the same (cf. *Poetics* 4, where representation and the delight in it come from human nature). What about a play like *Richard III*? Is this a tragedy or

reason for Aristotle to say *sphodra*. Indeed, Aristotle gives later his own example of this plot-type, in what Halliwell calls "an extremely vexed passage," about the clever but villainous Sisyphus being a legitimate protagonist of tragedy (18.1456a19-25). As Halliwell says, this (vexed passage about Sisyphus) "appears to count as tragic those plots in which a wicked figure falls into misfortune (*in contradiction of 53a1-4*) [my italics]."[619] Yet, contrary to Halliwell's claim, Chapter 18 is *not* a contradiction with 53a1-4 (which is the passage from Chapter 13 about the thoroughly villainous agent), because Sisyphus is villainous but not "*thoroughly* villainous."[620]

Thus, since no other published rebuttal of my argument (about the three plot types of Chapter 13 without pity and fear) exists to my knowledge, the only objections that seem worth considering are those coming from AnonC. I cover these arguments rigorously because other readers will probably have the same view and, again, because even some of those sympathetic to my claim that *katharsis* cannot exist authentically in *Dramatics* 6 have been very reluctant to exclude pity and fear there.

Regarding my assertion that pity and fear should not be in the definition of tragedy because three

---

comedy, in Aristotle's terms? Surely a tragedy, and yet Richard is indubitably wicked to some extent, albeit "better than us" in many ways (position, wealth, fighting ability, etc.). Does the play generate pity and fear? Most if not all of the audience will feel at least pity for the murdered young twins, and some, I would argue, might even feel those two emotions for Richard, because of his lost or wasted potential. Others might only feel antipathy, for more reasons when I discuss Sisyphus. At any rate, to emphasize, dramas "along the lines" of *Richard III* would be considered not comedies but tragedies by Aristotle. That is, given his views in Chapters 13, 15 and 18, he would not exclude from tragedy a plot involving a king like Richard III who was only mildly wicked and did not murder twins. Nor, given his strictures, would Aristotle exclude from tragedy a king who unfairly plotted to attain the throne and exiled the real heir(s), and who dies at the end when the heirs reclaim it in battle. The issue of where this type of plot falls exactly within a ranking of plots is a different issue and not our concern in this book. Presumably, though, this kind of tragic play would not be the best, given Chapter 13, where someone who is wicked cannot be the protagonist of the finest plot. That honor is reserved in Chapter 13 for an admirable person who makes a mistake.

619   *Op. cit.*, 1986, p. 32.

620   AnonC queries: "How do you know Sisyphus was the protagonist in the plot Aristotle is referring to, and not (e.g.) the opponent in a double plot?" I answer: We know nothing, apparently, of this play, other than who the lead character is. However, Sisyphus is merely given as an example in Chapter 18 in the passage in which villains (and not just "intermediate noble" men like Oedipus) can be protagonists in tragedy. I discuss this in detail later, but for the moment suffice it to say that throughout his treatise, except for one passage in Chapter 13 when explicitly dealing with "double structures," Aristotle speaks of the primary protagonist. It would be astonishing if he were to switch now to double plots and to one of dual protagonists without noting it and without specifying the other protagonist. At any rate, let us grant AnonC his point for the sake of argument. Nevertheless, the double-structure is still a tragedy, not a comedy, and not all double-structures require the protagonists to end up both sadly or both happily. Aristotle only gives in Chapter 13 Aegisthus and Orestes walking off as friends as an example, and that type of play was still a tragedy, just the second-best type (from the perspective of structure).

of the four tragic plot-patterns in Chapter 13 have no pity and fear, AnonC states, very briefly and without explanation: (I) "[This is] a weak argument: tragedy is defined as an imitation of a complete action, but there are tragedies with episodic (and therefore not complete) plots." He also states that (II) "similarly there are one-legged bipeds and rational animals incapable of thought," which implies that exceptions to a rule do not necessarily undercut it. I gather that "rational animals incapable of thought" are in effect sleeping because if they are wholly incapable of thought it is hard to imagine how they could be rational. In other words, we should consider these two plot-types in Chapter 13 to be the exceptions that do not undercut the "rule" of tragedy with pity and fear. Finally, (III): AnonC also says of the three plot-patterns in Chapter 13, "they are candidates only in the thin sense that they are considered—but they are not treated as having a serious claim."

My rejoinder to these points follows, going from the two weakest arguments—(I) and (III)—to the strongest one (II).

Regarding (I): I assume that AnonC means that episodic (incomplete) plots are exceptions to the rule, viz., to the definition; and that, because no one complains about "complete [action]" being in the definition, I therefore should not complain about pity and fear being in the definition. However, contrary to what AnonC states, episodic plots are not incomplete, and hence, since they do not provide an exception to "completeness" in the definition, are irrelevant in this context. First, for Aristotle they are a sub-category of simple plots, and a simple plot is explained as having a single action that has a transformation (of fortune) continuously, with no recognition or reversal (9.1451b33-10.1452a15). The episodic plot, however, shows neither probability nor necessity in the events (1451b34-35), *yet is still complete*, one reason being that Aristotle immediately says:

> such [tragedies] are composed by inferior poets because of themselves, *but by good ones because of the actors*. For in composing competition pieces, they extend the plot beyond its potential and are often compelled to distort the sequence [my italics] (1451b36-1452a1).

Thus, for Aristotle, episodic plots, like other simple plots, are not only complete but often shown in the competitions by good dramatists. Those composers presumably would not be writing incomplete plots. They are just the worst kind of plots, but Aristotle never excludes them showing a transformation of, say, a virtuous man from good to bad fortune or vice-versa,—they do it with randomly displayed incidents, whereas in a simple plot the transformation happens logically but with no reversal or recognition. The episodic plot may, or may not, have pity and fear, and indeed may show the "misfortune to fortune" allowed in *Dramatics* 6, of which more later. However, nothing that Aristotle says about episodic plots gives us a clue about how much pity and fear they might have (or not), in part surely because he cares not a jot for these worse kinds of plot. Nevertheless, especially when written by "good poets," they are indeed complete for Aristotle, the crucial consideration for the moment,—just the worse kind of (complete) plot.

Regarding (III), namely, that the three plot-patterns are candidates only in the thin sense of being considered but that they are not treated as having a serious claim: First, Aristotle does not treat the plot-patterns jokingly and spends half a chapter explaining why pity and fear are inappropriate for them, and thus why none of them is the best plot. Hence, they are surely candidates that Aristotle considers worth discussing, and that none of them is the winning plot type is not the issue here. Rather, the question for us is whether they are legitimate tragic plots even while having no pity and fear. They indeed are not comedic nor are they plots for satyr plays, at least as considered in Chapter 13. Also, why they are "thin" is puzzling, because one of the plot-types involves a virtuous protagonist going from good to bad fortune! This covers a number of the most admirable surviving ancient Greek tragedies, including Euripides' *The Trojan Women* and possibly Sophocle's *Antigone,* the latter of which, on a common if not universal interpretation, ends tragically for the heroine and her beloved Haemon. On that common interpretation, both are seemingly very virtuous and in good fortune before Antigone's brother Polyneices is killed and left unburied at the beginning of the play. Moreover, Antigone's burying her brother against Creon's wishes is arguably not a mistake or a character flaw but obeisance to a higher law than the foibles of a political leader. Butcher long ago presaged this point by writing the following (leaving aside his view that tragedy was literature for Aristotle):

> A sovereign authority has been claimed for him [Aristotle] by those who possessed no first-hand knowledge of his writings... A far truer respect would have been shown him had it been frankly acknowledged, that in this *Poetics* there are oversights and omissions which cannot be altogether set down to the fragmentary character of the book; that his judgments are based on literary models which, perfect as they are in their kind, do not exhaust the possibilities of literature;...that, for example, the *requisites laid down in chap. xiii for the character of the tragic protagonist would exclude from the first rank of art some of the noblest figures of the Greek drama,—Antigone, Clytemnestra, and possibly Prometheus* [my italics].[621]

In no way, then, does AnonC's criticism (III)—that the three plot-types are "thin" and not seriously considered—appear even remotely plausible.

We now examine the strongest argument (II), again another exception-that-proves-the-rule case: AnonC implies that we have one-legged individuals like Tom, who very sadly lost one leg in a war but are still indubitably classified as human beings, even though the definition of human typically for Aristotle is a "two-legged (rational) animal."[622] Thus, because exceptions exist that do not necessar-

---

621    Butcher, *op. cit.*, p. ix. Very shortly, I discuss briefly Woodruff's different interpretation of *Antigone*, but even for him there are other so-called tragedies that make my point, like the *Trojan Women* (and I highly recommend his treatment in an appendix of Hegel and *Antigone*).

622    Cf. *Nicomachean Ethics* I 13, where the rationative capacity is suggested to be distinctive to man; *De An-*

ily undercut the legitimacy of definitions, the essential conditions of tragedy with pity and fear are still legitimate because the three "loser" plot-patterns are mere exceptions that prove this particular "rule."[623] However, for the following reasons, this claim still drastically fails.

First, these plot *types* are not three individual exceptions (like Tom in the case of a two-legged animal), namely, drama A by dramatist X, drama B by Y, and drama C by Z. Rather, they are three plot-*patterns*, each pattern of which could have, and presumably did have, many instantiations (just as teenage, middle-aged and octogenarians are three types of human, with many instances of each). If anything, the one pity-and-fear-inducing plot pattern, which is the best plot in Chapter 13 and which is explained using *Oedipus*, is the exception. Just as there are many more common or typical men than "best" men (who presumably have, say, wisdom), so the best tragic plot, which would be consid-

---

*ima* III 11, 434a6-7, narrows the distinctiveness to "deliberative imagination." However, Joseph Owens (under whom I studied the *Metaphysics*) states that "Aristotle does not use the later Greek definition 'rational animal'" and Owens points to the definitions of man as "biped animal" and "biped animal featherless" in *Metaphysics* Z 12, following Plato *(The Doctrine of Being in the Aristotelian Metaphysics*, Toronto: Pontifical Institute of Medieval Studies, 3rd ed., 1978, first publ. 1951).

    None of these definitions has a laudatory function, like wisdom, built into them, and with good reason (for one can rationate or deliberate wrongly). The "neutral" definition (of what a man is), therefore, is different from an account of excellent men in the sense given in, say, *Nicomachean Ethics*. Likewise, the (neutral) definition of art or tragedy would be different from good art or tragedy, respectively. Indeed, "having a complex plot" is a requirement for the finest tragedy, as agreed upon by all scholars, and yet is missing from the definition. So, anyone who suggests that a standard of excellence—say, pity and fear—should be in the definition seemingly does not understand the difference between a neutral definition for Aristotle and the additional criterion (or criteria) of what makes an example best. One instance is Pakaluk, *op. cit.*, given his account discussed above and especially his claim: "Aristotle holds that a thing is good or bad if it has those traits that enable it to carry out its function well; if a good tragedy is one that is so constructed as to evoke these emotions [of pity and fear], then the evoking of such emotions *must be the function of tragedy* [my italics; no pagination on webpage]." Pakaluk then wrongly suggests that the function of a *good* tragedy should be in the definition of *mere* tragedy.

623    There are some, including Pierluigi Donini (*La tragedia e la vita. Saggi sulla Poetica di Aristotele*, Alessandria: Edizioni dell'Orso, 2004, pp. 87-106) and Veloso, who deny that the plot types in Chapter 13 are tragic ones, the latter indicating that "Enfin, il n'est pas bizarre de mentionner des muthoi qui ne sont pas tragiques le contexte de *Poét*. 13, puisque l'auteur dit justement qu'il est évident que le meilleur ne doit pas être ainsi" ["Thus, it is not bizarre to mention plots that are not tragic in the context of *Poetics* 13, because the author says justly that it is evident that the best one should not be so"] (private correspondence, 2013, my transl., long before I articulated my upcoming list of counter-examples in this chapter). This may ultimately be a matter of intuition, but the fact that Aristotle continues in Chapter 13 to discuss different kinds of tragedies—including the one that has a double ending of Aegisthus and Orestes exiting as friends—without ruling them out as tragedies, in order to argue why some are the best, adds weight I believe to the view that all plots in Chapter 13 are tragic types. Moreover, insofar as dramatic representations had plots, there were generally only three possibilities in Aristotle's time: tragedy, comedy and satyr plays, and the plot-types that Aristotle is discussing hardly seem to be types of comedy or of satyr plays. Finally, although epic could have transformations, etc., Chapters 13 and 14 seem without question a discussion of tragedies, as all the references to the plays there make clear.

ered for a prize in a competition, is presumably also much rarer than all of the other tragic plot-types, which Aristotle lists throughout the treatise. Certainly, the winners in competitions are much more unique than all the other tragedies. Let us review now, then, those types, and see indeed that the seemingly ideal, best complex plot-type with pity and fear—which are the minimal, if not sufficient, requirements in Chapter 13—is a small fraction of the plot-types of tragedy in general that exist for Aristotle. We start at the beginning of the treatise and end in Chapter 18.

Insofar as plots are discussed in Chapters 1-8, they are only concerned with happiness and unhappiness (e.g., 6.1450a17-19), or with going from fortune to misfortune *or misfortune to fortune* (e.g., 7.1451a11-15). This last option is crucial in this context. There is no condition in Chapters 1-8 (apart from the disputed clause in the definition) that pity and fear have to be included, and when giving the conditions of the object (or "subject"[624]) of mimesis in *Dramatics* 2, Aristotle only gives good men (in action), not good men suffering enough to cause pity and fear. A Platonic type of play, showing a noble character going from misfortune to fortune by striving ethically in the structure of the events (on stage, with the music, dance, and spectacle) must be considered a tragedy under the conditions Aristotle gives within the first eight chapters. Absolutely no requirement that a tragedy end badly occurs there, and apart from the dubious *katharsis*, pity and fear clause, absolutely no implication occurs in the expanded discussion of plot in Chapters 6-7 that there must be so much suffering (whether in the beginning, middle or end of the play) that pity and fear follows necessarily in all cases. Tragedy for Aristotle is not like tragedy for us, which after Julius Caesar Scaliger came, as we see in the Appendix, to mean necessarily a play ending very painfully. Tragedies for Aristotle at least through the end of *Dramatics* 8 need not, and often did not, have both pity and fear, especially if "misfortune to fortune" is depicted, as confirmed below. In short, tragedy means merely for him serious drama (that fulfill the essential conditions in the definition as developed in the six necessary conditions of *Dramatics* 6).

I have already noted the three plot-types at the beginning of Chapter 13 that Aristotle explicitly says have no pity and fear, including the one with a virtuous protagonist going from fortune to misfortune. We find at the end of the same chapter a fourth plot-type (having a "double-structure") that we can easily deduce does not have a relevant pity and fear. By *relevant* pity and fear I mean the kind of emotions that the great teleologist Aristotle cares about during the discussion of Chapters 13-14, namely the one or ones happening at the end of the play, as I demonstrate in detail in *Aristotle's Favorite Tragedy: Oedipus or Cresphontes?* That is, Aristotle would not deny that many different emotions could be felt at some points during a play but he is always concerned in these two chapters with the dominant, ending emotion (or set of emotions). Thus, even though pity and fear might have been felt

---

624 Whalley argues that "subject" is more satisfactory here for the Greek "of what" (*op. cit.*, 1997, pp. 46-8). My view holds no matter which way we translate the Greek.

in the middle or toward the end of a play with a virtuous character going from fortune to misfortune, the ending causes the pity and fear to be dispelled. The play then becomes *miaron* (disgusting or shocking). This is why Sophocles's *Antigone* for Aristotle would not have pity and fear, as Butcher himself saw, even if Butcher did not recognize the fuller ramifications.[625] To return now to the "double-structure" plot-type: Aristotle says that many others avow this type to be the best kind *of tragedy*, an example being Orestes not killing Aegisthus and both walking off as friends. However, Aristotle adds, the pleasure is more like comedy than like tragedy, and thus it seems impossible that the play had a relevant pity and fear (as part of its outcome). All of this means four of the five tragic plot-types of Chapter 13 (the fifth being the Oedipus-type) do not have the relevant pair of emotions.

Aristotle also discusses five plot-types in Chapter 14, with the type that must include *Oedipus* repeated. He freshly introduces the criteria of whether an agent knows or not that he is harming a family member (or friend) and whether the agent carries out the deed. Aristotle accordingly ranks the resulting four possible plot-types. The *Antigone*-type that is *miaron* and that has no *pathos* is worst. The *Medea*-type in which the agent knowingly kills a family member is next to worst. The type in which an agent unknowingly kills a family member and only recognizes the relation afterward (which must include *Oedipus*) is only second-best, and the type that ends happily, with examples including *Cresphontes*[626] and *Iphigenia (in Tauris),* is best. In *Aristotle's Favorite Tragedy* I resolve the perennial debate by specialists concerning how Aristotle can rank happily-ending tragedies over the seeming paradigm in Chapter 13 of *Oedipus*, but I need not cover this topic here.[627] It is sufficient to

---

625 While revising this section for the 2nd edition, I became aware of Paul Woodruff's fascinating *Antigone, op. cit.,* 2001, noted already concerning the report of the sacrifice of Cleon's elder son. For Woodruff, the play is perhaps badly titled because Creon is the main figure in the drama. Moreover, like Oedipus after his own *hamartia*, Creon suffers horribly, at least in the sense that he loses much of his family. Thus, for Woodruff, there would be pity (and presumably fear). Antigone is less than innocent in going against the laws and thus is not fully *epieikēs*, at least for the Athenians. I assumed the interpretation of the play that Butcher and others have had, namely, that she is a heroine who fights for natural justice against sometimes arbitrary and unjust man-made laws. It is too difficult for this book to determine what Aristotle himself might have thought precisely about Antigone. Perhaps a better example, then, for our purposes here would be a play that Woodruff suggests, Euripides' *The Trojan Women* (private correspondence). The protagonists do seem without question to be *epieikēs* and yet suffer for no good reason. On Aristotle's account, the play would not have (a relevant) pity and fear because it would be *miaron*. Similarly, with any play, including newly created ones, in which the main protagonist is *epieikēs*. Thus, my conclusions about the illegitimacy of pity and fear in a definition for all tragedy hold no matter how one interprets Sophocles' *Antigone*.

626 This appears to be a lost play by Euripides. According to Lessing, in his Essay No. 37, *op. cit., Hamburg Dramaturgy,* "Aristotle refers to this *Kresphontes* without the name of an author, but as in Cicero and other classics we find reference to a *Kresphontes* of Euripides, he can scarcely have meant any other work than this" (p. 105). To my knowledge, Lessing's view has not been challenged in over 200 years, and for good reason.

627 Paul Schollmeier ("Purgation of Pitiableness and Fearfulness," in *Hermes: Zeitschr. für klassische Philologie,* Vol. 122, 1994, 289-99) is one of the admirable few who acknowledge the ranking in Chapter 14 and

Chapter 6: Pity and Fear in the Definition of Tragedy

demonstrate for our purposes in this book that pity and fear are not in many legitimate tragedy-types for Aristotle. Apart, then, from the second-best-type plays like *Oedipus* none of those other four plot-types in Chapter 14 has a relevant pity, much less, therefore, a relevant pity *and* fear, as I now explain.

Aristotle explicitly says that the worst plot such as *Antigone* is *miaron*. We can easily deduce that the third best *Medea*-type plot is also *miaros/miaron*.[628] Yet, being *miaron* rules out the two worse plot-types in Chapter 14 from having pity and fear, just as in Chapter 13 the virtuous person going to misfortune has no pity (and fear) because such a result is *miaron*. *A fortiori,* the two types of worst plays in Chapter 14 cannot have both *pity and fear*, even if fear is felt at some point before or during the outcome. Yet, both emotions are required by the extant manuscripts in the definition of tragedy. By the way, Aristotle explicitly says in Chapter 14 that the second-best play, which must include *Oedipus,* is **not** *miaron*, because, we can also easily deduce, the title figure *unknowingly* kills his father and marries his mother.[629] All of this entails that six of the seven plot-types discussed so far in Chapters 13-14 have no relevant pity, with, again, the *Oedipus*-type being the one exception.

The next plot-type in Chapter 14 that has no pity (and *a fortiori* no pity *and* fear) deals with enemies and was recognized by, for instance, even Belfiore herself: She notes that the topic in Chapter 14 is "good (tragic) plots" and adds that, there, Aristotle "excludes those in which enemies or neutrals harm one another, *saying that these lack pity and fear* (1453b17-19) [2009, p. 639; my italics]." Actually, Aristotle never says that they lack pity *and fear*, only that they lack pity, but there is no reason to quibble about this point now, because, again, without pity a drama would not satisfy the current definition of tragedy. A play with noble enemies causing suffering to each other is still a tragedy and

---

who keeps the happily-ending tragedies on top. However, his view is vitiated, I believe, by various caveats on keeping catharsis, pity, and fear in the definition of tragedy and by ignoring almost all the problems articulated in this book that stem from keeping the catharsis clause there.

628   Belfiore correctly deduces, too, that a mother *knowingly* killing her (innocent) child for Aristotle is *miaron*; cf. my *Aristotle's Favorite Tragedy*, 2018, pp. 14 and 27.

629   *Miaron* is seemingly as equivocal as the other Greek terms we have examined. This is one time the translation of *miaros* as "shocking," which Janko uses, is not fully appropriate in my view, for indeed the realization is shocking in the sense of being utterly surprising, for *both* Oedipus and the audience. How could Aristotle deny that? However, for Oedipus and Jocasta, what has happened as a result of the luckless killing at the crossroads (including the incest) is also extremely odious. Otherwise, neither of them would have committed a self-blinding and a suicide, respectively, out of shame and disgrace (cf. *Rhetoric* 2.6 for Aristotle's detailed account of shame). Hence, Aristotle seemingly implies that the plot of the *Oedipus* is not *miaron qua* odious *from the perspective of the audience,* because, again, the events must be odious to the characters in the play. All of this suggests to me that emotions in these discussions are at least primarily felt (or not) by the audience, rather than by the hypothetical characters within the drama. I would not rule out, however, that the dramatic characters sometimes feel similar, "hypothetical" emotions, given Aristotle's general views of mimesis, especially as given in *Politics* VIII 5.

not a comedy, given the strictures of *Dramatics* 2, when good or serious men in tragedy are contrasted with the vulgar men of comedy.

The final plot-type in Chapter 14 that can be deduced to have no pity and fear as the relevant set of emotions—namely, the best play-type of Chapter 14—ends happily, as did the double-structure plot of Chapter 13. The reasons are similar, but not identical, as we can quickly determine: Aristotle suggests the plot-type in Chapter 13 is not plausibly developed, and becomes comical as a result of the silly ending, whereas the best plot in Chapter 14 involves the recognition and reversal stemming from a very natural and plausible cause.[630] Why the pleasure resulting from that plausible recognition is different from the kind of mixed comic-tragic pleasure gets explained at the end of my *Aristotle's Favorite Tragedy*, but what both plot-types have in common is, again, the happy ending, and this would rule out pity and fear being the relevant, dominant set of emotions.

The score in Chapters 13-14 is, therefore, one plot-type such as *Oedipus* with (relevant) pity and fear and eight not having *both* (relevant) emotions. As part of demonstrating all of this in more detail in *Aristotle's Favorite Tragedy*, I also demonstrate that the *Antigone* of Chapter 14 must be the version by Euripides that ends happily (which is why Aristotle says it is *apathes* "without suffering"). This goes against the long-prevailing tradition in which all scholars to my knowledge have assumed it was by Sophocles and have attempted a variety of explanations to handle Aristotle's puzzling description. I give the reasons why Euripides' *Antigone* is *miaron,* which is to say, in summary, why this version of the play goes against the Aristotelian precept not to drastically change popular myths. I also explain why *Oedipus* only deserves for Aristotle the silver medal, as it were, in Chapter 14. Again, however, these two topics are beyond the scope of this book: I need only demonstrate for the matter at hand that many legitimate tragedies—including the best plot-types of Chapter 14—for Aristotle do not have a relevant pity (and *a fortiori* could not have the pity and fear required by the clause in the definition).

To summarize this section: The two plot-types of the virtuous protagonist going to misfortune (which would include, for example, Sophocles' *Antigone* or *The Trojan Woman*) and of Euripides' *Antigone* are explicitly "disgusting" (*miaron*) for Aristotle, although for different grounds, as is explained in *Aristotle's Favorite Tragedy*. The plot-type that must include *Medea* can also be deduced to be disgusting even though all three plot-types could have generated, and presumably did generate some, pity and fear (and anger, hope, sympathy and a host of other emotions) throughout the course of the play, until the ending, when the relevant (set of) emotion(s) was established. Yet pity and fear are explicitly thrust out for Aristotle because of the disgust in Chapter 13 and the same presumably

---

630  Aristotle explains at least six types of natural recognition (not depending on supernatural phenomena or on *deus ex machina*) in Chapter 16.

## Chapter 6: Pity and Fear in the Definition of Tragedy

holds for Chapter 14. It follows that, likewise, joyful dénouements would also thrust out any ending pity and fear, and, thus, the best plots of Chapter 14 do not relevantly have those emotions. It also is certain that the latter half of Chapter 14 is perfectly consistent with the rest of the treatise in terms of allowing the ending in tragedy to be fortunate or unfortunate. Chapter 13 oddly excludes the ending of good fortune from the *best* plots. Aristotle recognizes that a bad man can go from misfortune to fortune, but he does not consider a good man going to fortune, perhaps because this obviously would not generate pity and fear. To emphasize, pity and fear are important for the *sub-type* of tragedy he is examining in that chapter, which explains the omission of the plot ending in good fortune.[631] Whether this means Chapters 13 and the first half of Chapter 14, which forms a unit with Chapter 13, were interpolated from another treatise by Aristotle or whether we are missing sections of a much larger work in which Aristotle distinguishes different sub-types of tragedy and restricts one of them to an unhappy ending is something that cannot be fully addressed in this book.[632] A third option, of course, is that in lecture Aristotle explained some of the oddities we have (for instance, restricting the discussion from Chapters 9-13 to certain sub-types of plays that end unhappily), which suffices to rebut Halliwell's criticisms that are my immediate focus. However, even this option does not explain the kind of chaotic ordering of the extant chapters. For instance, Chapter 12 on the chorus and the quantitative parts interrupts the discussion of the qualitative parts in general and plot in particular. The long examination of plot seems finished at the end of Chapter 14, and Chapter 15 introduces the details of character, the second most important condition in the explanation of tragedy in *Dramatics* 6. However, Aristotle then returns to plot in Chapter 16. More on this topic later.

Additional sub-types of tragedy that do not have *both* pity and fear continue to be shown in *Dramatics* 14-18. I did not mention that Aristotle remarks at the beginning of Chapter 14 (1453b8-10) on plays that are only monstrous and not "fearful," saying that they have nothing in common with

---

631 This helps explain why Aristotle's statement in Chapter 11, which Halliwell used to criticize me, is a "hypothesis" that pity and fear are part of some tragedy, rather than part of the definition that applies to all tragedy. Aristotle in Chapter 11, as we just saw a few pages back, also noted plays could go to misfortune *or fortune*. Presumably the pity and fear would apply only to the first type of ending, with misfortune. Who pities or fears fortune?

632 The first half of Chapter 14 continues the discussion of pity and fear, at least until Aristotle sets forth new criteria for the ranking of the four types in the latter half of Chapter 14, a ranking that completely—and puzzlingly—ignores the ranking and pity and fear of Chapter 13. As is explained in the history of the *Dramatics* in the Appendix, Dacier did not agree with the "arbitrary" chapter divisions as given first in 1550. Rather he split Chapter 14 into two different chapters. I would break the chapter below where he did, keeping all of the discussion of pity and fear together. To emphasize: Starting with 1453b23, Aristotle begins the discussion and then the ranking of the four plot-types that in no way recognizes the different ranking in Chapter 13. In my opinion, this second half of Chapter 14 could not have reasonably followed Chapter 13 directly in an original manuscript. Again, all of this gets discussed in detail in my *Aristotle's Favorite Tragedy* (*op. cit.*).

tragedy.⁶³³ However, this statement must only be a figure of speech (like the earlier claim that a whole can have no magnitude) because these plays surely were not considered comedies and would have been performed as tragedies. Confirmation of this comes in Chapter 18, and its mention of "tragedy of spectacle," if we follow Janko in his interpretation of the corrupted Greek word, which might be *opsis* but which might also be "simple" (*haplē*), which Tarán and Gutas prefer on paleographical grounds. To turn to that passage, Aristotle writes:

> There are four kinds of tragedy (for we said that its parts too are of the same number): (i) the complex tragedy, the whole of which is reversal and recognition; (ii) the tragedy of suffering, e.g., the [tragedies called] *Ajax* and *Ixion*; (iii) the tragedy of character, e.g., the *Women of Phthia* and the *Peleus*; (iv) the fourth [kind] is spectacle, e.g., the *Daughters of Phorcys*, the *Prometheus* and [dramas set] in Hades (1455b33-56a4).

This passage does not establish too much, in part because it may not even have been in the *Dramatics* that initially contained Chapters 1-8. There have never been four parts of tragedy listed or discussed, and the definition emphatically gives six.⁶³⁴ Yet I am assuming for this book that the *Dramatics* was unified. If at least the general principles were consistent for Aristotle across multiple texts that are now the single treatise, then the following seems reasonable: First, tragedies of spectacle had been spoken of in Chapter 14, as we just saw, and sometimes included results that were "monstrous." Aristotle wanted to denigrate those plays by rhetorically excluding them from tragedy but that they must be tragedies at least in the broad sense, and, e.g., not comedies or satyr plays, is confirmed here in Chapter 18, when they are recognized as a sub-type, at least if *opsis* is the missing Greek word. Anoth-

---

633   D.W. Lucas remarks on the mysteriousness of this passage and believes it might refer to the kind of spectacular effects that, e.g., were attributed to Aeschylus's scary masks and that caused women (supposedly) to faint (*op. cit.*, pp. 150-1). In my view, it is entirely possible that the passage also refers to plays made infamous by, e.g., Phrynichus, who with the *Fall of Miletus* (approximately 494 BCE) was fined because he made the Athenians recall a devastating and very painful episode in their history (the recent defeat and massacre of their allies by the Persians). Indeed, the Athenians apparently then passed a law that forbade such types of representation. Aristotle could not have been ignorant of such an infamous tragedy, given the list he made of dramas performed in Athens (cf. Whalley, *op. cit.*, p. 9) and it aligns with his claim in Chapter 13 that showing a virtuous man going from good to bad fortune has no pity and fear but is shocking (*miaron*). One cannot show any suffering and expect pity and fear to result: as we have also already seen with *Medea,* one might get shockingness or a "monstrosity." A dramatist for Aristotle has at least intuitively to recognize the ethical considerations that cause pity and fear, and realize when too much suffering causes neither but rather disgust or terrible anguish or perhaps something else equally undesirable. I say "perhaps" because the dramatist may purposefully wish to cause anger, a legitimate emotion for tragedy in *Dramatics* 19, which itself may immediately follow disgust, of which more later. However, I underscore that all of this demonstrates that Aristotle's view of the possible legitimate psychological effects of tragedy is much richer and more sophisticated than previously thought.

634   As noted, the text is corrupt and the fourth sub-type could be "simple" or "spectacular." The fact that the same thing—having four types "like tragedy"—is said of epic also in the first sentence of Chapter 24 (1459b8-10) suggests that Chapter 24 also came from another text, and that the *Poetics* is an amalgamation of different Aristotelian texts, but I leave aside this whole issue in this book.

er reason Aristotle can exclude the plays of spectacle from tragedy at the beginning of Chapter 14 even without being rhetorical is that he concentrates there on the sub-type or a mixture of sub-types that involve pity and fear, and in this restricted sense of tragedy, they are excluded. Second, complex tragedies are amply discussed in the middle chapters. However, tragedies of suffering and of character are missing from our earlier chapters. Moreover, it is extremely peculiar for Aristotle to be specifying a "tragedy of suffering" on the view that pity and fear are authentic in *Dramatics* 6, for if by definition all tragedy has pity and fear, which require significant suffering, why would there be a distinct sub-type of "tragedy of suffering"? It makes no sense unless of course the pity and fear clause was never written by Aristotle in Chapter 6 or unless this type of tragedy in Chapter 18 is supposed to convey *extraordinary* suffering, with little emphasis on, say, the amazement or enthrallment that Aristotle mentions when describing the reversal or recognition of complex tragedy (6.1450a33-34; 18.1456a19; 24.1460a12-18). Yet a tragedy of extraordinary suffering is still very suspect: What would "extraordinary suffering" entail when, as we just saw, suffering already entails great pain or killing,—maybe torturing Iphigenia for hours or days in a malicious manner, with a purposefully very blunt knife, before sacrificing her? Surely this would evoke *miaron* and not pity and fear. One might claim that the suffering of Ajax, and his suicide, is more extraordinary than, say, the suffering of Sophocles' *Antigone*, but I venture only a few warriors would agree with this. Most audience members would probably say that Antigone's suffering is equally terrible, and at least *Antigone* follows Aristotle's recommendation that family member harms family member (Creon in effect causing Haemon's death and his wife's suicide). Again, then, it becomes hard to see how the tragedy of suffering adds any more suffering to the known Greek tragedies with horrible endings.

In any event, "tragedy of character" itself may cover the virtuous man going from misfortune to fortune, which Aristotle omitted as a plot-type in Chapter 13 but which without a doubt is given as a possibility in Chapter 6. Presumably, howsoever they end, these tragedies "of character" were concerned with "decision-making" as described in Chapters 6 and 15, be it in speech or, as Aristotle says, in some kind of choice pertaining to action (e.g., 15.1454a15-19), choice being for Aristotle what helps determine character. These tragedies were quite possibly the type favored by Platonists or by anyone sympathetic to some of Plato's views, whether or not they accepted his claim in the *Republic* that tragedy should be banned in the ideal state. I might add that literary theorists who have complained about plot having to be above character in Chapter 6 can now get their fill of character for Aristotle.

In summary: Whatever we think of the four sub-types in Chapter 18, three of them are set *against* tragedy of suffering, insofar as they are different sub-types. Although complex tragedy may have pity *and* fear, there are many examples throughout the treatise of complex tragedy having neither emotion (the three plot-types in Chapter 13) or only one, fear, at most (e.g., the "double-structure" plot at the end of Chapter 13). Moreover, spectacular tragedy can cause terror but not fear. Yet having one emotion (either pity or fear but not both) is not sufficient on the traditional view, because—need I repeat?—the *katharsis*, pity and fear clause in the definition requires both emotions in tragedies (again, *rare* exceptions aside). Besides, one gets the strong impression by early in Chapter 18 that the goal of *complex tragedy* is more to give amazement or enthrallment than to give pity and fear, even if pity or fear or both are *sometimes* found in those tragedies. However, many passages in the treatise would need to be reconciled with this impression before one could assert it confidently, and they are topics for the future, because the relationship between pity or fear and amazement seems very complex, given the various statements in the treatise.[635] It would have been very tidy to read that pity or fear is the goal of "tragedies of suffering" that end unhappily, like the *Oedipus* of Chapters 13-14 or the *Ajax*, and that "complex tragedy" has as its primary goal amazement because of the reversal and recognition. Aristotle's theory, though, is not so simplistic, and complex tragedies at times seemingly have any of these four combinations with the relevant amazement: pity or fear or both or neither. To add to the possible permutations: The four sub-types naturally could be mixed by a dramatist, with, e.g., a resulting tragedy of complex suffering and spectacle, just as dramatists sometimes create tragi-comedies. In any event, these are in my view part of the "hard issues" of the treatise that Woodruff very prudently in my opinion suggests scholars should be focussing on, rather than, e.g., on the meaning of *katharsis* in *Dramatics* 6.[636] Only by ridding the definition of the whole *katharsis*, pity and fear clause, though, will we be able to see and get a basic grip on these "hard issues" most

---

635 Various scholars too numerous to list have remarked that pity and fear necessarily go together. However, Aristotle separates them in Chapter 13 (1453a3-5) and never says that they are necessarily connected. The dramatist has to fulfill both of the conditions there, not just one, or he only gets one emotion. Moreover, if they were necessarily connected, why would Aristotle need to mention both repeatedly? If someone is human, she has lungs necessarily; there is no reason always to say "human and lungs." Moreover, pity is never discussed in the whole chapter dealing with fear in *Nicomachean Ethics* III 6. Recall also the rigorous permutations of this topic that Lessing engaged in and said must be examined deeply (as seen in the Appendix). For an excellent account of why pity and fear need to be treated separately, even if *at times* they are correlated, see Butcher, *op. cit.*, espec. pp. 255-66.

636 "The *Poetics* is a ruin of a book; much has been lost, and the smaller surviving fragments do not help with reconstructing his theory of tragedy. In reading the *Poetics*, and seeking for the Aristotelian purpose of tragedy, we may be like visitors to an archeological site. Here are most of the remains of an arch; some stones are missing, and the remaining ones are damaged by time. How are we to reconstruct the arch? One hypothesis would be that the arch stood (when it stood) only because it was locked by a keystone, which has now been lost. What can we learn about the keystone from the stones that have survived? That is the mode of search for those who think there is a keystone and it is katharsis... Perhaps, however, the original arch had nothing but more stones of the kind we have seen, so that it depended equally on all of its stones, including the ones that we now see on the ground. *Then we would do our best to study the stones we have, as being equally important as those that are lost. Then we would have less speculation ahead of us and, to break the analogy, more hard work with the text.* This is the model I prefer. It steers us back to the *entire* text... [my italics]" (Woodruff, 2009, p. 263).

## Chapter 6: Pity and Fear in the Definition of Tragedy

efficaciously—at least as much as possible, given, in my view, the incomplete, or mixed, nature of the texts that remain.[637]

Let us continue with our list of plot-types that do not involve both pity and fear, and recall the passage from late in Chapter 18 that Halliwell called "vexed":

> [The poet] ought to remember what we have often said, and not compose a tragedy with an epic structure... e.g., if someone were to compose [a tragedy with] the whole plot of the *Iliad*... [T]hose [tragedians] who composed a *Sack of Troy* as a whole and not in part like Euripides[638]...either fail or compete badly, since even Agathon failed in this one respect. In reversals and in simple incidents, *they aim to arouse the amazement (thaumastos) which they desire; for this is tragic and morally satisfying. This is possible when someone who is clever but villainous is deceived, like Sisyphus, or someone who is brave but unjust is defeated* [my italics] (1456a11-23).

Notice that the tragedians aim to arouse amazement, not catharsis through pity and fear. The moral satisfaction is important, too, which was stressed in Chapter 13. Moreover, the arousal of tragic, morally satisfying amazement can be accomplished not only through reversal (which would make a plot complex) but even through simple incidents (which I gather is part of a simple plot). Recall, besides, that the plot with Sisyphus was used before by me to help prove that the three plot-types not having pity and fear in Chapter 13 are nevertheless *tragic* plot-types. Otherwise, again, in Chapter 13 Aristotle would not have emphasized the "thoroughly" villainous man having neither pity nor fear, and could have simply said that the villainous man in going from good to bad fortune has no pity or fear. None of this entails, however, the universal affirmative statement that *all* plots with "clever villains" being deceived in every case have, or should have, both pity and fear.[639] Moral satisfaction appears

---

[637] The even better title of the treatise, were I to write a tome following the insights of de Montmollin, Else, and others, and following some of the remarks in this book, might be *The Collected Texts of Aristotle on "Musical" Drama*. This would immediately warn readers that the work was not necessarily written as a single, organic whole work.

[638] By "part" Aristotle means a single action, which is what a tragedian should do, Euripides being an exemplar in this case.

[639] I am far from the first to look at the problem of trying to maintain both pity and fear in all tragedies that subscribe to Aristotelian principles. To anticipate an account in the Appendix, Gordon Pocock reports while discussing Corneille: "...in a long discussion of Aristotle's theory of tragedy, he is at pains to separate catharsis by pity from catharsis by fear..." (in "Corneille and The Critics," *Corneille and Racine: Problems of Tragic Form*, Cambridge: Cambridge Univ. Pr., 1973, p. 19). As indicated, Lessing was also extremely fascinated with this topic and its importance.

For a worthwhile recent examination of pity and fear in Aristotle and Plato, see Dana Lacourse Munteanu, *Tragic Pathos: Pity and Fear in Greek Philosophy and Tragedy* (Cambridge: Cambridge Univ. Pr.) 2012. Whereas Halliwell writes as if pity, fear, and catharsis are necessarily interconnected in the *Poetics*, Munteanu takes a more grounded approach, in my opinion, realizing that pity and fear have a "proper pleasure" that is not necessarily catharsis, and saying, quite wisely, that

...my analysis of the Aristotelian tragic emotions in this book does not rely on the presence and into be a pre-condition of the correct kind of response, and, to emphasize, indeed was a requirement in 13.1452b38-39, as we saw before. Moreover, in Chapter 15 *good* character is the primary consideration concerning the second most important element in tragedy from Chapter 6, character itself. Because the reversal in a plot need not always go from fortune to misfortune given the previous chapters (6, 13 and 14), Aristotle also seems to be suggesting therefore in Chapter 18 that "This [the amazement and moral satisfaction] is possible [*even*] when someone who is clever but villainous is deceived, like Sisyphus." In other words, we do not always need an extremely good protagonist like Merope in the *Cresphontes* recognizing her son before he is to die to generate the amazement and moral satisfaction. Even the upending of a clever scoundrel, or—to take the other combination that Aristotle mentions—a brave but unjust king (like Richard III) can suffice, assuming other principles of tragedy are adhered to, although the degree and kind of moral satisfaction will depend on the protagonist, their precise outcome, and their precise characteristics.

Ironically, these plot-types of Chapter 18 involving protagonists who are not thoroughly villainous are consistent with the traditional *katharsis*, pity and fear clause. Having a reversal and therefore being complex, some of these plots even have one precondition of being the best one (although whether they satisfy all of the other preconditions is another matter). Not too much should be made of this, though, because these plots types are equally consistent with Aristotle focussing at times in the middle chapters on a narrow notion of tragedy, which is my view, involving pity and fear. The plot-types in Chapter 18 are also consistent with my broad notion of tragedy (from Chapters 1-8) that removes the pity and fear clause in Chapter 6! That is, Aristotle is not saying in Chapter 18 that partly admirable villains will always engender pity and fear if they suffer. Again, pity is only felt for those undeserving of the suffering, and villains insofar as they are vicious deserve no pity. The nub of the matter is that typically the protagonists are not perfectly bad (or perfectly good) but a mixture. They are different from Oedipus in that they do not make an egregious mistake on one occasion but have a disposition to act in mildly, or moderately, vicious ways consistently or always, while having other,

---

terpretation of catharsis in the definition, and it would not be influenced by the removal of the controversial term, and/or by the removal of pity and fear from the definition (p. 238).

Curiously, though, for the reason that follows, she also says the following:

Scott 2003 and Veloso 2007 have recently revived the argument that there is no room for catharsis at all in the definition of tragedy in the *Poetics*, as the passage is corrupt. In addition, Veloso 2007, 280-2, argues that the words pity and fear in the definition appear to be part of the catharsis gloss, so they should be eliminated as well. I find certain points in Veloso's article convincing, yet not quite sufficient to overthrow the tradition (p. 238).

Given that she says "in addition," I wonder whether she read my article thoroughly, because as can be easily seen from my "Purging," *op. cit*, 2003, pp. 249ff, when I begin arguing against Petruševski, I athetize the whole catharsis clause and not just the word catharsis. In any event, not caring one way or the other to solve the problem of catharsis, she provides a very up-to-date and even-handed synopsis of the different positions on catharsis.

admirable qualities.

In brief, then, the "vexed" plot-types in Chapter 18 may cause either pity or fear, or neither, or both. The result would depend on the way the dramatist interweaves the various elements, themes, and character traits. In some plays, there may be no pity, because the villain is defeated and, insofar as he is a villain, deserves no pity. Maybe there is fear, which we would *not* have, however, if he were thoroughly villainous because in that case we (somewhat virtuous audience members) would not then identify with him and "identification" is a requirement of fear in Chapter 13. Thus, even with mild villainy a proper audience could be suitably gratified. The protagonist's multiple good traits (like intelligence in the case of Sisyphus) may be commendable, and in those plays a possible mildness of villainy and the greater redeeming qualities of the clever character might even cause *some* pity and fear. There is self-evidently a whole continuum of possibilities for not only mixing positive and negative qualities in a protagonist but generating a similar continuum of pity or fear or both—or not, especially if the play ends happily and no great suffering occurs. Misfortune may only be the loss of victory (as the "defeat" mentioned above concerning the unjust but brave man might suggest) or may involve death. Likewise, a mild or moderate villain being deceived, as happens with Sisyphus, might result in him not gaining power (given one myth about him) or might result in his punishment of eternally rolling a rock up a hill. We do not know the exact plot, which might take liberties with the myth.

To reiterate: It is noteworthy that these "vexed" plot-types seem *secondarily* at best to have pity and fear, if and when they have both, for the two emotions are not at issue here. Indeed, they are not even mentioned! Rather, Aristotle stresses amazement and moral satisfaction, the latter of which, again, in Chapter 13 had been presented as a requirement for the best plots (of that chapter) and the former of which has been typically identified with the cognitive response to the reversals and recognitions of complex plots (such as given in the best, happily-ending plays of Chapter 14). Curiously, then, at the opportune moment to suggest that the moderate villain might be the subject of pity or fear (or both or neither), Aristotle chooses to concentrate on amazement and moral satisfaction.[640] Here, then, at still another time, particular tragic plot-types do not *require* both pity and fear as their goal or as one of their prime concerns.

Let us now summarize the plot-types in the treatise not having *both* pity and fear:
- The tragedies, including Platonic-type ones, in Chapters 1-8 that have no discussion of pity and fear applied to them, which Aristotle sympathizes with to a great extent, given his

---

[640] It has been said to me that Aristotle does not mention pity and fear because they are presupposed by the previous discussions, but then why does he discuss amazement and moral satisfaction, which had also been discussed?

statement in Chapter 15 that "first and foremost, the characters should be good" [1454a16]. They presumably are especially the ones that Aristotle says go from "misfortune to fortune."

- The three plot-types in Chapter 13 explicitly without pity and fear, one of which is the virtuous person going from fortune to misfortune.
- "Double-structured plots" at the end of Chapter 13, which we can easily deduce would not have *both* pity and fear and which are considered to be the best plots by some others, according to Aristotle, but only second-best for himself. They were and would be performed as tragedy, not as comedy.
- The kinds of spectacular tragedy noted at the beginning of Chapter 14 that give horror or terror, as opposed to the proper fear.
- The various plot-types in Chapter 14 that are, e.g., enemy versus enemy or enemy versus friend, which again have no pity, Aristotle expressly says.
- The *Antigone*-type play of Chapter 14 (by Euripides) that ends happily, which again could not have any relevant pity for two reasons, because Aristotle explicitly says it (i) is *miaron* and (ii) has no suffering.
- The *Medea*-type play because it must also be *miaron*.
- The best plot-types of tragedy in Chapter 14, *Cresphontes, Helle,* and the *Iphigenia*, which, in ending happily, cannot have the relevant pity.
- Chapter 18's three sub-types of tragedy that are set against "tragedy of suffering," including complex tragedy. Complex tragedy is usually the best type for Aristotle. Its distinguishing traits are reversals and recognitions and the psychological result throughout the treatise is cognitive amazement or the like, not pity and fear (even if some individual plays might also have pity and fear because they mix perhaps tragedy of suffering with complex tragedy or any other relevant sub-type).
- The "vexed" passage of Chapter 18, which suggests that sometimes the audience feels pity and fear for a mildly villainous character and sometimes not, again, depending both on the particular mixture of virtue and vice and on the way the plot is developed (the plots can undoubtedly trigger amazement and moral satisfaction, given Aristotle's explicit statements at this point).

In short, given all of the plot-types examined above without both pity and fear, it would be a "Fallacy of Composition" to assume that for Aristotle all tragedies must have both emotions just because the exceptional, best plot-type in Chapter 13—repeated as only the second-best type in Chapter 14—has them. It is much more reasonable to reconcile all of these issues fundamentally, as much as they can be resolved with the texts we have, by deducing that Aristotle was focussing on a specific sub-type (or two) of tragedy in those middle chapters, perhaps the "tragedy of suffering" of Chapter 18 or a com-

## Chapter 6: Pity and Fear in the Definition of Tragedy

bination of "tragedy of suffering" with "complex tragedy." Anyone who claims that the *Dramatics* is a series of lecture notes or that Aristotle filled in gaps in lecture or that we have lost texts must, to be consistent, recognize that the Northern Greek easily could have narrowed the discussion in the middle chapters, probably starting in Chapter 9 as discussed above, to one more of these sub-types.

It should be very obvious now why we cannot follow AnonC in considering the three plot-types of Chapter 13 to be mere exceptions that prove the rule. It follows, even more strongly, that neither pity nor fear can be an essential condition of tragedy. We can also see, therefore, why Halliwell should not be ignoring the inconsistencies of Chapters 6 and 13 in the respect just discussed and why he should not have said in his own "Appendix":

> ...since it becomes abundantly clear in *Poetics* 9 onwards that Aristotle regards pity and fear as central to the experience of tragedy, there is every reason why reference to them should be found, as it is, in the definition of the genre.[641]

To the contrary, given not only the three plot-patterns of Chapter 13 but the other examples in the list above, both pity *and* fear are not central to the experience of tragedy, even if they are central to the one plot-type like *Oedipus*. To argue that the other plot-types are exceptions that prove the rule, as AnonC has done, may show mettle or a die-hard loyalty in defending the traditional view. Certainly, we must consider these types of arguments in order to remove any remaining doubt about the authenticity of pity and fear in Chapter 6. However, AnonC's view is completely unconvincing on a sustained examination of the rest of the *Dramatics*, if my arguments above are even approximately correct.

I can now imagine Halliwell and Veloso becoming "strange bedfellows" from this point onwards regarding this particular matter because Halliwell might decide to follow Veloso, given that the latter claims that two of the plot-types in *Dramatics* 13, dealing with evil and very wicked men, are not tragic plot-types at all because they had been excluded by *Dramatics* 2.[642] This is, on the surface, a legitimate worry, and in effect, both scholars might contest White, who I reported in Chapter 6 saying insightfully (and correctly in my view) of Aristotle in *Dramatics* 13: "his claim is not that no tragedies were or could be built on any of these patterns, but only that 'the finest tragedies' avoid them."[643] Veloso does not give the precise reason for excluding the two plots with evil or very wicked men, suggesting it seems to me that *Dramatics* 2 is requiring that men be good in all respects or that only (moderately) good men can be shown in tragedy. Yet, *Dramatics* 2 only distinguishes admirable men from vulgar men, and Aristotle says in the final statement there that "Tragedy too is distinguished from comedy by precisely this difference; comedy prefers to represent people who are worse than

---

641 Halliwell, 2011, p.264.
642 Veloso, 2007, p. 274.
643 White, *op. cit.* p. 229.

those who exist, tragedy people who are better" [1448a17-19]. Leaving aside that Aristotle only says "prefers," which suggests a mixture of good and bad protagonists could be shown in tragedy (especially if they are all aristocrats), *Dramatics* 2 only seems to require some kind of significant goodness, not perfect goodness, which means the good character can have some reprehensible traits. This is consistent with the important case of the moderately vicious man going from good to bad fortune, e.g., Sisyphus in Chapter 18, which Veloso never takes into account. Moreover, and most crucially, Veloso has no argument as to why the remaining plot-type, the representation of a virtuous (*epieikēs*) individual in Chapter 13 going from good to bad fortune, cannot be a tragedy,—it would just not be the kind of best tragedy Aristotle prefers in the precise context of Chapter 13. Indeed, as Richard Sorabji has remarked, "this [the exclusion of pity from a good man going from fortune to misfortune] seems to contradict the *Rhetoric* [2.8, 1385b34] since the *Rhetoric* preserves pity especially for victims who are good (*epieikeis*)."[644] "Seems" in Sorabji's remark is undoubtedly an understatement.

Veloso's suggestion that perhaps tragedy only applies to a not-extremely-virtuous man generates (as he very sensibly acknowledges) a tension with Chapter 2 before he leaves the issue unresolved and proceeds to other and better reasons why pity and fear cannot be in Chapter 6. However, if, indeed, tragedy in general (as opposed merely to the best plot-pattern of a sub-type of tragedy in Chapter 13) *only* applies to a moderately virtuous man, then, as Veloso suggests, a tension surely exists between Chapter 13 and Chapter 2. Part of that tension exists because Aristotle switches back and forth not only in those two chapters but in the rest of the treatise between a concern for dramatic characters that are better, the same, or worse than us—which could be an issue of reputation, political power, money, intelligence and so forth—and dramatic characters who are virtuous in the full sense, involving justice and benevolence and the like. What Veloso does not say, though, that is more germane to the debate at hand (whether or not the three plot-patterns in Chapter 13 are mere exceptions that prove the definition of tragedy) is that Chapter 13 then also generates an extreme tension with Chapter 6 and the use of *spoudaios* in the definition of tragedy, which itself collects the division of Chapter 2. The reasons follow.

If *spoudaios* means "good" in the sense of "perfectly virtuous" then one could argue that, according to the definition in Chapter 6, no evil character of any kind—slight, moderate or extreme—can be shown in tragedy for Aristotle, and we would then hear Plato not only applauding loudly in his grave but dancing a confined *sikinnis*. However, this would then contradict not only the implication in Chapter 13 that moderately evil men can generate pity and fear in going from good to bad fortune but the

---

644    Richard Sorabji, *Emotion and Peace of Mind: From Stoic Agitation to Christian Temptation* (Oxford: Oxford Univ. Press) 2000, p. 25. As I have argued, *Poetics* 13 also seems to generate severe tension with *Poetics* 6, and Sorabji completely misses or stays silent on this point.

outright example of Sisyphus being a legitimate protagonist, and in similar cases probably deserving a little pity and fear. This restriction to completely virtuous men would also then contradict intermediately virtuous men like Oedipus being ideal protagonists (because he seemingly is prone to anger in killing a stranger, who turns out to be his father, and because he does not do enough research to realize he was marrying his mother). It would also contradict Chapter 15, when Aristotle only rules out *unnecessarily* villainous men at 1454a29, which I failed to mention above. Mildly or moderately villainous ones or perhaps even thoroughly villainous ones needed to make the plot believable presumably are implicitly permitted in tragedy for him. Thus, I believe it is important to take *spoudaios* in the more restricted sense of "serious" or "admirable" in *Poetics* 6, or "good" in a general sense without necessarily implying complete virtue—*but not ruling it out either. Spoudaios* suggests—but only suggests—goodness in the sense of complete virtue. As the cases of Oedipus and Sisyphus prove, people who are legitimate protagonists often are good and bad, in almost any mixture, and although "serious" people may be more good than not, they are not necessarily virtuous in all respects because of their seriousness, nobility, or the like. *Spoudaios*, then, can mean someone who has many of the virtues—e.g., intelligence, courage, temperance, wit, or generosity—but not all, or it can mean a genuinely virtuous person in all respects.

Chapters 2 and 6, therefore, allow protagonists other than moderately good ones in tragedy, contrary to what Veloso (or Halliwell) might try to maintain, and that protagonist might go from misfortune to fortune. Such a play would surely be a "tragedy" (*tragōidia*) in Aristotle's sense of the word, especially if it had choice, reasoning, speech, music, dance, and spectacle. Those chapters even allow moderate villains to be the protagonists of tragedy as long as they have some redeeming qualities.[645]

---

645 Veloso or Halliwell might say that Chapter 2 and 6 only refer to the primary protagonist and that secondary characters or other protagonists can be wicked, although not inordinately wicked, given the restrictions of Chapter 15. Indeed, Aristotle seems to be speaking of main protagonists in Chapter 13. Yet if there are multiple protagonists—like the two or three in *Antigone*—I think that possible line of argument fails *insofar as it is supposed to be evidence that the three plot-types in Chapter 13 do not fall under tragedy in the Aristotelian sense*. Either a single noble protagonist is wicked in one or two ways, but is still smart, powerful and courageous, and thus an allowable subject for tragedy, if not the best tragedy, or multiple, appropriate protagonists are developed in ways that do not lead to comic results but that are varied, one protagonist going to good fortune, another to bad, but logically and not like the inane "double-structure" plot discussed above of Aegisthus and Orestes. Again, this latter type (of realistically developed endings with multiple protagonists) may not be the best tragedy for Aristotle, but surely would still be a tragedy. Without the simplistic notion that all tragedy has to evoke pity and fear, Aristotle's theory becomes much more viable as a theory that covers all, or almost all, ancient and modern tragedy, although I cannot argue fully for this point in this book, given considerations of space.

    I should also report what Veloso does say in this respect: Because of the many contradictions or inconsistencies with other parts of the *Poetics*, including Chapter 14, he believes—as indicated in private correspondence—that Chapter 13 is a "*variante d'auteur*," suggesting a different treatise or a different context even in an original *Dramatics* by Aristotle. This possibility, with which I am very sympathetic, exposes too many issues

To emphasize: The *spoudaios* might be entirely virtuous, but might at other times be mostly virtuous with a few flaws (like Oedipus) or just moderately virtuous, and indeed might even be a Richard-the-III[rd] type of man like Sisyphus: significantly unjust but very intelligent, brave, and witty. Also, to refine some statements from before: A very virtuous man or *epieikēs*[646] could be the recommended primary hero (or one of the protagonists) in tragedy, if he is going from bad to good fortune. He could be the hero of a Platonic-type tragedy, again, a plot-type not discussed in Chapter 13, but one that follows the strictures in Chapters 1-8, and one that would surely be a tragedy and not a comedy for Aristotle.[647] (I have suggested that this might fall under "tragedy of character.") Moreover, and this is a new point: The *epieikēs* could even be shown going from good to bad fortune, especially if the dramatist attempted to inspire anger at the way the virtuous man was treated,—because what would the resulting emotion typically be otherwise after the disgust (*miaron*) noted in Chapter 13 was felt at such a plot? Surely this would be a tragedy and not a comedy for Aristotle, *especially since he lists anger as one of the legitimate emotions immediately alongside pity and fear in Ch*apter 19 at 1456b1. That this type of drama—or the other tragedies with moderately villainous but clever protagonists—would not be the best (for at least one sub-type of tragedy) according to Chapter 13 is not at issue here, and can be granted immediately. However, this might be precisely the reason a playwright creates such a plot—to be unique and thus to gain a victory one time, but not necessarily to repeat this plot type consistently over the years. Again, just because a play does not follow the Oedipan model does not make it non-tragedy, and the best and worst tragedies of Chapter 14 are ample proof of this.

To summarize: Resolving (i) the exclusion of pity and fear in three of the plot-types in Chapter 13 with (ii) the inclusion of pity and fear at other times in Chapters 9-14 is one issue. Harmonizing, or better yet, revealing the inconsistency between those three plot-types in Chapter 13 (and the other plays in Chapters 13-14 that have no pity) with the *katharsis*, pity and fear clause in Chapter 6 is another issue and my primary concern in this book. Regarding the latter issue, I unfortunately suggested in 2003

---

to address in this work, but is irrelevant for the moment concerning Halliwell, because he accepts that Chapter 13 is part of the original treatise (*op. cit.*, 1986, p. 33). Nevertheless, see his work (1986, pp. 32ff) for a very impressive list of the additional, notorious major inconsistencies in the *Dramatics*,—a list that ironically does not include catharsis in Chapter 6. I say "ironically" because, as my own and Veloso's work have shown (*op. cit.*, 2003 and 2007 respectively), and as the rest of this book reveals, that single word in that location, which of course is connected with pity and fear, arguably causes almost as many inconsistencies or outright major contradictions as the other, top major issues combined!

646 As Freese says when translating Aristotle's *Rhetoric* 2.1: "*epieikēs* and *spoudaios* both = *agathos* ["good" or "virtuous"]. In a restricted sense *epieikēs* is 'respectable', *spoudaios* 'serious'" (*Aristotle in 23 Volumes*, Vol. 22, *op. cit.*, 1926).

647 I am not sure why Aristotle ignores this plot-type. Perhaps there is no dilemma with it, and everyone, even Plato, agrees that it is a justifiable kind of tragic plot. Hence it may have no philosophical interest for Aristotle. At any rate, *Dramatics* 15 fills in more details for this option.

Chapter 6: Pity and Fear in the Definition of Tragedy

that because Aristotle focusses on the best plots in Chapter 13, we can explain for that reason alone why pity and fear need not be in *Dramatics* 6, which is partly right but, for the reasons given, incomplete. My better, and arguably insuperable, explanation is that Aristotle switches in Chapter 9 to a sub-type (or to sub-types) of tragedy involving pity and fear and *then* brings his ongoing concern for the best tragedies into the most precise focus by concentrating on the best plots (of that sub-type) in Chapter 13 and the beginning of Chapter 14. This explanation is much more effective and entirely sufficient. It is wholly consistent with all the passages throughout the treatise and with pity and fear being inauthentic in Chapter 6. Why in the middle chapters Aristotle decides to narrow the conception of tragedy to the kind that has pity and fear is a very interesting question. (Again, if oral explanation is permitted, as it is by Halliwell, the narrowing could have been accomplished by a slight emphasis of the voice at 1452a2 and pointing to a diagram, were Aristotle using one,[648] or by uttering a simple additional sentence.) There are any number of answers. Perhaps the type of tragedy with pity and fear poses the most interesting questions philosophically because there is a historical antecedent at times for such types of tragedies going back to Gorgias. Besides, as we will see soon, Aeschylus and Sophocles most often, if not always, had their tragedies end sorrowfully (leaving aside the satyr play that came at the end). Alternatively, Aristotle may have wished to focus on one or two of the four different sub-types of tragedy from Chapter 18. Perhaps he wrote about all of them, and we are missing the rest of the discussion. In any event, to emphasize one last time, since this narrower conception of tragedy is a different sense of tragedy from the broad sense in Chapters 1-8, no contradiction occurs between Chapters 13 and Chapter 6 if pity and fear are excised in the definition of tragedy. All of this redeems Aristotle, Veloso, and myself. Another option is that some of the extant passages in the *Dramatics* or even some of the chapters come from different Aristotelian works. This option would explain in and of itself the outright contradiction between the best plots of Chapters 13 and 14, along with Aristotle in the ranking of Chapter 14 not even being aware of what he just wrote in Chapter 13.[649]

---

[648] Cf. Natali, *op. cit.*, on Aristotle using tables and diagrams while teaching, pp. 113-7.

[649] Whether the other parts of the *Poetics* are earlier or later or better or worse Aristotelian theories than Chapters 1-8 is a different—and extraordinarily complicated—matter, and one that, for instance, de Montmollin tried in his own way to solve (*op. cit.*, 1951). At least another large book would be necessary even to begin to address the many related issues and possibilities, especially given my correction in this book of the two fundamental misconceptions. However, I offer a few introductory thoughts in passing. If Veloso and I are correct in denying the authenticity of pity and fear in *Poetics* 6, we all may have more solid grounds in the future for tackling the question of whether the *Dramatics* is truly a unified whole or whether large sections of that whole are missing or whether, as I believe, the treatise is an agglomeration of different Aristotelian texts. The middle chapters may well have been written at a different time by Aristotle and combined by a later editor with parts of the original *Dramatics* (including Chapter 14). I mentioned already that Natali reports Strabo indicating that the bumbling editor was Apellicon of Teos, whereas Plutarch can be interpreted as suggesting the bumbler instead was Tyrannion the grammarian, who re-ordered the texts, or possibly even Andronicus, although the latter is said only to publish the texts and make a catalog (*op. cit.*, 2013, pp. 102-3). This scenario makes Apellicon or Tyrannion or both the prime suspects in my opinion. Apart from the evidence already given (like the four

Let the above suffice for our purposes, because if we enter more deeply into the related issues, like the possibility that the chapters come from different texts by Aristotle, we will never extract ourselves in the space allotted here from the morass of questions (and, again, I address much more the dilemma of the inconsistent best plots of Chapters 13 and 14 in *Aristotle's Favorite Tragedy*). However, if scholars, including Halliwell, wish to continue advocating the authenticity of pity and fear in the definition of tragedy, the burden of proof is on them to reconcile how those *essential* conditions are consistent with, e.g., three of the tragic plot-patterns in Chapter 13 (and the other types in the whole list above) not having both pity and fear, my primary and important concern in this chapter. Another burden for them is to demonstrate how the middle chapters can be internally consistent concerning those two emotions. That is, how do the best, happily ending tragedies like *Cresphontes* have a relevant (ending) pity and fear? It will not be good enough to say the pity and fear happened in the middle of the play. Pity and fear surely could happen in the middle of a play about a virtuous hero going from fortune to misfortune but Aristotle is emphatic: Such a play is disgusting and thus has no pity and fear (in the relevant way).

Two final points should be emphasized. First, Halliwell's support of Bernays regarding a purposefully excised explanation of *katharsis* in Chapter 6 is manifestly doubly problematic (leaving aside that, in addition to the explanation, Bernays would need to demonstrate why Aristotle drops *katharsis* in all the places the Northern Greek discusses the end of tragedy). *Again, we are missing an expansion in Chapters 6-7 of pity and fear, too*. To say that the two emotions are explained in Chapter 13, a point I brought up concerning Petruševski, is not sufficient to handle the oddity that all other terms in the definition are developed more in Chapters 6-7, but not pity and fear. Even given Petruševski's solution, namely, the correction of **katharsin pathēmatōn** to **sustasin pragmatōn**, pity and fear should have been briefly discussed, like the other essential conditions, or at least postponed explicitly until later. Thus, some additional missing text on Halliwell's and Bernays's view in Chapter 6 is required to explain these two emotions or at least to show Aristotle indicating that they will be covered later. On their view, the missing texts keep getting larger and larger, hardly a favorable sign. Second, neither can we accept Halliwell's implicit claim that *katharsis*, pity, and fear all stand or fall together in the *katharsis* clause, for they are separate words and separate issues, as noted before concerning Munteanu's work. Although I gravely doubt the success of such an approach, pity and fear

---

types of tragedy and the "four parts" in Chapter 18 when actually six exist in Chapter 6), another ground of the "patchwork theory" that Else agrees with and dealt with throughout his book is, for example, that Chapter 12 focusses on the chorus and then Chapter 13 returns inexplicably to the discussion of plot, which is the focus of Chapters 7–11. Rather, Aristotle should have been going onto another of the six necessary elements of tragedy that he starts to explain after the definition in Chapter 6, probably character, the second most important (which is covered of course in Chapter 15). At least most, if not all, of Chapters 20-22 on language appears to come from a grammatical treatise, and Chapter 25 from the *Homeric Problems*.

might somehow be justified in the definition by Halliwell appealing to still *yet another* lost discussion of the two terms in Chapters 1-5. However, even in that case, those two words do not necessarily pull in *katharsis* as a result (nor, of course, do they resolve the problems just mentioned, that no critical term in the *katharsis* clause is described again in the derivation of the necessary conditions in Chapter 6). Rather, following Chapter 14 (1453b10-13), it may be that the goal of tragedy was *pleasure* through pity and fear. Therefore, even if my arguments of this Unit can be proven wrong, it might still be that Petruševski was fundamentally right in rejecting *katharsis* but keeping pity and fear in conjunction with the arrangement of incidents. Hence, Halliwell should not just summarily dismiss this last option without argument, as he does, because Petruševski's solution makes the treatise much more coherent and consistent than the traditional *katharsis* clause, and someone now may be able more convincingly to advance a Petruševskian-type solution. Indeed, as I just discovered when implementing the final editorial corrections (to the first edition), and as I discuss in the Post-Postscript below, Marwan Rashed has started down that path in an article in June 2016. Let this suffice, though, for the rejection of pity and fear in the definition of tragedy,—otherwise this section threatens, if the reader will allow me this quip, to become frightfully long.

This takes us to Halliwell's fourth and final set of arguments, which is not so much against my 2003 article (viz., Chapter 5 above) as an alleged omission on my part. Halliwell claims:

> (S⁴) Aristotle's appeal to 'the stated function of tragedy' (*ho ēn tēs tragodias ergon*) at *Poet.* 6.1450a30-1 is most readily understood as a reference back to the catharsis clause of the definition. If that clause were deleted, as Scott proposes, the reference back would have to be to plot as the 'end' (*telos*) of tragedy (see Scott 2003: 248, cf. 244; as a *back* reference, it cannot be to the notion of tragic pleasure in chapter 14). But that would render the rest of Aristotle's sentence at 1450a31-3 vacuous, making it say in effect that a tragedy 'with a plot' (but deficient in character, etc.) will 'much better achieve' a plot.

To understand this most clearly, and as part of my final reply, which comprises three rejoinders, let us first re-examine the relevant passage by Aristotle, which we saw once before in my Chapter 3:

> ...if [a poet] puts in sequence speeches (*rhēseis*) full of character, well-composed in diction and reasoning, he will not achieve what was [agreed to be] the function (*ergon*) of tragedy; a tragedy that employs these less adequately, but has a plot (i.e. structure of incidents), will achieve it much more.[650]

The first rejoinder, then, to Halliwell is that Aristotle's statement is not vacuous at all on my interpretation. To flesh out some of the points made before, the wider context for this passage is Aristotle arguing that plot is higher, and more important, than character, during the ranking of the six necessary elements of *tragōidia* (and when I use "tragedy" at any point from now on, the reader should consider it a technical term that does not necessarily entail tragic endings). At that point, Aristotle

---
650   1450a29-33.

justifies his claim that plot is the soul of, and indispensable for, tragedy whereas character is not (the case of "metaphysical primacy" that I discussed in Chapter 3). He now says, first, that a composer could string together "character-laden" speeches[651], well composed in language[652] and reasoning. However, this means that the composer only assembles three of the six necessary elements of tragedy: the character (second-most important), the reasoning (the third), and the language (the fourth) (1450a38-b20). Plot, music-dance, and spectacle are being left off, the latter two being unnecessary to support the argument that plot is higher than character. This "assemblage-of-three-elements," though, is not truly a tragedy, Aristotle implies, because it does not have all the six necessary elements,—indeed, it does not even have a plot, the soul of tragedy! Some (like Plato) might call it a (literary) tragedy, or something of the sort, which is perhaps another ramification of Aristotle's remark. All of this is, in effect, Aristotle's first point, or strongly implied by it. Aristotle then adds the second option: The dramatist could employ the most important element, plot (as "enacted sequence of actions," done by the actors on stage), theoretically possible and historically done even with mere dance or pantomime on at least some occasions in the early evolution of tragedy, as I showed in Chapters 2-3.[653] The dramatist could combine these coherent stage actions with the three elements just noted that themselves, as Aristotle says, are *now* very poorly composed. Aristotle adds that, still, even with the three last elements poorly composed, this option will give the function (*ergon*) of tragedy much better than the "three-element-assemblage" that has no plot at all. In summary: On the first alternative, an audience member would get the impact or *dunamis* of only three of the "secondary" six parts of tragedy—an actor reciting speeches even reflecting characters—but would not get the function at all of tragedy, strictly speaking, because the first alternative has no plot *per se*.

Another reason that Aristotle's passage is not vacuous is that Aristotle may be subtly rejecting the views of those, like Chaeremon, who were writing plays only to be read and who were then dispensing with the performing tradition (the "structure of actions" onstage). Plato himself may also be an implied target here, because of his characterization of tragedy as a composition of speeches. We noted this above concerning the *Phaedrus* (again, Aristotle uses the exact word that Plato uses, *rhēseis*, when Aristotle lays out the first option, the one containing good speeches but no plot *per se*). In any event, there is nothing wrong with Aristotle saying that you will not get the effect of a plot unless you have a plot in the first place (and we must not forget that the context of Aristotle's argument is to rank

---

651    Speeches with character are speeches in which the speaker reveals a decision or makes a choice. As Aristotle adds almost immediately at 1450b8-11, that "this is why those speeches in which the speaker decides or avoids nothing at all do not have character."

652    One can make a character-laden speech (showing clearly the speaker's decisions or choices that make the speech a character-flavored one) with awkward uses of language, so it is not redundant for Aristotle to add "well-composed in language."

653    Originally in Scott, *op. cit.*, 1999, espec. pp. 20-37.

## Chapter 6: Pity and Fear in the Definition of Tragedy

plot above character). In short: To say that the second alternative gives more the function of tragedy is an example of litotes, understatement for the sake of emphasis. *Only* the second alternative has the primary necessary element (plot), which is so important that even with other, poor elements it overshadows superb writing, superb character, and superb reasoning,—what one would find, it seems, in good literature or Plato's conception of tragedy. Aristotle's remark has upset literary theorists for generations, none of them recognizing that he discusses drama and plot in a way that is apart from literature *per se,* as we saw in Unit 1.[654] Thus, Halliwell's critique claiming vacuity on this point utterly fails.

The second rejoinder to Halliwell is that one need not accept the interpretation of the Greek text as given by either himself or, I might add, by Janko. Take Janko's own bracketed "agreed to be" in the passage that is the focus of this discussion: "...if [a poet] puts in sequence speeches (*rhēseis*) full of character, well-composed in diction and reasoning, he will not achieve what was [agreed to be] the function (*ergon*) of tragedy..." (*eti ean tis ephexēs thē rhēseis ēthikas kai lexei kai dianoia eu pepoiēmenas, ou poiēsei ho ēn tēs tragōdias ergon...*). Although admittedly one legitimate rendering, with *ho ēn* an idiom in which "the imperfect may refer to a topic previously discussed,"[655] other translators much more known than I as masters of ancient Greek render the passage "he [the poet] will not achieve the function of tragedy."[656] This translation means, of course, that we would not have to search for a previous mention of the function of tragedy. Yet, for the sake of rigor, let us accept Janko's reading and Halliwell's similar "*stated* function of tragedy," which takes us to the third and final rejoinder.

Halliwell suggests that function (*ergon*) and end (*telos*) are the same. However, this need not be the case, an option Halliwell never explores in this context. Plot in tragedy is clearly the end (*telos*) in the context of this discussion in Chapter 6 (1450a21-22), perhaps the goal of the dramatist putting together all the elements in combination with the chorus, whereas the function (*ergon*) has been traditionally to give *katharsis*. I demonstrate in the next chapter that the function is to give (the proper) pleasure or delight to the audience.[657] Once we see this distinction between function and end, at least

---

654 Notice that all of Aristotle's arguments given here are intended only to support the importance of plot over the other necessary elements, and that the Northern Greek is not suggesting that the finest tragedy will *not* be superb in all or most of the elements, a different point and one outside of our scope here. Indeed, later, complex plot also becomes, for instance, a condition for the finest tragedy.

655 H.W. Smyth *Greek Grammar* §1903. I am beholden to AnonC for this point.

656 *Aristotle. Aristotle in 23 Volumes*, Vol. 23, translated by W. H. Fyfe. Cambridge, MA, Harvard University Press; London, William Heinemann Ltd., 1932.

657 This is why I agree with Woodruff on almost, but not, everything that he says here:
"The aim is a certain kind of action, not a quality" (50a17); "the actions and the story are the aim (*telos*) of tragedy, and the aim is the most important of all [of the elements of tragedy]" (50a21-22).

four possibilities for the "stated *function* of tragedy" exist that evade Halliwell's objection, which I now summarize and then detail in order below:

- A) the function of dramatic representations to give pleasure, as stated in Chapter 4;
- B) the *praxeos mimesis* [the representation of an action] at 6.1449b36;
- C) a lost sentence or two earlier in the treatise, whether in Chapter 6 or before (but not in the location of the current *katharsis*, pity and fear clause);
- D) the legitimate goal of tragedy in Chapter 6, written by Aristotle and lost, which *katharsis* has replaced, and which, unlike *katharsis*, is actually consistent with the rest of the *Dramatics*.

(A) Pleasure is given as the function of representations in Chapter 4, and representations include tragedy, indeed all drama, along with epic. As I prove in the next chapter, this is consistent with all the other discussions in the treatise in which pleasure is given as the goal, or the function, of dramatists and epic makers (in, e.g., Chapters 14, 23, and 26). Any objection that Aristotle does not use the exact word *ergon* in Chapter 4 when he describes the delight that mankind gets by nature from representation is handled, I believe, by the obviousness of the case, including the subsequent statements showing that pleasure is indeed the goal of tragedy and epic (leaving aside, of course, the disputed *katharsis* clause). It is also consistent with Callicles in the *Gorgias* and shows Aristotle to be following the typical commonsensical view, not a surprising approach for an empiricist and a view that hardly needs belaboring on his, or anyone's, part.

(B) As D.W. Lucas notes, two of the greatest commentators of the *Dramatics,* Ingram Bywater and Johannes Vahlen, understand "the *ergon* to be the production of a *praxeos mimesis* ["mimesis of an

---

By "actions" Aristotle apparently means whatever is presented on stage through mimesis, not the behavior by which the performers represent those actions (50a16); similarly, the agents ("those acting," *hoi prattontes*) are what we would call the characters who are represented by the performers. To say that action is the aim of tragedy, in context, means that the other elements of tragedy (such as character) serve the larger aim of achieving mimesis of action. But it cannot mean that the mimesis of action is the final aim of tragedy. If the mimesis of action had no further aim, any action would do. *But we have seen that tragedy must select those actions that have the power to arouse pity and fear.* So action serves the arousal of emotion, and therefore it is not at the top of the hierarchy of aims in tragedy [my italics] (*op. cit.*, 2009, pp. 612-3).

Given the arguments of this chapter, I must disagree with the italicized statement (unless of course a specific sub-type of tragedy, like "tragedy of suffering," were in scope, but it is not for Woodruff). Tragedy in the broad sense could have pleasure, or amazement in reversals and recognitions, or anger or any other number of psychological states as its goal, often intermixed. The "proper pleasure" typically results from a total *dunamis* that captured any one or more of the full range of human responses, which makes Aristotle's theory much more viable as a relevant theory across the ages, as the Appendix demonstrates.

## Chapter 6: Pity and Fear in the Definition of Tragedy

action"] (cf 49b36), which a mere sequence of speeches could not achieve."[658]

(C) The previous reference to the function of tragedy, before Chapter 6, was lost. Halliwell himself can hardly object fairly to this solution, as suggested before, given his own explicit willingness to appeal to lost passages or oral explanations. Again, once one starts appealing in his way to oral accounts, one invites (almost) all theories, but why the loss of the legitimate goal of tragedy and the subsequent wrongful interpolation of *katharsis* in *Dramatics* 6 are different and *sui generis* in this regard is because of the incredible and massive inconsistencies that ensue by keeping the word.

(D) This is a variation of (C): At least *katharsis* in the definition was added to replace lost or damaged words or to provide what an editor thought must be a required final cause. Instead, any one of these following options on the surface could have been the antecedent of "the stated function of tragedy," again, written initially where *katharsis* now janglingly sits:

(i) "**...to provide a particular intellectual enjoyment**," following *Dramatics* 4. This is similar to the goal of epic and tragedy in Chapters 23-26, which Aristotle gives as the relevant pleasure. This option also fits with *Politics* VIII 3, 5 and 7, a crucial consideration for any Aristotelian interpretation, and does not entail that non-intellectual pleasures, like emotional or aesthetical ones, cannot be felt, just that the enjoyment is the primary function.[659]

(ii) Speaking of VIII 7: Just as the discussion of "reasoning" (*dianoia*), one of the six necessary elements, is pushed by Aristotle in Chapter 19 at 1456a35 to the *Rhetoric,* the goal of tragedy is pushed to the *Politics* VIII 7: "... **to fulfill the aims spoken of in my *Politics***" (with emphasis on pleasure, following VIII 3, 5, and 7, but allowing the other goals—education, *katharsis*, relaxation, and recreation—*if* and when appropriate).

(iii) "**...to provide the total *dunamis* ("power" or "potential") of the parts**," each *dunamis* being referred to or alluded to in various chapters—the *dunamis* of music-dance in Chapters 1 and 6; the *dunamis* of plot in Chapter 9 and of spectacle in Chapter 6; and the *dunamis* of verse versus prose in Chapter 6 (1450b13-15). Without a doubt, for Aristotle tragedy is a complex made up of parts and its total *dunamis* would be complex also.

(iv) Petruševski's solution, which keeps pity and fear and substitutes **sustasin pragmatōn** ["arrangement of incidents"] for **katharsin pathēmatōn** ["*katharsis* of sufferings"] and which Halliwell rejects without reason.

---

658 Lucas, *op. cit.*, p. 103-4.

659 To reiterate: The most important passages are arguably 1338a11ff and 1338b2-3, in which Aristotle stresses that it is the intellectual delight during leisure that is the end of (political) life and that always seeking the useful does not become the free and noble soul. As noted, these are the types of passages that have caused many commentators like Spengel to, e.g., reject Bernays' view that *katharsis* in Chapter 6 could be purgation and is the goal of tragedy.

Perhaps I have missed a formulation, namely, any other phrase that Aristotle might have made, consistent with the other remarks in the *Dramatics* on the goals of tragedy or drama in general, and one better than the current *katharsis*. However, the four options suffice for my purpose here, to explain a possible previously stated function of tragedy. With this, I conclude the rebuttal of Halliwell and the other classicists who have not only directly criticized me but who have indirectly criticized the other doubters insofar as we share common ground. Every one of Halliwell's significant criticisms fails, and in other circumstances I would not even concede the two insignificant points about pity and fear that I allowed him, in order to get to the most critical matters.

## Two Final Moves

In this *agon* about *katharsis* in *Dramatics* 6, its defenders might think they have two final moves. The first advocates novel uses of *katharsis* and the second ironically appeals to Aristotle's empiricism. I take up both moves, addressing first the apparent, newest favorite son of the profession.

This son is a compound meaning of *katharsis* and seemingly stems from, or is well represented by, Halliwell's "La psychologie morale de la catharsis: un essai de reconstruction,"[660] which was also developed in English in 2011.[661] Rejecting the traditional interpretation of *katharsis* as a "purgation" of emotions, Halliwell says tragic *katharsis* is "not just the conversion and integration of otherwise painful emotions into the pleasurable experience of mimetic art: it is the psychological benefit accruing from this conversion."[662] This notion of *katharsis* attempts to combine in a complex (and admittedly at times very intriguing) way psychological, aesthetical, and ethical phenomena, and is associated with pleasure but not identifiable with it,—and for good reason, given, as Halliwell himself acknowledges, that "Aristotle speaks separately of the pleasure(s) and the catharsis arising from certain kinds of mimetic art."[663]

Yet, this new meaning fails on Halliwell's own principles! The complex meaning does not fit well with his grounded observation, when he argues against Veloso, that Aristotle in *Politics* VIII 7 expects the reader to understand the term immediately and without further explanation.[664] Moreover, the paradigm of *katharsis* in VIII 7 is the sacred rites, where the individuals sing and dance and experience

---

660  Stephen Halliwell, "La psychologie morale de la catharsis: un essai de reconstruction," *Les Etudes Philosophiques*, Number 64, 2003-4, pp. 499-51. My Ph.D. supervisor, Sparshott, actually gave a very similar solution back in 1983, *op. cit.*
661  Halliwell, *op. cit.*, 2011.
662  Halliwell, *op. cit.*, 2011, p. 253.
663  Halliwell, *op. cit.*, 2011, p. 253.
664  Halliwell, *op. cit.*, 2011, pp. 263-5.

Chapter 6: Pity and Fear in the Definition of Tragedy

*katharsis* as a result. They are not trying to present mimetic art as their primary goal. Nevertheless, let me emphasize that some of Halliwell's observations have great worth, even if a slight transposition is necessary, to understand how Aristotle used *katharsis* in his younger years, whether concerning comedy, dithyramb, sacred rituals, "music" or any other event that Aristotle might have applied *katharsis* to, *including perhaps occasional instances of tragedy*, following *Politics* VIII 7. I am only claiming that the very helpful insights of Halliwell (and many others, including perhaps even the terrorist-labeling Marx) do not support *katharsis being in Dramatics 6*. We can easily see that there are two fatal problems in general with any novel conception of *katharsis*: First, as just seen, even on Halliwell's own account, a novel conception would inappropriately move the term away from the typical ancient Greek meanings. Second, novel conceptions are still open to the same objections as the standard and well-known meanings of *katharsis*. They all set up fatal inconsistencies with biological definition being used without an appropriate division of *katharsis* in Chapters 1-5, with no following explanation of the term in Chapters 6 and 7, and with no subsequent mention in the rest of the *Dramatics* where we would reasonably expect the term.[665] The only way possible that the purveyors of *katharsis* could partially succeed is if they *identify katharsis* with pleasure, but we have just seen that even Halliwell would (properly) reject that.

Finally, defenders of *katharsis* in *Dramatics* 6 might hold that tragedy for Aristotle always had and should have *katharsis* as a goal by pointing to his empiricism and by downplaying somehow that he also presents a philosophical theory of drama in the *Dramatics*. Their final move would go something like this: All fourteen surviving tragedies by Aeschylus and Sophocles appear to end painfully enough that *katharsis* (whatever it means) through pity and fear would seemingly be appropriate to the genre as a necessary condition and Aristotle's theory with *katharsis* in the definition captures this.

However, this claim would be as groundless as asserting that because all standing (portions of) walls

---

665    Sachs takes a unique but, in my view, indefensible position in trying to solve at least one of the three objections (he does not recognize the other two problems), saying:
> I believe that the word *catharsis* drops out of the *Poetics* because the word wonder, *to thaumaston*, replaces it, first in chapter 9, where Aristotle argues that pity and fear arise most of all where wonder does, and finally in chapters 24 and 25, where he singles out wonder as the aim of the poetic art itself, into which the aim of tragedy in particular merges... Aristotle's use of the word *catharsis* is not a technical reference to purgation or purification but a beautiful metaphor for the peculiar tragic pleasure, the feeling of being washing or cleansed (*op. cit.*, 1995, p. 27).

Apart from not recognizing the strictures from the *Topics* described before that forbid metaphor in a definition, Sachs ignores the blatant statements of Aristotle as discussed here in my Chapters 3, 4, 6 (and upcoming in 7), in which pleasure (not wonder or amazement) is given as the *ultimate* goal. Although to his credit Sachs brings in pleasure at the end, and even though Aristotle indeed has wonder or amazement at times as one of the intermediate goals of plots, Aristotle says amazement is *more applicable to epic* (24.1460a13-18). Presumably, wonder is too.

in Pompeii have one window, all of the walls there before Vesuvius erupted had to have one window (allowing only very rare exceptions). Many walls on higher floors could have had multiple windows. Moreover, as a philosophical theory of architecture, this erroneous claim would suggest further, more remarkably, that walls always should continue to have only one window—perhaps because one window lets in less heat—and that walls *in the definition of a house* should therefore include only one window! Analogously with the current definition of tragedy: Aristotle could not help but be aware that his definition covers not only historical tragedies *but future tragedies* and how they all could and should be created as tragedies,—and, as now given, always with *katharsis* (of pity and fear) as the goal. He also recognizes tragedy and comedy as the only two dramatic genres in ancient Greece and leaves aside the satyr play, for completely mysterious reasons. As a result, this "final move" appealing to his empiricism to defend the catharsis clause entails that Platonic-type tragedy or any of the other possible goals of serious drama should be shunned for Aristotle. Were he, though, to be so prescriptive, indeed, benightedly narrow-minded, it is even more stunning that he would not explain *katharsis* in the various later places in which he discusses the goals of the dramatist, such as in Chapter 4, when pleasures in representations are introduced, or in Chapter 14, when it is pleasure through pity and fear that is the goal, or similarly in Chapters 23-26, when the comparison between epic and tragedy is often done with pleasure and never with catharsis, or when he allows in Chapters 7, 11 and 14 that tragedies can end happily.

Nevertheless, despite the oddity of Aristotle subordinating philosophical principles to empirical ones on the current hypothesis, let us continue to ignore for a moment the philosophical tenets that for Aristotle presumably hold as long as human nature holds (given Chapter 4 and his claims that *mimesis* is natural or biological). I return to the empirical history. The "final move" trying to use history to defend *katharsis* in *Dramatics* 6 ignores what was happening more closely to Aristotle's life. Regarding the progression of drama and as mentioned above, five of Euripides's eighteen surviving plays end happily: *Cresphontes, Helen, Ion, Iphigenia in Tauris,* and *Orestes*—which is of course one shy of 33%. Moreover, we do not have any of the tragedies of, say, Agathon or of any dramatist of the entire fourth century BCE. Yet, the model of dramatic composition has seemingly changed from *Dramatics* 13 to Chapter 14, where, as we saw above, the *Oedipus*-type explicitly comes in second best. With no doubt whatsoever, in Chapter 14 the happily ending plays are best for Aristotle.

In the time of the three great tragedians of the fifth century, any *katharsis* may have been a result of the satyr play that finished their tragedies, when the tragic experience, at least at the competitions, was a four-part performance. I only develop this topic a little more here because of limitations of space and because the topic opens up too many new, vast questions. Edith Hall says:

Most hold that the satyr play must have functioned to create a sense of release or relief from the psychological tension of the foregoing tragedies... Satyr drama also sends its spectator out to the festival not only laughing rather than crying but reassured of his place in a joyous...collective.[666]

As we saw in my Chapter 4, Aristotle himself says in *Politics* VIII 7 that *katharsis* gives a relief (1341b14-15), and typically scholars recognize this while always assuming that the *katharsis* had to occur in the three parts of tragedy *before* the satyr play or as a result of those three plays.[667] Yet it is possible, and arguably much more probable, that many, or all, of the times the *katharsis* was a result *of* the satyr play. No specialist in Aristotelian philosophy to my knowledge has ever explored this very sensible possibility in the context of this whole debate. Bernd Seidensticker states that:

> From the end of the sixth century on each tragedian admitted to the tragedy competition had to produce not only three tragedies but also a satyr-play to serve as a cheerful epilogue. The tetralogy structure was only given up in the second half of the fourth century (*terminus ante quem 340/39...*).[668]

This means that the long-established tradition of a four-part experience of "tragedy" would have been seen continually by Aristotle from his first exposure at about eighteen years old in 366/365 until he was about thirty-six, when he left Athens after Plato's death in 348/347 and when the Academy's directorship was taken over by Speusippus. Curiously, though, Aristotle says nothing in the *Dramatics* about tragedy as a tetralogy despite recording such fine-grained details as Sophocles introducing scene-painting and despite the well-known fact that, for instance, Aeschylus won at least one prize for his satyr plays.[669] Besides, Aeschylus' *Oresteia* is three acts, as it were, of one long plot. During *Dramatics* 4's whole discussion of the history of tragedy, a tragedy is treated as a single unit. Of course, Aristotle's analysis of tragedy in the *Dramatics* could have been meant to apply only to the portion of the "tragic tetralogy" that we think was tragedy *per se*, *one* of the three plays that form part of the trilogy (rather than the whole trilogy as a unit, comprising, as it were, three "acts," and even less to the tetralogy). However, it is still extremely odd—to put it mildly—that nothing is even mentioned in

---

666 Edith Hall, *Greek Tragedy: Suffering under the Sun* (Oxford: Oxford Univ. Press), 2010, p. 237. By the way, this is the type of reason why someone *might* argue comedy or satyr play is better *at times* than tragedy, whether or not Aristotle followed suit in his lost work on comedy. Griffith confirms Hall's view, stating: "Since antiquity, satyr plays have been viewed primarily as a contrast to, or relief from the tragedies that preceded them. I shall not dispute this view, for it is obviously correct, at least in some respects" (Mark Griffith, *Greek Satyr Play: Five Studies, op. cit.*, 2015, p. 15).

667 E.g., Jonathan Lear stresses, "katharsis provides a relief" but never considers whether it might be as a result of the satyr play that ends tragedy in the sixth and fifth centuries BCE (in "Katharsis," *Essays on Aristotle's Poetics*, ed. A.O. Rorty, *op. cit.*, p. 328; orig. publ. as "Katharsis," *Phronesis*, 33/3, 1988, 297-326).

668 Bernd Seidensticker, "Dithyramb, Comedy, and Satyr-Play," *A Companion to Greek Tragedy,* ed. Justina Gregory (Oxford: Blackwell) 2005, p. 43.

669 I am grateful to Nickolas Pappas for reminding me of this. The largest fragment of a satyr play by Aeschylus to survive is *Dictyulci* ("The Net Fishers"), and the only satyr play to survive in its entirety is Euripides' *Cyclops*.

passing in his history in Chapter 4 in this regard, unless, as proposed before concerning Themistius and the discussion of Thespis being missing, part of Chapter 4 is lost. Why would Aristotle not even note that he means one of the three plays of a trilogy and that he is leaving aside the satyr-play, especially if the one long story of the *Oresteia* (with three "acts," as it were) allows the dramatist to present the longest plot, which according to Chapter 6, 1451a9-11, is therefore the finest (as long as it is clearly observable or memorable)?

I have no answer to these questions. Moreover, I cannot help but wonder both (i) if the satyr-play was considered part of the whole experience of "tragedy" by Aristotle in his earlier work, say, *On Poets*, and (ii) if he did not locate at least some *katharsis* in that final, fourth "act," perhaps even more than, say, in the last play of the trilogy. This account might help explain why no explanation of *katharsis* occurs in our extant *Dramatics*. Any *katharsis* in a tragedy with a harrowing ending did not occur in that part of the tragic experience but during the satyr play. If there was no painful ending, the pleasantness of the play required no *katharsis* (amazement and moral satisfaction would suffice at least sometimes, as happens in Chapter 18 with plays involving characters like clever villains such as Sisyphus going from fortune to misfortune or as happens with the *Cresphontes*-type play). Naturally, another option is that satyr play is closer to comedy than to tragedy and was discussed in the lost manuscript on comedy.

In any event, when Aristotle returned to Athens in 335, at the age of about forty-nine, and started seeing tragedy again after a lapse of thirteen years (for it is hard to imagine that there were full-fledged Athenian-type productions in Lesbos and his other residences during his self-imposed exile), tragedy no longer had satyr-plays. Quite a change from 347! Especially if the *Dramatics* or at least major parts of it are late, post-335, as many scholars think, the change in dramatic practice might also help explain why no focus whatsoever is put on satyr-plays,—the tragic competitions did not incorporate them anymore (or again, the focus was always on one part of the whole trilogy, the tragic play *per se*). Whatever the answers to these fascinating questions, some of the ones truly worth exploring in the future, we see even more reason why Aristotle's allowing a protagonist to go from "misfortune to fortune" is an important part of the expanded discussion of the definition of tragedy (7.1451a11-15). We also become more aware of the other locations noted earlier where Aristotle specifies the transformation from fortune to misfortune *or vice-versa*. Given that the dramatist did not have the satyr play to lighten the audience's mood after either a dreadful finale or possibly even three dreadful finales in a row (one for each part of the trilogy), the kind of play that ended well in Chapter 14, like Euripides' five examples, may well have become much more dominant. Dramatists liked prizes, acclaim and anything that gave the audience pleasure, as Aristotle says at the end of Chapter 13: "The dramatists follow the spectators, composing to suit their wishes" and it hardly takes a rigorous empiricist to realize that people love pleasant endings even in serious drama. This observation might also explain the contradiction between the best tragedies in Chapters 13 and 14. The earlier plays like *Oedipus* could end with great suffering because the satyr play would put the audience back in a positive mood, but plays that ended happily might be more popular when the satyr "act" was omitted, and hence the new considerations and the new ranking in the latter half of Chapter 14, written much later than Chapter 13 (and the first part of Chapter 14).[670]

Whatever the answers to these dilemmas, they are topics that deserve a much more rigorous examination in my opinion. That they do not get suitable attention generally, is, I believe, in part because not only is a discussion of the satyr play missing in the extant treatise but because scholars are still fixated on a single word, or a single clause, in the definition of tragedy that is out of place. In any event, this possible "final move" by traditionalists and the empirical claims about tragedy in the fifth century will not justify keeping *katharsis* in the definition of tragedy, if for no other reason than this "final move" still does not even touch half, much less all, of the stunning inconsistencies that result from *katharsis* being in that definition.

## Conclusion to Chapter 6

Although the manuscript tradition is obviously extremely important and foundational, arguably *in some circumstances* paleography is to philosophical soundness as character is to plot (where soundness includes consistency and truth for a thinker like Aristotle). One cannot ascribe outright nonsense or blatant inconsistency across *many* indubitable doctrines, including those internal to the *Dramatics,* for the sake of maintaining a single word or clause in an alleged "archetype" (even assuming we could all agree on what it was), and I say this with full knowledge of how contentious this will be for many scholars. However, they are then reminded that all of them have atetized other words or passages for decades or centuries on the same principle and with arguably much less reason. Thus, I must disagree entirely with Tarán and Gutas on one claim. Despite their diligence, brilliance, extremely high standards, and the acknowledged benefits they have provided with the *Editio Maior* to all scholars interested in a deep study of the *Dramatics*, they say:

> The text of the passage [the *katharsis* clause in Chapter 6] is not in dispute, though its interpretation is... The context and the agreement of B [one of the two extant Greek manuscripts] and Σ [the basis of the Syro-Arabic tradition] leave no doubt as to what Aristotle wrote.[671]

---

[670] However, if only for the sake of argument, my solution in *Aristotle's Favorite Tragedy: Oedipus or Cresphontes?* assumes the chapters exist together.

[671] Tarán and Gutas, *op. cit.*, p. 247.

To the contrary, there surely could be a difference between what Aristotle wrote and the archetype, given Tarán's own claim noted earlier that the archetype came at least 700 years after the Northern Greek! Hence, the "no doubt" rather in my view should be applied to the conclusion that someone other than Aristotle wrote the *katharsis* clause in some manuscript closer to the true original, one which had been damaged.

Some scholars have asked, and others will surely continue to ask "But who interpolated the word *katharsis*?", suggesting that if the "doubters" cannot answer this, we cannot continue to defend the athetesis of the word (or of the surrounding clause). I already discussed two possible options, Apellicon or Tyrannion, but there could be many others who were responsible. To see, however, how overly restrictive this requirement of finding the culprit would be, consider the following: No one who ever recommends other atheteses ever provides the name of the ancient editor or copyist writing the illegitimate text. Moreover, assume that a perfect copy of the *Dramatics* is discovered next week in some cave in Egypt, and it has as the goal of tragedy one of the first four options above, say, "the proper pleasure." This option itself harmonizes with not only the rest of the *Dramatics* but the rest of Aristotle's accepted definitory, ethical and political theory. Would that give us any more insight in determining how the current version got corrupted and who wrote *katharsis*? None whatsoever,— there is no direct discussion of the matter in antiquity, and the indirect issues have been summarized above in footnotes, in discussing Natali and Barnes (and Apellicon and Tyrannion). Besides, I have proffered already the sensible guess that the *Politics* VIII 7 and *On Poets* (which would be better titled *On "Musical" Composers*, following Diotima) were used by someone to justify the interpolation. Again, Tarán and Gutas stress that no commentary on the *Dramatics* exists either from ancient or early Byzantine times. The treatise was ignored. Hence, although it would be satisfying to know who the culprit was that interpolated *katharsis*, it is not necessary that the precise cause of the interpolation be cited to support the arguments for bracketing *katharsis* as spurious. The egregious philosophical inconsistencies themselves justify the bracketing. Hence, whatever happened *after* an "alleged primary manuscript" began getting copied over 1400 years ago is, albeit of vital historical and paleographical interest, less relevant in *this* particular context than the philosophical consistency of Aristotle's doctrines. In order of precedence, those doctrines internal to the *Dramatics* surely are first, then those internal to the whole Aristotelian corpus and then finally those from other authors. In short, Tarán and Gutas *qua* paleographers and I *qua* philosopher can all be right *in our own spheres*, complementing each other.

We return full circle to von Wilamowitz's ironic suggestion that it would have been better had we moderns, like the ancients, never seen Aristotle's definition with *katharsis*. Halliwell somewhat similarly writes wistfully in 2002 that "a temporary moratorium on discussion of the subject [of *katharsis* in

## Chapter 6: Pity and Fear in the Definition of Tragedy

Chapter 6 would be] a consummation devoutly to be wished."[672] I trust, and hope for his sake, that this book might bring his wish to completion, indeed not only temporarily but permanently (but, again, with respect *only* to *Dramatics* 6), and allow scholars like himself to focus on the correct and more fruitful application of *katharsis* in general or in other texts for Aristotle or to the related topics introduced above. To continue Halliwell's adaptation of Hamlet's "To be or not to be" speech: Catharsis in *Dramatics* 6 can now shuffle off this mortal coil, and, if I myself have been partially responsible for murdering the concept with a bare bodkin, then I am only helping a group of Aristotle-lovers starting with von Wilamowitz, Otte, Gudeman, Smerdel, Petruševski, Freire, and Brunius, and continuing now with at least Veloso and Marwan Rashed.

I finish this thought with the words of Nickolas Pappas, who summarizes the history and the issues pertaining to *katharsis* in Aristotle's *Dramatics* and then states:

> On this... proposal, the definition's phrase about catharsis is not Aristotle's language at all but a later insertion that scholars should excise (Petruševksi 1954; Scott 2003; Veloso 2007)... Omitting a difficult passage from ancient texts must be a last resort. But one must recall the long unsatisfying history of attempts to make sense of catharsis. The debates over catharsis might be as intractable as they are, and textual support so indirect, because the task is impossible. The time of the last resort might have arrived.[673]

To begin ending this chapter: Tragedy (*tragōidia*) seemingly comes from *tragos* and *aoidē/oidē*, and apparently either meant for the ancients something like "song of the goat" or "the song of the spelt" (because *tragos* could also mean the wheat, or spelt, that was fermented into the type of beer associated with Dionysian-type performances like the dithyramb from which tragedy came [4.1449a11]).[674] It was often a far cry from *our* notion of tragedy, which now always suggests something horrible occuring, especially at the end, and proof of this are the best plots in *Dramatics* 14 that end happily. Therefore, although pity and fear were surely in some historical or theoretical *sub-types of* tragedy for Aristotle (whether as an audience response or built into the structure of the play or both), the two emotions need not have been—and explicitly were not according to him—in all or even most of them, given the examination above. Consequently, neither of those emotions should be an essential condition in a definition of tragedy in general and Aristotle could not have been so incompetent as to miss

---

672   *Op. cit.*, 2002, p. 206.

673   Nickolas Pappas, "Aristotle," in *Routledge Companion to Aesthetics*, 2nd and 3rd editions, eds. Berys Gaut and Dominic McIver Lopes (New York, 2005 and 2013), pp. 19-20 and p. 16, respectively. Pappas had essentially the same conclusion in the 2nd edition, 2005, even before Veloso's article in 2007 provided additional support. Pappas saw no reason to change his mind eight years later, well before the much more substantial evidence in this book was composed.

674   I owe the alternative explanation of *tragōidia* as "song of the spelt" to Jane E. Harrison, *Prolegomena to the Study of Greek Religion* (Princeton: Princeton University Press) 1922.

that fact.[675]

At this point, I can be more emphatic, and revisit a statement in "Purging the *Poetics*," as reprinted in the previous chapter but buried in a footnote (#545):

> **At *Laws* 7, 817b, 'tragedy' is a very broad term, being simply contrasted with comedy and only meaning serious drama dealing with noble or good people.** Nothing disastrous need be implied, as Susan Sauvé Meyer asserts when discussing Plato's passage: 'Here "tragedy" is used as an honorific label, and the essential feature of the "tragic" is the "portrayal of the finest and best life" (*mimēsis tou kallistou kai aristou biou*, 817b4). **According to this conception of "tragedy," the tragic imitates the best life, in contrast with comedy, which imitates low life.** *So understood, labelling something as "tragic" does not imply that it is regrettable. (There is nothing particularly tragic about tragedy in this sense.) Such connotations do accompany the Aristotelian analysis of tragedy as involving disaster and reversal, but this does not seem to be Plato's conception—witness his description of Homer as a tragedian in Republic X (605c)'...*
>
> With one caveat resulting from my earlier analyses, I am fully in accord with Sauvé Mey-

---

[675] One last comment by an anonymous reader of this chapter deserves airing (when an earlier version of this chapter was submitted for publication as an independent article, and then rebuffed). He or she says in part:

> ...only a tiny minority of scholars reject the presence of catharsis in the definition of tragedy in *Poet.* ch. 6... The relevant words are transmitted in both Greek MSS A and B, in the Syriac, in the Arabic, and in the Latin translation (see now the edition of Gutas and Tarán). They were in the archetype of the text. *There is simply no doubt about them* [my italics].

How the reviewer can state in the same breath that "there is simply no doubt about them [the words in the catharsis clause]" while acknowledging that at least a "tiny minority of scholars" (which means at least already eight published ones) are rejecting or considering rejecting the relevance of catharsis in *Dramatics* 6 is puzzling. It would be tedious to give the rest of the reviewer's statements but, in short, it was clear that he or she criticized my position without reading my *OSAP* 2003, i.e., Chapter 5 above, on which the whole article was grounded. As with Marx, this reflects the attitude that no one can rationally question the authenticity of catharsis,—so why even read the arguments by anyone like Petruševksi, myself or Veloso (even though Tarán and Gutas, to their credit, treat Petruševksi with respect)?

Finally, to give another example of the faulty logic employed by the same reviewer: He or she says: "the term *miaros* which is the opposite of *katharos*, in ch. 13 *is the clearest reference to catharsis in the extant Poetics*. [Scott] does not even mention it [my italics]." Indeed, there was no reason to mention *miaros* ("shocking" or "disgusting") in the article I submitted, because, again, the concept had already been discussed in *OSAP* 2003, which had been cited as being foundational. To repeat what was said there, *miaros* enters in Chapters 13 when, e.g., Aristotle says that a plot having a virtuous man going from good to bad fortune *has neither pity nor fear* but is *miaron* (13.1452b36). It also enters in Chapter 14 for the *Antigone* by Euripides and for the second-best play that must include *Oedipus*, but for Aristotle as *not* applying to the latter. However, I did not discuss these two instances in 2003. How this usage of *miaron* in Chapters 13-14, though, justifies "catharsis *of pity and fear*" being in the definition of tragedy is imaginable only by the kind of logic (or state of mind) that Cratinus employed when getting inebriated before writing dithyrambs in order, he himself said, to be authentically Dionysian. Aristotelian logic, or the propositional calculus, surely entails that if there is no pity and fear in that type of tragic plot, as Aristotle explicitly says, then *there can be no catharsis of pity and fear for that type of plot*.

er: the Aristotelian analysis involving disaster and reversal, though, pertains only to the best [sub-type of] tragedy [as discussed in *Dramatics* 13]. If the opposite were the case, Aristotle would have established it in *Poetics* 1–6, when describing the differences between tragedy and the other genres [my italics and my additional comments in square brackets to clarify my discussion in 2003: In that year I implied "best tragedy" *in general*, rather than the best tragedy *of Chapter 13*, which is what I should have said].

It is also noteworthy that Lillian Lawler, in her very rigorous study of dance in ancient Greek theatre, indicates that **the term 'tragedy' was used equally broadly**, or even more broadly, at times. While speaking of late writers and lexicographers of antiquity, she says: 'Philoxenus the dithyrambist, for example, is called *tragikos* by a scholiast on Aristophanes' *Plutus* (290). By some late authors **the word seems to be used literally, as coming from *tragos*, "goat," and referring to the dances of the satyr play**; we may instance *Etymologicum Magnum* 764, s.v. "tragoedia," where tragedy and the satyr play are obviously confused, and where the choruses are said at times to imitate the *schēmata* of goats. **Many modern scholars think that in the lexicographers the word tragikos means merely "pertaining to the drama"'**... [my bolding/italics]

In short, *tragōidia* should normally *not* be translated as "tragedy," especially given that Aristotle says three times in his treatise that *tragōidia* can show the protagonist(s) going from misfortune to fortune and given that the finest examples of *tragōidia* in Chapter 14 are the plays ending happily, like *Cresphontes*. Rather, *tragōidia* should be translated as something like "serious drama." However, given the degree of completion of this book, with the first edition and Volume 1 of the second edition already published, and given how long the discussion might be to determine the most suitable English translation because of the centuries of usage, I leave it to the future to push for this change in any new translation or commentary. As already suggested, for the rest of this book and any future discussion of *tragōidia* in Aristotle's and Plato's work, one might assume that "tragedy" is being used more broadly, not as something necessarily implying a tragic result. In other words, *tragōidia* should be used in Plato's sense as just highlighted by Meyer or in Aristotle's sense as authentically defined in *Dramatics* 6. By "authentically defined," I mean without the clause containing catharsis, pity, and fear, which has obscured for centuries how *tragōidia* can end happily. The only time *tragōidia* could be translated unproblematically as "tragedy" is when dealing with the sub-type of *tragōidia* in Chapter 13 that has pity and fear, perhaps the "tragedy of suffering" of Chapter 18, although "could" is not necessarily "should," considering the ambiguity that would still result in other circumstances. The crucial consideration here is that Aristotle follows Plato with his authentic part of the definition of *tragōidia* in *Dramatics* 6.

The natural questions that arise from the foregoing are: How did pity and fear then also get written into the definition? What are the sub-type(s) of tragedy to which pity and fear apply and to which these two emotions are necessary rather than contingent? Might some sub-types having pity and fear also have *katharsis*, secondarily or primarily, as an intermediate goal, even though Aristotle only talks about the pleasure through pity and fear in Chapter 14? What is the goal of tragedy instead for him, given that the whole *katharsis* clause, including pity and fear, should be athetized in the definition? How does Aristotle really respond to Plato's attack on tragedy and comedy, especially given Aristotle's sympathy with Plato in many ways in, e.g., Chapter 15 and especially given Plato's own positive use of catharsis? Taking into account *Politics* VIII 7 and considering that *katharsis* is not a core consideration of tragedy of Aristotle's mature years, what is the role of catharsis in his theory of *poiēsis,* whether *poiēsis* is theatrical art, music, or poetry in the Gorgian sense? Is Aristotle's more correct theory of drama as described in this book still relevant in any important ways today and for future tragedy and drama in general, or is this all of mere historical interest?

The last question is covered in Chapter 9. Three of the other questions—regarding the true goal(s) of tragedy, how Aristotle responds (or not) to Plato without *katharsis*, and the real role of *katharsis* in drama for Aristotle—are relatively easy to answer concerning the fundamental issues and are actually for the most part right under our nose in the Aristotelian corpus once we get rid of the smelly red herring (the *katharsis* clause) in the definition of tragedy. Nevertheless, the full answers require two chapters more, given concerns of rigor. As noted in the Introduction, Chapter 7 covers the real goal(s) and the response to Plato, and Chapter 8 explores the issues for *katharsis*, which take us necessarily into comedy again for Aristotle.

I finish this chapter by addressing the other three questions. How pity and fear entered the definition is probably the same way that *katharsis* entered, and without discovering other texts, we will never know for sure. Probably the same editor who interpolated *katharsis* also interpolated pity and fear. The best guess for the whole interpolation, based on the extant textual evidence, is that he took Aristotle's statements from *Politics* VIII 7, *On Poets*, and the legitimate uses of pity and fear in the middle chapters of the *Dramatics* to justify the interpolation, not being careful enough to recognize the resulting serious inconsistencies throughout the whole treatise. However, as noted, the fact that the discrepancies were ignored or downplayed for well over 450 years, until, for instance, Smerdel (or Gudeman or both) began complaining strenuously about *katharsis* in *Dramatics* 6, and until Petruševski shortly thereafter cut half the Gordian knot, shows that even a well-intentioned editor could easily have made an innocent mistake.

Determining which sub-types of tragedy have pity and fear—and whether any of those sub-types also have *katharsis* as a crucial or even important goal, whether intermediate or final—is, I believe, the most difficult of all of these topics. Answering them would involve understanding why Aristotle gives four sub-types (and four corresponding parts) of tragedy in Chapter 18 and the corresponding four types of epic in the first sentence of Chapter 24 when he says the four sub-types match the tragic ones.

## Chapter 6: Pity and Fear in the Definition of Tragedy

This issue, though, itself leads to a host of related dilemmas that I already alluded to above. Since the four types (and the four parts) of tragedy had never been discussed previously by the Northern Greek, does this factor—and other considerations that, for example, de Montmollin, Else and Whalley themselves realized after their thorough, lifelong studies of the text—not show that the treatise is actually an amalgamation of Aristotelian texts, cobbled together for reasons that Strabo and Plutarch at least partially gave? Would the realization that our extant treatise has chapters written at different times, and perhaps even in slightly different contexts, not help, e.g., resolve the contradiction of the best plots in Chapters 13 and 14 (or at least confirm the solution I give in *Aristotle's Favorite Tragedy*)? The prospect that our text is not a unified one scared at least one editor to whom I submitted a chapter of this book a few years ago as an independent, preliminary article for a journal in ancient philosophy. He wondered (before rejecting the article for publication) where we go if the treatise was not one original text, which was one of the options I merely suggested, as I do now. My answer on reflection is "Where reason and good scholarship take us." Certainly, the prospect did not stop Else, de Montmollin and Whalley from doing very illuminating work on the treatise. As I suggested in passing, one possible approach, and I stress it is merely one, is to consider the first eight chapters as being the core part of the treatise we might call the *Dramatics*. No one to my knowledge has questioned any of those chapters as being outside of the book (although a few words or passages have been considered spurious, even apart from the clause with catharsis, pity, and fear). Then we add any chapters that are consistent with this core, provisionally think of them as the treatise and consider the remaining sections to be other works or fragments of Aristotle on drama, poetry, and "music," of which Diogenes Laertius lists many for Aristotle. In any event, however we proceed in the near or far future, the *katharsis* clause with pity and fear in *Dramatics* 6 must be ignored, given the arguments above. The ultimate potential rewards are too great, and, on the alternative approach, the amount of suffering to be incurred again for another 450 years while the *katharsis* clause is attempted to be understood, and shown to be consistent somehow with the rest of Aristotle's theories, would be too *miaron*. And certainly too Sisyphean.

## Postscript

E. Lobel impressively showed that the two earliest Greek manuscripts, A and B, each have their own merits and his final remarks are worth noting:

> The necessary conclusion is that A and B…are independently descended but have at least one ancestor in common (p. 17) and "As things are, we are bound to proceed on the assumption that only A and B are competent witnesses to the *paradosis* [the tradition as passed on from one generation to the next], though not therefore the only MSS [= "manuscripts"], which contain what Aristotle wrote, *which may once or many times have been*

*regained by conjecture* [my italics and explanations in brackets].[676]

As highlighted multiple times, the new critical edition of the manuscript tradition of the *Dramatics* by Tarán and Gutas improves in many ways upon Lobel.[677] Still, to repeat what they say:

> There is no extant ancient commentary on the *Poetics*, nor any evidence that there ever was one in ancient or early Byzantine times... the Greek tradition has provided us with only two primary witnesses, one of which (B) is not even complete and is seriously damaged.[678]

The doubters, including myself, will always grant that *katharsis* was in some "*alleged* primary manuscript" that formed the basis for A and B and any other copy (especially the two that Tarán and Gutas note form the foundation of the critical edition, along with the Syro-Arabic and the Latin translation from a Greek manuscript by William of Moerbeke). However, as noted, no matter how important and fascinating the paleographic issues are—and, again, they are *often* the most important and certainly the most fundamental—in this case they do not help settle the arguments that the doubters have put forth, which reflect such massive inconsistencies with the rest of the *Dramatics* that it is virtually impossible that Aristotle himself could have written *katharsis* in Chapter 6. It is very admirable, indeed necessary, to attempt to establish Aristotle's true original manuscript and to explain at *all* reasonable costs seeming discrepancies with uncontentious Aristotelian theory. This approach is what some have called "exegetical responsibility." Let us grant (and not just hypothetically) that Tarán and Gutas have established what at least the "alleged primary ms" was, which Tarán calls Ω, despite the dozen or so "mistakes and interpolations" that he pinpoints the archetype having.[679] Let us sincerely praise them for not only being exegetically responsible to the extreme but raising the standard to the highest level for the paleography. Yet they have not addressed the contradictions I have presented above—which Tarán explicitly says he is not concerned with. Even if he recognizes one crucial one with *katharsis*, there is no sign he recognizes, e.g., the discrepancies between *Dramatics* 6 and the biological divisions in Chapters 1-5. Nor does either philologist recognize the Diotiman sense of *poiēsis*, which means, given the arguments of Unit 1, that they do not even come close to realizing the true nature of, e.g., tragedy or drama for Aristotle.[680] Occasionally, if only occasionally, exegetical

---

[676] E. Lobel, *The Greek Manuscripts of Aristotle's Poetics* (Oxford: Oxford University Press for the Bibliographical Society) 1933, p. 48.

[677] Tarán and Gutas, *op. cit.*, 2012.

[678] *Op. cit.*, p. 156.

[679] Tarán and Gutas, *op. cit.*, pp. 148-9. As Tarán says "Clearly, then, the archetype contained mistakes and interpolations" (p. 149).

[680] Tarán says:
Concerning the principles and assumptions that have guided me in the selection and utilization of the material, I should state that these textual and interpretive notes [which he gives to elucidate his recommended Greek text of the *Dramatics*] are written from the point of view of what I take *Aristotle* to be trying to say. That is, I do not challenge his statements as to whether he is right or wrong,

*philosophical* responsibility must outweigh exegetical textual responsibility. Alternatively, to put the matter in the paleographers's own terms and to repeat what I once said, *sometimes* the exegetical responsibility to the rest of the entire Greek manuscript, twenty-six chapters, the result of Aristotle's sweat and blood that never received due recognition in antiquity, must outweigh a single word (or clause) that destroys the integrity of his thought.

## Post-Postscript: Marwan Rashed's Agreement and Disagreement

Marwan Rashed (Université de Paris Sorbonne and the Institut Universitaire de France) is one of the foremost, if not the foremost, paleographer in the world on Aristotle, according to some Oxford-Cambridge ancient Greek philosophers. Given the historical antagonism, whether real or merely playful, between the British and the French, this praise is stellar indeed. During the final edit of the first edition of this book, a draft of his new work "*Katharsis versus mimèsis:* simulation des émotions

---

> *nor do I ask if he is consistent in his views or not, etc.* Aristotle's famous definition of Tragedy... serves as an example. It is probably the most discussed sentence of the *Poetics*, but the text is firmly established;... Hence, my comment on this sentence is brief, *for we can be reasonably certain that the text adopted here and by a majority of the editors is **as close as possible** to what Aristotle wrote* [my italics and my boldfacing] (p. 221).

First, throughout the book, Tarán is often concerned with consistency regarding the philological issues and uses that criterion many times to help settle the Greek text, although he never seems to realize how ambiguous some of the Greek musical terms are for Aristotle (similar to *mimēsis* and our "play"). What he means, I gather, is that he is not concerned with consistency of the important philosophical views, which is my concern. Without that concern, though, I cannot agree with the "the text adopted here...is as close as possible to what Aristotle wrote." Athetize the catharsis clause and come to agreement on some of the philosophical issues of *Dramatics* 1 that I describe in this book and *then*, I believe we will be as close as possible to what Aristotle wrote in those passages (concerning the surviving texts, because my arguments show, I believe, that much is missing). Second, all of this still leaves some interpretations open. What, for example, are the two natural causes of *Dramatics* 4 and how do we settle the contradiction of the best plot in Chapters 13-14? Tarán challenges and refutes (or accepts) other interpretations, for instance, with regards to the correctness of the views of classification and literature in *Dramatics* 1. Thus, for him to suggest that he is not challenging whether statements are right or wrong is disingenuous. All commentators and translators (as Tarán well recognizes in other places) must hypothesize to some extent what Aristotle means, and in taking a stance they suggest what is "right" for Aristotle, whether or not they claim that this is a better theory or not than, say, Plato's. For example, Tarán's claims that the *Dramatics* is about tragedy, comedy, and epic as forms of literature (*op. cit.*, pp. 224-9). I claim that some crucial words like *poiēsis* are meant by Aristotle differently, following Plato, and that tragedy and drama in general are not forms of literature *per se*. Both of us cannot be right on that matter and the issue is not one of paleography (because I gladly accept and appreciate his paleographical insights) but of philosophical interpretation. Does Aristotle use *poiēsis* in the Diotiman sense or the Gorgian sense? Paleography (or philology) will not necessarily settle the matter, because it does not in this case for Tarán and Gutas; empirical knowledge, history, consistency (which means understanding the rest of Aristotle's corpus), and issues like organic unity, which both Plato and Aristotle explicitly consider important as we saw in discussing how the *Dramatics* follows the *Phaedrus*, often will.

et définition aristotélicienne de la tragédie"[681] was brought to my attention. In that article, he agrees with those following Petruševski, like myself and Veloso, that catharsis cannot be legitimate in the definition of tragedy and that if anywhere it was explained in the lost tract on comedy. Rashed independently of my arguments above refutes some of Halliwell's criticisms against myself and Veloso.

Rashed then offers his own solution, but one that hearkens back to Petruševski and Freire, not one that accepts the whole suppression of the catharsis, pity and fear clause, which Veloso and I advocate. In other words, Rashed wishes to keep pity and fear in the definition and he considers a fascinating option in which *mimēsis* is instead the goal in the definition (in lieu of *katharsis*). As I said in 2003 (and in Chapter 5 above), were my solution not to be accepted—that is, if someone like Halliwell or Rashed can rebut, for instance, the arguments I give in this chapter and re-authenticate pity and fear in the definition—the type of solution that Petruševski and now Rashed give (with his own variation) should be the one accepted or explored more. In any event, as Rashed, Veloso and I all agree, catharsis should never again be considered a legitimate part of the definition.

To detail my disagreements here with Rashed would be redundant, because they are already in effect given above, and because he neither had the benefit of this book nor of my earlier *Aristotle's Favorite Tragedy: Oedipus or Cresphontes?* which originally appeared only in February 2016, just a few weeks before I was sent his own work. In that small book, I demonstrate in even more detail than I do in this one that eight of the nine plot-types covered in *Dramatics* 13 and 14 do not have pity in the relevant sense and thus that pity could not reasonably for Aristotle be in a definition that should apply to all tragedies (and of course I have just shown plot-types in other chapters in *Dramatics* 2 through 18 that have no pity for Aristotle). The happily ending tragedies in general for Aristotle like *Cresphontes* are the best, as is explicitly stated in Chapter 14 when they are ranked above the *Oedipus*-type. Besides, just as the plot-type of the virtuous person going to misfortune has no pity and fear because it is *miaron* (shocking or disgusting), so the best, happily ending plot has no pity. That is, there may have been some pity before the end in *both* of these two plot-types, but Aristotle does not consider that pity to be relevant. Instead, the ending emotion or set of emotions are crucial for the paradigmatic teleologist. Thus, I prefer to wait to hear what Rashed says to my arguments in this and *Aristotle's Favorite Tragedy*, if he cares to read them, before adding anything more.

To emphasize one final time: Having catharsis in the definition of tragedy would be like having "blond hair" in the definition of man. Having also "pity and fear" there would be like having "three-stranded braided blond hair" in the definition. Even if blond is removed, "braided" still restricts the denotation

---

681 Marwan Rashed, "*Katharsis versus mimèsis*: simulation des émotions et définition aristotélicienne de la tragédie," in *Littérature: Aristote, l'aventure par les concepts* (publ. Larousse) No. 182, June, 2016, 60-77.

## Chapter 6: Pity and Fear in the Definition of Tragedy

of the definition much too much, and obviously "three-stranded" even more drastically. In a setting that gives Rashed his full due, I would argue that the goal of tragedy is not mimesis, but rather pleasure, as I explain in detail in general in the next chapter. Apart from Aristotle only giving *plot* as an end in *Dramatics* 6 and giving pleasure or some variant of pleasure as the goal in many other places (again, all detailed in my next chapter), it appears mimesis is always part of the material or formal cause in the *Dramatics*. However, Rashed only gives his solution at the very end of his article, and it would be fascinating to hear how he develops his insights. In the analysis of *Dramatics* 4, I show that Aristotle's two natural causes of the art forms like tragedy are mimesis and "music and dance," which often exist for pleasure. I emphasize that they are natural dispositions for Aristotle (and for Plato) but, like a desire for nutrition, are something that then we strive to satisfy or attain on occasion. Perhaps in this way, mimesis could be the goal, but whether it would be the goal in the definition when it was already the root of the definition is one interesting question. I gave arguments in Chapter 3 about how tragedy could not be reduced to literature, arguments which suggest the contrary, and I also noted that the *Topics* forbids duplicate terms in a definition. As the French say, though, *on verra*. "We'll see."

Be this as it may, I am extremely grateful to Rashed for ignoring the *ad hominem* arguments against Veloso and myself—and indeed for mentioning them for what they are—and for applying his very formidable skills to tackling this issue. Repeating in effect the praise of the English critics Dryden, Gildon, and Rymer for Dacier, as I describe in the Appendix, some modern British scholars appear to be entirely correct about a modern French philosopher.

### *Note to the 2nd Edition*

Immediately before publication of this Volume 2, another example of the type of *ad hominem* remarks that Rashed called out came to my attention. In Pierre Somville's recent French translation of the *Poetics*, Somville adds a note that comprises his entire response to the views of Petruševski, Freire, Brunius, myself and Veloso on the legitimacy of *katharsis* in the definition of tragedy, saying only of Veloso's article from *Oxford Studies in Ancient Philosophy* (2007), *op. cit.*, that "Claudio William Veloso, qui en vient à considérer la définition de la katharsis comme une interpolation de basse époque ('Aristotle's *Poetics* Without *Katharsis*, Fear or Pity', *Oxford Studies in Ancient Philosophy*...) aura fait parler de lui" (in R. Bodéüs, ed., *Aristote, Oeuvres. Éthiques, Politique, Rhétorique, Poétique, Métaphysique. Bibliothèque de la Pléiade.* Paris: Gallimard, 2014, pp. 1500-1518; in particular p. 1511-1512 n. 4). As Florence Fournier, founder of the French School of the Caucasus, translates (and explains in square brackets): "Claudio William Veloso, who comes to consider the definition of catharsis an interpolation from the Late Period...will have made speak people about him" [i.e., people spoke about him in the past but that moment is finished]."

Now, first, Veloso and all others only consider the definition *of tragedy*, not of *katharsis*, whose definition does not exist, but this is minor and excusable sloppiness on the part of Somville. However, given that Somville provides no arguments, he either impugns Veloso personally or is horse-blinkered in his view of the recent developments or both. If he suggests that Veloso was only concerned with causing a mini-scandal (recall Marx calling Veloso a "terrorist" for daring to argue that *katharsis* in *Dramatics* 6 is not authentic), then Somville implies that *Oxford Studies* and the editor at the time, David Sedley, one of the most respected specialists of ancient Greek philosophy in the world in the last 40 years, would publish an article that is mere self-aggrandizement or that Sedley could not recognize self-aggrandizement as opposed to legitimate scholarship. This is *miaron* (shocking or disgusting) and Somville would be insulting not only those associated with *Oxford Studies* but the works that Veloso explicitly followed.

If, on the other hand, Somville merely reports his understanding of the professional development because 6 years had passed in French circles without any "takers" for Veloso's view (until Rashed, who published in 2016), then Somville is horse-blinkered and ignores what happens in English scholarship, despite his being aware of *Oxford Studies in Ancient Philosophy*. If he actually had read Veloso's article and saw that it followed mine in many ways, it would not have been too difficult to ascertain that Pappas in 2005 and 2013 (*op. cit.*) and Woodruff in 2009 (*op. cit.*) published, respectively, that my view, which Veloso follows, might be the solution or at least should be considered. Halliwell offered his rebuttal in 2011 (*op. cit.*) to both Veloso and myself and clearly the debate was continuing right before Somville's contribution appeared. Of course, Somville might be both impugning Veloso and reporting his own view of the professional development. At any rate, Somville could, and arguably, should have simply stayed neutral and written something (in French, naturally) like ""cf., for example, Veloso (*OSAP* 2007) for the view that Aristotle did not write katharsis, pity, and fear."

I should add that Somville's remark is typical of the desperation of some of the "Old Guard," those who have recently tried to protect the authenticity of catharsis in the definition of tragedy but usually without even replying to the arguments of Veloso or myself. I exclude other members of the "Old Guard" like Stephen Halliwell, who, as seen earlier, had, and has, the curiosity, intellectual courage and professional integrity to try to answer the arguments of myself and Veloso, even if his answer ultimately fails (and I emphasize the "if," because readers of this book and Veloso's new one will determine whether Veloso and I have solidly rebutted his answer or not). At least Halliwell's approach does philosophy and himself credit and contributes to a deeper understanding of Aristotle.

# Unit 3: The Real Goal of Tragedy and Comedy

*Aristotle on Dramatic Musical Composition*

# Chapter 7: The Real Goal of Tragedy and Aristotle's Response without Catharsis to Plato's Attack on Tragedy and Comedy

Given the arguments in Unit 2 that the whole *katharsis* clause should be bracketed as spurious, I now answer two of the questions that immediately arise:
1) What is the goal of tragedy instead for Aristotle or are there multiple possible goals?
2) Because Aristotle would allow both tragedy and comedy in the ideal state, how does he reply to Plato's attacks in the *Republic* on "tragic" (= serious) and comedic drama if he does not resort to *katharsis*?

Let us examine these questions in order.

## Section 1: The Goals of Tragedy

Once the *katharsis* clause in *Dramatics* 6 is athetized, or at least provisionally put aside, we can quickly establish the goals of tragedy for Aristotle. The plural "goals" is important, because not only the *Dramatics* but the *Politics* show that there is more than one goal of tragedy or of the musical arts for him, even if one is primary, and here I support this claim. It will be sufficient merely to establish the multiple options on Aristotle's view and to counteract the previous impression that there is only one, namely, *katharsis*, whatever that term means. I leave it to another time or to others to develop this point more fully, and indeed many, including Woodruff recently, have already presented in detail various options, even if those scholars are typically presenting the options as mutually exclusive.[682] To anticipate my conclusion: For Aristotle, tragedians could combine the goals in any way they see fit, even though being legitimate is not the same as being the most laudatory. I proceed in the order the goals are given or suggested in the *Dramatics*.

As we noticed in detail before, but for other reasons, in Chapter 4 Aristotle says that there are two natural causes "of (the art of) dramatic musicals" (*tēn poiētikēn*). Again, the text is ambiguous, with Aristotle adding that man is most inclined of all species to representations and uses it for learning and that we get delight from representations and learning. Aristotle states a few passages later at 1448b20-21 that *by nature* we are given to representation and to "music and dance" (*harmonia kai rhuthmos*.) The two causes, then, of the art of dramatic musicals are either:

[1] Delight in representation and delight in learning; or,

---

[682] Woodruff himself seems to leave the door at least slightly ajar for there being multiple goals, saying "What then is the aim of tragedy as Aristotle understands it? The text does not warrant a simple answer; the most plausible answers will make use of all of them" (*op. cit.*, 2009, p. 614).

[2] (a) Delight in both representation and learning, and (b) the propensity for music and dance.

I prefer option [2], but for this book it does not matter which option is correct. Delight in representation (the genus of tragedy) is crucial no matter which interpretation one takes, and, as we saw, dramatists according to Aristotle create to give the audience that delight. Still, a caution might be helpful: Previous scholars have debated whether learning is a legitimate goal of tragedy, especially, for instance, in the context of determining whether *katharsis* can mean clarification in Chapter 6 and how learning can be delightful, all of which is paradoxical given that learning is painful according to the *Politics* VIII.[683] Once we strip away the issue of *katharsis*, though, we can understand without impediment that the *delight* in learning, not merely learning, is what is apropos here, because learning in and of itself is not ultimately the primary focus of Aristotle's concern in this context. This emphasis on delight becomes clearer when we proceed through Chapter 4 and find him discussing the pleasure in viewing images even of corpses if the image is proficiently done [1448b10-13]. At any rate, the delight in representation and the delight in learning are not necessarily the only or prime goals of tragedy (as a species of representation), merely the two first mentioned in the treatise.[684] Whether at least one of them is primary will be determined later. It hardly seems as if the propensity for music and dance is a goal or final cause rather than some efficient or formal cause. Hence, I leave that propensity aside in this context, although one might well argue that just as the propensity to acquire nutrition makes eating sometimes a goal in life, so does a natural propensity to sing and dance make singing and dancing sometimes a goal.

---

683 "For amusement does not go with learning—learning is a painful process" (5.1339a29).

684 Weinberg says:
Castelvetro specifically rejects any profit or utility as the end of poetry. The sole end…is to delight, to give pleasure and recreation… The position is reiterated on several occasions, notably in his discussion of purgation in tragedy; *he finds Aristotle in agreement with him on the matter of pleasure and sees the utilitarian notion of purgation (as he interprets it) as a contradiction on Aristotle's part*:
For if poetry was invented principally for pleasure, and not for utility, *as he demonstrated in the passage where he spoke of the origin of poetry in general*, why should he now insist that tragedy, which is a part of poetry, should seek utility above all else? (275. 30) (Bernard Weinberg, "Castelvetro's Theory of Poetics," in *Critics and Criticism: Ancient and Modern*, ed. R.S. Crane, Chicago: Univ. of Chicago Pr., 1952, pp. 349-71; p. 354; my italics throughout).
As one can see in the Appendix, Castelvetro was primarily concerned with giving his own view, but he tries to reconcile the issue for Aristotle by claiming that pleasure means (for the Greek) "the purgation and the expulsion of fear and of pity from human souls…" (Weinberg, *op. cit.*, 355). This view of pleasure, however, is indefensible, as we see through this chapter and book. Naturally, Castelvetro was at the forefront of commentaries, and it would have been very unreasonable for him to start questioning then the authenticity of the catharsis clause, at the very beginning of the exegesis of the *Dramatics*. Yet ironically he is perfectly correct about the importance of pleasure for Aristotle.

## Chapter 7: The Real Goal of Tragedy and Aristotle's Response to Plato

In Chapter 6, Aristotle says explicitly that the plot, "the structure of the incidents," is the end (*telos*) of tragedy, and is the most important element (1450a22-24). This end is not the same kind of end or goal as delight in representation or delight in learning, which themselves seem to be final causes, as becomes clearer later in Chapter 13. There, in a passage we examine in more detail below, Aristotle states that giving delight in representation is a goal for dramatists wishing to please the audience and to win a prize. I therefore treat delight in representation as if it could sometimes be at least a final cause or end for him, in that it is a psychological goal for the audience. On the other hand, plot appears to be something like the end for the *creator* of tragedy, something he himself should aim towards so that the audience can at least experience the play, no matter what the psychological goal is (be it pleasure or anything else). From the perspective of the audience, plot might be considered more appropriately part of the material or formal cause with respect to the creative process. That is, just as bronze is the material cause of a certain sculpture, so plot is part of the materials or form of tragedy, being in fact a derived necessary element from the essential conditions *per se* of tragedy in *Dramatics* 6 (as we saw above in Chapter 2). Plot does not on the surface, then, seem to fall cleanly into one of Aristotle's four causes, being suggested to be a final cause from one perspective (by being an "end") and yet being part of either the formal or material cause from another perspective. As a result, the relevant passages pose difficulties for anyone's interpretation of the treatise (which also goes to show that there is no simple way sometimes to apply the doctrine of the four causes). Whatever the solution to this difficulty, however, one matter is clear: Anytime one asks, "What is the goal of tragedy?" that person should be prepared to specify for whom or from what perspective, to help narrow the possible answers. If "end" is the same as "goal," as I assume it is in this context,[685] then already we have by this point in Chapter 6 three possible goals for tragedy for Aristotle. Alternatively, if delight in representation and delight in learning count only as two variations *of delight*, then we have two possible goals, and again I leave aside for the sake of brevity how the propensity to sing and dance might lead to those two activities being goals on occasion.

Aristotle notes further in *Dramatics* 6, in a passage that I examined in replying to Halliwell, that an author could compose speeches in sequence with character and fine diction but no plot (that is, no structure of incidents). However, Aristotle adds, the function (*ergon*) of tragedy is achieved better even if these elements are less worthy, but there is a plot *per se* (1450a29-33). He then states, and this is the crucial point for us now, that not only are the reversals and recognitions the most important aspects which enthrall (*psuchagōgei*) us but that these are part of the plot (1450a33-34). All of this

---

[685] I use "end," "goal," "aim" and "final cause" synonymously here, and do not think anything important hinges on a difference between them. Aristotle says "the end (*telos*) is something ultimate" and "the ultimate thing for the sake of which [the final cause] is also an end" (*Metaphysics* V 25, 1021b25-31, tr. W. D. Ross, in Barnes, *The Complete Works of Aristotle, op. cit.*; the Greek is from the Loeb Classical edition, *Aristotle in 23 Volumes*, XVII, Cambridge, MA: Harvard Univ. Pr., 1933 first printing, 1980 reprint).

suggests that it is the delight—the enthrallment—in viewing representations of a certain sort that is the goal, or at least part of the goal, of tragedy (not *katharsis* through pity and fear).[686] Moreover, he immediately adds that it is the same as in painting: Seeing random colors would not be as "delightful" or "gladdening" (*euphraneien*) as a black-and-white outline, with the black-and-white outline being clearly for him the analog of the plot—that is, of a representation.[687] Twice, then, a synonym of pleasure is given as the goal: enthrallment and then gladdening. Again, the pleasant psychological result is crucial and, in this way, Chapter 6 seems entirely consistent with Chapter 4. Indeed, the final focus on the pleasure in images in Chapter 4 that we saw once before is now in effect repeated in Chapter 6 with the pleasure experienced while viewing a black-and-white outline.

The next relevant passage mentioning the aim of tragedy occurs at the beginning of Chapter 13. Aristotle says: "... we must perhaps discuss next what [poets] should aim at and what they should beware of in constructing plots, i.e., how tragedy will achieve its function" (1452b28-31). As noted a few times, though, he never then discusses how *katharsis* might result via pity and fear, even though the two emotions are employed repeatedly throughout the chapter. Rather, after specifying three of the four plot patterns that do not even have pity and fear,[688] he then continues focusing on the best plots and he repeats the goal of pleasure. That is, he notes the goal of some dramatists while comparing (i)

---

[686] In mentioning *psuchagōgei*, it is worth recalling what Francesca Schironi reports:
"...Aristarchus...never defines Homeric poetry as "useful" or remarks on the *sophia* of the poet. This can be seen in conjunction with the idea that Homer does not aim at *didaskalia* [instruction] but at *psuchagōgia*..." (Francesca Schironi, "Theory into Practice: Aristotelian Principles in Aristarchean Philology," *Classical Philology* 104, 2009, 279–316, p. 309)
It is well known that Aristotle concentrated on, and admired, Homer; recall e.g., the *Homeric Problems*.

[687] This passage helps to show that Aristotle would accept formal art, even if he prefers mimetic art, as I argued in other ways in my *op. cit.,* 2005. What I did not emphasize there is that Aristotle writes *chudēn* (random) in making the comparison. What about if the colors were put together in an ordered way, albeit showing no "original?" There would be more pleasure on that side, maybe even equal to, or greater than, than a simple black-and-white outline. It would surely depend on the painter and the particular work. Why Aristotle presents the issue like this may be out of deference to Plato, who said, as we saw in Chapter 1, that all art is mimetic. However, whether Aristotle reports here that the Greeks were already doing some 20th-century type of formalistic painting is impossible to determine from this passage. He might refer to such a practice but speaks merely theoretically, and I leave the matter to specialists in ancient painting.

[688] I add a point to those given in the previous chapter. Most often scholars, intentionally or not, skirt the issue of the three tragic plots without pity and fear being inconsistent with the definition of tragedy or leave the matter ambiguous. For example, after summarizing accurately *Dramatics* 13, Sorabji says that "the plot must not show a good man (*epieikês*) brought from good to bad fortune" (*op. cit.,* 2000, p. 24). Does Sorabji mean that the dramatist must not show a virtuous man suffering while creating the *finest* plots with pity and fear (which is a legitimate claim because this is Aristotle's discussion of the sub-type of tragedy examined in Chapter 13) or while creating *any* tragic play (which leads to the extreme inconsistency with Chapter 6, in which pity and fear are supposedly required)? To repeat what was said above by Butcher regarding Sophocles' *Antigone*: Sorabji's stricture would rule out some famous protagonists and classical tragedies as being tragedies.

plots having a double structure with (ii) plots having a single structure, giving as an example of double structure Orestes and Aegisthus exiting as friends. Aristotle says, and this is the crucial point of Chapter 13 for us now, that "this is not the *pleasure* (*hēdonē*) [that comes] from tragedy, but is more particular to comedy [my italics]."[689] He immediately adds that dramatists create this way because they wish to suit the audience, implying that the dramatists wish to gain favor or win a competition. Thus, winning a competition is a goal of tragedy for some dramatists—no surprise here, I imagine, for any reader who is not hypnotized by *katharsis*—and one might properly claim that even this goal is a means to the further ultimate end of gaining fame and prizes, which themselves lead to pleasure, which itself is part of happiness for Aristotle. Note, again, that Aristotle does not remove this type of double-structured plot from the category of tragedy—just as he had not removed the kind of plot that involves a virtuous (or a thoroughly wicked) man going from fortune to misfortune—rather, he explicitly indicates that this kind of double-structured plot is merely second-best and that the pleasure is *more* particular to comedy (not only particular to comedy).[690] Clearly, then, for him, good empiricist that he is, one goal of tragedy for some dramatists is to win competitions. The other goal, however, that is strongly implied, is to provide pleasure, as with comedy, even though both dramatic forms give slightly different sorts—and it is by providing the audience pleasure, the implication is, that the dramatist succeeds. Finally, the further—and more interesting—implications at this point, at least for me, are as follows. First, there is a generic form of pleasure for the dramatic arts, with tragedy and comedy having particular types of that pleasure. Second, Aristotle leaves open the question whether, just because the type of play with a double-structure is "second best," that its kind of pleasure is *necessarily* worse—it might indeed be worse if, as Aristotle is suggesting, we want *pure* tragic pleasure as given by the sub-type of tragedy as covered in Chapter 13, but it might be equally good in its own right, as a mixed genre, of which nothing is said in our extant treatise (but which might have been

---

689  1453a35-36, tr. Janko, *op. cit.*

690  As mentioned, I agree with Janko's translation here of *mallon* as "more," and not with Munteanu's, where "rather" is rendered instead: "Yet, it is not the pleasure [to expect] from tragedy, but rather the pleasure proper to comedy" (Munteanu, *op. cit.*, p. 115). Yet, as she herself admits on the same page, this kind of "double-structured" play was very popular for Athenian audiences as tragedy, and not as comedy, and so my important point holds: Aristotle is in no way removing this kind of play from the category of tragedy—the plot-type just becomes "second-best" and there could be some kind of tragic pleasure involved, even if at the end the pleasure gets mixed with a more comic pleasure.

 The same experience happens nowadays with, e.g., *Swan Lake*. This "tragic" ballet originally ended, and typically still does, with the two beloveds, Odette-Odile and Prince Siegfried, dying, their deaths causing the evil sorcerer Rothbart to die also. However, the Russians have sometimes made the ending happy, having Siegfried kill Rothbart by ripping off a wing, thereby freeing the swan maidens. If you do not know which version of the ballet you will get, until close to the very end you will have the same pleasure (and other emotions) from both, including possibly some pity or fear (if any). But the saccharine Russian version will then add a different emotion in closing. Thus, tragic pleasure is not simple but, like the full tragic *dunamis*, very complex for an event that can last hours.

discussed in his theory of comedy).[691]

Aristotle repeats two more times in the next paragraph (at the beginning of Chapter 14) that we should seek the right kind of *pleasure* from tragedy, and not, for instance, what is only monstrous. He also emphatically states that the dramatist should use mimesis to produce the pleasure from pity and fear (14.1453b11-13). Again, *katharsis* never even enters the discussion, and it is pleasure that is still the goal. Moreover, given that there were different kinds of *katharsis* in ancient Greece, as seen in various discussions throughout this book, including those that Plato conveys, Aristotle could have said that we should seek the right kind of *katharsis*—but he does not. The final times that Aristotle at least alludes to the goal of tragedy occur in the last chapters of the book, starting with his loose definition of epic in Chapter 23. There, as we saw before, he states: "...*just as in tragedies*, [the epic poet] should construct plots that are dramatic ... about a single whole action that is complete ... *so that it will produce the pleasure (hēdonē) particular to it*" (1459a17-21, tr. Janko; my italics). The "just as in tragedies" strongly suggests that tragedies too have pleasure particular to them, again obviously continuing the theme of the many passages already cited.

This statement in Chapter 23 raises the question why Aristotle did not similarly add pleasure as the goal of tragedy in its own definition in Chapter 6. In a way, this is a silly question, given the work of the doubters now claiming that *katharsis* was wrongly added as a goal. For them, the original manuscript was corrupted at that spot and the original goal lost (assuming Aristotle gave the final cause at the end of the definition), or the *katharsis* clause was wrongfully added, or both. Hence, Aristotle may well have written *hēdonē* instead, of which more later. The better question for the moment might be, how could Aristotle have written only one particular goal for tragedy, considering the goals already noted above, for instance, a (proper) pleasure and winning a competition? Are not the three or four goals listed in *Politics* VIII 7—education, intellectual enjoyment, amusement/relaxation, and *katharsis*—also all applicable, just as they are all applicable for "music" (albeit at different times, depending on the kind of "music" and on the kinds of audience, e.g., whether they are children or not)? Furthermore, as introduced in my Chapter 6, there are four sub-categories of tragedy that Aristotle lists in *Dramatics* 18, and perhaps each had a slightly different goal, and a slightly different pleasure. We are getting ahead of ourselves, though. One option is that Aristotle listed no goal in the definition of tragedy, simply because there is no single goal. However, although possible, this does not seem

---

[691] I owe this last point to Munteanu, who has perspicaciously indicated (in private correspondence) the need to separate the issue of proper pleasure from the evaluation of the plot-type. Consider (in my own words): If one only cares about the monetary value of gold, purity is better; yet if one cares about using the gold for a wedding ring, then practical considerations such as additional strength make impurity, namely, adding a tiny bit of nickel, better. The same (in my view, although I am not sure for Munteanu) could hold for pure and impure tragic pleasures, but whether Aristotle discussed this in the lost section of comedy, we do not know.

plausible because we have already seen some explicit goals listed in the *Dramatics* and most, if not all, are reducible to pleasure, whether conceived generically or particularly. Why would he give, then, the goal for epic and not for tragedy? Another option, then, is that Aristotle originally wrote the generic pleasure that is common to all the subcategories as the goal of tragedy (and recall the first two options given in reply to Halliwell in the last chapter). I acknowledge that "generic" may confuse here, because the aesthetical pleasures are a mere subset of pleasure in general for Aristotle, as is commonly known and as will be shown with some textual evidence soon. Perhaps, then, "specific" (or species-related) pleasure would be better.

To return, then, to the possibility that there are many goals of tragedy for him: Maybe the differences between them were notable, and maybe there were too many for him to include in the definition, so he skirted the issue. One might think, at first impression, that it would have been inappropriate for him to use the same phrase "particular pleasure" as given for epic, the reason being that there appears on the surface to be only one form of epic whereas tragedy has four subcategories, which entails that the cases are not similar. However, even this is extremely doubtful because, as we saw before, in Chapter 24 epic is said to have the same four kinds, or at least the same number of kinds, as tragedy. It stands to reason that the pleasure for each would be slightly different, just as the spectacular or simple tragedy would give slightly different pleasures from a complex one, with all kinds of "special effects" (costumes and scenery) in the former but probably not as much in the latter (and the latter being the finer plot).[692] Certainly, the pleasure of viewing fine scenery is different from the pleasure of hearing

---

692  In addition to there being the four sub-types of epic, each sub-type could be (i) only spoken, or (ii) spoken and accompanied with instrumental music, or (iii) only "chanted" or sung, or (iv) sung with an instrument. Thus, sixteen possibilities exist. Classicists debate whether epic at the time of Plato and Aristotle had music or was only spoken (certainly in earlier days it was at least sometimes accompanied by a lyre, as we noted before concerning the *Odyssey*, Book 8, 250ff). Aristotle gives mixed messages in the *Dramatics*, although I present evidence throughout this book why he believes epic rhapsodes used music (at least as "chanting" or song) and "acting/gesturing/dancing," that is, body movements or facial expressions. It appears to me that epic rhapsodes were so well understood by the general public to be chanting that Aristotle takes it as a given and speaks about the epic verses as if they were merely language, just as nowadays we can speak about the words of an operatic or vocal libretto without having to emphasize that they are sung. The performed "musical" context is understood.

Sufficient proof that rhapsodes at least typically sang (or "chanted") comes from Plato's *Ion*. At the beginning of the dialog, Ion arrives from a musical competition in Epidauras that not only included epic rhapsodes reciting Homer, but "other musical competitions" (*tēs allēs ge mousikēs*) (530a). This might mean "music" in the sense of Muses, including strictly linguistic poetry, but the following passages reveal that the rhapsode sings, with Socrates saying: "...you [Ion], the rhapsodists and actors, and the men whose poems you **chant** (**hadete** ta poiēmata) (532d); also, "You are **chanting**, say, the story of Odysseus as he leaped up to the dais..." (ē ton Odyssea hotan epi ton oudon ephallomenon **hadēs**) (535b); and similarly other passages involving the epic rhapsode using *melos* (e.g., 534-536c) (transl. in this footnote are by Lane Cooper, from *The Collected Dialogues of Plato*, ed. E. Hamilton and H. Cairns, Princeton: Princeton Univ. Pr., 1961, eleventh printing 1982).

and understanding fine language, or from apperceiving the kind of plot that can also be expressed in dance and pantomime. Thus, considering that Aristotle states that epic has four sub-types, then because Aristotle considers "proper pleasure" in the quasi-definition of epic to be appropriate, he could have considered a single corresponding pleasure to be appropriate for a definition of tragedy that also entails the four sub-types of *Dramatics* 18.

Perhaps, as yet another option, Aristotle listed *all* of the goals of tragedy, but that would mean the manuscript was changed drastically to arrive at the extant version, something which is possible given the view of some scholars, like Bernays and Halliwell, who think that a large section of Chapter 6 could have been lost (or purposely deleted, in the case of Bernays). In any event, if the amount of space that exists in the current manuscripts for the goal of tragedy as *katharsis* (that is, the whole *katharsis* clause) was what contained the initial formulation, then I presume that Aristotle gave only the generic goal for all of the sub-types of tragedy as (intellectual) pleasure or something similar.

---

On the other hand, recall what Nagy says:
At the feast of the Panathenaia of Athens, celebrated in the late summer, there were competitions in the performances of tunes played on the *kithara* or on the *aulos*, also of lyric songs sung to instrumental accompaniment by the *kithara* or by the *aulos*, **and also of epic poetry recited without any instrumental accompaniment** [my bolding]("Epic," 2009, p. 21)...
... we read in the Aristotelian *Constitution of the Athenians* (60.1), where the author refers to these same Panathenaic categories of competition and where the overall competition is specified as the 'competition [*agōn*] in *mousikē*'.

What does the author mean by *mousikē* here? In Aristotelian usage, this word is a shorthand way of saying *mousikē tekhnē*, meaning 'craft of the Muses', that is, 'musical craft' in the etymological sense of the word *musical*. It is misleading, however, to think of ancient Greek *mousikē* in the modern sense of 'music', since the categories of 'musical' performers at the Panathenaia included rhapsodes. The performative medium of rhapsodes in the era of Aristotle was *recitative* and thus not 'musical' in the modern sense of the word. By *recitative*, to be more precise, I mean (1) performed without singing and (2) performed without the instrumental accompaniment of the *kithara* or the *aulos*. In this era, the competitive performances of the Homeric *Iliad* and *Odyssey* by rhapsodes at the Panathenaia were 'musical' only in an etymological sense, and the medium of the rhapsode was in fact closer to what we call 'poetry' and farther from what we call 'music' in the modern sense of the word. Still, the fact remains that the performances of rhapsodes belonged to what is called the 'competition [*agōn*] in *mousikē*', just like the performances of citharodes (*kithara*-singers), citharists (*kithara*-players), auletes (*aulos*-players), and so on (p. 23).

Yet Nagy gives no evidence, at least in this work, that the "recital" could not be a type of chanting, and his view seems contradicted by Plato's statements. Nevertheless, even if he is perfectly correct in saying the rhapsodes performed without singing, this only supports my claim earlier that there were different forms of epic performance (with sixteen possibilities total). However, Aristotle and Plato themselves focus only on the ones with some form of singing/chanting or instrumental playing. Thus, given the *Ion,* the "reciting" may be a "chanting" or at least a "quasi-singing" of the words, and thus, music *in our sense* was indeed part of the rhapsodic, epic experience, even granting that no instrument was used. Finally, where is the textual evidence that *mousikē* for Aristotle meant "craft of the Muses," given that we saw in Chapter 4 Aristotle explicitly characterizing *mousikē* as *melopoiias kai rhuthmōn* (music and dance) in *Politics* VIII 7?

## Chapter 7: The Real Goal of Tragedy and Aristotle's Response to Plato

There would not have been enough space to give a variety of goals. Further justification for this possibility includes the following: Unlike *katharsis* and like all the other elements, pleasure had been laid out in the previous "divisions" in Chapter 4, as we saw above, which accords with the biological division leading to the rigorous definition. Moreover, pleasure and its variants—"delightfulness" and "enthrallment"—are noted in Chapter 6 as being associated with plots, which means that the goal of pleasure in effect gets discussed in the chapter, just like all the other elements in the definition. Moreover, we are in the process now of seeing the numerous times pleasure as the goal of tragedy is mentioned after Chapter 6. Hence, if pleasure of some kind had been originally written as the goal of tragedy, the rest of the chapter and the treatise provides a very fitting follow-up. Indeed, it is telling that Aristotle cites pleasure/enjoyment as the goal of tragedy in more instances in Chapter 6 alone than he mentions a relevant *katharsis* in the whole treatise (two versus one).[693]

---

693   I recall only one author (Watson, *op. cit.* 2012, p 63 and 80-1) suggesting that Aristotle does not discuss catharsis in Chapter 6 because it is the final cause, whereas the other conditions, which are discussed in depth, are the other causes. I take it that, just as the efficient cause of the sculpture is the sculptor (or the art the sculptor has), the efficient cause of the tragedy is the dramatist and any other artist who helps create it (perhaps the actors or musicians if they contribute to the creation of the language, expression, and actions, as opposed to merely acting as interpreters).

I say "presumably" because there is no easy mapping of causes to Aristotle's theory of biological definition, at least that I am aware of, and it is questionable how one would map: As given at the beginning of this unit, and as stated in the *Metaphysics* and *Physics*, the formal cause can be *a shape or a definition*. Does this formal cause *qua* definition, then, only include the material, efficient and final causes or does the formal cause *qua* definition include all four of the causes with even another, embedded formal cause? If the latter, we seem to have an infinite regress. However, if the formal cause *qua* definition includes only "shape," presumably we are fine. Take a definition of Aristotle's example, sculpture: Assume the definition includes the material cause (say, bronze or more generically "hard material"), efficient cause (sculptor), and final cause (pleasure); can it not also include "shape" or "three-dimensional volume" without danger of the regress, or does "hard material" not already imply a certain shape in any given case? How does this apply to tragedy? The material cause is language, music, dance, spectacle, and so forth, namely, the means, objects and manners of mimesis; the efficient cause is the dramatist; the final cause, say, pleasure; and I have assumed the formal cause is the definition, which lists the various other causes. What about the equivalent of "shape"? Is it something like magnitude and related considerations, or the manner of mimesis? Alternatively, are actors not as much part of the material aspects as they are part of the efficient cause?

Fendt has a different way of applying the four causes to the *Dramatics,* and he says: "*Katharsis* is the final cause of tragedy when we examine it with a view to its relation to an audience, but that examination is not entered upon in *Poetics*, it is an other of *Poetics* [his words as given]" (*op. cit.*, 1997, pp. 253-4). He also adds: "In that logos tragedy would be understood as a dramatic *mimesis praxeos* (form) in sweetened speech (matter) which through incidents arousing pity and fear (efficient cause) accomplishes a *katharsis* of such *pathemata* (final cause)" (p. 249-50). So he includes a "form" within a formal cause (definition), although it is not clear to me whether this means "shape" or "formal cause," and if the latter how a potential regress gets blocked, or why that may not be worrisome. At any rate, one might differentiate between a near efficient cause, Fendt's "incidents arousing pity and fear" (which should be transposed for me to "incidents arousing pleasure" unless we are dealing with only a sub-type of tragedy) and a remote efficient cause, or a series of remote efficient causes, going back to the the "first cause," namely, the dramatist (and perhaps actors) who created the drama to begin with.

Let us now finish proceeding through the *Dramatics* in order to account for any remaining specified aims of tragedy. Later, in Chapter 24, 1460a13-18, Aristotle notes that the dramatist should put what is amazing into his tragedies but that epic can generate amazement better because of the constraints of stage representation for tragedy. Again, tragedy is fully dramatic whereas epic "recitation" omits orchestral art and spectacle, and at the best is partially dramatic in terms of spoken (or, better yet, sung) plot construction, according to Chapter 23, 1459a19. The crucial point for us now immediately follows: Aristotle says that what is amazing is pleasant, and people give embellishments to stories *in order to please*. Again, the importance of the creators pleasing—not providing *katharsis*—is at the forefront.

We find the last mention of the goal of tragedy in Chapter 26, when Aristotle debates whether epic or tragedy is the better art form. Even though epic had been said to give more pleasure because of more amazement, Aristotle now asserts that tragedy is the superior art form. Tragedy provides the pleasures of spectacle and *mousikē* (again, usually translated as "music" but translated better, I have argued, as "music-dance" or "orchestral art"). Immediately thereafter, Aristotle adds at 1462b1-3 that tragedy gives a more concentrated, and therefore better, *pleasure* than epic, and in the final few sentences, almost at the very end of the whole chapter and of the extant treatise, he concludes:

> So if tragedy is superior in all these ways, and also in [achieving] the function of art (for tragedy and epic should produce *not a random pleasure [hēdonēn], but the one we have mentioned*), it is obvious that it will be superior to epic as it achieves its end more than epic does [my italics]" (1462b12-15).

Aristotle could have argued in Chapters 23 through 26 that *katharsis* is also the end of epic and that a tragic catharsis is better than an epic catharsis. However, he does not. Rather, he expressly says that tragedy should achieve not a random pleasure but the one mentioned, whatever that refers to in the text, unless it is a lost passage.[694] Thus, without question some kind of pleasure is the primary goal of tragedy and of epic. Let me restate this with a slightly different twist. Considering also that Aristotle says at the very beginning of Chapter 24 (1459b8-12) that the parts of epic except for spectacle and "choral composition" (*melopoiia*) are the same as for tragedy, including reversals, recognitions, suf-

---

I am not claiming in this book to have given the only possible application of the four causes to the definition of tragedy, only one helpful one. This whole topic deserves at least an article, if not more.

In any event, no matter the quantity of scholars who have thought that the final cause was discussed in another treatise or lost section, given their latitude with respect to the need to discuss catharsis further in the extant treatise, or should I say lassitude?, those scholars should then allow equal latitude about pleasure being the goal of tragedy in Chapter 6. At least pleasure is noted twice in Chapter 6, in some form, as discussed.

694   Recall from Chapter 6 the discussion of the "stated function" of tragedy in *Dramatics* 6. The function either is, e.g., the delight in *Dramatics* 4 at seeing representations or the *praxeos mimesis* or a lost passage on the purpose of tragedy. This passage may well have been the passage now being referred to, but one that (unlike *praxeos mimesis*) mentioned the importance of pleasure.

## Chapter 7: The Real Goal of Tragedy and Aristotle's Response to Plato

ferings, reasonings and language (*lexis*), he *should* have argued—to emphasize my conclusion from Chapter 6 above—that epic's goal was also *katharsis*, were *katharsis* truly the goal of tragedy.[695] Yet he does no such thing, and again the words *katharsis*, pity and fear are completely missing in this whole discussion of epic. Pleasure is always the goal of both tragedy and epic for Aristotle in the *Dramatics* (leaving aside, of course, the suspicious phrase in the definition).

This concludes the internal review of the goals of tragedy in the *Dramatics*. There are different ends for tragedy, from different perspectives, and some are noted or strongly implied but not necessarily approved outright (dramatists trying to obtain favor from the audience or to obtain a prize in the competitions). However, once *katharsis* in Chapter 6 is ignored, it should be amply clear that (the proper) pleasures or enjoyments of various kinds are always the primary purposes of tragedy and epic for Aristotle. This emphasis on pleasure has been confirmed in part by many previous scholars, including Lear and Hutton, who themselves, unfortunately, dealt with the issue while unnecessarily burdening themselves with the view that *katharsis* must be taken into account for all tragedy.[696]

What about the only other evidence from the whole Aristotelian corpus that pertains to the goal of tragedy, but that has been taken to suggest that *katharsis* is legitimately a part of our extant *Dramatics* 6 and thus the goal of tragedy, namely, the statement in *Politics* VIII 7 examined in detail above in Chapter 4? We reviewed this passage earlier in the context of examining the correct meaning of the musical terms, but I repeat it:

> ... we maintain further that "music [in the Greek sense]" (*mousikē*) should be studied, not for the sake of one, but of many benefits, that is to say, with a view to (1) education, (2a) purgation [*katharsis*] (the word 'purgation' we use at present without explanation, but when hereafter we speak of *poiētikēs* ["musical composition" or "dramatic musical composition"], we will treat the subject with more precision); "music" may also serve for (3) for intellectual enjoyment, for (2b or 4) relaxation and for recreation after exertion (my translation, following Jowett, 1341b35-41).

---

695  I will not even attempt to list the various scholars who have tried to identify catharsis with pleasure or who have tried to show that some indirect allusion to pity and fear occur in the chapters on epic in order to harmonize these chapters with the catharsis clause in Chapter 6. Suffice it to say that if one has to resort to these devices to justify catharsis being in Chapter 6, one has paid a much higher cost than athetizing the catharsis clause, for the first approach contradicts everything we know about Aristotle's conception of both catharsis and pleasure and the second is too little and too late. Even an ardent defender of catharsis such as Halliwell indicates that pleasure and catharsis cannot be identified with each other, as we saw above. Cf. Scott, 2003, p. 247-8.

696  For Hutton's view, see his *op. cit.* and the summary in Scott, 2003, p. 240. Lear's view (*op. cit.*) is fairly well-known and was noted briefly above. To repeat, he says (p. 328) that "Katharsis provides a relief: it is either itself *pleasurable* or it helps to explain the proper *pleasure* that is derived from tragedy [my italics]." However, Lear's insight is more appropriate to *Politics* VIII 7 than to the *Dramatics,* and he continues to accept not only the whole catharsis clause but the literary view of tragedy; cf. his footnote 72.

We have seen already that *katharsis* cannot be legitimate in *Dramatics* 6 and that VIII 7 in no way supports the ostensible legitimacy, and we will examine in the next chapter how VIII 7 actually supports the possibility that *katharsis* was mostly, or entirely, important for Aristotle with respect to comedy when he wrote the *Dramatics*. However, the crucial point now is that "music," and by implication "dramatic musical composition," should be studied "not for the sake of one, but of many benefits." That is, if the goals of "music" are different from the goals of tragedy, then we must discount anything said in VIII 7 as being relevant to the *Dramatics* or at least to its Chapter 6. If the goals can be the same, especially given that I have demonstrated above that music and dance are necessary parts of tragedy, then tragedy should, or could, have multiple goals. Furthermore, although it may well be that the education of children would not be one of the goals of tragedy, it seems impossible to dismiss intellectual enjoyment as a, or indeed *the*, goal, given *Dramatics* 4 and all the other instances in the *Dramatics* when pleasure is invoked as the goal. In short, then, not only does VIII 7 provide no sustainable evidence that *katharsis* is the primary goal of tragedy but it supports the views on pleasure explained above, for intellectual enjoyment is a kind of pleasure. Many others, including Kraut and Veloso,[697] as we saw to some extent in Chapter 4, have given the detailed reasons why the best aim of "music" and (at least for Veloso) of tragedy from the perspective of *Politics* VIII 7 and the *Nicomachean Ethics* must be enjoyment (in intellectual pursuits). I need not add anything more on this subject, other than to underscore that their reasons mesh superbly with the findings above of the goals of tragedy internal to the *Dramatics*.

Catharsis is not necessarily ruled out in VIII 7 as a possible secondary or tertiary goal of at least some tragedies. However, that is an issue to be resolved in the future given the considerations discussed above, namely, whether any sub-type of tragedy that Aristotle discusses in *Dramatics* 13 and 14, in having pity and fear, also has *katharsis* as its goal. That subtype of tragedy might only have pleasure as the ultimate goal, as explicitly specified in Chapter 14, with *katharsis* perhaps being only the intermediate goal or *katharsis* playing no role whatsoever or very rarely. Also notice I say "if the goals of 'music' are different from the goals of tragedy," which is a large "if." It is still an open question whether the goals of "music" in VIII 7 can be applied to tragedy. This is a fascinating question, and not settled as quickly as one, might wish. "Music" is obviously different from tragedy, even if tragedy includes it as a part, and in *Dramatics* 25, as emphasized, Aristotle expressly says that different arts have different principles—or, more exactly, that other arts (*technes*) do not have the same principles

---

[697] Veloso, *OSAP* 2007, p. 266; Kraut also aptly says: "He [Aristotle] thinks that properly listening to music of the right sort is one of the virtuous activities in which happiness consists, and that it therefore does not need to serve some further purpose in order to be justified... Because of the close connection... to happiness, this must be considered the most important use of music..." (*op. cit.*, p. 206). Hence, when modern school administrators try to justify "music" (or music and dance) by saying that the students then get better at math, one should point those administrators to Aristotle's discussion in Book VIII.

as "'music'-verse" (*poiētikēs*) (1460b13-15). I discuss this issue more in Chapter 9, and I touched upon it already when, e.g., examining Aristotle's view in *Dramatics* 26 that music and dance add more (and seemingly a different type of) pleasure than the primarily literary form of epic (which *secondarily* has music and dance *qua* ordered gestures for Plato and Aristotle). The whole topic of both the *dunamis* and related pleasures of the different elements of tragedy, or of any complex art form, though, would take at least a few chapters and probably even at least a few books to explore rigorously.

This covers all of the relevant passages from the Aristotelian corpus pertaining to the end of tragedy.

In conclusion: the internal evidence of the *Dramatics* clearly shows that pleasure of some sort (in mimesis, in learning, in music and dance, in amazement, in reversals and recognitions) is the goal of tragedy. This goal coincides, as emphasized, with the commonsensical view that Callicles holds in Plato's *Gorgias* when he confirms with Socrates that all music for the lyre and dithyramb and all tragedy is created primarily for the pleasure of the audience (502a-b), whether or not Socrates concurs. *Politics* VIII 7 can be taken to suggest that the listed goals *may* be relevant to tragedy rather than to the practices that Aristotle explicitly mentions: sacred rituals (which give *katharsis*) or dithyramb or other "musical" performance, any or all of which could have pity, fear or "frenziedness." However, the relevance to other practices like tragedy (or comedy) has to be supported with other argumentation, above and beyond simply asserting that the mere mention of pity and fear proves the relevance for tragedy. Given the arguments from Chapters 5 and 6 above, according to which many legitimate tragedies for Aristotle have neither pity nor fear, the relevance of catharsis to dramatic forms like tragedy probably will be accomplished more effectively via the "musical" aspects than via the two *combined* emotions of pity and fear or of "frenziedness" (and, for instance, I discussed how fear by itself is catharted for Plato using movement). In short, no significant consideration impedes the conclusion that pleasure is the goal of tragedy for Aristotle.

## Section 2: Aristotle's Response to Plato

### Section 2a: How Aristotle Agrees—and Disagrees—with Plato on Tragedy

In *Dramatics* 2 and 6, by definition, tragedy requires "admirable" or "good" (*spoudaios*) men in action. In *Dramatics* 15, Aristotle says that characters should be first and foremost good, which is completely Platonic. We also saw before how extensively Plato employed *katharsis* in his own theories. Why, then, would Aristotle reject Plato's conclusion that the ideal state should ban tragedy, and where does he part company with his mentor? Is the parting an issue of *katharsis*, with the student hoisting the master on the master's own petard, in spite of the term being illegitimate in the definition? If not, where is the parting? To start answering this, let us re-examine some basics. If Janko is a reliable guide in this respect, as I think he is, there are four Platonic attacks that Aristotle seemingly must deflect to defend tragedy (treating for the moment Janko's use of "poet" as a synecdoche for "dramatist" or "composer"):

i) Poets compose under inspiration, not by using reason.

ii) Poetry teaches the wrong things.

iii) Poetry is mimesis (imitation), at two removes from reality.

iv) Poetry encourages the emotions of those who perform or listen to it [drama or epic].[698]

The only attack by Plato, it appears, that *katharsis* could reasonably parry, and hence the only relevant issue for this book, is (iv), which itself implies Plato's further statement that the emotions then start undercutting reason and corrupting the individuals.[699] This eruption of emotion is traditionally

---

698   Janko, *op. cit.*, 1987, p. xi.

699   Perhaps (ii) would also be addressed if *katharsis* can mean "clarification," but many including myself have destroyed that possibility, as discussed in Chapter 5. Fendt reports on the common view that the *Dramatics* is an answer to Plato, and also gives some of the scholars who deny this, citing, e.g., on the full continuum Nickolas Pappas, Alexander Nehamas, Martha Nussbaum, and Leon Golden. With the title of this chapter, I myself only mean to suggest that the *Dramatics* is an indirect reply to Plato, of which more later. For the moment, suffice it to say that Aristotle presents his theory of drama and he cannot but help realize it will be understood by anyone knowing the issues as an option to some views—albeit a confirmation of other views—of his mentor, so in that sense it is at least an (indirect or oblique) reply *in the relevant respects*.

Fendt himself presents a fresh approach on a number of different issues in the *Dramatics*, but considerations of space do not permit me to address all of the interesting topics he raises, partly because he sometimes takes the traditional conceptual framework and accepts the legitimacy of the catharsis clause. Still, as an indication of why I appreciate his methods and approach, let me take up one related topic in this context. As he says:

> The *Poetics* is, then, not an answer to any of Plato's supposed problems with drama, for it considers tragedy in itself, without relation to its audience. We can see from what he [Aristotle] has said in the earlier chapters, however, that an investigation of the worth of tragedy would be a very complex undertaking, *for it would have to consider the permutations of two sets of three kinds of character, since we would have to consider the effects of better, equal, and worse poets (or voices) on better, equal and worse audiences.*
>
> *There would be, then, nine possible effects of tragedy*, and three possible effects if we consider that tragedy can only be written by a character which mimics the good. Tragic catharsis is, then, not one thing, but at least three. Considering the complexity of the problem, it is no surprise that Aristotle puts it off to get clear about the thing "in itself" first.
>
> So, then, critics like Alexander Nehamas are right in their claim that Aristotle is not answering Plato's charges in *Republic* X in writing the *Poetics*. (That Aristotle is answering Plato is a rather standard view.) They are wrong, however, in their reasoning… (Fendt, *op. cit.*, 1997, p. 251-2).

I just explained in part, and the rest of this chapter explains additionally, why I agree and disagree with Fendt's claim that "critics like…Nehamas are right in their claim that Aristotle is not answering Plato's charges." The sub-topic about permutations is a complex issue that deserves its own treatment, but, as suggested above, too many have thought that catharsis must have one meaning in the context of the arts for Aristotle, when indeed, like pleasure, it may have variants.

for commentators what *katharsis* addresses: Somehow the emotions (pity and fear especially) are catharted and reason is not threatened. I therefore leave aside for this book any in-depth examination of the first three attacks, although I believe Aristotle has adequate answers to them in, e.g., *Dramatics* 25, often understood in the secondary literature. Suffice it to say in passing that, in reply to the three attacks respectively, Aristotle claims that: art is production in accordance with right reason (*Nicomachean Ethics* VI 4); dramatic musical composition is not primarily designed to teach, but to "entertain," ideally in a profound way; and mimesis is natural and thus part of reality, not removed from it (*Dramatics* 4).

In order to determine now precisely whether and how Aristotle parts company with his mentor regarding the assertion that tragedy unduly encourages the emotions, recall the example that Plato gives while attacking tragedy in *Republic* X (605d-606b)—of a dramatized hero lamenting too much, causing the audience not only to pity him inordinately but also to predispose themselves to pity afterwards, weakening their own characters. For the sake of clarity, let us divide the Platonic criticism into two assertions, the second of which is bifurcated:

1. The hero laments too much in a tragedy (that is, in general terms, he acts wrongly).
2. The audience will be entranced by a pleasurable treatment of the lamentation, and the better the dramatist, the more pleasurable and compelling the play will be. In this case, the audience members will then improperly sympathize with the hero and his inordinate suffering, causing them to pity either others or themselves unduly in their private lives. In short, the pleasurable experience ultimately corrupts character, by fostering bad emotions at the expense of reason and self-control.

However, as we now see, Aristotle in the particular case of lamenting heroes *accepts* (1) and thus does not need to reply to Plato, with *katharsis* or anything else. If we generalize the specific case, however, we see a divergence, but one based on their views of ethics, not on using *katharsis*. Aristotle would, however, utterly reject (2), but, again, for reasons having nothing to do with *katharsis*. The textual evidence follows.

**Versus (1): The hero laments too much in a tragedy**

In *Dramatics* 15, as earlier remarked, Aristotle says that characters should be first and foremost good. What he adds that I did not mention is that characters should also be appropriate, life-like, and consistent, and he then notes further "an example ... of the unsuitable and inappropriate, [is] the lament of Odysseus in the *Scylla*... (1454a30). Thus, Aristotle's "reply" to Plato concerning the overly lamenting hero is no reply at all. Aristotle agrees with his mentor. In tragedy, the hero should not lament too much; merely appropriately, if at all. If you wish to know what "appropriate" conveys, read the *Nicomachean Ethics,* especially with respect to the doctrine of the mean in Book II, Chapters 6 through 8 (of which more below). By extension and in general terms, Aristotle implies that one should not show unethical behavior in tragedy, as Plato prefers. However, Aristotle allows in *Dramatics* 15, 1454a29 and 1454b13-14, that an evil person could be shown as "appropriate," that is, if necessary to the plot, and in one way this is very Platonic although in another way not, because Plato seemingly does not allow *any* unethical character to be represented. In other words, Aristotle's ethics sometimes, but only sometimes, diverge from Plato's ethics, if significantly at those moments. In these cases, we detect divergence between the two thinkers and a quick overview of a few parts of the *Nicomachean Ethics* reflects the important differences with regards to tragedy in general.

Lamenting or feeling pity for Aristotle is perfectly fine, with certain restrictions:

> ... both *fear and confidence and appetite and anger and pity* and in general *pleasure and pain* may be felt both too much and too little, and in both cases not well; but **to feel them at the right times, with reference to the right objects, towards the right people, with the right motive, and in the right way, is what is both intermediate and best, and this is characteristic of virtue** [my italics] (*NE* II 6, 1106b13ff).

> ... No one would reproach a man blind from birth or by disease or from a blow, but rather pity him (*NE* III 5, 1114a26-27).

First, in my view, the bolded statement is one of the most important, and most under-rated, of Aristotle's ethical principles, and is as crucial for him as the Ten Commandments for Christians or the Categorical Imperative for Immanuel Kant. I call it Aristotle's Core Principle of Virtue, and it involves five conditions to be fulfilled to determine whether an emotion or action is virtuous. Second, pity and fear at times can be completely acceptable, and in fact not to have them at those times is blameworthy. Moderation is crucial (nothing new here for readers of Aristotle).[700] One would be genuinely a monster if, for instance, one felt no pity when coming across a person blinded after protecting his country in war or when discovering that one's own kind-hearted, generous and honest best friend was maimed by a plane falling out of the sky. Similarly, one would be inordinately rash (and thus unethical in Aristotle's sense of having no practical wisdom) if one felt no fear when being confronted by an earthquake or a tidal wave—like the "Celts" whom Aristotle discusses at *Nicomachean Ethics* III, Chapter 7, 1115b25ff, to make this point. In short, a hero could and should lament, but only appropriately, and insofar as Plato was implying that a hero could not lament at all, Aristotle disagrees, and similarly for other ethical or unethical behavior. Aristotle, however, very much disagrees with Plato's second assertion, which is also why he would not ban tragedy in the ideal state. Let us examine that assertion.

---

[700] Even Plato accepts the importance of moderation at *Republic III*, 389d, so simply to be moderate is not sufficient to be "anti-Platonic" in this whole context. Whether Aristotle's ethical theory is different in kind or merely different in degree with respect to moderation is a fascinating question but one I leave aside here.

Chapter 7: The Real Goal of Tragedy and Aristotle's Response to Plato

**Versus (2): The audience will be entranced by a pleasurable treatment of the theme ...; the audience will then inordinately sympathize with the hero and his suffering.**

Plato had said in related remarks in the *Republic*:

> Mixed styles [of music (*harmonia*) and dance (*rhuthmos*)] fit the inferior—they are most pleasant to the children, their tutors, and the vast majority (III, 397c-d, my transl.)...

> Decent people get affected by a hero's lamenting, and the better the poet, the more influential the lamenting will have on even decent people, who will then start pitying themselves inappropriately in real life (X, 605d-606b).[701]

The pleasure Plato refers to, then, would not be taken directly in the inappropriate, *extreme* lamenting or wrongful conduct *per se* on the part of the protagonist. Instead, the pleasurable way in which seemingly even necessary evil parts of a theme or story get presented *initially* causes reason ultimately to get seduced. The audience subsequently accepts the lamentation as, not laudatory, but acceptable (because, again, the *wonderfully wrought* hero is doing it). The more potent the dramatist, meaning the more capable he is of presenting the tragedy in all its aspects in dramatic musical composition, the more capable he is of captivating and thereby corrupting the audience. The wrongness of the behavior is not directly at issue here, because insofar as it is extreme and therefore inappropriate, it has already been covered above, and Aristotle agrees with Plato that *certain* kinds of inappropriate behavior are in and of themselves out of place for a hero in tragedy. Plato's worry, however, still occurs for moderately or "necessary" evils being mimicked *if they are represented well*, e.g., very beautifully or captivatingly.

Aristotle's reply, though, to (2)—that the pleasantness of the representation triggers a process leading to undue sympathy—comes from the *Nicomachean Ethics* and the *Dramatics*. Those texts easily reveal that Aristotle would not accept that presenting the bad behavior in a pleasurable, "dressed-up" way persuades the relevant audience to accept wrong behavior and to feel *inordinate* pity, just as dressing up literally a vicious murderer in beautiful, fashionable clothes would not for Aristotle cause any rational or ethical person to accept the murderer's behavior.[702] No murderer ever argues in trial "I was wearing Armani at the time you claim I killed the victim; therefore, I must be innocent." In short, the audience members would not lose their critical faculties and become "entranced," nor—even if they were delighted by the pleasurable treatment of the song, spectacle, costumes and so forth—would they take the next step and sympathize with the related, despicable behavior. Let us

---

701   All translations of the *Republic* by G.M.A. Grube and C.D.C Reeve (in *op. cit.*, *Plato: The Complete Works,* ed. by John Cooper) unless noted. My own translations modify theirs, for words discussed previously in this book.

702   By relevant audience, I mean one with typical, and reasonably good, values. Children or thieves/murderers are presumably not the kind of audience Aristotle is concerned with, although older adolescents might be a concern, of which more soon.

review Aristotle's texts for support of these claims.

As a preliminary remark, the word *katharsis* does not appear in the *Nicomachean Ethics*, which as an argument from silence reflects how unimportant *katharsis* is for Aristotle's mature ethical theory.[703] Rather, the doctrines instead of the temperate and self-restrained person, and fighting with oneself in cases of *akrasia* ("weak will" or "lack of control"), arguably suffice to handle Plato's worry about being overcome because of the pleasure. That is, neither temperate nor self-restrained individuals would allow the pleasures of the theater to affect their judgment of the correctness of related behavior, just as the temptation of a sweet would not cause a temperate or self-controlled individual to forget that sweets may not be healthy. Indeed, in *Nicomachean Ethics* III 10, in a passage that is rarely, if ever mentioned by scholars dealing with *katharsis* and tragedy (even Halliwell misses it when discussing other passages in the *Nicomachean Ethics* indirectly pertaining to *katharsis*, as just footnoted), Aristotle discusses briefly those individuals who delight extravagantly in painting, music or the theatre, and rejects the idea that they are self-indulgent, because he believes the term "temperate" refers to the bodily pleasures and not to the "intellectual" or "aesthetical" ones. Nevertheless, he qualifies all of this, adding "yet it would seem possible to delight even in these [aesthetical pleasures] either *as one should* or to excess *or to a deficient degree* [my emphases]" (1118a6-7). For Aristotle, then, one should take delight in the theatre, but following the Core Principle of Virtue. The mention of "excess or to a deficient degree" takes us back to that Core Principle, in which Aristotle talks about feeling pleasure too much or too little: Feeling pleasure *in the proper amount*, at the right time, *with respect to the right objects* (which means one does not take pleasure in evil actions), etc. Hence, the reply to Plato in this context is still in effect Aristotle's famous doctrine of the Mean,[704] not of *katharsis*. Were Aristotle to have written that *katharsis* is the goal of tragedy, designed to purge either (i) potentially illegitimate emotions of pity and fear or (ii) inordinate emotions caused by pleasurable treatments of a theme, he could, should and would have added in *Dramatics* 6 something like "only if those emo-

---

703  Halliwell says (*op. cit.*, 2003-4, p. 507):
En *Éthique à Nicomaque* 1171a29-34, un passage négligé par les commentateurs de la *Politique*, Aristote utilise deux fois le même verbe *kouphizesthai* («alléger») pour désigner le soulagement de la douleur ou de la détresse émotionnelles *(lupeîsthai)* quand ceux qui sont dans le malheur tirent leur soutien de la sympathie de leurs amis *(sunalgeîn)*. ["In *NE* 1171a29-34, a passage neglected by commentators of the *Politics*, Aristotle uses two times the same verb *kouphizesthai* ("alleviate," "lighten" or "relieve") to designate the relief of grief or of the emotional distress *(lupeîsthai)* when those who are in woe derive their support from the sympathy of their friends *(sunalgeîn)*" (my translation).]
Although illuminating, this, and Halliwell's accompanying discussion, are not sufficient to show, e.g., why and how Aristotle would advocate using catharsis on two emotions that can be appropriate.

704  The "mean" pertains to virtues, which are the "intermediate" or the "mean" between extremes. Thus, courage is the "mean" between cowardice and rash bravery; wit is the "mean" between buffoonery and boorishness.

tions are extreme or have improper objects and need to be moderated." Optionally, he would and should have mentioned *katharsis* in one of his passages just noted in the *Nicomachean Ethics*. Better yet, given his own principles of definition, he would have done both: mention *katharsis* in the *Ethics* and explain it or moderation correctly in the definition of tragedy.

Now, a Platonist might object and say that the passage in *Nicomachean Ethics* III 10 is merely a remark about going to the theater or seeing paintings too much, which is perhaps wrong on Aristotle's theory because such a habit causes people to neglect business or family or other important values. Thus, the Platonist might add, Aristotle's claim does not address the problem of aesthetic pleasure enticing people to accept inordinately bad emotions or bad behavior. In reply, however, even though admittedly Aristotle's comment is brief, it also, along with other guidelines as given in the Core Principle, suggests that the aesthetic pleasure does not overrule, e.g., character evaluation. That is, Aristotle ranks character well above the language, music-dance, and spectacle in the list of six necessary conditions. It follows, since the aesthetics pleasure relates to those last three conditions, that any aesthetic pleasure will not be more important than character, which according to *Dramatics* 15 must be good, appropriate, etc. Moreover, merely in making all of these distinctions and speaking of the different powers (*dunamis*) of the different parts of tragedy, Aristotle is at least implicitly laying the groundwork for being able to evaluate one part independently of a different part. Indeed, the comparison of tragedy and epic shows how well he recognizes that the individual aspects of each art form can augment or detract from its worth. Thus, he could, and would, readily admit that the masked protagonist in *The Phantom of the Opera* sings heart-rending melodies exquisitely, but he would point out that no typical audience member feels saddened by the just desserts the Phantom gets at the end for his deplorable attempt to kidnap and enslave the young singer Christine. Nor would any typical, non-pathological audience member be tempted then to start kidnapping singers in real life just because the Phantom sings so well.

Moreover, Aristotle never spells out in detail in Chapter 13 *why* and *how* the excellent person going from fortune to misfortune involves disgust rather than pity and fear. Thus, given the high level of the discussion in the *Ethics*, similarly there is no reason for him to explain in detail why or how the aesthetic pleasures do not encourage any possibly related bad behavior. These might be fascinating topics, but they belong to another time and another book. Nevertheless, without a doubt, Aristotle writes in Chapter 13 that only revulsion is felt towards a virtuous person going to misfortune, in spite of him saying in the *Rhetoric*, as we saw, that the virtuous person is most deserving of pity. It suffices here to show that aesthetic pleasure in general is also subject to the doctrine of the Mean or the Core Principle of Virtue and that Aristotle would not accept that "dressing up" actions hoodwinks any ordinarily intelligent audience member into ignoring the foulness of any evil deed. The Core Principle is not simple and involves as we saw five conditions, and it surely is the case that any particular evaluation of a tragedy, or one action within the tragedy, may or may not satisfy one or more of the five conditions. Another tragedy, or another event in the same or different tragedy, likewise may or may not satisfy those conditions. No simple statement can cover all, or even most, of the cases regarding the *details*. Thus, as in *Dramatics* 13, the details in *Nicomachean Ethics* III 10 are missing as to why and how Aristotle's statement helps him reject Plato's worry about pleasure unduly affecting one's morality. Nevertheless, the arguments and evidence above show that the general principles of the Mean, especially the Core Principle itself, suffice for Aristotle to counter Plato's attack on drama.

Confirmation of all this—and especially the claim that one should take delight in the theatrical (or aesthetical) pleasures in the proper way—is spread throughout the *Dramatics*. As we have seen in many ways already, pleasure comes from many aspects of tragedy—reversals and recognition, the mimesis, the song and dance and spectacle, and so forth—and is never spoken of negatively, subject to perhaps one oddity. Aristotle writes in Chapter 14 the passage that many people focus on for other reasons:

> Those [poets] who use spectacle to produce what is only monstrous and not terrifying have nothing in common with tragedy. For we should not seek every [kind of] pleasure from tragedy, but [only] the sort which is particular to it. Since the poet should use representation to produce the pleasure [arising] from pity and terror, it is obvious that this must be put into the incidents.[705]

Without question, as this passage implies, tragedians can create different kinds of pleasures in different ways (and there is a pleasure associated with monstrous representations, which should be no less, and perhaps no more, surprising than having a pleasure associated with pity and fear). However, for Aristotle, the tragedians—at least the composers of the sub-kinds of tragedies that in my view he is speaking of in this context—should *not* create the *irrelevant* pleasures. Nevertheless, that the tragedians can and should create not only the "particular pleasure" pertaining to pity and fear (for at least some sub-types of tragedies) but pleasure in other ways becomes very obvious later when, as we saw, Aristotle states in Chapter 26 that music and spectacle give the kind of pleasure that allows us to rank tragedy over epic.

Further confirmation of Aristotle's reply to Plato without *katharsis* occurs in the final chapters of the *Dramatics*. For instance in Chapter 25, when Aristotle takes up a host of criticisms on art, epic composition, and tragedy, he leaves aside the moral issues, as if they had already been covered earlier, probably with his principles from Chapters 13 through 15 on moral imperatives and good character. He examines the various "aesthetical" or epistemic issues, including the defense of artistic falsehoods that Janko lists as part of the four Platonic attacks, which we saw above: how the representation

---

705   1453b7ff, tr. Janko, *op. cit.*

should be done in terms of accuracy; how errors can be defended; how seeming untruths can be justified; and so forth. As Aristotle concludes that long chapter:

> So the criticisms that people make are of five kinds—that things are impossible, improbable, harmful, contradictory, or incorrect in terms of [another] art. Solutions must be looked for among the items we have stated; there are twelve of them (1461b21-25, transl. Janko).

Had Aristotle thought *katharsis* countered Plato's relevant criticism, it is puzzling why in this whole section of "refuting criticisms," Aristotle would not have responded with the doctrine of *katharsis* to the attacks on tragedy or "poetry" in general, insofar as there is any linkage to the corruption of character. One explanation is that Aristotle thought he had covered the criticisms already with his other chapters (or with another book). However, let us grant for the sake of rigor that Aristotle chose to address merely some, but not all, of the Platonic and non-Platonic criticisms in Chapter 25, even if Plato is not named (perhaps out of politeness to his mentor). Nevertheless, further confirmation that Aristotle continues to respond to Plato in the final chapters of the *Dramatics* by not employing *katharsis* in defense of tragic drama—or even of epic—arises at the beginning of Chapter 26 when he ranks epic and tragedy. As we saw in my Chapter 2, Aristotle rebuts Plato's criticism in *Republic* III of tragedy, namely, that it has vulgar or too much movement, in order for Aristotle to rank tragedy over epic. Aristotle thereby shows in *Dramatics* 26 that Plato's own criticism applies in some ways to epic, even if Plato had not intended this art form, his favorite, to be a target, because epic also emphasizes heroic movement and action. For Plato in the *Republic*, drama uses "acting" or gestures, which for him are inherently vulgar, rather than the nobler use of language (associated more with epic):

> Good men having (only) unfortunate periods can be imitated, and ideally mostly in narrative (which means, as I [Socrates] explained above, not dramatically, as actors in tragedy and comedy do) (III, 396c)...
>
> Inferior people will enact anything and everything, no matter how unworthy, and will use only a little narration (397a) ...
>
> Music (*harmonia*) and dance (*rhuthmos*) that have little variation are best; the music and dance that have many variations are worse (397b-c, my translation).[706]

As we saw before to some extent, Aristotle rejects Plato's position, devoting almost half of Chapter 26 to explaining why such criticism about movement or vulgar movement is ungrounded and why tragedy is therefore better than epic. For instance, we will recall that he says the charge is not against the composition but the actor's delivery and that even in epic Sosistratus gestured too much, a direct reply to Plato's views, using many of the same terms in effect that Plato himself had used in the

---

[706] As should be unsurprising, given my Chapter 2, throughout these passages in the *Republic* pertaining to drama in the theater, all or virtually all translators continue to miss the correct meaning of *harmonia* and *rhuthmos* as "music and dance."

*Republic*.[707] Why, then, Aristotle responds still another time (in *Dramatics* 26) to a criticism of the *Republic* and yet, again, completely ignores the one criticism pertaining to the corruption of character that results from inordinate emotion is tough to explain unless, as suggested, he either agreed with Plato on the matter or felt he had already responded elsewhere.[708]

Given all of this, even if a tragedian presents a "reasonably necessary" representation of an evil deed with such powerful expression that the music-dance-language is the part that is remembered later by even "decent" audiences, to use Plato's concept, the audiences nevertheless on Aristotle's view would still not be seduced by those pleasurable trappings into believing that the concomitant, unethical behavior is justified. They would not then, e.g., begin pitying themselves inordinately or, following the *Phantom of the Opera*, start kidnapping singers in real life. They would realize that the necessary aesthetic conditions in the list from Chapter 6 were fulfilled well, but that the importance of character, the second-most important necessary condition, failed.

To give one final example, albeit from modern musical theater: the songs in *Carousel* may entrance me and I may consider the barker Billy Bigelow to be like Sisyphus in having mixed virtues and vices. The latter consideration would allow a modicum of pity *at times*. Nevertheless, none of this causes me to sympathize either with Billy's conspiracy to rob the money-carrying employer or with Billy committing suicide. The songs and music certainly cause me in no way to consider plausible either his ascent to heaven or return to earth. In other words, the songs in no way cause me to reject good empiricism and accept a fantastical theology. Thus, to use Aristotle's technical vocabulary: the very mellifluous music of the production undercuts neither my practical nor theoretical wisdom (assuming I have them) nor my ethics in general.

To begin finishing these issues: The virtue of cleverness (or intelligence) of the villainous Sisyphus, or the brave quality of the unjust king of Chapter 18 (like Richard III), might cause *some* pity, but even that is questionable depending on the various factors, as already explained in Chapter 6. To re-

---

707    Woodruff says: "But when Aristotle's main purpose in a text is to refute a Platonic doctrine, as in *Ethics* 1.6 or *Politics* 2.2, he makes it clear that this is his target. In the *Poetics* he does no such thing." ("Aristotle's *Poetics*: The Aim of Tragedy," p. 621.) In general, I think Woodruff is right, but I must quibble with his last sentence, and point to the discussion of vulgar movement here as a counter-example, if one of the only ones or indeed perhaps the only one. Again, Plato had ranked epic highest in the *Republic* and the *Laws*; Aristotle rejects that ranking in Chapter 26, even if he does not name Plato. On the other hand, Woodruff might be entirely right, in spite of my views as articulated so far, if the refutation of Plato is not Aristotle's *main* purpose (as Woodruff states precisely), but only a *secondary* one. That is, perhaps Aristotle's main purpose was to rank tragedy over epic, and the Platonic type view entered only in support, secondarily, of that ranking.

708    I find it impossible to believe that somehow Aristotle just missed Plato's attack on tragedy pertaining to the emotions being corrupted.

iterate, Aristotle's doctrine from the *Nicomachean Ethics* would not grant that any reasonably ethical audience member could overlook the bad aspects of character, no matter how delightfully wrought the literary and "musical" passages were in representing Sisyphus or Richard III. Even adolescents can distinguish between the finery of apparel and the wearer committing a vile deed like a murder. Thus, the onlookers, or at least the onlookers worth speaking about, for Aristotle would not be overly affected emotionally by the vicious qualities of any delightfully wrought protagonist, and the onlookers would not find the *unethical* qualities worth emulating. Thus, the initial inordinate pity and then ultimate inordinate self-pity never happen. Likewise, with other emotions, and yet, if the audience members are astute at making distinctions, as discussed or alluded to in *Dramatics* 6, 18, 25, and 26, they might praise the "music," while stressing that this has less weight overall than character. In short: Aristotle does not think that portraying inappropriate behavior in very pleasurable ways (with mixed-styled "melodies" or mixed-style song-dance), especially if the underlying behavior is necessary to the plot, will cause an audience to begin abandoning their moral scruples. Again, *katharsis* plays no role here whatsoever in any part of his theory.

To summarize and conclude this section: In *Dramatics* 15, Aristotle explicitly bans inordinate lamenting. By implication, he forbids any genuinely unethical character unless it is necessary for the plot. By the way, making a mistake, *hamartia*, may not be, strictly speaking for Aristotle, a flaw in character in Chapter 13 but an isolated action that sadly can cause great anguish, one that permits a relatively good man like Oedipus to be the object of pity and fear.[709] Even Plato allows, as we saw, that a good man could be shown, ideally in narrative, having an unfortunate period in his life (and we can now understand why Plato wants the narrative, because then the "musical" elements would not exist and thus could not seduce the audience as much). Any ordinate lamenting or any evil that is necessary to the plot, which for Plato might be so "dressed up" with pleasurable music, dance and poetry as to make the evil superficially palatable, eventually causing extreme emotions that overrule reason, is a different story and a different worry. However, Aristotle's doctrine in the *Nicomachean Ethics* and his distinctions in the *Dramatics* block this worry.

In the *Nicomachean Ethics,* pity and fear can be proper emotions for Aristotle. Thus, showing pity and fear can be valid for at least some sub-types of tragedy, and he never says in the *Dramatics* that dramatists should either dissolve (wholly or partially) pity and fear in those cases or moderate those

---

709   My thanks to Frank Gonzalez for reminding me that the flaw (*hamartia*) of Oedipus may not necessarily be one of character in Aristotle's technical sense of that word. Nevertheless, I believe that Aristotle can also accept that heroes even have one or more minor character flaws and still be part of the best plot, as briefly touched on in Chapter 6 above. If they have no flaws whatsoever, then according to Chapter 13, it appears that even if they make some kind of minor mistake, the plot will not be pitiable or fearful but disgusting (*miaron*), were it to show them going from good to bad fortune.

emotions, although it is reasonable to suppose that the *Nicomachean Ethics* does the latter, and only the latter, for him. Thus, on my view of tragedy in (the middle chapters of) the *Dramatics*, pity and fear could be created on purpose by a playwright *not necessarily to be removed entirely or moderated* but to make tragedy sometimes the analog of bittersweet chocolate, which itself should not be cloyingly sweet.[710] In this way, my interpretation differs greatly from most or all of the traditional views, which, typically because of the distorting inclusion of *katharsis* in Chapter 6 and the (ungrounded) misapplication of *Politics* VIII 7, assume that pity and fear are included as a first step to be "catharted," whatever this means. On my account and following Chapters 13 and 14, some, just not all, tragedies as defined by *Dramatics* 1-8, might have pity and fear purposefully included, and purposefully kept by the tragedian for the outcome, as "flavor." In other words, pity and fear can be desirably shown emotions in the right circumstance but would have to be shown in the right way, in the right (moderate) amount, etc. Pity and fear *might* be incorporated to caution the audience as a secondary goal ("the moral of the story is never to get overly angry, and, e.g., to kill a strange man who might be your father if he insults you at a crossroads"). It may even be that a dramatist organizes a serious story, generating pity and fear that are extreme, and then through the resolution of the plot *moderates* them through a *katharsis* as also caused by the drama. He could, if clever enough, conceivably even do it without one of the finest plots, that is, without a complex one (involving by definition reversal or recognition)—rather, he might be able to accomplish it through a simple plot. These considerations do not mean, though, that every other tragedy should follow suit.

Following the Horatian principles that were often combined with Aristotelian ones historically, as we glimpse in the Appendix, the tragedian might even compose his work (but presumably only on occasion) so that, in part or whole, it functions as an educational experience of some type, in line with one of the goals of "music" in *Politics* VIII 7. Nevertheless, the *Dramatics* itself and the rest of the *Politics* clearly show that pleasure or enjoyment is the better, and primary, goal—and here the goal of education, insofar as it applies to tragedy, secondarily functions probably only for adults, as "on-going" education similar to having a "moral to the story." Adults tend to forget certain considerations in the whirlwind of life, and it is sometimes appropriate to remind them of ethical—or practical or political or cultural or romantic—principles. I gave an example of this a few sentences back, with respect to killing a strange man even if he insults you, because it is doubtful that for Aristotle children would be

---

710   Woodruff refreshingly says while introducing the topic of the meaning of catharsis:
  Now, as we shall see, a good tragedy arouses the emotions of pity and fear for appropriate objects, and there is nothing false or corrupting or dirty about pity and fear in themselves or as they are experienced by a tragic audience. It follows that there is nothing foul in our emotions to clean or to purify or to purge, and we are left with a serious problem of interpretation (*op. cit.*, 2009, p. 619).
Halliwell, *op. cit.*, 1986, p. 197, is another, among many, who recognizes at times that pity and fear are not necessarily bad emotions to be drained, in spite of him wishing to keep catharsis in *Dramatics* 6.

educated *per se* in the theater, given the statement in VIII 7 that Doric "music" is for education and the "modes" of action and passion for the theater. Even, this, though is vague, and one could make the argument that *at times* older children or adolescents could, and should, for Aristotle be taken by parents or other caring adults to paradigms of excellent tragedy (which perhaps had some Dorian "music" in it along with minimal passionate "music"). On the other hand, they might be excluded still from specific sub-types that involve extreme suffering, pity, and fear so that the adolescents are not too emotionally affected.

One final comment to finish this section: Those, like Destrée, who need to see the benefit of tragedy *beyond* pleasure on Aristotle's part,[711] in my view do not understand deeply enough Aristotle's ethics or are too Platonic, blindly following Plato in his challenge in *Republic* X: "We would change our mind [about banning tragedy and comedy] if poetry could be shown to be not only pleasurable but beneficial" (607d-e). *Eudaimonia*, short for "(under the protection of) a good (*eu*) demon (*daimon*)," is typically translated as "happiness" and involves pleasure as an end in and of itself for Aristotle in the *Nicomachean Ethics*, at least on the "total goods" view of *Eudaimonia*. That is, *eudaimonia* consists in the totality of goods: health, wealth, friendship, long life, pleasure, "virtue" or excellence, etc. Hence, receiving pleasure from tragedy appears to be sufficient justification in and of itself as part of happiness *per se*. No other benefit is required. On a second common interpretation of *eudaimonia*, the "dominant ends" view, contemplation is what one primarily strives for in life, and the other goods are a means to that end. However, when one goes to tragedy one contemplates it, and indeed, the word for contemplation, *theoria,* stems from "watching at the theater," so contemplating tragedy aligns even more perfectly with Aristotle's notion of happiness. Both the "total goods" view and the "dominant ends" view, then, harmonize very fittingly with the position of those like Veloso, Kraut, and myself, who claim that the best, albeit not necessarily the only, goal of tragedy is intellectual enjoyment or aesthetical enjoyment or a combination of the two (all of which has emotional effects in

---

711    Destrée, *op. cit.*, espec. pp. 30-1. Destrée says that catharsis should have a translation that is ethical without requiring tragedy to be a moral lesson and that any meaning should show the benefit beyond pleasure (in order to reply to Plato's attack). The body of this chapter presents the reasons why Destrée misses the mark on the second conjunct and why the first conjunct is not even relevant for *Dramatics* 6 anymore (given that Aristotle could not have written the word *katharsis* there). Where, however, Destrée touches on the truth is in realizing that, because of *Politics VIII* 7, catharsis *might* be *one* of the secondary benefits of the musical or orchestral arts, and indirectly at least might give *additional* benefits for drama or at least for other theatrical musical arts that could augment Aristotle's use of suitable pleasure as a reply to Plato. To put this in a fuller context, consider another, very incisive and very correct Aristotelian view:

> Aristotle's overall conclusion concerning music is that, since it has 'the power to induce a certain character of the soul…, it must be applied to education, and the young must be educated in it.' Music is all the more valuable in educating the young, says Aristotle, because it is pleasant. This argument will be repeated by many subsequent critics, including Horace and Sidney (Habib, *op. cit.*, p. 49).

any number of ways, depending on the details of any performance). In short, with a proper pleasure, no other benefit is needed, although other benefits may naturally be optional or secondary, and the best dramatists might, as stated at the beginning of this chapter, actually combine multiple goals in many different ways, given my interpretation of Aristotle. It follows that although *on occasion* dramatists *could* instruct, it is *not* their *primary* job to teach values, which is why Lessing and others who antedated or follow Destrée in this respect are wrong, insofar as they suggest the opposite. Rather, dramatists need "only" to understand proper values, at least at some intuitive level (admittedly, not always an easy matter), and incorporate them as necessary in their work; otherwise, they risk alienating the sympathy of audiences and reducing the audience's crucial pleasure in the overall experience. In other words, *ethics is in the service of art*, not vice-versa.

That is it: Aristotle's reply to Plato regarding both tragedy and undue emotions like inappropriate lamentation. Not much was needed but this makes sense, given that Aristotle agrees with his mentor already in so many fundamental ways about life and "tragedy" *qua* serious drama. There is nothing mysterious here for those familiar with Aristotle's ethics, especially if one pays very close attention to the *Dramatics* while ignoring *katharsis* in Chapter 6.[712] If more proof is needed regarding how Aristotle disagrees with Plato without resorting to *katharsis*, it comes in the next section.

## Section 2b: Aristotle's Defense of Comedy against Plato

Plato tenders separate arguments against comedy in *Republic* III and X, albeit interwoven at times with his criticisms of tragedy, and gives reasons for banning it also from the ideal state, reasons that are similar but different from those banning tragedy. How does Aristotle respond in this case? The secondary literature is much sparser on this topic, mainly because the second part of our *Dramatics* appears to be lost unless the *Tractatus Coisilianus* contains at least some authentic passages. Nevertheless, Aristotle's answer to Plato concerning comedy in one way is straightforward and simpler than the "response" to tragedy noted above. Still, that answer in no way involves *katharsis*. Following to

---

[712] What Aristotle does not say in the *Dramatics* is in one way more fascinating than what he does say (although perhaps he at least implies as much in the *Politics*). If pleasure causes one to take on behavior that one normally does not have, as Plato strongly suggests during his attack on drama, then pleasurable treatments of a theme—again, be it with song, dance, verse, spectacle, or plot construction—could equally well cause immoral people (at least those not hopelessly incorrigible) to be better after they see superb tragedy. Plato never considers this option in the context of his attack in the *Republic*, another reason why his total censorship, rather than the more constrained censorship advocated by Aristotle that we explore more below, seems overly reactionary. As one historical account has it (if my memory serves me well, because I have forgotten the source), this might have been a mark of a once aspiring playwright permanently embittered at being rejected by people of the lower classes. Of course, Plato might believe that by adulthood one's character is set, and, to some extent, this is true for Aristotle. However, there is arguably a "grey" period between adolescence and full adulthood (maybe age 12-24) within which young adults are still amenable to very significant change.

some extent Plato of the *Laws* II,⁷¹³ he says in *Politics* VII 17 that:

> the legislator should not allow youth to be spectators of iambi or of comedy until they are of an age to sit at the public tables and to drink strong wine; *by that time education will have armed them against the evil influences of such representations* (1336b19-22, my italics).

(Iambic is the verse form for lampoons, as Aristotle says in *Dramatics* 4, 1448b30-33.) Surely this means, among other things, that Aristotle believes education can inoculate the audience against the criticisms that Plato levels in the *Republic*, namely:

> We should not represent worthwhile people overcome by laughter, because violent changes in mood tend to follow (388e)…

> (Decent people get affected by a hero's lamenting, and the better the poet, the more influential the lamenting will have on even decent people, who will then start pitying themselves inappropriately in real life [605d-606b]…) *The same argument applies to comedy: if you partake in, and therefore encourage, laughter, you increase the chances you will be the butt of jokes in real life* (606c, my italics).

Presumably, Aristotle's short comment in the *Politics* about only allowing youth to see comedy after they can drink strong wine publicly means that for him adults will not have violent changes in mood or even if they do, these changes will not be inimical to character. Indeed, they are probably beneficial—laughter immediately relieving stress or anxiety and replacing it with calmness or delight, just as *katharsis* would and should do, of which more below. Nor will the typical, and properly educated, audience be worried about being the butt of jokes in real life, for they will merely laugh at the behavior of the ugly, ridiculous or vulgar men (who as Aristotle says in *Dramatics* 5 are not painful and destructive, 1449a32-37). The audience will also very easily recognize that they behave probably very differently from the dramatic characters —in effect, turning laughter of the bad or the irrational into the ally of pleasure in the good and the rational.⁷¹⁴ Besides, a proper willingness to engage in self-deprecation at times is often the mark of a witty person, and if the audience realizes they act the same irrational way, they can silently and without public shame make changes to their life. Only the fool thinks that anyone can be perfect. Thus, mocking the bad and reinforcing that some behavior is ridiculous while simultaneously giving a proper pleasure can be very beneficial support for ethical values that were presumably taught in previous circumstances. Nevertheless, comedy cannot go *too* far in being licentious. Aristotle again follows Plato in some respects, indicating:

> There is nothing which the legislator should be more careful to drive away than indecen-

---

713    As the Athenian says: "How then shall we encourage them to take readily to singing? Shall we not pass a law that, in the first place, no children under eighteen may touch wine at all, teaching that it is wrong to pour fire upon fire either in body or in soul…?" (666a, transl. Bury, *op. cit.*).

714    For more on this theme and irrationality being the focus of comedy or laughter, see Richard Patterson, "The Platonic Art of Comedy and Tragedy," *Philosophy and Literature* 6, 1982, (1-2):76-93.

cy of speech… and… clearly we should also banish pictures or speeches from the stage[715] which are indecent…" [*Politics* VII 17, 1336b4ff].

Surprisingly (or not), for Aristotle even comedy involves an ethical dimension. Nevertheless, this dimension is secondary for him in one sense, even if it is more fundamental in another. That is, similar to the tragedian, the comedian's primary task is not to instruct, merely to understand somehow proper values and presuppose them in developing best the plot, dialogue, choral music and dance, and comic aspects. However, this need not restrict the comedian, like Aristophanes, from perhaps secondarily engaging in the goals of VIII 7 or even combining the goal of enjoyment with such ends as "adult" education or political satire or, as we shall see, *katharsis*. In the *Frogs,* Aeschylus asks Euripides what he looks for in a good dramatist and the latter replies, "Technical skill—and he should teach a lesson, make people into better citizens."[716] Although Aristotle would undoubtedly agree with the remark about technical skill, he would relegate the teaching to a secondary goal. That is, *especially given his chapter-long discussion in the Nicomachean Ethics IV 8 of wit and proper laughter as a virtue between boorishness and buffoonery*, he would remind Aristophanes that the comedian's own goal is not necessarily to teach but to provide the equivalent proper pleasure (with the appropriate values subsumed, perhaps in line with *Dramatics* 15). Indeed, as Halliwell has brilliantly observed in his *Greek Laughter*, this chapter of the *Nicomachean Ethics* reveals Aristotle's system to be one of the only ethical systems, if not the only one, that makes wit a virtue—so even in getting people to laugh *correctly*, one is making them better![717]

---

715   AnonC correctly says "from the stage" is missing in the Greek, but what is there—*praxeōn mimēsin*—surely covers such types of representation, given their place in Athenian life and given the same words in the definition of tragedy in *Dramatics* 6. Thus, Jowett's translation arguably is allowable, and my point still holds. I accept, though, AnonC's possible astute implication that the banishment for Aristotle should also be in other places that involve *praxeōn mimēsin*, and for us that would include perhaps journalism and documentaries. Of course, the crucial consideration becomes how we define "indecent." Also, nothing is implied as far as I can tell whether adults can watch "indecent" actions in private, and Aristotle's lack of criticism of the sacred rites that apparently had orgiastic behavior at times suggests he only speaks of public performance in VII 17, especially if funded by the state.

716   Ll. 1009-1010, *op. cit.*, tr. Barrett.

717   Stephen Halliwell, *Greek Laughter* (Cambridge Univ. Pr., NY) 2008. Halliwell says: "Aristotle's is the most sophisticated attempt made in antiquity to reach a philosophical accommodation with laughter, indeed literally to make a virtue out of it" (p. 307). AnonC says, in his unfailing attempt to question almost every major point I made in the earlier draft:

> In *EE* [*Eudemian Ethics*] 3.7 wittiness is one of several dispositions which Aristotle does not count as virtues, since they relate to affects without *prohairesis* (1234a24-30). In *NE* [*Nicomachean Ethics*] 2.7 he classifies things differently, but it is not clear even here that he counts wittiness as a virtue strictly speaking. (He does, of course, still think that it is a good thing.)"

*Prohairesis* is "choice" or "volition" or the like. Leaving aside the discrepancy between the *EE* and the *NE*, which is beyond the scope of this book, it is puzzling why AnonC doubts Aristotle considers wit a "virtue strictly speaking" in the *NE*. It is listed there as an intermediate, or mean, between buffoonery and boorishness, as the

## Chapter 7: The Real Goal of Tragedy and Aristotle's Response to Plato

Again, then, we have a concise and clear answer to Plato, if one calls it an answer, rather than a substantially overlapping agreement because *initially* the account very much follows Platonic principles for youth and accepts banishment of indecent pictures or speeches. Equally clear, though, is that Aristotle then diverges from his mentor concerning *adults*: *They* would be able to see comedy, even though *Dramatics* 2 and 5 acknowledge that it represents "inferior" or "vulgar" men. The reason, again, is the audience's education—part of which is spelled out in *Politics* VII and VIII and part of which involves the doctrine of the mean, with its own relevant emphasis on habits (which is an integral part of training for Aristotle). Other theory of the *Nicomachean Ethics* fills in the blanks.

I also believe that Aristotle speaks only of comedy and not tragedy with respect to restricting youths until they are old enough to drink strong wine publicly. The implication is that youth (maybe 13-18?) could see tragedy, if only for pleasure or for habituation in the right kind of pleasure. The reasons are these: In *Dramatics* 26, Aristotle ranks tragedy above epic with explicit reasons that I discussed in great detail in Chapter 2. Often scholars assume that comedy always comes below tragedy and even below epic for him, even though Aristotle never says that anywhere. Indeed, at times Aristotle praises comedy over tragedy, for example, for having used universals in the plot before tragedy (*Dramatics* 9). Nevertheless, even if the other positive comments about comedy in *Dramatics* 2 through 9 entice us to accept that, for him, comedy and tragedy can be equally beneficial art forms for adults in their own right, at least at times, it is impossible I contend that for Aristotle tragedy would be *always* a lesser art form than comedy, especially regarding morality.[718] Therefore, those youth close to adult-

---

same kind of "intermediate" that includes truthfulness and modesty (*NE* 2.7, 1108a23-26). I link arms, then, with Halliwell on this issue.

718      I stress "in their own right." Whether comedy is ranked equal with tragedy and above epic is unknown. Take a common position:
> Also classical in outlook is Aristotle's insistence on distinguishing clearly between different genres in a hierarchical manner: comedy, which deals with "low" characters and trivial matter, ranks lowest; epic, which includes various plots and lengthy narration, falls below tragedy, which is more concentrated and produces a greater effect of unity (Habib, *op. cit.*, p. 60).

Tragedy is argued to be better than epic in Chapter 26. Yet Aristotle does *not* bring comedy into this comparison, and it would be fascinating to see how he compared it with tragedy *and to epic*, were we to discover any lost chapter in which he ranks them all. On the surface, comedy has advantages over epic, in the same way that tragedy does, regarding choral song, dance, and spectacle, and in being more compressed; on the other hand, it deals with "inferior" men or maybe with vulgar themes. In any event, it is hard to see why the competition about the best dramatist in, for example, the *Frogs* is a "trivial matter." The *Frogs* is without question a comedy and yet it deals with three great poets (Aeschylus, Sophocles, and Euripides) and Dionysus. Epic deals with good characters, but always more than comedies like the *Frogs*? There are thoroughly nasty scoundrels in epic. Regarding tragedy and comedy, both have spectacle, music, and dance, and a greater intensity because of a shorter duration than epic, so they are equal in that respect. Other considerations would necessarily enter and determine the matter. Does comedy, e.g., give more catharsis to help it, even though tragedy has the advantage of showing good men? One can only speculate on these topics but I would not assume Aristotle places tragedy and

hood would presumably be allowed to see tragedy, or at least tragedy properly done in all respects. This final qualification is important, and I am not claiming that the adolescents, especially the very young ones, could or would see *all* types or sub-types of tragedy or would experience tragedy in and of itself *necessarily* for education, in the sense that it was a required part of rearing. Rather it would be optional and might harden any good ethical principles they have already learned, but perhaps only learned abstractly, that is, the principles that have not been applied to (at least a few) particular cases, especially if "tragedies of (good) character" were the type that they were allowed to see. Aristotle himself growing up in Stagira had no access to tragedy (as a full spectacular theatre art), although perhaps he saw wandering bands of "Thespians." He therefore presumably realized it was not absolutely crucial for education, but still he might have seen its value for others or himself once in Athens. There is a very good chance he saw as much of it as he could after joining the Academy at 18 years of age.

I acknowledge that in the *Politics* Aristotle discusses Theodorus, whom he calls a tragic actor (at 1336b29) when he explains his reasons (in the passage we just read above about wine) for keeping the youth away from "such representations" as comedy. Theoretically, it is possible that "such representations" refers to drama in general, including tragedy, but I believe the discussion suggests that Aristotle refers only to comedic or evil representations. Theodorus is cited as a way to emphasize that we like what we see first, so children should first see (only) good things. Hence, Aristotle might well have allowed adolescents into admirable tragedies while excluding them from mediocre ones (along with *all* comedy) in his ideal *polis*. We see, though, that these issues start getting too complicated for our current needs, and so I leave the topic for future examination.

To summarize this section: Aristotle follows Plato with respect not only to preventing the youth from seeing comedy but to banning indecent speeches and depictions for all, so indeed Aristotle accepts *partial* censorship for theatrical events (if only for at least state-funded events, say, the "competitions"). However, the "provincial" Stagirite who gets associated with Macedonia[719] does not follow his

---

epic *always* above comedy, in all respects, as the Western dramatic tradition invariably, and in my view rashly, tends to assume, especially taking into account *Dramatics* 9, as mentioned above and given the statements by the Neo-Platonists Iamblichus and Proclus. Certainly, I would not claim without *much* more evidence that comedy is *necessarily* lower than epic for Aristotle. Both Aristophanes and, e.g., Molière chose to create comedy, not epic, which suggests what two great artists themselves thought of the latter art form.

719   Aristotle's birthplace, Stagira, is part of the Chalcidian peninsula in modern-day Northern Greece. It is often reported that Aristotle was Macedonian, because of the ties of his father, physician to King Philip and the Macedonian court (and I once wrongly said the same thing myself, in print). However, for a better, more in-depth view on this matter, see Natali, *op. cit.*, 2013, pp. 6-8. Based on his book, we can safely call Aristotle "a Northern Greek." I wish to suggest (not only because of my own and Natali's book) that remarkably this man from an area with no significant record of full dramatic performances develops as an adult a sophisticated and grounded theory of musical drama, including tragedy and comedy, which typically for aestheticians grounds

## Chapter 7: The Real Goal of Tragedy and Aristotle's Response to Plato

sophisticated, urban Athenian mentor with respect to completely banning drama: every adult can see any tragedy (because it ideally at least concentrates on good characters, appropriately shown), and perhaps some adolescents can see some sub-types or examples of tragedy also (like tragedy of character). Moreover, adults can see comedy. A proper education, then, not *katharsis*, protects adults from comedy, and by implication also protects them from tragedies with bad conduct, such as those with heroes unsuitably lamenting or clever villains sometimes acting inappropriately, even if the villains are pleasurably expressed on stage (using all the means of mimesis) by otherwise excellent dramatists. All of this supports my arguments above relating to the *Nicomachean Ethics* and reflects that Aristotle's Core Principle of Virtue helps counter Plato's attacks on tragedy (when Aristotle does not agree with his mentor).

In finishing, let me stress an additional, explicit agreement of Aristotle and Plato on the topic of *katharsis*. We have also seen above that Plato uses *katharsis* extensively in his own theories, and thus in at least some way Aristotle's recommendation of specific practices which result in *katharsis* was very Platonic. Recall, for example, the discussion of Griffith and Korybantism in Chapter 1 above, and in particular that in the *Laws* VII, 790d-791a: The Athenian Stranger (presumably representing Plato himself), after noting that nurses treat fractious babies better with motion (rocking in the arms) than with stillness and with tunes rather than silence, recommends the Bacchic rite for those suffering from Korybantism. He says further that the source is fear (*phobos*) in the soul and he lauds the music and dance necessary to cause the external shaking to overpower the internal frenzy and to calm the person. Aristotle follows his mentor in this regard in VIII 7 and suggests that not only music but bodily movement is a crucial part of sacred rituals and that *katharsis* often results. We saw this above in Chapter 4 when discussing the passage with "frenziedness." Far, then, from hoisting Plato on Plato's own petard here, Aristotle follows him in using motion and music to provide relief. Therefore, anyone arguing that *katharsis* is Aristotle's weapon against his mentor would have to handle this kind of case.

---

most of Western dramatic theory. This is a tribute not only to Plato's inspiration and core values but to Aristotle's own wide-ranging curiosity and ability to explain a vast number of important topics. Developing philosophical expertise "only" requires a (good) mentor or three; understanding well musical drama at a philosophical level—and debating a sophisticated mentor's expertise effectively—requires also time-consuming experience of very complex, expensive-to-produce, and thus relatively infrequent events.

*Aristotle on Dramatic Musical Composition*

# Chapter 8: The Real Role of Catharsis and the Importance of Comedy

We are now ready to grasp how *katharsis* might truly function in Aristotle's theory of the theatrical arts, as presented in the *Dramatics* and *Politics*. To summarize what we know from the previous chapters: In the extant texts, *katharsis* functions as the primary goal of tragedy neither in the *Dramatics* nor *Politics* VIII nor anywhere else (like the *Nicomachean Ethics*) in any way whatsoever. Nor is *katharsis* ever used by Aristotle in extant texts to help counter Plato's attacks on tragedy or comedy. Aristotle indicates that *katharsis* is useful at times in the musical arts in VIII 7 when he expressly replies to criticisms there from the *Republic* pertaining to the Phrygian mode (as used, e.g., with the dithyramb) or when he speaks of therapeutic results of the sacred rites and related practices, one—but only one—of which I have deduced might be a sub-type of tragedy. Even then the *katharsis* would be a secondary benefit behind enjoyment. I should also repeat that the only other time in *Politics* VIII that Aristotle uses *katharsis* is in Chapter 6 at 1341a23. The *aulos* should be used not in education but for exciting (*orgiastikon*) performances that have the effect of *katharsis*. Again, this remark suggests events like sacred rites or dithyramb as much as, or more than, tragedy.

What else do we know that can help us determine how Aristotle applied *katharsis*, given that it seems impossible that *katharsis* was initially explained in, and applied to, our extant *Dramatics*? Only two realistic possibilities exist, given the reference in VIII 7 *en tois peri poiētikēs*: *katharsis* was explained in the part of the *Dramatics* on comedy that is lost,[720] as briefly presented before when discussing Halliwell, or the notion was examined in a book with a similar title, completely lost. That book could be the earlier *On Poets* (= *On "Musical" Composers*, in my view, given the arguments about the Diotiman meaning of *poiētēs*) or one of the many other books that Diogenes Laertius lists Aristotle wrote on music, drama, and poetry.[721] Of course, *katharsis* might have been explained both in an early and later work. Other considerations suggesting that the explanation of *katharsis* was either in a treatment of comedy or in another lost work (which could also have included comedy) are the following. Halliwell, who gives perhaps the first rigorous chronological study of the age of the *Dramatics,* says this treatise had its roots in Aristotle's early thought but received attention in the late years and "is perhaps most likely, as it stands...the first book of a treatise used for instruction in the full course of study and enquiry offered in the Lyceum during the last decade and a half of Aristotle's life."[722] Woodruff also concludes: "We seem to have everything he [Aristotle] wrote about tragedy."[723]

---

720   Or that is perhaps saved in part in the *Tractatus*.
721   Diogenes Laertius, *op. cit.*
722   Halliwell, 1986, p. 330.
723   Woodruff, 2009, p. 620.

I myself noted the stunning omission of satyr plays, which were always included in (performed) tragedy before Aristotle took a thirteen-year hiatus from Athens and which were not included when he returned. Unless sections of Chapter 4 are lost, the omission gives further evidence that the treatise was written, or at least finalized, late in Aristotle's life. To return, though, to *On Poets/On "Musical" Composers* (*peri poiētōn* in three books, according to Diogenes Laertius): As alluded to above, it sometimes got confused with our *Dramatics*, according to Janko. As he indicates:

> The *On Poets*, sometimes called by the same title as the *Poetics* in antiquity, was one of Aristotle's "exoteric" or published works. These were in dialogue form ... it was also read and quoted more widely, at least until late antiquity, when the *Poetics* drove it out of circulation, perhaps because of a mistaken belief that the esoteric works contained Aristotle's "real" or "secret" teaching.[724]

What can we now determine from all of this evidence, scant as it is, leaving aside the option that Aristotle himself drove *On Poets/On "Musical" Composers* out of circulation because his views had matured? First, even if some commentators called two works by the same title, Aristotle could not have been confused about his own books, and he also speaks at the very end of Chapter 15 of his "published works"(*ekdedomenois logois*), which are universally agreed to be the exoteric works like *peri poiētōn*. Thus, he would not have said *en tois peri poiētikēs* in VIII 7 if he had meant *peri poiētōn* or *ekdedomenois logois*. Unless, then, *peri poiētikēs* refers to a wholly lost work, we can deduce that it implies the work which starts off with precisely those words, our own *Dramatics*. However, again, even if that other work is lost, there is no reason that Aristotle could not be repeating some of that discussion in the *Dramatics*, especially if the concept being discussed is even as remotely important as, say, pleasure, which itself is discussed throughout the *Dramatics*, *Politics* and *Nicomachean Ethics*. In summary, because *katharsis* is never explained (or applied where we would expect) in the extant *Dramatics*, the best option given the textual evidence is that it was examined in the lost part on comedy. Dacier, then, was correct as have been some more recent commentators like W. D. Ross, as I recounted above and as I recount more in the Appendix. However, contrary to what Dacier and others following him assumed, why that explanation would *not* have been applied back to tragedy or epic or both in any fundamental way was already discussed above with respect to Halliwell, because of what Aristotle says at the end of Chapter 26, namely, that the discussion of tragedy and epic is finished.

The conclusion that *katharsis* was explained in the lost section on comedy seems supported by what we began to discuss in Chapter 4. Let us review and then continue that discussion. What was clear was that in *Politics* VIII 7 *poiēsis* seems to be used for musical art, with the given examples being the Phrygian mode, oboe-playing, and the dithyramb. Presumably, then, *poiētikē* has a similar meaning. Aristotle is not using the term in the broad sense of "production" in VIII 7. Likewise, he is not using

---

[724] *Op. cit.*, 1987, p. 175.

## Chapter 8: The Real Role of Catharsis and the Importance of Comedy

it in the Gorgian sense. The reason is, again, that no purely literary art or any other art than "music" (as orchestral art) is in the discussion of VIII 7 (or VIII 5-6). Hence, to use *poiētikē* in a way different from "musical composition" would mean that within a few sentences Aristotle changes the sense of a group of words based on *poiēsis,* with no obvious change of context, which is possible but not at all likely. As merely introduced before, this leaves three good alternatives for the meaning of *poiētikē* and hence the kind of treatise he is possibly referring to. From broadest to narrowest, the meanings are: (1) "art" via synecdoche, given *Dramatics* 25 where he mentions "*poiētikēs* and other arts (*technes*)"; (2) Diotima's "narrow" usage as "'music' [in the Greek sense] along with verse;" or (3) Aristotle's own sense in the *Dramatics* as the slightly restricted Diotiman one, "*dramatic* musical composition."

I suggested at the end of Chapter 4 that Aristotle may refer to a treatise different from our *Dramatics* because there is no evidence that dithyramb, which is highlighted in *Politics* VIII 7, is to be discussed in the section on comedy. However, on reflection, that suggestion is too hasty. The textual evidence strongly suggests that *poiētikē* has to mean his own sense as found in the *Dramatics*, for these reasons: First, even though Aristotle only promises to discuss comedy, he may have compared or contrasted it to dithyramb concerning a few points, and we have no evidence that dithyramb was *not* discussed briefly. Second, regarding "*poiētikēs* and other arts (*technes*)," the beginning of *Dramatics* 25 has Aristotle introducing painting and other "image-making," so the "*other* arts" (rather than the "similar arts," which he could have written) are presumably arts like these, and *poiētikēs* therefore seemingly, although not conclusively, has the meaning it has at the beginning of the *Dramatics*, which I have shown is music-verse-dance-plot. This supports then (3), if only very lightly.[725] More importantly, the evidence of the *Rhetoric*, which many other scholars have noted independently of my work, supports all of this. In that treatise, one finds two occurrences of the exact same reference as in *Politics* VIII 7 when Aristotle speaks of discussing the ludicrous *en tois peri poiētikēs* (I 11, 1372a1) and when, in mentioning Gorgias combating earnestness with jests and vice versa, he indicates that jests have been classified *en tois peri poiētikēs* (III 18, 1419b5). These references about jests rule out a treatise on (the theory of) aural music *per se*. Language had to have been at least part of the discussion also. It seems probable, then, that our *Dramatics* (in its extended form with a lost section on comedy) is meant, and indeed, as I noted once before, the categorization of jests that exists in the *Tractatus* strikes me as one authentic Aristotelian part, if the only one there, and is probably what the *Rhetoric* is referencing.

---

725    Even if, as some believe, Chapter 25 is from the *Homeric Problems* and Aristotle is primarily discussing epic, I have already shown that it has the three means of mimesis in its own way, plus the secondary notion of plot as given in Chapter 23. At the worse, the two senses of *poiētikēs*—Diotima's and Aristotle's own—could very easily have been differentiated at the Lyceum, in lecture.

Recall again, now, our discussion above of the Neo-Platonists reporting Aristotle countering Plato with "satisfaction of the emotions in due measure" through purification[726] of the emotions with respect to *both* tragedy and comedy *in the dialogue* against Plato, i.e., the early book known as "*On Poets/On "Musical" Composers.*"[727] Given all of the above, the reasonable options for where *katharsis* was "explained" by Aristotle follow:

- He applied *katharsis* to both tragedy and comedy in *On "Musical" Composers* and dropped it for *both* arts in the *Dramatics* (but the complete omission seems ruled out by *Politics* and *Rhetoric*).
- He applied *katharsis* only to comedy (and not tragedy) in *On "Musical" Composers* and then either kept it in the lost text of *Dramatics* or dropped it as he got older (but this option is ruled out by the Neo-Platonists, with respect to the early dialogue, and by the *Politics* and *Rhetoric* with respect to the *Dramatics*).
- He applied *katharsis* only to tragedy in *On "Musical" Composers* and then dropped it in later years for tragedy in *The Dramatics* (but this is ruled out by the Neo-Platonists).
- He applied *katharsis* to both tragedy and comedy in *On "Musical" Composers* and dropped it for tragedy, but left it as a, or the, goal of comedy when he wrote the *Dramatics* (this is consistent with *Politics, Rhetoric*, and the Neo-Platonists).

The last option, then, is the most viable one.[728] Whatever the circumstance with the earlier *On "Musical" Composers* (a.k.a. *On Poets*), *katharsis* was only explained in the *Dramatics* in the lost section on comedy and then presumably applied only crucially to comedy (and perhaps to satyr plays, if that

---

726    The term that Proclus uses is not catharsis but a synonym, *aphosiōsis* (expiation, purification). Iamblichus uses *katharsis*.

727    It is fitting to give here an example of how classicists in general have misconstrued the issue for generations (and I certainly have made my own mistakes, as the Postscript in Chapter 5 above shows). Destrée says (*op. cit.*, 2011, p. 15) in speaking about catharsis in *Dramatics* 6, in a phrase that I partially examined in another context: "D'un point de vue strictement philologique et historique, notre texte n'a rien de suspect. Rappelons que Jamblique, puis Proclus parlent d'une catharsis comique et tragique en se référant à Aristote…" ["From a strictly philological or historical point of view, our text has nothing suspicious. We recall that Iamblichus, then Proclus speak of a comic and tragic catharsis while referring to Aristotle."] Thus, Destrée assumes that catharsis in *Dramatics* 6 is warranted, as evidenced by these two Neo-Platonists. However, the Neo-Platonists referred to Aristotle's previous work or they had no idea the *Dramatics* had been corrupted if they even had access to it or both. *Nothing* the Neo-Platonists say point to catharsis being precisely in *Dramatics* 6 as opposed to some other Aristotelian text, especially the more known, exoteric one; cf. Veloso, *op. cit.*, 2007, pp. 256-7.

728    Rashed says: "Aristote traitait de la *catharsis* à l'occasion de son discours sur la comédie. C'est à ce passage qu'il fait référence au livre VIII de la *Politique* (*op. cit.*, p. 18). ["Aristotle treated catharsis during his discourse on comedy. It is to this passage that he makes reference in book VIII of the *Politics*" (my transl.]" I myself eagerly await more details in the future from Rashed regarding catharsis in comedy, for his short article only laid the basic groundwork.

genre was discussed there also). I have recognized that Aristotle might have *remarked* in the lost section on comedy how *katharsis* or some sub-type of *katharsis* could be applied *peripherally* to a, or the, sub-type of tragedy that has pity and fear. However, anyone proposing this has to explain away the goal of tragedy with pity and fear in *Dramatics* 14 as pleasure, which may not be difficult to do, if, as in *Politics* VIII 7, the pleasure comes as a result of the relief from *katharsis*. Nevertheless, any explanation of how *katharsis* in the lost manuscript applies to tragedy (or to epic or both) would entail even more discussion of tragedy (and of epic) after the final statement of *Dramatics* 26 that the discussion of tragedy and epic is finished. Furthermore, recall the possibility that the satyr play may have generated *katharsis* in a tragic tetralogy. If the satyr play could accomplish the phenomenon for the antecedent trilogy, what we call tragedies, with horrible endings, then comedy may well have done something similar, for reasons that follow. I should acknowledge immediately, though, that the following is mere guesswork, if educated guesswork, and that future research and scholarship would determine the most plausible and most precise answers. The best that we can do now, given the current textual evidence, is to state the scope of *katharsis* in the context of the "musical" arts that include language as a part. We have no idea what Aristotle said (apart from what I suggested above), although perhaps some previous commentators throughout five centuries, in trying to solve the mystery of what *katharsis* in *Dramatics* 6 meant, lucked upon some of the points. Nevertheless, to emphasize a final time, even if tragedy was one kind of theatrical experiences for which *katharsis* was (at least sometimes) applicable, Aristotle seemingly discussing *katharsis* in the lost comic portion of the *Dramatics* entails that *katharsis* has much more relevance to comedy (or to "music" or music composed for comedy) for him than to tragedy.[729]

How or why, then, might *katharsis* have been used by Aristotle to show the benefit of comedy or of "music" and—perhaps secondarily—of some, and only some, sub-type(s) of tragedy? Starting with the last option: Stripped of the burden now of reconciling how *katharsis* has to apply to all tragedy, researchers can more effectively explore when *katharsis* might have been applicable *on occasion* for

---

[729] Comedy in earlier, lost Aristotelian work may well have had a broader sense than is found in our *Dramatics* and may have included satyr plays. Cf. Watson (2012, pp. 137-8), who has some intriguing thoughts about the genre,—thoughts which can be appreciated even if one accepts, as I do, that possibly the only authentic part of the *Tractatus Coisilianus* may be the categorization of jests. In my view, Watson's book repays reading for graduate students as interested in general Aristotelian principles as for aesthetical ones, even if it is to become also with respect to the *Tractatus per se* "widely admired and widely disbelieved," a phrase I borrow from him and one that was originally applied to Janko's similar work on comedy (*op. cit.*, 1984). To start laying any groundwork (or not) for why satyr play may have been discussed in the lost manuscript on comedy and because we have already seen that the satyr play may have been responsible for a *katharsis qua* relief, see Griffith, *Greek Satyr Play, op. cit.*, 2015, pp. 16ff. Griffith describes the similarities (and differences) between the satyr play and Old Comedy before presenting the benefits of satyr plays themselves, whether already recognized or newly formulated by himself.

Aristotle to tragedy. Even then *katharsis* will probably be a secondary goal, aiming ultimately toward pleasure (as indicated by the "pleasure in pity and fear" of *Dramatics* 14). One might take much from the existing massive secondary literature on *katharsis*, but that literature must be employed with great caution. With regard to the second art form, "music," and to extend my brief comments in Chapter 5: Although the current professions of music therapy and dance therapy offer interesting hints on what Aristotle *might* have said, I will not begin to speculate here on his view of *katharsis* in music and dance (including those in the sacred rituals). Again, if suitably qualified, the previous research on *katharsis* may apply at least at times to music and dance themselves. One place to start is perhaps with Iamblichus, who is cited by Janko, and who arguably antedates Freud's notion of repression by about 2000 years, as we saw in part once before:[730]

> Some of the ceremonies that are regularly carried out in the holy places ... produce what is useful for us, or purify (*kathairei*) us in some way and release our emotions as human beings, or avert some other of the evils that can happen to us... *The potentialities of the human emotions that are in us become more violent if they are hemmed in on every side.* But if they are briefly put into activity and to the point of due proportion they feel delight in moderation, are satisfied and, purified (*apokathairomen*) by this means, are halted by persuasion and not by force. For this reason, by *observing* others' emotions *in both comedy and tragedy*, we can check our own emotions, render them more moderate and purify them, and by *seeing and hearing* shameful things in some of the holy rites we are released from the harm that derives from them in actuality [my italics] (Iamblichus, *On The Mysteries 1.11*).[731]

Again, notice that it is not only aural music but *visual* activity that is the focus here, all of which, as suggested before, supports my reading of *Politics* VIII 7, which itself discusses *katharsis* relative to the sacred rites and indirectly to other arts like dithyramb. That is, "Seeing...shameful things" helps confirm my view that the *melos* of the sacred rites in *Politics* VIII 7 is not just tune but the associated body movement.

With regard, however, to comedy, the focus of the rest of this chapter: Maybe Aristotle spoke of laughter lightening the soul, following obvious empirical evidence, giving relief and *katharsis* in that way (and "gallows humor" is a similar phenomenon long known). Maybe he developed his virtue of

---

730   In spite of my disagreements with him on the nature of tragedy, Janko is one of the scholars most deserving of praise for having helped piece together recently discovered fragments in order to give us all more insights into ancient aesthetical theory. For another take on Janko's work, though, and why he should not be perhaps exploiting that material always in exactly the manner he wants, see Malcolm Heath, "Aristotle *On Poets*: A Critical Evaluation of Richard Janko's Edition of the Fragments," *Studia Humaniora Tartuensia*, vol. 14.A.1 (2013), ISSN 1406-6203, http://sht.ut.ee.

731   Richard Janko, *Philodemus: ON POEMS, Books 3-4 with the fragments of Aristotle ON POETS* [The Philodemus Translation Project: *Philodemus: The Aesthetic Works*, Volume I/3, Series Editors D.L. Blank, R. Janko, D. Obbink] (Oxford: Oxford Univ. Pr.) 2011, pp. 458-9.

## Chapter 8: The Real Role of Catharsis and the Importance of Comedy

wit and its relation to laughter from the chapter that is too often neglected in the context of the issues of this book, *Nicomachean Ethics* IV 8, and applied that virtue to comic drama ("virtue" is used here in the classic Greek sense of excellence, not, as I mention for non-Greek specialists, in the modern Victorian sense that often implies chastity). Maybe the effectiveness of satyr plays was additional empirical evidence for him for the worth of *katharsis* in a comic representation, as I suggested above with Hall's account of satyr drama "sending its spectator out...not only laughing rather than crying but reassured of his place in a joyous...collective."[732] These issues are not simple, though. We should not forget that Plato at *Philebus* 48a declares via Socrates that "the spectators of a tragedy sometimes feel pleasure and weep at once," and that at 50b he adds "when we see a comedy, do you realize that here again we have a mixture of pain and pleasure?" This last quotation verifies some commonality between tragedy and comedy (of both having pleasure and pain) that I alluded to before (in discuss-

---

732  Hall, *op. cit.*, 2010, p. 237. I re-iterate that this is the type of reason why someone *might* argue comedy or satyr play is better *at times* than tragedy, whether or not Aristotle did it in his lost work, especially if the comic dramatist is as brilliant as Aristophanes.

A final remark on the satyr play: I had doubts about Mark Griffith's views regarding Aristotle and the satyr play for the following reasons. Griffith does not acknowledge that the satyr play could have been covered in lost texts, such as in *Dramatics* 4 or a manuscript on comedy. Nor does he realize that pity and fear may not apply at many times in the relevant way to *tragōidia* as an art form that, like the *Cresphontes*, can end happily. Nor does he consider the ramifications of Aristotle having a "tri-focal" ethical view of drama in *Dramatics* 2 as representing those "better, equal to, or worse than ourselves" when Griffith considers the Northern Greek to have a limited "bi-focal" view of the historical practice. Nevertheless, his *Greek Satyr Play: Five Studies*, op. cit., 2015, is an excellent introduction to the genre as a whole and the new scholarly interest in it.

I should add a private, gracious reply by Griffith in response to correspondence that shows more agreement between our views than might be gleaned merely by reading *Greek Satyr Play* and that addresses my concern about Aristotle's "bi-focal" view:

> My decision to begin the 'Middlebrow' article by referring to Aristotle's largely binary organization (high/low, tragedy/comedy, 2 books) of *Peri Poiêtikês*, with one book focusing primarily on tragedy, the other focusing on {something else, apparently = "comedy"}, was not intended to amount to an absolute declaration that Aristotle had no room for a discussion of satyr-drama, or that he cared all that much about 2 vs 3 divisions of drama (or "*poiesis*" in general). It was intended as a starting-point for my rather (too) wide-ranging exploration of several different eras and theorists of Greek dramatic (and other) genres. I usually think of Aristotle as a thinker who is (admirably) comfortable shifting his analytical structures from one context to another; so if you prefer to insist that he really thinks of drama as essentially functioning in three genres, rather than two, I have no quarrel with you (April 29, 2018).

Again, in my view and depending on the lost manuscripts, Aristotle may have considered satyr play *either* a subgenre of a whole *theoretical* genre of comedy (different from the historical tradition of specific Athenian comedy) or a third type of drama. I say this in spite of Griffith astutely observing that "In particular, I show...that the vocabulary of satyr drama is in general very closely aligned with that of tragedy (and not with that of comedy), most notably in the usage of compound adjectives..." (*Greek Satyr Play*, p. 11). For Aristotle, language is only one element that gives part of the total *dunamis* of a dramatic form. I make no commitment and emphasize Aristotle may have held either position but hope that Griffith's own very impressive work in general and the research he cites may one day help give us an answer to my particular questions.

ing the double structure of Chapter 13 with Aegisthus and Orestes leaving as friends). I believe this commonality is too unrecognized in Aristotelian exegesis.[733]

At any rate, maybe comedy (at least New Comedy) was more relevant in this situation than the satyr play, because the latter may have been too vulgar for the Athenians of Aristotle's time, even if comedy was similar to it in some respects. Hence comedy may have had a more appropriate *katharsis*, similar to the kind associated rightly or wrongly for centuries with tragedy (again, I emphasize that there may be different kinds of *katharsis* for Aristotle, just as there are different pleasures). Urbane Athenians may have been so bored by slapstick satyrs that they never experienced the sought-after, most desirable *katharsis* in that respect. However, on some accounts satyr plays also had become fairly sophisticated by Aristotle's time, and Griffith's new work that I have cited throughout this book, *Greek Satyr Play* provides more evidence, if unintended, for this conclusion. There are a host of other options, and with respect to some of the most recent work in this area, Sorabji imagines (with suitable caveats) what emotions comedy might have catharted, even though unsurprisingly he follows the traditional view that *Politics* VIII 7 refers to tragedy and that *katharsis* is legitimate in *Dramatics* 6.[734] Another rich source, although more for establishing the context of comedy, laughter, and wit in ancient Greece than for getting at the precise issues in this chapter's setting, is the aforementioned *Greek Laughter* by Halliwell. He remains non-committal there on whether and how *katharsis* was applicable to comedy for Aristotle and directly spends but one sentence on the whole matter, persuasively saying:

> Whether or not he [Aristotle] believed that comic drama in the theatre involved a *katharsis* of its audiences' emotions (perhaps by aligning laughter not with hostile derision but with an ethically moderate response to human foibles), he does seem to have regarded the virtuous enjoyment of laughter in circumstances of social relaxation as a kind of implicit

---

[733] A recent article by Paul Schollmeier takes the unusual, but worthwhile, tack of finding some commonality in tragedy and comedy ("Aristotle on Comedy," in *International Philosophical Inquiry*, Vol. 40, Num. 3-4, Spring-Summer 2016, 146-162). Although I disagree with a number of his points because he assumes the legitimacy of catharsis, pity, and fear for all tragedy, nevertheless I appreciate his fresh look at the issues on comedy.

[734] *Op. cit.* 2000. See pp. 24-5 for Sorabji's unquestioned acceptance of the catharsis clause in *Dramatics* 6, but also for an illuminating summary (concerning pity and fear) of the differences and similarities between the *Dramatics* and the *Rhetoric*. More to the point regarding catharsis in comedy, and how it might pertain to, e.g., contempt or scorn, see pp. 288-93. Sorabji is one of the few who keeps in mind that pity and fear get listed along with *enthousiasmos* in *Politics* VIII 7, and he discusses the latter at times. I have yet to understand, though, why he and others translate *enthousiasmos in this context* as "ecstasy" (or in other cases "enthusiasm" or "religious excitement"), for reasons given before pertaining to how it seems slightly pathological for Aristotle. Moreover, how Sorabji can also think that the one use of *poiēsis* in VIII 7 at 1342b4 means "poetry" when he is very clear that the discussion there is about "music" and not drama is also beyond me, but since that translation, as discussed in Chapter 4 in great detail, appears to have been an article of faith for hundreds of years for the entire profession, it might have been much more surprising had he taken a different stance. Sorabji introduces other fascinating points about the place of comedy and laughter into Christian times, which I recommend.

## Chapter 8: The Real Role of Catharsis and the Importance of Comedy

'education' of pleasures and sensibilities.[735]

That comedy is also used in general to effect *katharsis*, at least today, is I believe shown albeit unintentionally by Woodruff. He says in his "The Paradox of Comedy," which, like Hall's account regarding the satyr play earlier noted, never once uses the term *katharsis* in the whole article:

> The obvious virtue of laughter is that it takes objects that might otherwise engage our emotions and puts them outside the circle of our deepest concerns. If an embattled people can see their enemies as ridiculous, they will find them less terrifying; and those who can laugh at the unfortunate are spared the discomfort of pity. We are the same in relation to ourselves: a peaceful detachment comes with the gift of laughter at ourselves or our own circumstances. Generally, laughter negatives emotion, and comedy serves our lives *by detaching us from what would otherwise be painful emotions.*
>
> ... in theater laughter functions (as sometimes in real life) *to allow for the release of emotions otherwise too powerful to be admitted* [my italics].[736]

If getting rid of terror in the first example, minimizing pity in the second, and achieving a peaceful detachment by negativing painful emotions are not all examples of *katharsis* of the emotions, I have no idea what *katharsis* is—at least *qua* purgation.[737] It may be surprising for others that pity and terror enter the discussion of comedy for Woodruff, but for me this is very natural, given *Politics* VIII 7, where pity and fear apply to many more art forms than just tragedy. One can find occasional episodes of fear and pity in classical comedies by, e.g., Aristophanes, and recall Plato's statement in the *Philebus*, in which pleasure *and* pain apply to comedy along with tragedy. Similarly, I gather that if laughter functions to release unwanted emotions, because they are too powerful, this qualifies as cathartic. Why Woodruff never invokes *katharsis* in his article, however, was baffling to me, and even after receiving a very helpful private explanation I think the issue is still very open concerning what Aristotle himself thought.[738]

---

735   *Op. cit.*, 2008, pp. 328-9. Halliwell also refers us back to his prior work, *op. cit.*, 1986, pp. 274-5, which also is non-committal regarding comic catharsis, but which provides a valuable list of the previous thinkers who have taken a stance one way or the other on that topic. As was said there: "The specific issue of whether Aristotle would have posited a comic as well as a tragic *katharsis*, is only one, if a peculiarly obscure, aspect of this whole question [of how to reconstruct the core of Aristotle's theory of comedy]" (p. 274).

736   Paul Woodruff, "The Paradox of Comedy," *Philosophical Topics*, Vol 25, #1, Spring 1997, pp. 319-335; citations p. 319 and 321 respectively.

737   I presume the example of pity—more precisely, "of being spared the discomfort of pity"— which Woodfuff gives is a proper one for which pity is not necessarily required but perhaps "optional." That is, the possible targets of the pity, the unfortunate, may have brought a miserable state of affairs on themselves (say, by getting drunk before engaging in damaging actions) and may not strictly deserve pity on Aristotelian ethical grounds.

738   Woodruff writes (February, 2013, private correspondence):
　　Catharsis in comedy: I can explain why I do not mention it. I do not believe in it—quite emphatically. Laughter negatives emotions at the source. It may also release them, but in comic theater, generally, there is nothing to release. The emotion does not get started. So that solves that puzzle— why I do not say it. (Perhaps comedy has a cathartic role for fears people bring into the theater, but

I cannot help but believe Aristotle may have said something along the lines that Woodruff presents (even though Woodruff ironically rejects *katharsis* for comedy or at least rejects the view that pity and fear or other emotions should be aroused in comedy in order to cathart them). That is, I believe Aristotle would have emphasized, more than is usually considered, the importance of comedy in the theatre and of laughter in life, although the exact details are very open. The power of the relevant mimesis is too evident for an empiricist to ignore and the full chapter on proper wit and laughter in *Nicomachean Ethics* at least indirectly confirms this. Maybe Aristotle would have noted all the reasons above for using *katharsis* in that art form, with many more. I cannot say with any certainty, nor I gather can anyone else, but clearly comedy, wit, and laughter are vital to him in the theatrical setting, as also evidenced by the surviving portions of the *Dramatics* (especially chapters 3, 4, 5 and 9). In my view, Aristotelian comedy has been vastly underrated by most scholars from the Renaissance onwards, with notable and praiseworthy exceptions, some of whom have already been mentioned.[739]

## Conclusion of Units 2 and 3

My purpose in Units 2 and 3 has been fivefold:

- To continue the project started by Smerdel and Petruševski (and perhaps by Gudeman) in order

---

> that is another phenomenon entirely from releasing emotions evoked in the theater, and I have no special thoughts about that.) The best comedy, I think, keeps us poised between emotions almost getting underway and checked by laughter as they do. Not catharsis.

Woodruff may be right about comedy not generating emotions to release them, and maybe Aristotle thought the same. Instead, as Woodruff notes, perhaps it is an issue of the fears (and other emotions) that people bring into the theater, but to me these are equally important emotions to consider. I take absolutely no stance one way or the other for the moment on all these matters. In my view, these are all the kinds of questions that I believe should be examined rigorously in the future, when reconsidering Aristotle's dramatic theory vis-à-vis both comedy and tragedy without being side-tracked by catharsis in *Dramatics* 6.

739   Some good starting points in my opinion for becoming acquainted with the secondary literature are, apart from the authors and works mentioned already in this article (with Chapter X in Butcher, *op. cit.*, "The Generalising Power of Comedy" being perhaps one not-so-obvious starting point given the the title of his own book):

- Lane Cooper, *An Aristotelian Theory of Comedy, with an Adaptation of the Poetics, and a Translation of the Tractatus Coislinianus* (New York: Harcourt Brace) 1922. Available at:
  http://www.questia.com/library/7379692/an-aristotelian-theory-of-comedy-with-an-adaptation
- For how the Platonic-Aristotelian concepts influence theory of comedy, whether or not this is Paul Woodruff's main intent, see his "Rousseau, Molière, and the Ethics of Laughter," *Philosophy and Literature*, Vol. 1, # 3, Fall 1977.
- Leon Golden, *Aristotle on Tragic and Comic Mimesis* (Atlanta: Scholars Press) 1992.
- For a picture of how different types of catharsis are applicable to comedy, see Gene Fendt, "Resolution, catharsis, culture: *As You Like It*," *Philosophy and Literature* 19 (1995): 248-60; largely reprinted in *Love Song for the Life of the Mind: An Essay on the Purpose of Comedy* (Washington DC: Catholic University of America Press) 2007.

## Chapter 8: The Real Role of Catharsis and the Importance of Comedy

to end forever the excruciating, Sisyphean tradition of trying to explain *katharsis* in *Dramatics* 6, a tradition that, if I may mix metaphors, threatened to be like the thousand-mile animal in *Dramatics* 7 or another entity that is even more "unbounded" in Aristotle's view;
- to add weight to the side of those scholars who believe Aristotle also advocated comic or "musical" *katharsis*, however *katharsis* gets precisely applied to tragedy;
- to emphasize that *katharsis* may have been applied to some sub-type(s) of tragedy, and only to some sub-type(s), but with the correct considerations that still need to be articulated;
- to demonstrate the correct goal of tragedy for Aristotle as (a kind of) pleasure and how he replies to Plato's censorship without *katharsis*;
- and to begin motivating some initial, appropriate general questions about the future direction of these matters, the final topic and one that I examine further in the next chapter.

My purpose has not been to second-guess with respect to comedy or comic *katharsis* the lost, detailed theory of one of the most brilliant thinkers of all time, if not the most brilliant: metaphysician, scientist, ethicist, biologist, psychologist, logician, and theorist of drama and politics (and I leave aside how well he might have done the *emmelia*). I cannot do much more in the space I have because, if I am right with respect to the major points in this book, there will be many questions to resolve or to revisit and many books to be written, and certainly not by me, or not only by me. Aristotelian aesthetics begs for an extensive, fresh examination, especially concerning *katharsis* and comedy, with the understanding that *katharsis*, like pleasure, need not be univocal in the different arenas for which it is relevant.

Probably the most pertinent unanswered question in the context of "tragedy" *qua tragōidia*, which can end happily, is whether some sub-types of tragedy could have catharsis as their goal for Aristotle, even if they have pity and fear, given that Chapter 14 has pleasure through pity and fear being the explicit goal. Another greatly overlooked issue that in my view begs for extensive research is why Aristotle did not treat the satyr play at any length, although, to reiterate, perhaps this type of musical drama was a subset of comedy for him, or more related to comedy than to tragedy, and was therefore covered in the lost book. A third issue is historical: Why have none of the well-known commentators in over 465 years considered whether the Platonic-Diotiman meaning of *poiēsis* applies to Aristotle's aesthetics? Finally, the most challenging issue perhaps, and one that may never be solved, is trying to determine the truly authentic chapters or passages of the *Dramatics*. I have added weight in this book to the opinion of some of the greatest specialists of the treatise in the twentieth century that the work is a collection of related, but different, Aristotelian texts.[740] In my view, our understanding of

---

[740] This view is far from unanimous, though: Halliwell and Janko are two who consider the book to be an organic whole.

Aristotle's theory of drama would be much better served by taking the chapters that are clearly consistent with Chapters 1 through 8 and marking them as definite. Then, as once suggested, combine these with the other chapters or passages that are also very consistent as part of an organic whole and append the others as collected texts of Aristotle. Employ them as such, rather than trying to force all extant chapters to work as a single whole. This approach may prove to be much more effective because now at least we can better imagine the different possibilities from Aristotle's perspective with respect to the various issues in ancient Greek drama (or epic) rather than prolong generations of effort trying to reconcile passages that simply cannot be reconciled as such.

# Unit 4: The *Dramatics* and Its New Future

*Aristotle on Dramatic Musical Composition*

# Chapter 9: The Future of the *Dramatics*

**Section 1: Why Aristotle's *Dramatics* Directly Applies Nowadays Only to Musicals**

The principles of the *Dramatics,* insofar as tragedy is the topic, are most directly applicable to what we call today in the United States "(serious) Broadway musicals," rather than to so-called "straight plays," those without music. Examples of the latter are *The Crucible* by Arthur Miller or Athol Fugard's *The Road to Mecca* or (typical) revivals of *King Lear*. Broadway musicals like *West Side Story,* at least when they contain weighty themes and relatively admirable protagonists, as qualified with the discussion of Sisyphus in my Chapter 6, are the only plays that satisfy the conditions of *Dramatics* 6. Some other well-known examples are *Oklahoma!* and *Phantom of the Opera*. (Epic is now rarely ever created or "sung/chanted," that is, performed, so I leave aside this art for the rest of this book.) In addition, from what we can tell about the statements of comic drama in *Dramatics* 1 through 8, the lighter or more laugh-oriented forms of modern musical theater also come closest to Aristotelian comedy, at least in terms of "look" or in terms of satisfying the characteristics that seem part of the relevant "biological division" for that art. Comic examples are plays like *Anything Goes, Chicago* or *A Funny Thing Happened on the Way to the Forum,* and examples with a combination of weighty and comedic themes (that Aristotle recognizes in *Dramatics* 13) might be *Showboat, Man of La Mancha, The Sound of Music,* or *The Book of Mormon,* whether or not they have a "double-structure" plot that he denigrates at the end of Chapter 13.

Slight adjustments might have to be made for modern tragedies not following exactly the choral structure given in *Dramatics* 12 and for there being typically a more fluid transition between the choral aspects and the purely acted sections than was done in ancient Greece, leaving aside the lost plays of the fourth century BCE. However, those adjustments are minor considerations. They do not impact the essential and necessary conditions, which is all I am concerned with at this basic level. Furthermore, there is a substantial gray area in which it is hard to determine whether modern musicals would fall under tragedy or comedy, and they might be more like the *Frogs* or the more sophisticated New Comedy of fourth century BCE in many ways than anything else, regarding their content and plot development. Why *Frogs* is a comedy rather than a tragedy in the broad sense of *Dramatics* 1 through 8 is an interesting question, because the characters are noble personages (including a god) and extremely talented artists, the theme is grand (who is the best dramatist and why?), there is some kind of mild suffering and thus perhaps pity (Euripides must stay in Hades), and the play satisfies, for the most part, the conditions of tragedy in *Dramatics* 6. Of course, the god is somewhat silly, and there is much emphasis on laughter, both of which presumably compel the play to be classified as a comedy, even with the grand or famous personages. Still, one must wonder what mixture of comic elements are permitted in tragedy and vice versa (consider the comic elements in Shakespeare's *Romeo and Juliet*). The critical point for the moment, though, is that Aristotle's six conditions of tragedy do not apply to modern "straight" plays, because these modern plays generally have no singing and dancing chorus. Also, operatic performances, which fall under the category of music usually, are not the type of performance intended to be covered by the *Dramatics per se*, in spite of how much overlap exists between the ancient drama of the *Dramatics* and modern opera. As once noted, music in drama is, for Aristotle, fifth in the list of ranked conditions, below, for instance, language and plot, whereas music is usually considered the most crucial element in opera (and, if one claims the plot in opera is equally important, then we have a hybrid that makes the issues more difficult). Thus, Aristotle's treatise, unless one carefully extends its principles with substantial justification, also does not directly and fully apply to other similar modern art forms such as operettas, which to my knowledge are usually considered a species of opera, although if they are more like Broadway musicals, the story changes.

What does "carefully extends" mean? I start to answer in Section 2 below, but before examining that issue, let us cover some final remarks on the correct scope of the *Dramatics* if one wishes to try to apply it to our arts. Its principles as a whole, again, are not applicable to tragic literature, much less literature in general, be it poetry in our sense or novels or short stories, because literature has neither music (whether or not in the Greek sense) nor spectacle, two of the six necessary elements for tragedy from *Dramatics* 6. Moreover, much modern poetry has neither plot nor character in Aristotle's sense that minimally reflects choice and ethical values. Once we have gone through the arguments from Chapters 1 through 4 above, these conclusions are easily seen, and nothing more need be said on this score.

Another place for caution before I tackle the issue of extending musical dramatic principles to other arts: One has to be careful about speaking of modern tragedy and Aristotelian tragedy, as if they are the same, not only because the serious Broadway musical is closest to Aristotle's definition of tragedy but because of the ambiguity of the term "tragedy" itself. This ambiguity existed in ancient times, given, for instance, the difference even between Plato and Aristotle, and has increased at least as far back as Scaliger in the 1500's. Let us recall what Orgel says:

> Scaliger begins, naturally, with Aristotle on tragedy. He says he has no wish to impugn the classic definition but will merely add his own: 'Tragedy is the imitation through action [i.e., not through narration] of an important man's fortunes, *with an unhappy outcome* [my italics], and expressed in serious poetic language. Although Aristotle includes melody and song, they are not, as philosophers would say, of the essence of tragedy. ... Moreover, the term catharsis does not at all describe the effect of every plot." Scaliger, that is, finds Aristotle too limiting, and he expands the boundaries of the definition on pragmatic grounds. Melody and song are considered inessential because the printed version of a

Chapter 9: The Future of the *Dramatics*

tragedy does not cease to be a tragedy."⁷⁴¹

I leave aside how prudent Scaliger was to reject *katharsis* as being empirically relevant (and whether he would have "favored," to use Destrée's term, the doubters' claim about *katharsis* in *Dramatics* 6 had he heard the arguments of this book). Let us also leave aside the views that melody and song are "inessential," and that a printed play is sufficient to be a tragedy in the relevant sense, given my Chapters 2-3. The crucial consideration now is that tragedy *must* have an "unhappy outcome" for Scaliger, which also conflicts with the best plots of *Dramatics* 14 like *Cresphontes*. Moreover, unsurprisingly other authors historically posit different connotations of tragedy. The current meaning, or definition, of tragedy might involve a play with the following restrictions, and I do not give an exhaustive list, because we could surely devise quickly other variations. Tragedy might involve as its connotation:

(i) an unhappy ending, as Scaliger says (with perhaps the paradigm of *Oedipus*), with language being the only required and the most important element, but with music, dance, spectacle, and *katharsis* optional, and pity and fear not even mentioned;

(ii) those conditions like (i), with *katharsis* also required;

(iii) those conditions like (i), with pity and fear also required (following *Dramatics* 13);

(iv) those conditions like (ii) and (iii), with the *katharsis* coming *through* pity and fear (of course, the standard interpretation of the *Dramatics* for centuries);

(v) those conditions given in *Dramatics* 6 and explained in *Dramatics* 1-8, including the required plot, character, music, dance and spectacle (without the interpolated *katharsis*, pity, and fear clause), namely, true Aristotelian *tragōidia* ("tragedy"), which allows unhappy *or happy* endings.

Clearly, then, tragedy and *tragōidia* have had multiple senses. Scaliger's view, option (i), is perhaps the most common view today of tragedy, however one assigns historical credit to the conception. Literary versions and performances without song and dance—such as modern renditions of Shakespearean tragedies and, e.g., Miller's *Death of a Salesman*—are invariably considered paradigmatic tragedy for many, with their unhappy endings. In any event, the principles in the *Dramatics* intentionally and fully apply, at least in Chapters 1 through 8, to only (v) above. To ask "What is ideal tragedy?", then, will trigger very different answers depending on the notion of tragedy that interlocutors may be assuming, and, in order to stave off arguments at cross purposes, it is crucial that they agree on the notion they prefer to use for any particular discussion.

In other words, Aristotle's *tragōidia* (as defined in *Dramatics* 1-8) also covers the serious musical drama that has neither a killing of a protagonist nor an unhappy ending, along with, as noted, the tragic musical like *West Side Story* that does indeed result in very pitiable events like murder. Above

---

741 Stephen Orgel, *The Authentic Shakespeare, and Other Problems of the Early Modern Stage* (New York and London: Psychology Press/Routledge) 2002, p. 149.

and beyond the examples already mentioned are *Cabaret* (even though a protagonist gets battered during the play) and *Billy Elliot*. All have tension and maybe at least a little fear, perhaps even pity at times, but no killing or horrible ending (with perhaps some *caveats* for *Cabaret*). They are not comedies *per se*, even though they have occasional witty moments—again, like *Romeo and Juliet*. They are serious, even if most so-called Broadway "musicals" are comedic or are mixed comedic and serious. Because modern tragedy typically is more like Scaliger's conception, with an unhappy ending and typically with no music and dance, we moderns are usually working with a significant conceptual difference when thinking of Aristotle's "tragic drama" or "tragedy." (A balletic tragedy like *Giselle* would normally be called a tragic ballet or something similar, rather than simply "tragedy," in part because it has no language, and thus does not fall under Aristotle's "tragedy" either.) Given, therefore, that the principles of the *Dramatics* should be applied *directly* only to dramatic musical composition, were one to try to extend them in modern circumstances to other art forms, like literature, or what we might call tragic or comic literature, what are the issues?

## Section 2: The Dangers, and Rewards, of Extending the *Dramatics* to Literature or Other Arts

As we saw a few times, Aristotle clearly says in *Dramatics* 25 that there is not the same correctness in politics as in dramatic musical creation (*poiēitikēs*), nor is there in any other art (*techne*) as in dramatic musical creation (1460b13-15). The first disjunction means that art is autonomous, in some meaningful sense of the word "autonomous"; the second that dramatic musical creation has different principles from other arts. Those "other arts" are presumably painting, the nameless art of pure language, etc., but might refer now to new art forms like cinema, as many aestheticians have recognized historically, when, e.g., dramatic principles were sometimes and incorrectly assumed to rule cinema after the Lumière brothers helped give birth to it. Given that a different and unique means of mimesis is employed (film and light then, and now, with computers, digitalization), cinema has its own rules or its own "correctness," even though it might share some principles with drama and literature because it typically (but only typically) has, respectively, a plot and significant language. Various authors have tried to extend—or at least have proposed the viability of extending—Aristotle's theory from drama, commonly, though, conceived as literature, but the difficulty arises immediately in determining whether those principles are applicable as is or whether they must be modified.[742]

---

742    E.g, Fendt says:
        ...the *Poetics* is not (in the main) about mimesis in general, it is not about all the ways our feelings and moral states may be moved or shaped by art, but only about those mimeses which use language. Further, *it—at least what we have of it—is not concerned even with all the kinds of mimesis that use language, but only tragedy (epic being a subtype thereof) and comedy...* However, since the *Poetics* covers the most inclusive form of mimesis (or, since tragedy uses all the means the oth-

Chapter 9: The Future of the *Dramatics*

Consider a *seemingly* straightforward case, applying Aristotle's theory of performed tragedy to its first cousin, tragedy designed to be only read, the relatively new practice he mentions in the *Rhetoric*, with the example of Chaeremon.

As noted briefly in the Introduction, this form of purely literary tragedy becomes more like epic, which invites questions as to whether it can fulfill the same *dunamis* as performed tragedy. As we saw above in Chapter 3, in *Dramatics* 24 epic is said to be more amazing than tragedy because it is narrated and because it does not have the constraint of being shown on stage, as tragedy does. Thus it need not abide by the same temporal rules as tragedy (and can, for example, show scenes much more easily out of normal temporal sequence), and can ignore some obvious considerations that would be absurd on stage. In epic, this goes unnoticed, Aristotle says. An example he gives is Achilles chasing Hector with the rest of the armies standing and watching, even though, presumably, in the theater they could easily trip their enemy: Hector by a Greek or Achilles by a Trojan.
If merely written, why then should tragedy not take advantage of the same "amazingness" that epic

---

er arts use separately) *we may be able to read it as synecdochic of those mimeses which only use rhythm or language*, for all of those other mimeses will break into the same categories of character—better/worse or tragic/comic [my italics] (*op. cit.*, 1997, p. 254-5).

Fendt is right on a few points, such as Aristotle's focus on three and only three art forms, with epic being a "subtype" of tragedy. I trust, though, that Fendt uses "subtype" in a different sense from the four subtypes of tragedy in Chapter 18. That is, I assume Fendt means something like "subset," as having only some of the six necessary conditions of *Dramatics* 6, without the choral *melopoiia* or the spectacle. However, his suggestion at the end, namely, that Aristotle's principles could be applied to other art forms is both tantalizing and questionable. Although Fendt correctly delimits the scope of the *Dramatics* to the three art forms, he still assumes it is mimetic *language* (rather than mimesis as impersonation or emulation or representation or the like) that is fundamental, and he still thinks apparently that "rhythm" is some abstract, perhaps musical, quality.

Also, regarding the division "better/worse": Let us take *rhuthmos* more correctly as dance and explore some of the ramifications of Fendt's passage. One can certainly apply the division to this art form, as Blasis does, in one of the seminal works of ballet that is briefly covered in the Appendix. Actually, Blasis gives three kinds of dancing—noble, "demi-character," and comic/pastoral, sometimes called "character"—which seemingly correspond better to Aristotle's tripartite division in *Dramatics* 2 of people better, the same, or worse than ourselves. Indeed, Chapter 8 of Blasis's book (*op. cit.*) is devoted only to this. The distinctions can be easily grasped in the famous *Romeo and Juliet* with Galina Ulanova (on film, 1955), choreographed by Leonid Lavrosky for the Kirov Ballet: Count Paris dances always in the noble form, elementary steps while expending very little energy, with the kind of posture and dignity that Plato advocated; Romeo and friends dance in the demi-character mode with a much wider range of dynamics and steps, albeit still elegantly almost always; and the jester and peasants dance in the character mode, with an emphasis on great vigor and no real concern for dignity. The ethical qualities that each kind might portray could be similarly categorized, but, as discussed regarding the case of Sisyphus, impersonations could become very mixed. In *Giselle*, the peasant Hilarion is in some ways more ethical than the philandering Duke Albrecht, much as the ballet tries to paint Albrecht as the more sympathetic character because of Giselle's love for him. How the three types of dance and character allow, though, principles of the *Dramatics* to be applied to ballet is still a complicated issue, especially if the ballet is plotless.

has, along with its other advantages? However, by being merely written, purely literary tragedy then loses some advantages of performed drama. By dispensing with "music" and spectacle, two aspects of traditional, performed tragedy that cause it to be ranked over epic in *Dramatics* 26, purely literary tragedy restricts its *dunamis*, because the pleasures associated with those aspects become non-existent. Should, then, purely literary tragedy abide by the rules of (performed) tragedy *per se* or of epic, and how does one handle the inconsistencies that arise when the rules conflict? There is no easy answer to this, and the ultimate answer may be that dramatists, tragedians or authors, however they categorize themselves, take any option they choose but with awareness of the advantages and disadvantages of each approach. Hence, I assume now with this one simple example that we see the danger of not understanding the precise correct scope and goal of tragedy and of trying to extend the principles in the *Dramatics* even to something so closely related as purely literary tragedy. Let this suffice to caution theorists about applying the principles to other art forms, which are even more "remote."

This is not to say that the spirit of Aristotelian theory (logical analysis, empiricism, humanism and other qualities, as enumerated more below) should not be applied or re-applied to other art forms, only that there is no simple, mechanical transference of the principles in the *Dramatics* to those other art forms, given Aristotle's statement of the autonomy of the arts in *Dramatics* 25. The already proven worth over hundreds of years of that spirit for Western culture in drama suggests that, if applied correctly to the other art forms, we will gain other benefits that have not yet been realized. In other words, if a thinker—or a group of thinkers—can show with care, erudition and practical experience how principles in the *Dramatics* can be applied to other art forms, the correctly conceived *Dramatics* might well have additional value. These remarks can be transposed for *katharsis*, which, to emphasize one final time, might well be applicable *at times* for Aristotle for tragedy, as described above, in Chapters 5 through 8 of this book, although I trust *katharsis* would primarily be more applicable to comedy.

Modern serious musical theater has all the necessary elements of tragedy for Aristotle, but, as mentioned, need not follow the exact "quantitative" ordering given for the chorus in *Dramatics* 12. That ordering appeared to be a result of Athenian regulation, although I leave this topic for the experts in Athenian theater. In other words, given how independent Chapter 12 is from, say, plot and the other necessary qualitative conditions, the quantitative ordering is more a description of what happened in his day rather than a prescription of what always must be done, as the omission of any quantitative aspect in the definition proves. Thus, Chapter 12 in no crucial way blocks any attempt to apply the *Dramatics*, correctly understood, to more recent serious musical theater.

After modern musical theater (including comedy), probably the lowest-hanging fruit for Aristotle's principles are the so-called "straight" plays, insofar as they are performed nowadays only with actors. These plays have five of the six necessary elements of tragedy: plot, character, reasoning, language, and spectacle. They miss the music and dance, or orchestral art, of *Dramatics* 6. However, in spite of that missing element, presumably, the passages on plot— *insofar as they are not affected by the orchestral art*—would be applicable. Moreover, one needs to consider that pity, fear, and *katharsis* are not necessarily part of any relevant dramatic theory, even if on occasion they might be appropriate to a sub-type of tragedy. It may be that audience members only feel sympathy or empathy or concern or worry for characters in a play, but neither of these states of *pathos* should be mistaken for pity. An emotion like sympathy or empathy is merely one of the many possible reactions that are similar enough to pity to confuse audiences and critics, just as concern or worry is close enough to fear that spectators might believe they are fearing when they are really only worrying—and likewise for the theorists or reviewers writing about the phenomenon. It may also be—and I venture to say surely will be—that, as *Dramatics* 19 suggests, the full range of emotions are relevant to tragic drama in the Aristotelian sense, as long as proper pleasure is the ultimate goal. What "proper pleasure" as intellectual delight is, and whether, for instance, the four types of tragedy each have a slightly different pleasure, and what this proper pleasure shares or not with the pleasure of comedy would require a much larger book. This is not to foreclose on other types of enactment on stage for other purposes— didactic, patriotic or otherwise—but these are not in the scope of this, and Aristotle's, treatise, and thus Brechtians, and those who have other goals for drama, can go their own way without picking a quarrel. Just as there can be multiple goals of sports throughout our culture, money for professionals and recreation for hobbyists, to pick just two, so there might be multiple goals of drama or art, but that leads us into general aesthetics, and I already noted that this book is of much more limited scope.

## Concluding Remarks

It is often said that one's ethics depends on one's metaphysics or ontology. Thus, for instance, if one does not believe in God, one's ethics or morality will not depend on a Bible or another religious tract but perhaps on one of the three major system of philosophical ethics: Aristotle's "virtue" ethics, Epicureanism (or its variant, Jeremy Bentham's and J.S. Mill's "utilitarianism") or Kant's deontology ("rule-based" ethics). Similarly, although this is rarely said, one's political and dramatic theory arguably depends also on one's ontological beliefs. If, to continue the point, no God exists, then, we should not establish in politics a theocracy, whether based on Shariah law or not. Nor should we invoke a *deus ex machina* in plays to resolve endings, as Euripides did at times, if we wish plays to be as believable as possible (again, assuming one is forthright with one's beliefs and assuming one is writing for a similar, humanist audience). Although this point has been acknowledged or expressed in slightly different ways by some previous writers, it has been too little stressed in my opinion.[743] Aristotle is a humanist, in no way believing in gods in our sense (that is, in gods who care about human affairs[744]), all of which helps determine his dramatic principles. For instance, recognitions and resolutions are ideally created in plots through natural means, as listed at length in *Dramatics* 16: recognition of scars, use of memory, acquiring knowledge through a description that allows one to deduce the solution to a dramatic problem (for instance, the revelation by Tiresias in *Oedipus* that Oedipus had killed his father, which leads the king to realize he had married his mother), among other, purely natural possibilities. Not one way of recognition for Aristotle is a religious one, dependent on the existence of, and interference by gods, even if Aristotle pays some lip service to myth and the possibility of including it in the spoken parts of drama. Again, it is believability that is crucial for him in Chapters 15 and 24, and we saw before that believability is even more important than truth in one respect. He says in the former chapter:

> It is obvious that the solutions of plots too should come about as a result of the plot itself, and not from a contrivance, as in the *Medea* and in the passage about sailing home in the *Iliad*. A contrivance must be used for matters outside the drama—either previous events which are beyond human knowledge, or later ones that need to be foretold or announced. For we grant that the gods can see everything. There should be nothing improbable in the incidents; *otherwise, it should be outside the tragedy...* [my italics] (15.1454a37-b7).

As just suggested, this latter point about believability has been acknowledged by more than a few scholars before, who sometimes also have spoken correctly of how little any religious consideration enters into drama for Aristotle, including its origin, but I believe it needs additional emphasis. In part this is because the passage just given is often not explained with respect to "the gods can see everything," which itself suggests that Aristotle finds the gods important. Presumably, though, Aristotle merely means something like "for we grant that [*only*] the gods can see everything," because as is, the passage contributes nothing sensible to the discussion. By suggesting, however, that we are not like the gods—or something similar—Aristotle is implying, very sensibly, that the dramatist cannot rely on our having powers like gods, divining somehow connections or causes in the incidents of the play. Instead, as human beings, we can only experience the drama, and make inferences, in natural

---

[743] Halliwell is one of the admirable exceptions; cf. his thoughts on secularism in tragedy for Aristotle, 1986, espec. pp. 229-37.

[744] The Unmoved Mover of *Metaphysics* Lambda is Pure Actuality and pays no attention to nature, that is, to the universe of potentiality and movement. At best, it is, ironically, selfishly "thinking of itself thinking." Many specialists in Aristotle, including myself, believe that the Unmoved Mover was a product of his youthful thinking and that he gave it up in his mature years, considering the problems that ensue with the doctrine, some of which he acknowledges. All of this, however, is far beyond the scope of this book. Moreover, if he believes in immortal bodies and calls those "gods," those are far different from the Judaeo-Christian "God" with which many in our culture are generally concerned. Suffice it to say that in a work in progress—*Aristotle's "Not to Fear" Proof for the Necessary Eternity of the Universe without the Unmoved Mover* (expected publication 2019-20)—I cover these issues in depth.

## Chapter 9: The Future of the *Dramatics*

ways. Thus, it is crucial that nothing improbable be in the play, and that the connections or causes be made clear or deducible. Janko, who translated this passage, gives a very insightful account[745] of the examples of the *Medea* and the *Iliad* and concludes that the god on the "contrivance" (in early tragedy a type of crane that appeared) explained factors outside of the play. However, it appears that Aristotle only begrudgingly allows these contrivances, because of the practice of his time and presumably a need to accommodate an audience that in its own way was as religious as American audiences now can be. Yet, to emphasize, he in no way recommends such a practice in the rest of the *Dramatics*. Certainly, he at least implicitly recommends that some *natural* actions referred to in dialogue—for instance, that the person Oedipus killed was his father—can and should be outside the play (*exō tou dramatos*, 14.1453b32). Again, though, this is presumably for the reasons listed above regarding believability, or to setting up an unexpected reversal or recognition, or to keeping the play compressed sufficiently, as opposed to epic.

None of this is to say that Aristotle uses the omission of gods in drama for theological or metaphysical purposes, including relevant education, only that his principles are especially fitting for artists creating dramas in humanistic cultures. Arguments for or against the existence of god(s) belong to "first philosophy," or metaphysics.[746] Nevertheless, Aristotle's theory in the *Dramatics* is critical, being in some ways prescriptive (what makes a good plot, for example), in some ways descriptive (what poets have done effectively or poorly, how tragedy evolved, and so forth) and in other ways ethical or critical. In short, it is philosophical theory trying to give a "scientific understanding" of dramatic musical composition. Nevertheless, as we saw, Aristotle upholds the autonomy of artistic practices in Chapter 25, at least as much as one can uphold autonomy in a world in which no practice of any kind exists in complete isolation from other aspects of human life. In effect, Aristotle tries to treat the principles of drama comprehensively, and as I explain in this book, he covers all of its four causes while following the outline of achieving scientific knowledge based on Plato's *Phaedrus* or his own biological principles (namely, provide the differences and commonalities first, and then give the "causes"). In other

---

745    Janko, *op. cit.*, 1987, pp. 111-2.

746    Just as philosophy for medievalists was often "the handmaiden of theology," so art of all types (painting, certain types of architecture, music such as Bach chorales, etc.) for religious institutions has been their butlers,—their way of glorifying God and impressing both believers and non-believers. However, even those who have considered Aristotle to be a model thinker have misjudged his views or taken drastically different paths, in spite of their praise. For instance, Ayn Rand writes "Art is a selective re-creation of reality according to an artist's metaphysical value-judgments" (*The Romantic Manifesto: A Philosophy of Literature*, New American Library: New York, 1975 rev. ed., first publ. in 1971, p. 19), and she often praises Aristotle. He would presumably appreciate her praise, but would surely deny this definition, in part because it is much too narrow given his own account that we saw once before, as production in accordance with right reason. Moreover, "value" is a term of ethics and we saw how ethics for him was subsumed both to plot and to pleasure in his theory of drama, even if the composer wisely does not ignore ethics. Thus, "metaphysical value-judgments" is an oxymoron.

words, although his treatise is in part, and perhaps most importantly, theoretical, it is fundamentally empirical, grounding dramatic art in human nature (as in *Dramatics* 4)—on the biological and ontological status of human beings who function in natural ways and often with common psychological or epistemic concerns.[747] As indicated already, Aristotle's theory was presumably meant to apply to the plays of his day, or to plays written a month or two later, or a year or two later, or a hundred or thousand years later, as long as nature and human beings are essentially the same.

I see no reason to believe the Greeks were any different from us in important ways. We might be slightly bigger and have computers rather than other methods of calculating. We employ cars rather than carts, but these are differences in degree, at most, not differences in real kinds. We still have only five senses and the same organs and intellectual apparatus or "soul" (*psyche* for modern "barbarians," if I might gently tease some readers[748]). We still feel (or not) pity, fear, anger, joy, laughter, and other emotions. We still betray daily the same concerns for happiness that the Greeks had, involving love, friendship, pleasure, health and the like. It follows that insofar as Aristotle is correct in grounding his dramatic theory in human nature—and of how humans "act," the basis, of course, of the Greek term for drama—that his theory is still relevant nowadays, at least in general. He might be wrong in his notion of human nature—and maybe no less a biologist than Darwin was incorrect in believing him to be the greatest biologist who ever lived—and maybe as a consequence the foundation of his aesthetics is flimsy, or if "aesthetics" is too broad a depiction of Aristotle's view, his artistic or dramatic theory instead. However, all of that is a matter for extended discussion beyond this book. Aristotle may well be still right in many of the fundamentals of biology, like functionalism, and the crucial point now is that, insofar as our nature is the same as the ancient Greeks and insofar as his biology and psychology apply, any artistic or dramatic theory that correctly stems from human nature will continue to be valuable. I say this in spite of Aristotle not following the pre-Socratic Anaximander, who anticipated Darwin in thinking that man evolved from much simpler creatures. Aristotle also believed instead that the species was eternal, none of which, though, diminished him significantly in Darwin's eyes. Much of Aristotle's biological theory can be salvaged after removing that precept.

---

747  Hence, in part the emphasis on dramatists presenting themes that are "universal." R.G. Collingwood, in his *Principles of Art* (1938), takes a different approach and argues that art, presumably including drama, is the expression of an individual's "perturbation of the soul," and that concerns for universality are misjudged. Whether, though, his claims truly conflict necessarily with Aristotle's view or merely describe, or prescribe, a very rich phenomenon or set of phenomena from a particular and different perspective, perhaps with concepts that have different meanings, is yet another question for general aesthetics.

748  For the non-Greek reader, I reiterate that a *barbaros* was simply one who did not speak Greek. Although at the time some of them might have been considered "barbarians" in the sense that we give the word, it was not the case that the word necessarily implied that they ate children or were completely uncivilized or the like.

## Chapter 9: The Future of the *Dramatics*

Plato's and Aristotle's belief that music and dance stem from human nature also has been held (if only occasionally) by other thinkers historically, e.g., Adam Smith, well known for his *Wealth of Nations* (the shortened title of *An Inquiry into the Nature and Causes of the Wealth of Nations*, 1776). What is not known as much is that Smith was a professional philosopher, whose other seminal work, rarely mentioned nowadays, is *The Theory of Moral Sentiments* (1759). Citing no influence, he proposes views that hearken back to Plato and Aristotle, if not earlier:

> After the pleasures which arise from the gratification of the bodily appetites, *there seem to be none more natural to man than Music and Dancing*. In the progress of art and improvement they are, perhaps, the first and earliest pleasures of his own invention...
>
> ... *What the ancients called Rhythmus, what we call Time or Measure, is the connecting principle of those two arts*; Music consisting in a succession of a certain sort of sounds, and Dancing in a succession of a certain sort of steps, gestures, and motions, regulated according to time or measure, and thereby formed into a sort of whole or system; which in the one art is called a song or tune, and in the other a dance; *the time or measure of the dance corresponding always exactly with that of the song or tune which accompanies and directs it.*
>
> ... ***A pantomime dance may frequently answer the same purpose, and, by representing some adventure in love or war, may seem to give sense and meaning to a Music which might not otherwise appear to have any. It is more natural to mimic, by gestures and motions, the adventures of common life, than to express them in Verse or Poetry. The thought itself is more obvious,*** and ***the execution is much more easy*** [my italics and bolding].[749]

A few comments on this passage before continuing: The source for the meaning of *rhuthmos* is probably Aristoxenus. Otherwise, if Smith relies on Plato only using this notion of *rhuthmos* once, exceptionally, at *Laws* II at 672, then he ignores, e.g., 665a, and the more frequent uses of it in that book as the concrete "order of body movement (spatially or spatiotemporally)." Also, Smith wrongly suggests that the time of the dance always corresponds exactly with that of the tune, for which there is no good evidence. In Morris or other folk dancing, that is a good principle, but in fine art dance and ancient choreography there is little, if anything, to ground such a restrictive principle. Plato's view that the vocal music inspires dance (*Laws* VII 816a) in no way commits Plato to the further view that each musical beat has to have but one step. On the other hand, Smith recognizes, it appears, the difference

---

749    Adam Smith, *Of the Nature of that Imitation which takes place in what are called The Imitative Arts/ Of the Affinity between Music, Dancing, and Poetry*, from *Essays on Philosophical Subjects*, ed. W. P. D. Wightman and J. C. Bryce, vol. III of the *Glasgow Edition of the Works and Correspondence of Adam Smith* [1795] (Indianapolis: Liberty Fund, 1982). Available online at:
      http://oll.libertyfund.org/?option=com_staticxt&staticfile=show.php%3Ftitle=201&chapter=56033&layout=html&Itemid=27

For more on Smith's view of dance, cf. Francis Sparshott, *Off the Ground: First Steps to a Philosophical Consideration of the Dance* (Princeton: Princeton University Press) 1988, pp. 12, 40, 277, and 308.

between mere "formal" dancing (typically *rhuthmos* in orchestral art in Plato and Aristotle at least) and pantomime dancing (often *orchēsis* for the Greeks, I have shown). He also recognizes that it is the pantomime dance that gives the "sense and meaning to a Music which might not otherwise … have any," which is how I argued Aristotle perceives the matter in *Politics* VIII 5 and which itself followed *Laws* II in some ways. Finally, Smith notes the power and "obviousness" of dance over "Verse or Poetry," which in some ways is entirely in line with Plato's and Aristotle's views, as described in Unit 2. One might well wonder whether Smith was influenced by Thomas Rymer, who, we noted in Chapter 3 and who will be discussed more in the Appendix, himself called words in drama sometimes "heavy baggage."

In any event, to return to Aristotle: None of the above requires that every aspect of his theory in the *Dramatics* be correctly articulated or that we should take every statement as an infallible general principle, stemming from a perfect understanding of human nature and ontology. In other words, as Ben Jonson warned, we should not let Aristotle be a dictator.[750] For instance, the Northern Greek gives the types of stories that dramatists best realized in his day in *Dramatics* 13-14, based on the types of households that reflected the desired kind of suffering, pity, and fear in (a certain sub-type of) tragedy, or even the welcome averting of disaster at the last moment for plays like *Cresphontes*. This preference of Aristotle's does not mean all cultures, including American, French, Japanese or Greek, that create drama in the twenty-first century must confine themselves to those stories. Aristotle recounts what was happening in the Greece of his time because Greece was the only civilization to present drama. Yet his description, or prescription, of Chapters 13-14 arguably does not outweigh the prescriptions he gives in other parts of the treatise, including the option of presenting anything similar to what might have happened in the past, because, as he says, if something similar happened then it is possible that it could happen. Showing fiction or what could happen is part of the dramatist's task (*Dramatics* 9, 1451b16-32). Thus, the kind of story that the dramatist employs could be virtually anything, as long as absurdities do not result, given that one fundamental principle is to be believable.

As we have seen throughout this book, Aristotle also recognizes and explores various aspects of drama, including its autonomy as an art form despite the inescapable connection it has at times with ethics and politics. This connection in no way undercuts the crucial autonomy of art from the perspective of artistic theory, even if Aristotle attempts to understand related considerations when we deal with drama in a broader context, as sometimes we must. One cannot appeal to art to justify, e.g., spilling a neighbor's blood because one likes that color of red against green grass, a classical example in aesthetics to show that art cannot be given unlimited license in the name of creativity or visual delight. All of these considerations provide value to the Northern Greek's views, especially if his ethical

---

750   See the Appendix for the exact quotation.

## Chapter 9: The Future of the *Dramatics*

and political considerations are ones that we share, which arguably we do in many ways. Indeed, the ethical theory of the *Nicomachean Ethics* is, as mentioned, one of the three great systems influencing Western civilization.[751]

Consider what the modern literary historian M. A. R. Habib also says in these regards, which returns us full circle to the theme that opened this book, that the *Dramatics* has been the most important treatise on literature, drama and perhaps art in general for Western culture. He also confirms that many different cultures from many centuries have all found great worth in the *Dramatics* and will continue to find substantial worth in the treatise, even if he perpetuates the misconception that the work is fundamentally about literary theory:

> ... Aristotle's thought as a whole laid the foundation for the entire classical tradition of thought and literature in the Western world. *It may be useful to furnish a concise statement of the elements of Aristotle's classicism.*
>
> The most fundamental premise is a political one, namely, that the individual achieves his or her nature and purpose only within a society and a state. Our own notions of individualism, often Romantic in origin, were quite foreign to Aristotle. Poetry, for Aristotle, does not express what is unique about individuals but rather their universal characteristics, what they share with other members of society. While Aristotle grants to poetry a certain autonomy, it yet occupies a definite place within the state as an instrument of education and moral edification. Poetry is not, as in Romantic thought, exalted to an eminence beyond other pursuits...
>
> In addition to Aristotle's ethical and political dispositions, there are a number of epistemological and metaphysical principles which underlie his arguments and prescriptions in the *Poetics*. Some of these have already been mentioned: *Aristotle's empirical method, his acceptance of plurality, the teleology of both individual and state, and the principle of moderation. To these we might add the notions of unity, probability, necessity, rationality, universality, and truth.* All of these notions, together with Aristotle's ethical and political principles, underlie his views of the characteristics of good literature. *The issues at stake here include the meaning and desirability of realism, the presentation of character, the use of detail, the use of language, and the way in which various components of a literary work are mutually integrated and harmonized.*
>
> ... Aristotle's notions anticipate developments in several areas of literary criticism: the issue of poetic imitation, the connection between art and reality, the distinction between genres as well as between high and low art, the study of grammar and language, the psychological and moral effects of literature, the nature and function of the audience, the structure and rules of drama, as well as the notions of plot, narrative, and character. *All of these notions are still profoundly pervasive in our thinking about literature and the world* [my italics].[752]

---

751   By "ethical" here I mean from the perspective of philosophy and reason. Religious morality of course has great influence, for good or for bad, but is not within my focus.

752   Habib, *op. cit.*, 2005, pp. 49 & 60-1.

Not only are the various concepts that Habib lists still pervasive in dramatic musical theory, having sometimes occurred first in Aristotle's treatise, but, as Augusto Boal recognized (as seen in the Appendix), the concepts get applied nowadays also to non-musical plays, film, TV including "soap operas," and of course to much modern literature, despite, for instance, Virginia Woolf's diatribe against plot. One often reads in journals and newspapers the analytical tools or principles of the *Dramatics* as part of the typical discourse in cinema reviews and criticism: plot, character, probability, believability and so forth.[753] This is the case whether or not the modern writer understands that the con-

---

[753] Take a few cases culled mostly from the *New York Times*, all employing concepts stemming, knowingly or not, from Aristotle (and Plato). The cases reflect popular culture and show to some extent how widely and deeply the concepts have seeped into our consciousness:

In his review of Doris Lessing's novel *Ben, In the World*, Michiko Kakutani states "Because nothing feels very real in this novella, because Ben and everyone else seem like cardboard cut-outs, the reader feels neither pity nor fear for the characters, only a vague sense of irritation." ("His Weirdness Attracts Types Even More Weird," *NY Times*, Aug. 8, 2000, p. E6).

Stephen Holden's appraisal of the film *The Piano Teacher*, involving Walter being infatuated with his piano teacher Erika (Isabelle Huppert), contains Holden's criticism that "Erika's and Walter's tango doesn't track, mostly because Walter's changes of heart are too abrupt and seem determined by the plot rather than driven by character" (*The Piano Teacher*: Film Review "Kinky and Cruel Goings-On in the Conservatory," *NY Times*, Mar. 29, 2002, p. E15).

Michael Andreen, a consultant to the Chinese media firm Le Vision Pictures, which itself acquires or produces films for worldwide audiences, remarks: "Chinese audiences want more from Hollywood movies—not just spectacle, but stories that engage them" (as quoted by Michael Cieply, "U.S. Box Office Heroes Proving Mortal in China," *NY Times*, Apr. 28, 2013, p. BU 2).

Calin Peter Netzer discusses his film of 2014, which involves a young man accidentally killing a child in a car accident and then being placed in an awkward position by his mother, who given her position of power tries to get the charge of manslaughter dismissed in exchange for regaining control of the son. Netzer says "We were inspired by the news because accidents like this do happen in Romania. So we put it [the film] together with this pathological mother-son story. It's like a catharsis, therapeutic if you will" (Larry Rohter, "Romania's Overlooked New Wave," *NY Times*, Dec. 18, 2013: https://carpetbagger.blogs.nytimes.com/2013/12/18/romanias-overlooked-new-wave).

The penultimate case is most emphatic (leaving aside the questionable point about how much the *Dramatics* can be applied to film directly, when film in some ways is itself more like epic in being able to arrange temporal sequences more inventively). It is ironically also about the modern version of the culture to which Aristotle belonged. Alcestis Oberg writes about the reaction to the low-budget film *My Big Fat Greek Wedding* and it becoming one of the most profitable movies in history. She says:

> Hollywood is mystified by the success of [it]… Hollywood bigwigs…are still trying to comb through the nit-picking details of its "distribution," "limited screening" and "female audience appeal"—the useless measures by which they judge audiences—to understand why *Greek Wedding* is raking in more than their expensive summer blockbusters.
> The answer is simple: it's the story, stupid.
> More than 2,300 years ago, the Greek philosopher Aristotle wrote that a really good plot was the most important element of drama, followed by interesting characters, good diction, profound thought, nice scenery and tuneful songs. These elements sustained drama in all of its forms for two millennia—that is, until Hollywood honchos put expensive special effects first, substituted celebrity stars for true character development…and hung it all on a contrived, predictable or loopy plot

## Chapter 9: The Future of the *Dramatics*

cepts originated with Aristotle (or with Plato) or whether or not the writer understands what Plato's and Aristotle's views really are.

Thus, given all of the above, it would be surprising if Aristotle's views (to leave Plato aside for the moment) do not continue to have significant value for us now and long into the future, whether or not they are applied correctly. How much value that would precisely be is not something to discuss quickly, even if such a matter could be reasonably resolved. What criteria would be used to adjudicate such an issue or to measure it? In any event, the fact that so many different cultures for over 450 years have found inspiration in the *Dramatics* is not something to be disregarded without rigorous argument, especially if, as argued in this book, the treatise was often misunderstood, rejected or even ignored because of at least two major misconceptions.

---

("Maybe 'Greek Wedding' Will Wake Up Hollywood Bigwigs," *USA Today,* Sept. 12, 2002, p. 13A). Leaving aside, for instance, that even some ancient Greeks put special effects first, as Aristotle had complained about, the executives still do not seem to get the message, according to Brooks Barnes:

> Having tried 3-D films, earsplitting sound systems and even alcohol sales in pursuit of younger moviegoers, some theater chains are now installing undulating seats, scent machines and 270-degree screens... For an $8 premium, a Regal theater here even sprays patrons with water and pumps scents (burning rubber, gun powder) into the auditorium ("To Lure Young, Movie Theaters Shake, Smell and Spritz," *NY Times,* 11/29/2014: https://www.nytimes.com/2014/11/30/business/media/to-lure-young-movie-theaters-shake-smell-and-spritz.html).

## Final Postscript: New Dance-Related Scholarship

I had the pleasure of hearing Michel Briand present a paper at the annual conference of the Society of Dance History Scholars, in Athens, June 2015, where I was also presenting a paper on the unrecognized value of dance in Plato's and Aristotle's politics (essentially merely sections of this book). During subsequent correspondence, Briand offered some valuable feedback on the book, with some judicious advice and, in addition, comments on a few points that I have included in footnotes. Perhaps more importantly for some readers, he also introduced me to a wide source of scholarship, mostly from France, which had flown under my radar. To try to incorporate that work here would have postponed the appearance of this book for many more months, if not years. Nevertheless, because my intent is most of all to enable a fresh appraisal of Aristotle's *Dramatics* by correcting the fundamental misconceptions addressed above, I provide Briand's potentially valuable list for scholars who wish to delve more into the related topics in the future, in alphabetical order. At my request, Briand provided his own publications, including the collections they belong to, that might be of interest. Louis XIV, Menestrier, and Noverre might be smiling from Hades that so much theoretical attention is being given to dance, their beloved art form in France, whatever the focus in other countries.

### Greek Music, Dance and Theater

Briand, Michel. "Dance and theôria in Greek antiquity: Homer, Plato and Lucian of Samosate, beyond the distinction practice—theory," *Proceedings of the SDHS* (Society of Dance History Scholars) 2007 Symposium (Re-Thinking Practice and Theory/Repenser la pratique et la théorie), Centre National de la Danse, 2007, pp. 318-23.
- "La limite et l'envol: les fins paradoxales des épinicies de Pindare," *Commencer et finir. Débuts et fins dans les littératures grecque, latine et néolatine.* (Actes du colloque de Lyon (Lyon III—ENS LSH, Sept. 2006), 2008a, pp. 557-72.
- "Les épinicies de Pindare sont-elles lyriques? ou Du trouble dans les genres poétiques anciens," in D. Moncond'huy & H. Scepi, *Le genre de travers: littérature et transgénéricité*, La Licorne, PU de Rennes, 2008b, pp. 21-42.
- "La danse et la philologie: à partir du mouvement strophique dans les scholies anciennes à Pindare," S. David, C. Daude, E. Geny & C. Muckensturm-Poulle (eds.), Traduire les scholies de Pindare. De la traduction au commentaire: problèmes de méthode, avec une préface de Cl. Calame, *Dialogues d'histoire ancienne*, Supplément 2, PU de Franche-Comté, 2009a, 93-106.
- "Les épinicies de Pindare et de Bacchylide comme rites de passage: pragmatique et poétique de la fete et de la fiction méliques," in Philippe Hameau (dir.) avec la collab. de Christian Abry et Françoise Létoublon, *Les rites de passage. De la Grèce d'Homère à notre XXIe siècle*, Grenoble, Musée Dauphinois, 2010b, pp. 91-100.
- "Interplays between Politics and Amateurism: Ritual and Spectacle in Ancient Greece and

some Post-modern Experiments (Castellucci, Bagouet, Duboc, Halprin)," (SDHS 2010 Conference, Dance and Spectacle, 8-11 July, Univ. of Surrey, Gilford & The Place, London, UK), en ligne: http://sdhs.scripts.mit.edu/proceedings/2010/#papers, pp. 33-48, 2010d.

- "Danse—récit (et action)/danse matière (et création): pour une esthétique com-parée de l'antique et du contemporain, d'Homère et Lucien à Gallotta, Chopinot, Duboc, et retour," in Rémy Poignault (éd.), *Présence de la danse dans l'antiquité—Présence de l'Antiquité dans la danse*, Caesarodunum, XLII—XLIII, Clermont-Ferrand, 2013, pp. 409-23.

- "Liaison poétique, alliance rituelle: harmonia chez Pindare," in Pierre Gaye, Florence Malhomme, Gioia M. Rispoli, Anne Gabrièle Wersinger (dir.), *L'Harmonie, entre philosophie, science et arts, de l'Antiquité à l'âge moderne*, Atti della Accademia Pontaniana, n. s. vol. LIX suppl., 2010f, pp. 209-27

- "Light and Vision in Pindar's Olympian Odes: Interplays of Imagination and Performance," *The Look of Lyric. Proceedings of the network for the Study of Archaic and Classical Greek Song*, vol. 1, André P.M.H. Lardinois, Robert P. Martin & Anastasia-Erasmia Peponi (eds.), scheduled.

- "Gestures of grieving and mourning: a transhistoric dance-scheme," in Ken Pierce (ed.), Dance ACTions—Traditions and transformations. SDHS 36th Annual Conference, 2013, https://sdhs.org/proceedings/2013/pdf/Briand_22.pdf

- "Vision spectaculaire et vision imaginative dans la poésie mélique grecque. Le cas des épinicies de Pindare," in Régis Courtray (éd.), *Pallas: Regard et représentation dans l'Antiquité*, 92, 2013, pp. 115-31.

Calame, Claude. "From Choral Poetry to Tragic Stasimon: The Enactment of Women's Song," *Arion* 3: 135-152, 1994 (contains a comparison of Pindar's Partheneion 2 and the parodoi in Aeschylus' *Seven against Thebes* and in Euripides' *Phoenician Women*).

- "Performative aspects of the choral voice in Greek tragedy: civic identity in performance," in *Performance culture and Athenian democracy*, eds. S. Goldhill and R. Osborne. Cambridge. 125-53. 1999.

- "The Tragic Choral Group: Dramatic Roles and Social Functions," in *A Companion to Tragedy*, ed. R. Bushnell. Oxford: 215-33. 2005.

- "Choral Forms in Aristophanic Comedy: Musical Mimesis and Dramatic Performance in Classical Athens," in *Music and the Muses. The Culture of Mousike in the Classical Athenian City*, eds. P. Murray and P. Wilson. Oxford: 157-84. 2004.

Calame, Claude, and Florence Dupont, Bernard Lortat-Jacob and Maria Manca (dir.), *La voix actée. Pour une nouvelle ethnopoétique*, Paris: Éditions Kimé, 2010.

Catoni, Maria Luisa. *La communicazione non verbale nella grecia antica. Gli schemata nella danza, nell'arte, nella vita*, Torino: Bollati Boringhieri, 2008.

David, A. P. *The Dance of the Muses. Choral Theory and Ancient Greek Poetics*, Oxford: Oxford University Press, 2006.

Dupont, Florence. *L'invention de la littérature. De l'ivresse grecque au livre latin*, Paris: Éd. La Découverte, 1994.

- *Aristote ou le vampire du théâtre occidental*, Aubier: Libelles, 2007.

Gebauer, Gunter & Christoph Wulf. *Jeux, rituels, gestes. Les fondements mimétiques de l'action sociale*, Paris, Anthropos, 2004 (trad. C. Roger, de Spiel-Ritual-Geste. Mimetisches Handeln in der sozialen Welt, Hamburg: Rowohlt, 1998).

Lonsdale, Steven H. *Dance and Ritual Play in Greek Religion*, Baltimore: The Johns Hopkins University Press, 1993.

Klimis, S. *Archéologie du sujet tragique*, Paris: Kimé, 2003.
- *Le statut du mythe dans la Poétique d'Aristote. Les fondements philosophiques de la tragédie*, Bruxelles: Ousia, 1997.

Naerebout, Frits Gerard. *Attractive Performances. Ancient Greek Dance: Three Preliminary Studies*, Amsterdam: Gieben, 1997.

## **Roman Pantomime and Related**

Garelli, Marie-Hélène. *Danser le mythe. La pantomime et sa réception dans la culture antique*, Louvain/Paris: Peeters, 2007.

Greenberg, Mark (ed.). Thesaurus Cultus et Rituum Antiquorum (ThesCRA), t. II Purification. Initiation. Heroization. Apotheosis. Banquet. Dance. Music. Cult Images (Los Angeles: Getty Publications, 2004), especially L. Bruit-Zaidman, P. Schmitt-Pantel et al., "4a. Banquet," pp. 203-21, and H. A. Shapiro, "4.b Dance."

Webb, Ruth. *Demons and Dancers. Performance in Late Antiquity* (Cambridge, MA: Harvard University Press) 2009.

# Appendix

## A History of the Two Fundamental Misconceptions

The primary purpose of this appendix is to prove that not one well-known commentator of the so-called *Poetics* until my Ph.D. dissertation in 1992 considered Aristotle to be using *poiēsis* in the Platonic-Diotiman sense of the word, if only to argue that the Gorgian sense is better. Even considering just the most famous commentators, this history is necessarily lengthy, and the reader can imagine how many full *books* this history might have taken if all commentators since only the Renaissance were examined. All previous scholars before me had taken Aristotle to present literary theory in the treatise, with one caveat*:* As I demonstrate at the end, a few scholars claim he offers a much wider artistic or aesthetic theory, with literary works being mere examples of broad principles. Given my arguments in this book, which I imagine most if not all will have read before reading this appendix, I use interchangeably my rendering of Aristotle's technical title (stemming from the first two words in the treatise) as *Dramatics,* again short for *Dramatic "Musical" Composition.*

The second purpose is to show that even from the beginning of the commentaries starting with Avicenna the scholars were greatly puzzled by the word *katharsis* in the definition of tragedy. Indeed, the Arabic scholars either ignore it or treat it as an ethical term, moderation, unlike any accepted ancient Greek connotation. *Katharsis* has come to take on a host of meanings, especially in the twentieth century, far beyond the three ancient Greek senses. The history also reveals in more detail, for example, what I briefly discussed in Chapter 6, namely, that the extremely influential Jacob Bernays stunningly wrote in 1857 that an excerptor went through the *Dramatics* and purposefully removed the passages on *katharsis*, which for him explains why there is no explanation as seemingly promised by *Politics* VIII 7.

The third and final purpose is to present more of the criticisms that Aristotle has endured because of the alleged two misconceptions, above and beyond his having a "tin ear" for poetry, to bring us up to date on the status of his book at the beginning of the twenty-first century.

Professional aestheticians who are extremely familiar with the full tradition of the *Dramatics* may discover nothing substantially new. Nevertheless, perhaps all of them will find some surprising nuggets. Some of them may not know, for instance, either the work of two writers on drama in this context, Lope de Vega (1562–1635) and Thomas Rymer (c. 1643–1713), or the atypical but occasionally excellent intuitions of the commentator André Dacier (1651–1722), along with the generally unknown reports of dance theorists such as Claude-François Menestrier and Carlo Blasis. They are all rarely discussed in Anglo-American aesthetics.[754] Rymer and de Vega advocated the use of plot and action over text, even though they typically did it in their own names rather than as the correct Aristotelian view, ironically while citing Aristotle's authority in many related contexts. Nevertheless, this history is mostly for those not familiar with the long tradition of interpreting the *Dramatics*, to confirm that it unquestionably has been viewed in the manner I describe in the Introduction.

## The *Dramatics* from 322 BCE to the 11th Century CE

We have no way of knowing how ancient scholars took Aristotle's treatise.[755] As Tarán and Gutas say in their recent work, which, as noted, sets a new standard for the paleographical tradition:

> The *Poetics* has not been as well transmitted as many other Aristotelian works, as can be seen even in the greater number of emendations an editor must adopt. There are several related reasons for this difference. *There is no extant ancient commentary on the* Poetics, *nor any evidence that there ever was one in ancient or early Byzantine times...* The lack of the above shows that there was in ancient times no great interest in the *Poetics*, especially so among Aristotelian scholars. This accounts for the fact that our text was not copied as often as other Aristotelian treatises, and so the Greek tradition has provided us with only two primary witnesses, one of which (B) is not even complete and is seriously damaged [my italics].[756]

At most, a couple of attestations from late Hellenistic and Roman times survive that may refer to the *Dramatics*. However, trying to construct a theory of tragedy from them, much less of drama in general, would be like trying to demonstrate the shape of a building based on a handful of discovered stones, with no other record of how it was designed. However, it is worth reporting the attestations, if

---

754   I say "Anglo-American" loosely, because Great Britain seems, quite surprisingly, to have had little concern for aesthetics as a discipline, although it certainly has world-renowned thinkers in the related individual arts. I am not sure of recent developments, but while finishing my M.A. at Columbia University in the 1980s and choosing a program for the Ph.D., I examined Oxford and Cambridge. I discovered upon visiting both universities that they had no specialists in aesthetics, although, naturally, they had (and have) some of the best scholars in the world in ancient philosophy, my other interest. Perhaps this was the result in part of Bertrand Russell becoming disenchanted with aesthetics and maybe influencing others, as evidenced by a copy of correspondence that I was shown at the University of Toronto by the Russell specialist John G. Slater. Russell pens in a letter of Oct. 19, 1913, to Lucy Donnelly: "I feel sure learned aesthetics is rubbish, and that it ought to be a matter of literature and taste rather than science."

755   Two post-Aristotelian theorists, Lucian and Athenaeus, have been discussed at times already, insofar as they affect the theses in this book. Libanius wrote a treatise *Concerning Dance* in the 4th century CE, but it seems to have neither awareness of the *Dramatics* nor anything that would impact my conclusions. In part not to swell an already massive book, and given that Libanius writes almost 700 years after Aristotle, I leave it to others to show whether I was wrong to leave him out.

756   Tarán and Gutas, *op. cit.*, p. 156. Also, cf. Whalley, *op. cit.*, 1997, who gives an excellent summary of the whole manuscript tradition, pp. 4-7.

only for the assumptions and developments that underlie them. Francesca Schironi writes about the Alexandrian scholar and librarian Aristarchus of Samothrace (c. 217–145 BCE), who seems to have taken over as the head of the renowned library in Alexandria after Aristophanes of Byzantium:

> If what I am going to argue is sound, Aristarchus knew what the philosopher [Aristotle] had said about the affinity between these two genres [epic and tragedy] and therefore thought it legitimate to apply Aristotle's criteria for a good tragedy to epic poetry. The Alexandrians knew some of the Aristotelian works, and whether or not the *Poetics* was available to them, the dialogue *On Poets*, in which Aristotle discussed the same topics as in the *Poetics*, and the *Homeric Problems* were both known... The *Poetics* in particular does not seem to have enjoyed great popularity in antiquity: ancient sources are silent, and the earliest quotation is in Porphyry [c. 234–305 CE]...
>
> As I hope to have shown, Aristarchus seems to have been aware of Aristotelian reflections on poetry. In his work on Homer, he uses Aristotelian categories and critical concepts.[757]

"The *Poetics* ... does not seem to have enjoyed great popularity in antiquity" is either litotes, understatement for the sake of emphasis, or puts the matter so obliquely that it distorts the reality, as we shall see. Perhaps all of the Aristotelian concepts could have been known to Aristarchus via *On Poets* (as previously translated, even though the arguments of this book show the better title would be *On "Musical" Composers*). However, we know hardly anything about this exoteric work, and the concepts could have been known via another Peripatetic work (and we examined very briefly the miniature *On Tragedy*, which is another possible source). Nevertheless, the few scraps of *On Poets/On "Musical" Composers* that exist have references to the actors acting, which we saw in my Chapters 2 and 3 is the basis of the derivation of plot (*muthos*) in the first list of six necessary conditions.[758] Yet, with respect to applying principles to good epic from good tragedy (or vice-versa), Schironi ignores the adage of *Dramatics* 25 that each art form has its own principles. There are overlapping commonalities between epic and tragedy, in which case there are some grounds for her claim. However, as I showed in Chapter 9 there are clearly very important differences between the two art forms for Aristotle, and an uncritical acceptance historically of her type of claim in this respect has been one reason that dramatic principles have been misapplied to literature. This reason is irrespective of whether epic was truly literature *per se* in archaic and classical times, as opposed to a combined art of verse, music in the form of "singing" or musical accompaniment, and "dance-gesture," or whether there were different sub-species of epic, some with words only and some with chanting and gestures. Hence, Schironi's account in her otherwise often very impressive article is not completely sound, and she admits that no solid evidence exists for a copy of the *Dramatics* being held in the library in Alexandria or that Aristarchus had read it. This admission is partly why at the end she can only (properly) conclude, leaving aside the meaning of "poetry," that "Aristarchus seems to have been aware of *Aristotelian* reflections

---

757   Schironi, *op. cit.*, 2009, p. 282 and p. 312.
758   Cf. Janko, 1987, pp. 56-7.

on poetry [my italics]."⁷⁵⁹ Despite my aforementioned doubts regarding her article, and leaving aside the other, admittedly impressive parts, the most fascinating aspect of her report for us in this context is that it shows how quickly the performed art of drama was being subsumed under literary theory by the Alexandrians at the beginning of the second century BCE, only 125 to 150 years after Aristotle's death.

Janko gives more detail on the supposed first mention by Porphyry:⁷⁶⁰

> An important fragment of the lost portion of Aristotle's *Poetics* is the definition of synonyms preserved by Simplicius, which corresponds to Aristotle's own citation of the *Poetics* for synonyms in the *Rhetoric,* 3.2. 1404b37ff. I shall argue elsewhere that this derives from a discussion of the sources of verbal humour in the lost account of comedy and humour. Here it is my aim to show that Simplicius definitely derived the quotation from Porphyry, which pushes back the attestation of this part of the *Poetics* by more than two centuries (although the citation in the Antiatticist, *Poet.* Fr. 4 Kassel, is older still⁷⁶¹).

In short, the few tiny passages that make up a minuscule fraction of the *Dramatics* occur in texts published around 180 CE and 270 CE, over half a millennium after Aristotle's death. Other fragments seemingly refer to Aristotelian doctrine, as discovered in manuscripts during recent excavations of the city of Herculaneum, which, along with Pompeii was buried by the great eruption of Vesuvius in 79 CE. However, the fragments again appear to be related to the exoteric, widely publicized *On Poets* rather than the esoteric *Dramatics*.⁷⁶² We cannot assume, then, that just because Alexandrians and Romans took *poiēsis* in the Gorgian sense that Aristotle himself was treating not only this word but related concepts such as *muthos* (myth, fable or plot) in *their* way. As we proceed, I believe we will also see why the Emperor Justinian's ban on performed drama from about 530 CE onward was greatly responsible for the subsequent lack of interest in the treatise until the Renaissance revived tragedy and comedy. Besides, who would have been able to read the *Dramatics* after Justinian banned the schools of philosophy? However, none of this explains the lack of interest for 800 years, from 322 BCE, at Aristotle's death, to the time of Justinian. (This repressive emperor coincides with one of the last great Aristotelian commentators, if not the last, Simplicius, before Aristotelianism gets suppressed, only to be revived in non-Arabic culture by thinkers like Thomas Aquinas in the thirteenth century.) A historian of literary theory, Daniel Javitch, offers a possible account of the matter:

---

759   She, like many other philologists, translates *melopoiia* and *mousikē* in *Dramatics* 6 and 26 in other passages not reproduced above in the previously standard way, "music," which, as was demonstrated, completely and wrongly eviscerates tragedy of its dance.

760   "A Fragment of Aristotle's *Poetics* from Porphyry, concerning Synonymy," *The Classical Quarterly*, Vol. 32, No. 2 (1982), p. 323.

761   The Antiatticist *circa* 180 CE cites one very short example of word-play from the *Poetics*; cf. Janko, 1987, p. 164.

762   Cf. Janko, 1987, pp. 175-81, and especially his treatment of Philodemus.

Aristotle's view *of poems* in terms of the inherent or internal requirements of their forms was a minority view in the ancient world. Most ancient critics (Horace, among them) measure the effectiveness and value *of a poetic work* in terms of external standards of truthfulness and of morality, and not by the degree to which it contributed to realizing what Aristotle took to be its particular form and function. Moreover, the rhetorical orientation of these critics made them pre-occupied with the conditions imposed by the audience and not, as was Aristotle, with the composition of inherent and objective properties. This can explain why the *Poetics* was largely neglected in antiquity [my italics].[763]

Related to this is Tarán's very reasonable suggestion that the switch from rolled manuscripts to codices (equivalent to our book form), which started about the end of the second century CE and continued slowly for a few hundred years, may have been responsible for the section on comedy being lost, because if a text was not of great interest it never got recopied.[764] Until a better explanation comes along, if ever, I take it that these are some of the reasons why ancient and Byzantine scholars ignored Aristotle's treatise and why, starting with the Renaissance, subsequent scholars for generation after generation accepted the status quo of the two alleged misconceptions. Once the first Arabic commentators set the conceptual framework, perhaps inspired by the Alexandrians, that the *Dramatics* was primarily about literary theory and once the commentators passed the framework to the Latin scholars, it was extremely difficult to break the ensuing tradition by re-examining the ancient commentaries—*simply because there were none*.

Let us now proceed chronologically and review what scholars have said about the *Dramatics*, especially concerning the two misconceptions that I believe I have amply proved existed for centuries.

According to Ismail Dahiyat, at least a few translations of the *Dramatics* are known to have existed before the renowned Persian polymath and so-called "Father of Early Modern Medicine," Avicenna (980–1037), wrote the first commentary that focused solely on the *Dramatics*.[765] A previous commentary, which is only partial at best, had been given by al-Fārābī (c. 872–950), the so-called "second Aristotle," who spent most of his life in Baghdad. However, consider how al-Fārābī himself describes the treatise and what he gives for the definition of tragedy before we see that his account is not intended to be based solely on the *Dramatics*:

> The eighth [book of logic] contains the rules for analysing *poems* and the classes of *poetic statements* in use and those produced in each kind of situation. It also [contains] an enumeration of all things with which the discipline of *poetics* is connected, how many classes

---

763 Daniel Javitch, "The Assimilation of Aristotle's *Poetics* in sixteenth-century Italy," in *The Cambridge History of Literary Criticism: Volume 3, The Renaissance*, edited by Glyn P. Norton (Cambridge: Cambridge Univ. Pr.) 1999, p. 53.
764 Tarán and Gutas, *op. cit.*, p. 33.
765 Dahiyat, *op. cit.*, 1974, pp. 3-4.

of them there are, how many classes of *poems* and *poetic statements* there are, how each class is produced and from which things it is made, in connection with which things it becomes more excellent, more splendid, more brilliant and more pleasurable, and what qualities it ought to have so as to become maximally effective. This book is called *Poiētikē* in Greek, that is, the Book of *Poetry*...[766]

Tragedy is a kind of *poetry* having a particular metre, *affording pleasure* to all who hear or recite it. In tragedy good things are mentioned... Musicians used to sing tragedies before kings, and whenever a king died, they would insert in the tragedy certain additional melodies lamenting the dead king... [my italics][767]

We should note now the surprising omission by al-Fārābī of *katharsis* in the "definition," with pleasure being instead given as the goal (which, given what we saw in Chapter 7, is a remarkably sound observation on his part). However, leaving aside for the moment this sound observation, the lack of direct experience of dramatic performance is presumably part, but only part, of the reason that the Arabic commentaries are generally agreed, D.W. Lucas says, to have "cast but a fitful light on the subject."[768] As the Arabic specialist Gutas says of these passages by al-Fārābī, they had their origin not directly in Aristotle's *Dramatics*:

> but in a derivative textbook discussion of Greek **poetry** and **poetic meters**. In particular the **literary genres** of tragedy and comedy were little understood *as performance arts* among non-Greek speakers in the Hellenized Near East (and possibly even among the majority of Greek speakers with a classical Greek education) because they had stopped being part of public life in late antique societies [his own italics but my bolding].[769]

As mentioned, and as Gutas presumably implies, tragic performance stopped with Justinian. Further proof of Lucas's claim that the Arabic scholars cast but a fitful light on the subject of tragedy can be gleaned by examining the definitions of tragedy given in the Arabic translation attributed to Abū Bishr Mattā in about 932 from the Syriac edition, and then by the commentary of Avicenna, both of which came from Syriac translations and not directly from the Greek.[770] All of this, however, is subject to a *caveat* by Gutas that I present when examining Avicenna. Abū Bishr wrote no commentary on the treatise, but his translation is preserved in the National Library, Paris (MS, BN 2346), and was based on the Syriac version by Isḥāq ibn Hunain from about 900.[771] Note that Abū Bishr uses the Arabic word for

---

766     al-Fārābī, *The Enumeration of the Sciences*, in Taran and Gutas, as Test. 14, *op. cit.*, p. 94.

767     al-Fārābī, *Canons of the Arts of the Poets*, in Taran and Gutas, as Test. 15, *op. cit.*, p. 94.

768     D. W. Lucas, 1968, *op. cit.*, p. xxv. See also p. xxiii for a brief history of the Arabic texts and of the subsequent translations by D. S. Margoliouth in 1887 (who also gives apparently the first complete Latin rendering of the Arabic in 1911, but see the review by Tarán and Gutas, *op. cit.*, pp. 115-6, regarding the value of the work) and by J. Tkatsch, posthumously published in 1928 and 1932, as *Die arabische Übersetzung der Poetik des Aristotles und die Grundlage der Kritik des griechischen Textes,* 2 vols. (Vienna).

769     Tarán and Gutas, *op. cit.*, p. 95.

770     Dahiyat, *op. cit.*, pp. 4-6.

771     According to Dahiyat, *op. cit.*, p. 6.

"encomium" rather than for "tragedy":

> The art of encomium is an imitation and similitude of an action, voluntary, serious and complete; having magnitude and length; in useful speech, except each one of the kinds that are effective in the parts; not by promises; modifying the emotions and affections by mercy and fear, and purifying and cleansing those who are moved.[772]

This account of the definition is very similar, of course, to the definition of tragedy that we examined in Chapters 2-8. However, the notions of enactment (on stage) with spectacle versus narrative are wholly dropped in this translation, in lieu of "useful speech," which is perhaps not too surprising given that about 400 years earlier Justinian had banned the theater, a ban that lasted centuries and that meant subsequent generations of Europeans also never saw live performances until the Renaissance. (I should add that the repressive Christian Justinian closed Plato's Academy forever.) Moreover, Islam frowned upon human representation in different degrees, depending on the sect, and seemingly had no type of theater, as the Greeks once had. Thus, any Arabic (or Christian or secular) scholar in the 9th through 15th centuries would have been completely unfamiliar with the practice of staging tragedy and comedy that Aristotle wrote about (although of course they may have read about the history of such practices or seen the ruins of an amphitheater).[773] Curiously, though, Abū Bishr's definition of tragedy even omits "song," which al-Fārābī had included, although "useful" might have been developed to include song in texts I have not read. Catharsis, on the other hand, is indeed indicated. However, it is noteworthy that "Abū Bishr Mattā's translation … was not considered a reliable translation even by his own contemporaries."[774]

## Avicenna (980–1037)

Around 1020, after presenting his own views on poetry and discussing non-dramatic genres, Avicenna presents the *Dramatics* as having been formerly part of the *Organon*, a classic grouping of six treatises by Aristotle that themselves focus on logic and language.[775] *Organon* means "tool" or "instrument" and the books were construed to be the works that helped Aristotle analyze or carry out his philosophy in general. This grouping goes back to Aristotle's student Theophrastus, and Simplicius about 530 CE adds as its seventh and eighth "branches" the *Rhetoric* and the *Poetics*.[776] In this form, the organon was also accepted by al-Fārābī in the passage we saw above (he called it the "eighth book" there). Avicenna, who apparently knew neither Greek nor Syriac, intermixes his commentary with a summarized transla-

---

772 Dahiyat's transl, *op. cit.*, p. 6
773 I emphasize I am speaking of theater in the sense of Greek amphitheater. When discussing Averroes, I add some qualifications provided by James Monroe.
774 Dahiyat, *op. cit.*, p. 5.
775 Dahiyat, *op. cit.*, p. 12.
776 Dahiyat, *op. cit.*, p. 12.

tion of the *Dramatics*, using Abū Bishr's Arabic version, along with probably a second by Yaḥyā ibn ʿAdī, as his sources.[777]

Avicenna presents one chapter of his own view of *poēsis* and then summarizes Aristotle's *Dramatics* in the final seven chapters. The following gives an impression of his outlook concerning the themes of literature and *katharsis*. In the very first sentence of his first chapter, Avicenna says:

> We first say that *poetry is imaginative speech*, composed of utterances that are measured, commensurate—and, in Arabic, rhymed... The logician considers [poetry] only in so far as it is imaginative speech. Otherwise, the measure is the [proper] concern of the musicologist (in terms of investigation and general practice) and the prosodist (in terms of scansion and according to the practice of each nation). The rhymist considers rhyme... [my italics][778]

Avicenna then completes the chapter by developing the uses of poetry, as for instance in civil life or for wonder alone, and lists the twelve types of poetry almost verbatim to what al-Fārābī had given, and which, as such, have no basis anywhere in Aristotle:[779] tragedy, dithyramb, comedy, iambic (relating to maxims), "dramata" (which resembles iambic except that particular people are meant), didactic, "anthus" (a delightful kind with utterances composed "for their excellence and strangeness"), heroic epic, satyric, "poemata" (dealing with poetry itself), "*amphi geneseōs*" (poetry invented by Empedocles describing natural science), and acoustic (for instruction in the art of music). Al-Fārābī in his own words had culled them from the works of Aristotle, Themistius (whom I discussed in Chapter 3) and "other ancient writers, as well as the Commentators on their books."[780]

---

777   Dahiyat, *op. cit.*, p. 9. Further details are given by Gutas and summarized by Michael McOsker: According to Gutas, the first translation into Syriac was in the ninth century and was revised. Abū-Bišr Mattā ibn-Yūnus translated this revised Syriac version into Arabic. Finally, Avicenna indicates that the Arabic translation was itself revised twice. There are some additional quotations of it in Averroes, who quotes liberally, *probably* from the first revision, and is therefore occasionally useful. *The second, more thoroughgoing revision of Abū-Bišr's version implies the use of a second Greek MS. On these grounds, Gutas posits a MS Σ, the basis for the original Syriac translation, as well as Ψ, the MS used for the second revision of the Arabic.* ... Unfortunately, only one MS (Parisinus Arabus 2346) of the original Arabic translation, sloppily copied and damaged, exists [my italics]. (Michael McOsker, *Bryn Mawr Classical Review* 2012.11.26, also found at http://bmcr.brynmawr.edu/2012/2012-11-26.html; no page # on the web, the version used.)
I am unsure of the relation between the version by Yaḥyā ibn ʿAdī, which, as I understand Dahiyat, could have come from the same Greek manuscript that Abū-Bišr Mattā used, and the Greek Ψ which Gutas hypothesizes existed. In other words, did the Arabic translation get revised twice, based on one Greek manuscript or based on two Greek manuscripts? Would the different capabilities of a second scholar not allow for a "more thoroughgoing revision," even if only one Greek manuscript had existed in Persia? I defer to the Arabic specialists on this issue, and it has no bearing on the conclusions of this book.

778   Dahiyat, *op. cit.*, p. 61.

779   Dahiyat, *op. cit.*, pp. 66-8. This is not to say that some types cannot be found in Aristotle's work.

780   Dahiyat, *op. cit.*, p. 68.

Appendix: A Brief History of the Two Misconceptions

Starting in his second chapter, Avicenna begins summarizing the *Dramatics*, not offering anything that approaches a close translation of the text, but taking parts of Aristotle's texts that he can seemingly understand and interpolating his own explanations freely. I give just a few samples, and interested readers might see, e.g., Dahiyat's book for how the same approach and the same distortions are carried through to the end. Avicenna reports Aristotle's beginning of the *Dramatics*:

> As [Aristotle] said, let us now speak of poetry, its kinds and the characteristic of each kind; the principle of excellence in making likenesses and poetic fictions, i.e., imaginative utterances ... [at this point Avicenna skips the listing of arts that Aristotle notes are examples of mimesis, like dithyramb, tragedy, comedy, and double oboe- and kithara-playing].[781]

Later in *Dramatics* 1, as demonstrated in my Chapter 2, Aristotle mentions that orchestra-dancers, the *corps de ballet*, as it were, can through their gestured dancing alone convey *ethos* (character), *pathos* (emotion) and *praxis* ("action"), the last normally being something with an intent, as opposed to, say, mere breathing,[782] but Avicenna instead adds something that is not anywhere in *Dramatics* 1, whether or not it is true: "Rhythm without tone may be found in dancing; dancing, however, is better performed when accompanied by the proper tone—it makes [a stronger] effect on the soul."[783] Subsequently, when Avicenna discusses the history of "poetry" from *Dramatics* 4 he properly mentions the singers and dancers but confuses the role of Aeschylus and Sophocles, and reverses when the player gets added, if by "player" he means "performer" (because, as we saw a few times, Aristotle says the relevant language gets added late). As Avicenna says in his sections 9 and 10:

> 9. Tragedy grew from the ancient dithyramb; Comedy grew from the trivial, satirical poetry... then, the player's art was added to it [tragedy], and was utilized by the poets who combined speech with acting. Thus, the same thing came to be understood in two ways: one, according to language; and the other, according to the singer's appearance.
>
> 10. When old Aeschylus came, he mixed that with melodies and thus gave to tragedies songs that were used by the singers and dancers. He also introduced poetic dialogue, i.e., the reply and contest mentioned in the *Rhetoric*. Sophocles introduced the melodies played in theatres in the manner of jesting and lampooning. That had previously been rare and simple.

Yet, as we saw in Chapter 2, according to Aristotle, Aeschylus does not introduce dialogue; rather, he makes language the *main* element in tragedy, because the choral aspect, with music and dance, had existed first as the almost exclusive or predominant elements. Moreover, Sophocles

---

781    Dahiyat, *op. cit.*, p. 70.
782    Butcher gives a suitably brief account of the three types:
By *ēthē* are meant the characteristic moral qualities, the permanent dispositions of the mind, which reveal a certain condition of the will; *pathē* are the more transient emotions, the passing moods of feeling; *praxeis* are actions in the proper...sense... The *praxis* that art seeks to reproduce is...deeds, incidents, events, situation, [which are] being included under it so far as these spring from an inward act of will, or elicit some activity of thought or feeling (*op.cit.*, p. 123).
783    Dahiyat, *op. cit.*, pp. 71-2.

introduces the third actor and scene-painting (and himself has nothing to do with jesting language).

I finish with three sections from Avicenna's fourth chapter, which is almost exclusively devoted to the definition and subsequent explanation of tragedy in *Dramatics* 6:

> 5. Of Hexameters and Comedy, we will speak later, for the art of encomium and the imitation of noble deeds should have precedence over invective and ridicule.
>
> 6. Let us then define tragedy and say: Tragedy is an imitation of an action complete and noble, and elevated in rank; in very appropriate speech, not devoted to every particular part; affecting the particulars not with respect to quality but with respect to action—an imitation which moves souls to mercy ["pity"] and piety ["fear"].
>
> 7. By means of this definition, the nature of tragedy is shown in such a way as to indicate that in it all high and noble deeds are dealt with in pleasurable and measured speech, and in a manner that inclines souls to kindness and piety. It imitates actions because virtues and qualities do not lend themselves easily to imaginative representation, but are best known through actions. For the sake of such actions, tragedy is deliberately complemented with an additional rhythm and a harmonious melody in order to realize the tone fully; in this respect, the rhythm of the verse itself is enhanced by an additional rhythm. When tragedy is sung, such matters may also enter as gestures and the player's art—these make the imitation complete...[784]

Before remarking on this long passage, I should add that Avicenna then provides the final ranking of six necessary conditions that I examined in great detail in Chapters 2 and 3. After noting in order "fiction" (for our "plot"), "habit" (for our "character"), opinion (for our "thought" or "reasoning"), and [poetic] composition (for our "language" or "speech"), he states:

> 22. Fifth is melodious intonation. This is the most important of all; it has the greatest effect on the soul. As for {*the sixth necessary condition*} spectacle [lit., viewing and proof], it is that which fixes in the soul the import of diction and the necessity of its acceptance, in order to alleviate grief and produce the emotion proper to tragedy. It is not a matter of art; i.e., the [means of] persuasion mentioned in the *Rhetoric* are not proper to poetry. Tragedy is not based on argumentation and competition, nor on the player's art [my inserted qualification in pointed brackets] (p. 95).

The reader can see how far off these translations of Avicenna are (seen, of course, through the eyes of Dahiyat), given my Chapters 2 and 3, although often Avicenna reads the Greek-Arabic correctly. However, what is immediately clear follows. First, there is no translation here of the word *katharsis*, as Dahiyat himself says:

> nor in any part of the entire Commentary. The inference that one can make regarding this matter is that Avicenna seems to have the notion that the emotional effect of tragedy consists in moving the soul toward a philanthropic feeling of friendliness (*riqah*) and piety

---

784  Dahiyat, *op. cit.*, pp. 88-90.

(*taqwā*).[785]

Avicenna did not seem to understand how Aristotle could use *katharsis*, which is fascinating or baffling, because it appears he had a manuscript that had the word (that is, the Syriac translation for it). Probably Avicenna did not understand it whatsoever, and just skirted the problem of translating it. Next, Avicenna deduces that the verse of tragedy would have its own, inherent rhythm, and believes that another "rhythm" is added to it, along with the melody. Depending on how one reads the passage, either two or three rhythms are composed to exist together. Finally, note that he mentions actors and singing, but that he asserts that tragedy is not based on the player's art, as if one could have the tragedy by having the "poem"—for, after all, the subject was for him "poetry in measure." All of this entails that the player's art was an accessory, and not necessary. Moreover, the spectacle is mistaken for some psychological aspect or type of argumentation as found in the *Rhetoric*, rather than the theatrical accoutrements on stage.

## Averroes (1126–1198)

Averroes presents the third and final extant medieval Arabic account of tragedy in the *Dramatics*. The reason for me to present his account is not to understand the *Dramatics* better, for we will see that Ingram Bywater was also right when he said "Averroes is fairly at home in the more philosophical and grammatical parts of the book; but its meaning, as a theory of Greek Tragedy, was from first to last a hopeless enigma to the great Aristotelian of Cordova."[786] Instead, my purpose is to highlight the beginning of a specific tradition of the *Dramatics* in the late Middle Ages. This tradition regards the treatise as dealing with poetry *per se*, with music sometimes added to it, and also involves a curious—indeed brilliant and bold, if wrong—interpretation of *katharsis* that is not kept by the later commentators once the Greek manuscripts become widely known in the sixteenth century.

I should start by saying that Averroes also apparently knew no Greek and seemed to have used Abū Bishr Mattā's (Arabic) translation, again, itself based on the Syriac version of a Greek manuscript, plus perhaps the commentary of Avicenna.[787] Dahiyat adds:

> Averroes ... states that he aims at extracting from the *Poetics* only those "universal canons which are common to all or most nations, for a great deal of what is in it are canons peculiar to their poetry; and their conventions are analogously found in either Arabic discourse or other languages." Averroes finds that Greek tragedy and comedy are analogous to the *non-dramatic* Arabic genres of encomium and satire, and his method is to make as much as possible of the analogies. He sums up an Aristotelian statement ... *and then sets out*

---

785     Dahyiyat, *op. cit.*, p. 6.

786     Bywater, *op. cit.*, 1909, p. xxxii.

787     Cf. Dahiyat, p. 9; also, Mallette, p. 586; in addition, see *Averroes' Middle Commentary on Aristotle's Poetics*, translated and introduced by Charles Butterworth (South Bend, Indiana: St. Augustine's Press) 2000, p. xi.

*to explain it on the analogy and example of Arabic poetry, or literature (especially the Qur'ān)* [my italics].[788]

It is worth recalling that, even though Aristotle does not give one poem *per se* in the treatise, the examples of Arabic poetry comprise more than twenty of the eighty-one pages of Averroes's translation-commentary, on my count. As should not be surprising given the previous explanation and history of the theater from Justinian onward, Averroes seems to have no awareness of staged drama as it existed in Greece. This lack of awareness can be gleaned from a cursory examination of his translation-commentary, in which the best plots of *Dramatics* 13 and 14 are completely omitted, as are stage considerations (such as Aristotle's criticism of Carcinus in Chapter 17 for not paying attention to how the stage implementation could cause a play to fail).

Charles Butterworth writes in 1986 that he himself gives: "not only the first English translation from the Arabic original [of Averroes's *Middle Commentary*]; [but the] ... first translation of the Arabic text to be made in any language other than medieval Hebrew or Latin."[789] In Butterworth's lengthy introduction, not only the Greek poets but the Arabic ones are described as makers of images or imitations *in words*. Also, the Arabic poets are accorded even loftier status than the Greek practitioners.[790] Butterworth then asserts, "Poetry according to Aristotle and Averroes is, above all, imitative speech,"[791] but without offering any citation for the Greek. Moreover, Butterworth continues:

> A third consideration [about poetry] added by Aristotle—namely whether the object is represented narratively, dramatically, or by some combination of the two—is passed over in silence by Averroes, probably because of his basic confusion concerning the arts of tragedy and comedy. These two [are] understood by Averroes as eulogy and satire."[792]

We examined in Chapter 2 the difference between the two "manners of mimesis" as Aristotle gives them in *Dramatics* 3. For the moment, suffice it to say that Averroes asserts of tragedy and comedy in his first chapter (which is supposed to convey what *Dramatics* 1 says), "He [Aristotle] said: every poem and poetic statement is either satire or eulogy,"[793] treating them as types of poems. Moreover, as Averroes adds in that first chapter:

> With respect to poetical statement, imitation and representation come about by means of three things: harmonious tune, rhythm, and comparison itself [meaning "imitation" in the Arabic]. Each of these may occur separately from the others—like tune in flute-play-

---

788  Dahiyat, *op. cit.*, p. 11.

789  Butterworth published his first edition with Princeton University Press, 1986. The book was republished in 2000, as cited just above, and this latter one is the version I use.

790  Butterworth, *op. cit.*, p. 5.

791  Butterworth, *op. cit.*, p. 12.

792  Butterworth, *op. cit.*, 2000, p. 13.

793  Butterworth, *op. cit.*, 2000, p. 59.

ing; rhythm in dance; and representation in utterances, I mean, in imitative non-rhythmic statements. Or all three may be brought together—like what is found among us in the kind of poems called *muwashshahāt* and *azjāl*, these being the ones the people of this peninsula have devised in this tongue [the first is typically a love song and the latter something that troubadours sing and perform]. For it is in natural poems that the three things are brought together, and natural things are to be found only among natural nations. There is no melody in the poems of the Arabs. Indeed, they are meter alone or both meter and representation ["meter" alone presumably meaning verse, or what I have called the Gorgian sense of poetry/*poiēsis*]. Since this is the case, the imitative arts or those that effect imitation are three: the art of melody, the art of meter, and the art of making representative statements. *This latter is the logical art we shall investigate in this book* [my italics, and my explanations in brackets].[794]

Averroes separates verse from representation, which itself can also be found in prose. However, Averroes does not even require meter or verse for the representational language of tragedy, as we saw Aristotle does (recall that *metron* replaces *logos* at the end of *Dramatics* 1, as one of the three means of mimesis). Instead, Averroes interprets *logos* in Chapter 1, usually and correctly rendered as "language," as another form of "representation," and explains away verse as not being required to those who represent with language (which in one way is true at times for Aristotle, an example of which is Socratic dialogue in *Dramatics* 1, just not true for drama). Dance is recognized, but Averroes drops completely the passage by Aristotle in which the *corps de ballet* can convey pathos, ethos and "actions" with gestured *rhuthmos* (translated of course usually as "rhythm," perhaps because of Aristotle's account of *rhuthmos* in the *Rhetoric*, which Avicenna had explicitly referenced).

As fascinating as Averroes's account of the next few chapters is for how an Andalucian of the twelfth century who is one of the greatest thinkers in history would conceive tragedy, notwithstanding his lack of Greek or of real dramatic practice, and as informative as his account is of the Arabic poetry of his time,[795]

---

794   Butterworth, *op. cit.*, 2000, pp. 62-4.

795   For much more on the importance of song in Arabic culture of the time, and earlier, and how song was even more primary at times than language by itself, see James T. Monroe, "The Tune or the Words? (Singing Hispano-Arabic Strophic Poetry)," *Al-Qanṭara (Revista de Estudios Árabes)*, Vol. VIII, 1987, 265-317, espec. pp. 267, 274-5, 276, 279, 303, and (for the material directly on Averroes's passage above) 307ff. Monroe also added in private correspondence the following, which I think is important to share with anyone interested in exploring performance, and especially dance and music, in medieval Arabic culture, because from personal experience, I know how little dance historians know about dance in that period:

> As far as Averroes is concerned, although he had clearly never seen a Greek tragedy or comedy, on a popular level there do seem to have been dramatic performances of some sort in the Arab world. Witness the three shadow plays by Ibn Dānīyāl (d. 710/1310), composed in Egypt. In an article of mine, I further studied a *zajal* by the Andalusī poet Ibn Quzmān (d. 555/1166), in which that poet mimics a popular performance containing some form of dramatic representation ("Prolegomena to the Study of Ibn Quzmān: The Poet as Jongleur," *The Hispanic Ballad Today: History, Comparativism, Critical Bibliography*, Ed. Samuel G. Armistead, Antonio Sánchez-Romeralo, and Diego Catalán. Madrid: Cátedra-Seminario Menéndez Pidal and Gredos, 1979, vol. 3, pp. 77-129). In my

we must jump to Averroes's account of *Dramatics* 6 and the definition of tragedy, along with the derived six necessary conditions in the rest of that chapter. As Butterworth translates:

> He [Aristotle] said: the art of eulogy is brought into being when recourse is had to long poetic meters rather than short ones. Therefore recent poets have rejected the short poetic meters which used to be employed in this and other poetic arts. The meter most characteristic of it is the simple, non-compounded one. However, it ought not to be stretched out to such a length as to create aversion. *The definition that makes the substance of the art of eulogy understood is*: it is a comparison [i.e. being or essence here] and representation of a complete, virtuous voluntary deed—one that with respect to virtuous matters is universal in compass, not one that is particular in compass and pertains only to one or another virtuous matter. It is a representation *that affects souls moderately* by engendering compassion and fear in them [my italics].[796]

Only three points are noteworthy here, given the concerns of this book and the explanations in the earlier chapters. First, Averroes completely drops, at least in Butterworth's rendition,[797] the introduction to

---

> article, I provide what references were available to me on the subject of popular performances in al-Andalus. I would, therefore, tend to suspect that Averroes, rather than speaking out of total ignorance, may well be deliberately adjusting Aristotle in order to make him comprehensible, and even relevant, to his Arab audience, which was more familiar with the lyrical and classical *qaṣīda* ('ode'). In this respect, the *qaṣīda* embraces three subgenres: (1) *madīḥ* ('panegyric'), (2) *riṭā'* ('elegy'), and (3) *hijā'* ('satire'). The first two portray the individual, be he alive or dead, as loftier than normal, whereas the third portrays him as being below the norm. That is why Averroes refers to tragedy as *madīḥ* and to comedy as *hijā'*. In other words, he is attempting to convey the gist of what Aristotle meant by using Arabic literary examples that would be comprehensible to his audience of Arab readers who, in turn, knew nothing about Greek literature (private letter, Sept., 2015).

It is unclear how Monroe uses "dramatic," and whether it only means (as I suspect) a type of musical performance that has pantomimic elements or whether it means what Aristotle indicates it means, as something with spectacle. Also, I should add that in the "Prolegomena" Monroe gives ample examples of performance and dance being part of "musical" or "poetic" culture, e.g., a poem with those ululating in unison following ideally the leader, who are gently chided to "get moving!" (p. 79); etymologies of words that in a certain context mean performance, along with the use of castanets, an instrument used since Greek times by dancers (p. 87, ft. 31); and an impresario directing "musicians, singers, dancers, actors, and trained animals" (p. 97). Except for the trained animals, the description sounds like the artists that Plato and Aristotle speak about in drama (again, though, without the important scenery). Finally, while on the similarity *and dissimilarity* to Greek drama, I finish with one other fascinating report of Monroe's:

> As J.M. Landau has pointed out, dramatic performances in the Arab world are of three types: (a) mimicry, (b) the passion play, and (c) the shadow theater. Of these popular forms, the third contains elements that are closest to what concerns us here. While the origins of the shadow play are obscure, as are those of mimicry, *the theory has been advanced that they go back to the Greek mime, possibly through Byzantium* [my italics] ("Prolegomena," p. 97).

796    Butterworth, *op. cit.*, p. 73.

797    I offer Dahiyat's translation also, for comparison on to how *katharsis* gets translated,—or not:
The definition that expresses the essence of the art of encomium [tragedy] is that it is an imitation and similitude of an action, voluntary, noble and complete, which has a universal effect in noble matters, although not a particular effect in every one of the noble matters—an imitation that moves human beings to a moderate emotion by means of the pity (lit. "mercy") and fear it generates in

the definition at the beginning of *Dramatics* 6 in which Aristotle says he will speak of hexameter poetry (epic) and comedy later and in which Aristotle gives the definition "based on what had been said before." As emphasized repeatedly in Chapters 2-3, various scholars, including myself, have demonstrated that Aristotle's statement reflects him using biological division and collection to define. Second, as both Butterworth and Dahiyat independently show, the term *katharsis* is interpreted as "moderation," or to be precise "moderate (emotion)," which is the only time historically to my knowledge that such a rendering has been given in a "translation." Given what we saw in Chapter 6, it is a brilliant and very logical rendering because of Aristotle's ethical theory, and Averroes is bold to write it, especially if *katharsis* should be the goal of epic also and of any other "poetic" form that can engender pity and fear. However, the rendering is blatantly wrong as a translation of the Greek word, and many problems get swept under a rug by it. Finally, Averroes gives unnecessary words for the definition, but William Boggess shows that it was the Syriac translator who added the extra words to the *katharsis* clause that Averroes took faithfully and who is therefore really to blame for any augmentation in that particular regard.[798]

Let us continue to the only other passage we need examine in Averroes's commentary, which comes at the end of *Dramatics* 6, after Aristotle derives from the definition the six conditions that he says all tragedies have. We saw above how Avicenna treated them. Averroes himself writes:

> He [Aristotle] said: the parts of the art of eulogy must be six—mythic statements, characters, meter, beliefs, spectacle, and melody. A sign of this is that every poetical statement may be divided into something that is compared and that by means of which it is compared. There are three things by means of which something is compared: representation,[799] meter, and melody. There are also three things compared in eulogy: characters, beliefs, *and spectacle—I mean, discovery of the correctness of a belief.* Thus the parts of the art of eulogy are necessarily six.
>
> ... *Spectacle is what explains the correctness of belief. It is as though it were for them [the Greeks] a type of argumentation for the correctness of the eulogized belief.* None of this is found in the poems of the Arabs, though it is to be found in eulogistic scriptural statements.
>
> ... The fifth part in order is melody. Of these parts, it has the greatest influence on souls and is the most effective. *The sixth part is spectacle—I mean, giving argument for the correctness of a belief or the correctness of a deed, not by means of a persuasive statement for that is not appropriate for this art, but by means of a representative statement.* Indeed, the art of poetry and especially the art of eulogy, is not based on proving and disputing. That is why eulogy does not use the art of dissimulation and delivery the way

---

them (Dahiyat, *op. cit.*, p. 86).

798 William F. Boggess, "Hermannus Alemannus and Catharsis in the Mediaeval Latin *Poetics*," *Classical World*, Feb. 1969, pp. 212-4.

799 Butterworth notes "Averroes uses 'representation' (*muḥākāh*) and 'myth' (*khurāfah*) interchangeably," *op. cit.*, p. 76.

rhetoric does [my italics].[800]

Only a few points are needed now. "Mythic statements" is the translation of *muthos,* often "myth," but more correctly "plot" in all translations of the last few hundred years (for reasons we saw in Chapter 2). "Beliefs" is the translation of *dianoia.* The rest of the six parts are straightforward and almost match up with current translations, with one exception: "Spectacle" is the term that obviously completely eludes the Andalucian as it did Avicenna, which, again, may not be surprising given Justinian's ban on drama and the absence of the practice in Europe for 600 years by the time Averroes began writing.[801] As Butterworth indicates, Averroes misconstrues *nazar,* the Arabic word used for *opsis* (spectacle), for one of its other, common senses, namely speculation or reflection. Thus, when interpreting the *Dramatics,* Averroes ends by saying that "spectacle," means "discovery of the correctness of a belief," and it is explained with recourse to, and in contrast with, the *Rhetoric.*[802] Obviously, with spectacle (as the staging) removed, it is effortless to continue construing Aristotle as writing about myth-making or stories or literature in verse, that is, poetry in the Gorgian sense of the word, as the previous Arabic scholars had done.

To take stock so far: For the Arabic commentators, and the three extant commentaries, there was no questioning the nature of the enterprise for Aristotle. The treatise was about poetry or language, and anything dramatic or performative was a matter at most of the secondary, musical or non-argumentative stylistic considerations for Averroes or seemingly of optional troubadours' gestures for Avicenna. The commentators never considered even the possibility that tragedy could be an independent art of drama that merely used literature as a part, for they seemed not to realize what drama was for the Greeks and the notion of an amphitheater *with dramatic scenery* seems inconceivable to them. Moreover, concerning *katharsis,* even though Abū Bishr gave "… purifying and cleansing (those who are moved) …" in his translation, Avicenna drops the word *katharsis* and its related significance completely in his account, for reasons that are unknown. Averroes himself considers *katharsis* to mean "moderating (emotion)," but neither commentator notes the oddity of the concept missing in the rest of Aristotle's chapter, or, as we saw already with Avicenna, in the rest of Aristotle's book. Rebecca Gould may be perfectly right when

---

800   Butterworth, *op. cit.,* pp. 76-9.
801   O.B. Hardison, Jr. says (in *Poetics and Praxis, Understanding and Imagination: The Collected Essays of O.B. Hardison, Jr.,* ed. by Arthur Kinney, Athens: Univ. of Georgia Press, 1997) :
> …the confusion of the commentary [of Averroes] concerning poetic form produces a woefully distorted interpretation of the six "parts" of tragedy listed by Aristotle in *Poetics* 6…spectacle something called *consideratio,* by which Averroes seems to mean the gestures and facial expressions used by orators to emphasize their arguments (p. 30).

Also very pertinent to the themes of this book is that Hardison demonstrates (pp. 31-2) how Averroes changes the discussion of *Poetics* 12, of the chorus of tragedy, into terms from rhetoric, completely obliterating the function of the singing and dancing chorus. Hardison's enlightening and well-researched essay is valuable reading for anyone dealing with the tradition of the *Poetics* in the late medieval period.

802   Butterworth, *op. cit.,* p. 76.

## Appendix: A Brief History of the Two Misconceptions

she says "... it must be acknowledged that Ibn Rushd's [Averroes's] mistranslation—which is better understood as simply a variant interpretation—was one of the most productive misreadings in *world literary history* [my italics]."[803] However, whether as a mistranslation or, euphemistically, as a "vari-

---

803   Rebecca Gould, "The *Poetics* from Athens to al-Andalus: Ibn Rushd's Grounds for Comparison," *Modern Philology*, 112.1 (2014): 1-24, p. 24.   On a related point, although literary specialists are better equipped than I to judge the following with respect to literary issues, Gould might be able to advance her thesis without her over-simplification of Aristotelian truth, which hardly is sustainable, for reasons that immediately follow her additional statements:

> While Aristotle argued that, *pace* Plato, mimetic art partakes of truth, even the Stagirite was unable to do away entirely with the assumption that art's value is measured by the accuracy of its representation of the world. Islamic aesthetics by contrast emphasized the generative and even magical powers of the imagination. Herein lies a basic difference between Aristotle and his Arabic commentators: the distance between the world and its aesthetic representation is the beginning of *poiesis* in Arabic literary criticism. "The best poetry is that which lies the most [*khayr al-shi' rak-dhabuhu*]," runs a famous Arabic proverb that was cited by many Arabic rhetoricians, including al-Jurjānī. According to this logic, the distance between the world and its representation in literature is to be cultivated, theorized, and celebrated, whereas in the Platonic tradition this distance is a problem to be overcome. By privileging language over representation, poetry over drama, and the work of the imagination over conformity to representational aesthetics, Ibn Rushd [Averroes] was able to detach literary meaning from a correspondence theory of truth without relinquishing literature's capacity to intervene in the world. Aristotle, preoccupied as his treatise was by the concept of mimesis, assumed the dependency of art on reality and never sought to reverse that relation. Aristotle's concept of probability enabled him to demonstrate the efficacy of artistic representation in relation to other discourses (such as history), but, unlike Arabic and Persian theorists of poetics, Aristotle did not argue for poetry's ontological primacy in the world of representations. For Aristotle, as for Plato, poetry was always, at some level, subordinate to another level of discourse that was perceived as more proximate to truth. Indeed, the mere attempt to justify poetry (as against history) in terms of philosophy shows that, for Aristotle, philosophy was more important than poetry (pp. 15-6).

To address the many problems with Gould's passage, starting from the top: Aristotle certainly says in *Poetics* 25 that it is better for a poet to be convincing by representing something truthfully than not. However, truth is not an absolute requirement there. Indeed, being convincing is more important in poetry. In addition, a statement like "Oedipus killed his father" is not a truth-bearing sentence even though categorical in form, because there is no concern with saying "of what is that it is," Aristotle's notion of truth ("fictional truth" would be reporting what the poet said, accurately, but this is a different issue). Also, Aristotle emphasizes in Chapter 9 that the poet should express what might be and not what has been (although what has happened is *one* ground for showing what is possible). Aristotle's statement, also in Chapter 9, about poetry being more philosophical than history does not ground Gould's relevant claim. She needs to look at what Aristotle says about the worth of theoretical wisdom (and the worth of metaphysics) compared to art in the *Nicomachean Ethics* if she is concerned about ranking philosophy (including "first philosophy" or theology for Aristotle) against poetry. Yet, then, to be fair, she needs to ask the same about Arabic thought, and I strongly doubt that poetry in Islam will rank higher than the theological discourses of the *Qu'ran!* Besides, imagination is stressed by Aristotle in *Poetics* 17, although since the subject is tragedy, which I show is staged, the ability to be convincing requires that the imagination not be ridiculous. However, I venture to say that the same holds in Arabic poetry and that horses are not shown to have seventeen legs or forty-four wings with eyes on the back of their knees, even if in a religious context they might sprout two wings to take Mohammed to heaven. Besides, even though Aristotle prefers naturalistic

ant interpretation" or as a "productive misreading," Averroes's account of what Aristotle actually says and means was far from accurate in many ways, substantiating Bywater's evaluation. Nevertheless, that account laid the groundwork for other, typical misreadings, as we see now. Stephen Orgel, who describes the transition to the next historical period, remarks:

> Here is how Averroës renders the passage [regarding the definition of tragic drama]: tragedy "is an imitation which generates in the soul certain passions which incline people toward pity and fear and toward other similar passions, which it induces and promotes through what it makes the virtuous imagine about honorable behavior and morality." Obviously a good deal has been added to the clause to attempt to make sense of it, but one indubitably clear thing about it is that *pity and fear are conceived to be good things, and far from being purged, are what we are expected to end up with...* Nevertheless, despite all the confusions and lacunae, Averroës's notion that the Poetics *promulgates a view of drama* **as ethical rhetoric** *is one that* **persists long after the discovery and analysis of the Greek text**. Averroës in many respects continued to be the basis of Renaissance views of the essay, enabling it from the outset to be easily harmonized with Horace's *Art of Poetry* [my italics and bolding].[804]

## The Transition to the Renaissance

In the thirteenth and fourteenth centuries, two scholars—Herman the German ("Hermannus Alemannus") and Todros Todrosi of Arles—translated Averroes's commentary into, respectively, Latin in 1256 and Hebrew in 1337. Those translations became the basis of the late Medieval understanding of the *Dramatics*, despite a reputedly very faithful translation of the Greek by William of Moerbeke in 1278 that may have been requested by Thomas Aquinas (c. 1225–1275).[805] I rely on the specialists of that era, as quoted below, to report the more precise details. Three summaries shall suffice to confirm the fundamentals of the relevant account for our concerns. The first, by Mallette, recapitulates some of the points seen earlier and introduces newer historical phenomena:

> The great Aristotelian commentator ... Averroës wrote both a short commentary and a middle commentary on the *Poetics*. It was this middle, or medium-length, commentary that Hermannus translated into Latin, thus producing a Latin version of an Arabic version of a Syriac version of a Greek text. Hermannus's *De arte poetica* is a primer for the philologist working in the medieval Mediterranean. In its linguistic complexity, in the sea

---

depictions, he certainly allows depictions of myth and other "lies," as we will see throughout this book; cf. *Poetics* 24, 1460a19ff. Finally, as should have been clear by the end of my Chapter 9, we hardly know much about his views on literature *per se* including language in verse, Gould's topic. However, that epic can be and is, in Aristotle's words in Chapter 24, more amazing than tragedy because it is not shown on stage in and of itself suggests that Aristotle recognizes that (Greek) poetry could be just as imaginative as Arabic poetry and as little concerned with "the truth," in favor of more "amazing" poetical concerns *per se*.

804    Orgel, 2002, pp. 132-3.

805    Gould provides some of the textual evidence for Herman relying on "the assistance of the 'Saracens' residing at that time in Toledo," *op. cit.*, p. 1.

changes it underwent as it passed from language to language and culture to culture, the work both demands and thwarts philological precision... The most striking of the medieval innovations catches the reader without warning on the opening page of a modern edition of the text and has excited the most comment among modern historians. "Every poem," Aristotle says (according to Averroës and Hermannus), "and every poetic oration is either praise or vituperation"—thus did medieval readers understand the technical terms used by Aristotle, tragedy and comedy, and throughout his commentary Averroës uses the term *madīh* ... or "praise," when Aristotle speaks of tragedy, and *hijā'* ... or "vituperation," when he speaks of comedy.[806]

O.B. Hardison Jr. adds more along the same line:

> If the *Poetics* was unintelligible to Hermannus and his contemporaries, Averroes was not. Twenty-three manuscripts of the Hermannus translation survive, and it was printed in 1481,[807] thus becoming the first version of Aristotle's *literary theory* published during the Renaissance. Its compatibility with medieval critical ideas is attested by the fact that in 1278 William of Moerbeke, Bishop of Corinth, made a remarkably accurate translation from the Greek, which was, however ignored; William's translation exists in only two manuscripts, both dating from the thirteenth century, *and it was not printed until 1953.* The obvious moral of this tale is that the late Middle Ages was not prepared to assimilate the *Poetics.* On the other hand, Averroes' commentary was easy to assimilate.[808] The distortions which disconcert the modern reader are the very features which made the work intelligible and attractive to the medieval audience. In effect, it enlisted Aristotle in support of the most characteristic (and most un-Aristotelian) features of medieval poetic theory [my italics].[809]

Why the version of the Latin *Dramatics* by William of Moerbeke, which had *purgatio* ("purgation") for *katharsis,* was incomprehensible for over 200 years in the late Middle Ages is not explained, but it is touched upon by Boggess:

> Although William of Moerbeke, did, to be sure, anticipate one side of the Renaissance controversy by employing *purgatio* for catharsis, his Greco-Latin translation seems never to have been used until its discovery in our century. Hermannus' text, on the other hand, enjoyed wide authority from the time of St. Thomas Aquinas and Roger Bacon to the latter half of the sixteenth century. Its manuscript tradition and its *testimonia* in *florilegia* ["a

---

806   Mallette, *op. cit.*, 2009, p. 584.

807   Recall that Gutenberg's first press dates from around 1450 CE. Mallette reports twenty-four mss (*op. cit.*, p. 599), citing Boggess *et al* as references. Gould reports twenty-four also (*op. cit.*, p. 1). Concetta Greenfield reports only twenty-three, though, in Concetta Carestia Greenfield, *Humanist and Scholastic Poets, 1250-1500* (Lewisburg, PA: Bucknell Univ. Press) 1981, pp. 93-4. However, all specialists report only two manuscripts of William of Moerbeke and note the disproportion versus Averroes.

808   Hardison adds:
In his preface to the commentary on the *Poetics* Hermannus says that he planned to translate the *Poetics* itself into Latin but had to give up because of the difficulty of the vocabulary. His admission shows that the original was just as obscure to a thirteenth-century European as it was to Averroes (*op. cit.*, in Kinney, 1997, p. 26).

809   Hardison, *op. cit.*, in Kinney, 1997, p. 26

collection of excerpts from written texts"] and elsewhere have proven, moreover, that the *Poetics,* in this form, was taught and studied as a logical treatise [and not as one pertaining to drama *per se*] in the University of Paris during the fourteenth century. That the full discussion of catharsis did not flourish until the popularity of Averroes' commentary waned can scarcely be coincidental [both comments in brackets are mine].[810]

We saw in Unit 3 of this book reasons why the accurate translation by William of Moerbeke, using *purgatio* rather than Averroes's "moderation," itself a very central Aristotelian concept in the *Ethics,* might have been utterly baffling to those familiar with the rest of Aristotle's philosophy. Given, too, the absolute lack of personal acquaintance with staged drama in the thirteenth and fourteenth centuries—obviously still ongoing since Justinian's ban—it is also not surprising that the logical or linguistic aspects of the *Dramatics* took precedence. However, again, I leave it to specialists of the period to determine whether debates about drama ever arose. Aquinas, the great Aristotelian, does not provide either a translation or a commentary for the *Dramatics.* As Dahiyat reports,[811] Aquinas merely says in the *Commentary on the Posterior Analytics,* that, compared with dialectic or rhetoric, in poetry "a mere fancy inclines us to one side of a contradiction because of some representation ... for the task of the poet is to lead us to something virtuous by some excellent description."[812] Aquinas' remark smacks of Averroes's dramatic poetry as "ethical rhetoric."

The following account by the specialist Javitch (who, as we saw, offered a reasonable account of why the *Dramatics* was ignored during ancient and Byzantine times) completes for our purposes the history of the *Dramatics'* transition from medieval times to the Renaissance:

> ... because the kind of ethico-rhetorical terms into which Averroes recast Aristotle's poetics reflected prevailing notions of poetry well into the sixteenth century, Averroes' commentary on the *Poetics* was published, reprinted, and coexisted along with Giorgio Valla's 1498 Latin translation of Aristotle's text (the first to be published), and the 1508 Aldine printing of the Greek original.
>
> With the reacquisition of the Greek language in the course of the fifteenth century, and the recuperation of original Greek texts, learned Italians no longer had to depend on medieval refractions of the *Poetics.* Manuscripts of Aristotle's Greek text were being copied, were circulating, and were being studied in Italy as early as the 1470s. By 1480, or shortly thereafter, Angelo Poliziano was referring to the *Poetics* in his university lectures, as had Ermolao Barbaro before him. In fact, Poliziano appropriates some of Aristotle's views on *mimesis* in the reflections on comedy with which he begins his commentary on Terence's *Andria.* Yet despite the availability of the Greek text, and, eventually, of Giorgio Valla's (less than reliable and incomplete) Latin translation of it in 1498, the evidence suggests

---

810  Boggess, *op. cit.,* 1969, pp. 213-4.

811  Dahiyat, *op. cit.,* p. 18.

812  Thomas Aquinas, *Commentary on the Posterior Analytics by Aristotle,* trans. by F. R. Larcher (Albany, N.Y: Magi Books) 1970.

## Appendix: A Brief History of the Two Misconceptions

that Aristotle's theory had little relevance and value for its readers. It is telling that Giorgio Valla's own treatise on poetry, his *De poetica* (largely devoted to metrics), was much more indebted to Diomedes' *Ars grammatica* than to Aristotle, cited by Valla only occasionally and mostly for his views on the origins of drama. Even after Aldus published the Greek text in 1508 (as part of an anthology entitled *Rhetores graeci!*[813]), it had little impact. To be sure the *Poetics* was not dismissed or totally disregarded in Italy, as it was in other parts of Europe ('it has not much of good fruit', Juan Luis Vives would declare not untypically in his *De disciplinis* (1536), 'being wholly occupied in the observation of ancient *poems* [my italics], and in those subtleties, in which the Greeks are most pestiferous, and ... inept to boot'), but interest in the treatise only begins to grow once the Italians become more familiar with ancient Greek tragedy. It is hardly accidental that Alessandro de' Pazzi, the first writer to provide a relatively reliable Latin translation of the *Poetics* (composed in 1524; published in 1536) was also responsible for the first Latin and then vernacular translations of Sophocles and Euripides.

Pazzi's translation served to make Aristotle's text more accessible but only somewhat more intelligible. In the dedication to his first tragedy *Orbecche* (1541) Giovambattista Giraldi Cintio ... indicates how obscure and perplexing the text was to contemporary readers. Beyond Aristotle's characteristic obscurity, the treatise, writes Giraldi, 'remains so cryptic and dark that it takes much effort to understand his definition of tragedy'. It was at this very moment that the first sustained exegesis of the *Poetics* began. Bartolomeo Lombardi's lectures on the *Poetics* at Padua in 1541, continued by Vincenzo Maggi (who also lectured on the text at Ferrara in 1543), inaugurate a series of explications and retranslations by professors connected to the school of Aristotelian philosophy at Padua. With the appearance of Francesco Robortello's *Explicationes* (1548), the first of the commentaries to be published, a real upsurge of interest in the *Poetics* begins to manifest itself.[814]

I continue with the history, starting with Robortello, although readers interested in greater detail might return to Javitch himself. Before proceeding, though, I should underscore that all of Javitch's accounts of the treatise and the content therein as treated by the Italians are phrased in terms of poetry, poems, and metrics. Again, there is no hint that anyone even considered the possibility that tragedy was an independent art of drama nor that *poiēsis* might have a Diotiman meaning, if only to reject that option in order to justify the Gorgian sense. To return briefly to the second alleged misconception of this book, I offer a few additional points on *katharsis* by Orgel:

> ... Valla, in 1498, has tragedy 'completing through pity and fear the purgation of such habits' ... *Valla's word for Aristotle's pathemata, passions or emotions, is, oddly, disciplinae, what we have been trained to do (this is the word I have translated 'habits').* ... A generation later, Alessandro Pazzi, who in 1536 edited and published the Greek text with a Latin translation *that became the standard one*, has tragedy '*through pity and fear purging passions of this kind*' [my italics for the English].[815]

---

813  The subject being Greek rhetoric.

814  Javitch, *op. cit.*, in Kennedy, 1999, pp. 54-5.

815  Orgel, *op. cit.*, 2002, pp. 133-4. The easiest answer for the oddity of *disciplinae* being used is that Valla used manuscript A, which had *mathēmatōn katharsin* ("the catharsis of...learnings"), of which more later.

## Francesco Robortello (1516–1567)

Robortello is rarely recalled nowadays, but, as just suggested and as Bernard Weinberg also stresses, he was an important source for subsequent commentators in the fifteenth and sixteenth centuries.[816] Weinberg writes:

> If Aristotle's work, through its transformations and deformations, is at the basis of the classical doctrine in European criticism, Robortello's lengthy interpretation of the work is the first step in the formation of that doctrine.[817]

As we see now, that first step included setting or merely perpetuating from all the Arabic commentators the precedents regarding literature that I have contested in this book. The first step also solidifies what Pazzi accepted was the meaning of *katharsis*. Robortello says at the beginning of his *In Librum Aristotelis De Arte Poetica Explicationes*:

> Before attempting to unravel the fabric of this small treatise, it seems necessary to inquire into the nature of the poetic faculty and the power it has, the goal set for it and the subject matter out of which it accomplishes its task. This final item should be treated first, for everything else will rather conveniently follow from it. *The material basis, as it were, for the poetic faculty is discourse, as it is for all other activities that revolve around discourse.*
>
> There are two types of discourse, one that is said to originate from the mouth, the other springs from the depths of the heart and the recesses of the mind... one resides in expression (*prophorikos*), the other in conception... Since, then, poetry takes as its matter fictional and mythical discourse, clearly poetry's province is to shape myth and fiction in a suitable manner and no other art more properly devises fiction than poetry...
>
> What other end, then, shall we say the poetic mode has than to give delight by representation, description and imitation of all human actions, every emotion, and every thing, living or inanimate? And *since this imitation and representation occur through language, we hold that the end of poetry is discourse which imitates, just as in rhetoric it is language that persuades.* Cicero's excellent remark about comedy can be applied to poetry as a whole, namely that it is the imitation of life, the mirror of manners and the image of truth (*De Republica* 4. 13). That discourse may create a representation of the world is quite evident from the following train of reasoning, which is absolutely correct and quite unassailable. Thought receives images from objects. The mental images are expressed in words and speech. *It can be inferred, then, that the representation of everything is brought about by language, written or spoken.* The language of poetry does not represent the inner dispositions of virtues or vices but the very actions which result from any state. *As this state lies hidden in the mind and is not available to our vision, it can only be represented by actions, which everyone can perceive and judge.* But representation belongs not only to poetry but also to the stage. There are, however, differences between the two. For ac-

---

816    Bernard Weinberg, "Robortello on the *Poetics*," in *Critics and Criticism: Ancient and Modern*, ed. R. S. Crane, *op. cit.*, pp. 319-48.

817    *Op. cit.*, p. 319.

tors have the ability and power to imitate and represent character, the emotions, roles and actions of men so as to achieve plausibility and to persuade the audience and the spectators. *The poet exercises all his power merely in expressing and describing the morality of men, so that he creates, as it were, a silent representation set in language.* The actor, however, achieves a representation which is spoken and expresses what is to be represented by means of voice, speech, expression and gesture, **even though the actor's art is obviously dependent on poetry**.

Poetry and acting are both concerned with making the minds of the readers and listeners, respectively, disposed to receive the image of the object they are trying to represent. For representation or action on the stage unites in some way the image of the thing represented and enacted with the thought and imagination of men, as if it joins the entity itself with thought. Representation of this kind has great power in moving and inflaming men's minds to anger and fury, then in recalling them to kindness and assuaging them, in stirring them to compassion, weeping and tears, as well as to laughter and joy. **To complete its imitation properly, poetry needs no supports drawn from elsewhere, such as notes, songs, metres, mime and expression, and all the other devices which can be called theatrical**. *Nevertheless, it sometimes uses notes, masks and gestures and many other procedures; they greatly assist in introducing all kinds of affection and distress into men's minds.* **It is for this reason that Aristotle very clearly declares that notes, verses and such like are a part or means of the poetic mode** <1447b/25> [my italics and boldfacing throughout].[818]

This is all a crucial part of Robortello's doctrine. We should note, though, that, as Weinberg emphasizes,[819] it is as much *his* doctrine as it is Aristotle's, and that his avowed concern with explicating Aristotle's work is intertwined with his own concern to establish the "true," poetic theory. If, however, his statements are *only* his own, Robortello need not be construed of course as presenting Aristotle's meaning. But in this case, the title of his work—*In Librum Aristotelis De Arte Poetica Explicationes*—and his claim ultimately to explain Aristotle's small treatise become puzzling unless we take Robortello to have multiple goals. Moreover, Robortello's work becomes at times irrelevant for our purposes, and those who have thought that he tried to give Aristotle's meaning (at least in this passage)—and they appear to be more than a few—may have been misled. On the other hand, if Robortello is trying to give Aristotle's meaning, then we notice a seriously flawed method. Rather than uncovering Aristotle's intent as well as could be done on the basis of the textual evidence, Robortello seems to think that he must first "inquire into the nature of the poetic faculty [as he conceives it]" and then use the subsequent conclusions as a basis for "attempting to unravel the fabric of [the *Dramatics*]." But

---

818   Florence, 1548. From *Sources of Dramatic Theory 1: Plato to Congreve*, ed. and annotated by Michael J. Sidnell, with D. J. Conacher, Barbara Kerslake, Pia Kleber, C. J. McDonough, and Damiano Pietropaolo (Cambridge: Cambridge Univ. Press) 1991, pp. 84-97. The Bekker reference (in pointed brackets) has been interpolated by the translators.

819   "Much of the construction that Robortello puts upon passages in the *Poetics results from his own conception of the end of the poetic art* [my italics]. This he states succinctly in his Prologue and develops later in the course of the commentary" (Weinberg, *op. cit*., p. 320).

there is no demonstrable reason to think that Aristotle would have had the same picture of the "poetic faculty" as Robortello does, and thus there is no reason to think that the *Dramatics* could be explained on the basis of *Robortello's* conception of the poetic faculty, which is a Gorgian one. To my knowledge, Robortello never discusses whether Aristotle might be following Diotima's meaning of *poiēsis,* and we will see later that Robortello misses the point that representation and plot for Aristotle could be given through dance, like in our story-ballets. Robortello also, among other problems, reverses the priority of language and (gestured) enactment that was discussed in my Chapter 2.

Nevertheless, we need not determine whether Robortello's view of poetry is the correct one, nor need we give the precise reasons why his interpretation of Aristotle is right or wrong in many places. We need only recognize here that in Robortello's work we have the first, or one of the first, assumptions in European history stemming directly from the Greek manuscripts that Aristotle's *Dramatics* is dealing fundamentally with language or literary theory.[820] Also, we have in Robortello's work the first explicit denial stemming directly from the Greek manuscripts that performance is necessary (for Aristotle)—a view entirely consistent of course with his claiming that the performance is advantageous when added.[821]

---

820   When I originally wrote the Ph.D. dissertation (*op. cit.*, 1992) from which the following section is drawn, I said, long before Notomi published in his admirable, perhaps earth-shattering, study in 2011 that Gorgias was the first to use *poiēsis* as "poetry" *per se*:

> When the term 'poetry' comes to mean primarily the making of verse, I cannot say. Aristotle notes in his discussion in Chapter 1 of Empedocles that some people are using the term in that sense, and he obviously distances himself from such a usage. I have tried to show, primarily on the basis of Chapter 4 of the *Poetics*, that poets originally used music and dance with little or no language. Even at the time of Horace, the term *poetica* might mean 'dramatic composition' and might connote something that is not entirely linguistic (see, e.g., *The Satires and Epistles of Horace: A Modern English Verse Translation*, Smith Palmer Bovie, Chicago: University of Chicago Press, 1959; 4th impression, 1966, esp. pp. 244-5). Halliwell also discusses Horace in relation to the Aristotelian tradition (...1986, p. 288). Without doubt, the term 'poetry' is 'equivocal' in Aristotle's work, as Chapter[s] 1 and 25 of the *Poetics* especially show (Appendix A, footnote 240).

I discussed Notomi's findings in detail in Chapter 1.

821   Naturally, Robortello has a view that is much more sophisticated than I can present here in a synopsis. As Weinberg shows (*op. cit.*, p. 329ff, esp. p. 329 and p. 335), Robortello maintains that plot is the manner (of mimesis) of tragedy and that in the histrionics we obtain the plot or at least a different aspect of the plot. His view, which in fact has something in common with my own, also entails that the dramatist is concerned with the character in the language and that diction is part of the object of mimesis. The first three chapters of the *Dramatics*, however, contradict the way in which Robortello assigns elements to the three modes of mimesis, as I discussed when I explained the "2-1-3 pattern" in *Dramatics* 6 in Chapter 2. He also gives the impression that mere writing can give a plot, even while noting that epic does not have the "action" that tragedy does (Weinberg, *op. cit.* p. 336). This has the puzzling result that in tragedy two plots could be presented with one play, one through the histrionics and one through the language, but I am unsure how or if Robortello ever addresses this matter, and in any event, it is not something that seems to have any historical impact, if Weinberg is representative of the reaction. Of course, the plot could be considered the combination of histrionics and speech, but this sets up a tension with Aristotle's six

What about *katharsis*?  Unlike Avicenna but like Pazzi, Robortello recognizes it in the definition of tragedy and he also gives *katharsis* at least superficially the meaning of "purgation" (*purgatio* in Latin), following both Pazzi and William of Moerbeke (whether Robortello knew of the latter's translation or not).  Nevertheless, Robortello explicates it in great detail as a moral and educational concept, striving to reach the same result of moderation as the end, and so in that sense seems very consistent with Averroes.  The detail is far beyond the scope of this brief history and is given in large part in a fascinating article by Déborah Blocker.  In a very appropriate way, she speaks of Robortello dealing with the "Gordian knot" that results from Aristotle including the notion of *katharsis* in the definition of tragedy and how Robortello attempts to understand and explain it, roughly, by returning to the views of the neo-Platonist Proclus.[822]  A summary by Weinberg, though, must suffice for our purposes, in part because I already covered Proclus in Chapters 5, 6 and 8:

> In his commentary on that part of Aristotle's definition of tragedy relevant to purgation (1449b27), Robortello indicates in even greater detail how the spectators are benefited:
>
>> Thus when men are present at performances, and they hear and see people saying and doing things which very closely approach truth itself, they become accustomed to suffering, to fearing, to pitying; this, in turn, causes them, when they themselves undergo the common lot of all men, to suffer less and to fear less [*hence the Aristotelian moderation*]... The auditors and spectators of tragedies gain this benefit, which is really the greatest one, that, since the fate of all mortal men is the same and since there is nobody who is not subject to disasters, men learn to bear more easily the befalling of misfortune...
>
> The utility [*the end of catharsis*] is then *essentially an ethical one* ... they learn what characters and events are worthy of dread and of commiseration, [and] *they achieve a capacity to moderate their own passions* when adversity strikes.  In this utility Robortello sees an exact agreement between Aristotle and Plato (as interpreted by Proclus).
>
> [Robortello continues, according to Weinberg:] Aristotle approves of the opinion of Plato, in so far as he does not wish the imitation of the behaviour of wicked men to be made in tragedy or in any other poems, except perhaps in comedy [my italics and comments in brackets].[823]

We need not stop here to try to determine whether Robortello has captured Aristotle's theories combining drama, psychology, and ethics.  That was already accomplished for our purposes sufficiently in Units 2 and 3 (where we saw that purgation as either a medical or psycho-therapeutic account cannot mesh consistently with Aristotle's other well-known theory, and where we also discerned the

---

necessary conditions in which plot and language are differentiated.  Hence, it is better to say that the serious *drama* or the "tragedy" is a combination of plot and speech (and of the other four conditions).

822   Déborah Blocker, « Elucider et équivoquer: Francesco Robortello (ré)invente la catharsis », dans Stratégies de l'équivoque, numéro dirigé par J.-P. Cavaillé, *Cahiers du Centre de Recherches Historiques*, 33 (2004), pp. 109-40, espec. p. 124.

823   Weinberg, *op. cit.*, pp. 322-3.

problem of interpreting *katharsis* as "moderation" when Aristotle does not include a proper term for moderation in the definition of tragedy). The goal for the moment is simply to show how *katharsis* was finally taken very seriously in the first non-Arabic rigorous commentary on the *Dramatics* as "purgation." Nevertheless, one point might be made usefully in passing. Robortello's assertion that "... he [Aristotle] does not wish the imitation ... of wicked men" is ambiguous. Does Aristotle *wish* one thing *ideally* but allow another? Robortello in at least his tone and in having Aristotle agree with Plato is right in one respect but wrong in at least one other. Aristotle in *Dramatics* 13, 15 and 18 allows protagonists who are wicked to some extent, when they are necessary for the plot (although no more than necessary). Plato will not have them presented in drama *in any circumstances* in the ideal *polis*, as I discuss in Chapters 2 and 7.

### Julius Caesar Scaliger (1484–1558)

Another notable figure who furthers the tradition of the *Dramatics,* including the two alleged misconceptions, is Julius Caesar della Scala, or Scaliger. In the *Poetica*, which was published in 1561, three years after his death, Scaliger says as he discusses the history of language:

> [T]hus arose the established laws of speech. Later, language was adorned and embellished as with raiments, and then it appeared illustrious both in form and in spirit... Necessity demanded language in the search of the philosophers after truth, utility dictated its cultivation in statesmanship, **and pleasure drew it to the theatre**. The language of the philosophers, confined to exact, logical reasoning, was necessarily concise and adapted to the subject matter. On the other hand, in the forum and the camp less precise expression was permissible, governed by the subject, the place, the time, and the audience, and such speaking was called oratory. The third class contains two species, not very unlike, **which in common employ narration**, and use much embellishment. They differ, however, in that one professes to record the fixed truth ... while the other either adds a fictitious element to the truth, or imitates the truth by fiction, of course with more elaboration. While ... the name *history* came to be applied to the former alone ... on the other hand, the latter was called *poetry,* or *making,* because it narrated not only actual events, but also fictitious events as if they were actual, and represented them as they might be or ought to be. Wherefore the basis of all poetry is imitation...[824]

> The poet depicts ... a variety of fortunes; in fact, by so doing, he transforms himself almost into a second deity. Of those things which the Maker of all framed, the other sciences are, as it were, overseers; but since poetry fashions images of those things which are not, as well as images more beautiful than life of those things which are, it seems **unlike other literary forms**, such as history, which confine themselves to actual events, and rather to be another god, and to create. In view of this fact, its common title was furnished it, not by the agreement of men, but by the provident wisdom of nature. I must express my sur-

---

[824] From F.M. Padelford, trans., *Select Translations from Scaliger's Poetics*, Yale University Press, 1905; found in Hazard Adams, ed., *Critical Theory Since Plato*, New York: Harcourt Brace Jovanovich, Inc., 1971, pp. 136ff.

prise that when the learned Greeks had most happily defined the poet as the *maker,* our ancestors should be so unfair to themselves **as to limit the term to candle-makers**, for though usage has sanctioned this practice, etymologically it is absurd.[825]

Why does Horace question whether or not comedy is poetry? Forsooth, because it is humble, must it be denied the title of poetry? Surely an unfortunate ruling! **So far from comedy not being poetry, I would almost consider it the first and truest of all poetry, for comedy employs every kind of invention, and seeks for all kinds of material**... Was Lucan a poet? Surely he was. As usual, the grammarians deny this, and object that he wrote history... Verse is the property of the poet... Moreover, although Aristotle exercised ... censure so severely that he would refuse the name of poet to versifiers, yet in practice he speaks differently, and says: "As Empedocles poetically wrote (*epoiesen*)"; so he even calls Empedocles, who feigned not at all, a poet.

So our definition would be: *Comedy is a dramatic poem* ... written in a popular style...[826]

The definition of tragedy given by Aristotle is as follows: "Tragedy is an imitation of an action that is illustrious, complete, and of a certain magnitude, in embellished language, the different kinds of embellishments being variously employed in the different parts, and not in the form of narration, but through pity and fear effecting the purgation of such like passions." I do not wish to attack this definition other than by adding my own: *A tragedy is the imitation of the adversity of a distinguished man; it employs the form of action,* **presents a disastrous denouement,** *and is expressed in impressive metrical language.* **Though Aristotle adds harmony and song, they are not, as the philosophers say, of the essence of tragedy; its one and only essential is acting. ...** [his own italics but my bolding throughout][827]

As is apparent, Scaliger, even more than Robortello, is presenting his own view of poetry rather than attempting primarily to reconstruct previous theories. He uses Aristotle as a foil as much as a source of shared principles and identifies the poet with one who uses verse, in open (but partially mistaken) opposition to Aristotle's theory, as we saw when I discussed language and poetry in *Dramatics* 1. Scaliger also shows awareness of two of the three meanings of "poetry" at Aristotle's time, as "making" (even of candle-sticks) and Gorgias's "language in verse" (whether or not he recognizes the origin from Gorgias). Yet nothing is ever mentioned about Diotima's third meaning of "poetry," the making of "'music'-verse," and indeed Scaliger says: "Surely the *Symposium*, the *Phaedrus*, and other such monstrous productions, are not worth reading."[828] Given that the *Symposium* is "not worth reading," it is hard to imagine Scaliger even considering Diotima's meanings seriously.

---

825    *Ibid.*, p. 140

826    *Ibid.*, p. 141

827    *Ibid.*, p. 142

828    Scaliger, p. 140, *op. cit.* He gives no reasons why the dialogues are "monstrous," and I guess that it is because they portray male homosexuality without admonition.

Three further remarks are worth making about Scaliger. First, he claims that Aristotle allows Empedocles to be a poet, even though Empedocles "feigned not at all." Yet Aristotle had emphatically rejected Empedocles as a poet in *Dramatics* 1 (which, again, we saw in my Chapter 2). However, Scaliger is pinpointing a problem for scholars because Aristotle does seem to include Empedocles when discussing (the language of) poets in Chapter 25 (at 1461a24). The inconsistency in the *Dramatics* might be resolved if, e.g., Aristotle has different notions of "poet," as I discussed, or Chapter 25 is an interpolation from another work of Aristotle, as a number of commentators believe. Second, Scaliger says that "though Aristotle adds harmony and song, they are not, as the philosophers say, of the essence of tragedy." This suggests that Scaliger is maintaining his distance from Aristotle by merely disagreeing with the latter's claims (that tragedy has harmony and song). Nevertheless, Scaliger still seems to be allowing Aristotle his own view, and this seems preferable to the approach in which modern commentators state that song is not necessary to tragedy for Aristotle without explaining away that it is an *essential* condition in the definition. Scaliger adds "[tragedy's] one and only essential is acting." Yet, lest we think that this means he is advocating a performance view of Aristotelian tragedy (meaning acting *on stage*), consider what he adds:

> Tragedy and comedy are of the same genus, and share in common the name drama... The grammarians did some more false teaching about comedy when they said that it was poetry based upon imitation, *and consisted in gesticulation and delivery, for surely a comedy is no less a comedy if it be read in silence.* Then gesture is confined to recitation, and not all who read, recite [my italics].[829]

Thus, drama, including tragedy, is ultimately a species of literature for Scaliger, as it had been for Robortello. Scaliger, though, goes one step further concerning *katharsis*, after treating it in the definition as purgation, and says "the mention of 'purgation' is too restrictive, for not every subject produces this effect." He thus, to my knowledge, dispenses with the concept in his own view, along, by the way, with pity and fear. It appears sufficient in this regard for tragedy to have a "disastrous denouement," and quite appropriately and ironically he strikes upon pleasure as the reason for discourse in the theater. I take up this theme later when discussing how Aristotle's views have suffered because the empirical evidence suggests they are not appropriate to "tragedy" in general. All of this arguably confirms what Adams says of Scaliger in summarizing his thought, including the passages above:

> Scaliger was influenced by Aristotle and Horace, but perhaps more so by the rhetorical principles of Cicero and Quintilian... he runs the danger of reducing poetry to oratory. He adopts Horace's maxim that poetry should delight and teach, but emphasizes persuasion. Eventually he considers the poet's moral purpose paramount.[830]

Third, Scaliger leaves off (in his translation) the Greek word for the essential condition in the

---

829   *Ibid.* p. 142.
830   *Ibid.* p. 136.

definition of tragedy "through people acting" as the contrast to "not in the form of narration," all of which is crucial in determining that tragedy is an enacted art (on stage), as we saw in Chapters 2 and 3. Finally, it should be noted that Scaliger "almost considers it [comedy] the first and truest of all poetry." This is remarkable, given that to my knowledge all scholars believe that Aristotle ranked tragedy (and epic) above comedy, even though, as discussed in my main chapters, his only explicit ranking involves tragedy and epic. Scaliger's statement is still remarkable notwithstanding that Scaliger refers to his own notion of comedy and not to Aristotle's.

## Ludovico Castelvetro (1505–1571)

Nine years after Scaliger's treatise appeared, Castelvetro published his commentary *Poetica d'Aristotele vulgarizzata et sposta* (*The Poetics of Aristotle Translated and Explained*). Two of the doctrines that Castelvetro proposes are (i) the extreme unities of time, place and action, which became very influential subsequently but which are outside the scope of my concerns, and (ii) the importance of filling in historical episodes. The stress Castelvetro places on history and its relation to art in general is crucial, because it impacts his interpretation of Aristotle and may be illustrated by his example of Michelangelo restoring the missing part of a beard on the statue of a river god. The beard at the chin was so thick that it would have to hang to the god's navel, and yet the tip of the beard, which was all that remained below the chin, only touched the upper chest. This puzzled observers but Michelangelo showed that the missing part of the beard had been tied into a knot, which exhibited for Castelvetro how an artist might supplement history and what the value of such a creation might be. As Castelvetro says:

> The art to which poetry is most closely akin is the art of history. Indeed, their kinship is so intimate that, *if we possessed an adequate art of history, it would be unnecessary to write an art of poetry*, "since poetry derives all its light from the light of history"... The two arts differ in two respects only: history presents events which actually happened, poetry those which have not occurred but which might occur, and poetry uses verse whereas history uses prose. Otherwise they are so much alike that poetry may be defined as "a resemblance or imitation of history" [my italics].[831]

This priority on history appears to be the most basic tenet of Castelvetro's theory regarding the nature of poetry, and it reflects his conception of both history and poetry as modes of language. Castelvetro often concerns himself with the theatricality of drama, but this concern appears entirely consistent with the *theoretical* reducibility of tragedy to literature. Nothing stops him from assuming and developing fully the theory that tragedy conceived as literary production plus performance can and must, for instance, be unified with respect to time, place and action. Nor does anything stop him from

---

831   Weinberg, *op. cit.*, pp. 368-9

spending a large proportion of his treatise discussing aspects, such as costuming, that are theoretically extraneous but in practice commonplace. Castelvetro's acceptance of the reducibility of drama to literature, which follows Robortello, Scaliger and the Arabic commentators, even if those others did not describe the matter in this succinct fashion, has a double impact.

The first impact: Given his own concentration on the theatrical aspects of drama (which I am unable to capture here due to lack of space), any lack of denial on his part to the view that tragedy *is* reducible to the script becomes more inducement on the part of subsequent thinkers to accept the trend that the Arabic commentators and Robortello had begun—that is, to accept that *poiēsis*, even for Aristotle, was fundamentally a literary term with the other aspects secondary or tertiary. As suggested in the main chapters, it is as if a professor of drama in a theatre department, as opposed to a professor of literature, were to accept unquestioningly the claim that drama *is* most dependent on the script. The lack of a "selfish" argument on the part of the drama professor for theoretical equality of the dramatic (staged) elements (including actors acting) would suggest a greater objectivity to impartial observers and arguably has done more to convince those observers that drama is part of literature than an active argument on the part of the literature professor.

The second impact: The status of *katharsis* for Castelvetro is similar to that for Robortello. "For tragedy by means of the aforesaid passions, terror and pity, purges and expels those same passions from the hearts of men."[832] Castelvetro clearly does not understand easily this passage, and offers an explanation based on the frequency of deaths in an epidemic, as he says, to better understand "what Aristotle perhaps wanted to say but uttered darkly and scarcely hinted at, either because, as is often said, his remarks are brief notes for use in a larger work, or because he did not wish openly to censure the opinion of his master Plato..."[833] Whether Castelvetro succeeds with his explanation I leave aside here, except to note that his claiming that fewer objects of pity and fear (that is, just a few deaths) affect us more than a thousand deaths (which cause us to become accustomed to the suffering), in no way seems helpful to understanding the dilemma of *katharsis* as the end of tragedy, which we examined in depth in Unit 3. (His explanation has never been accepted by others, to my knowledge; following his reasoning a million deaths should affect us even less!) Castelvetro says later, even more stunningly, that this phenomenon of experiencing representational tragic events is actually pleasurable and "can quite properly be called *hedonē*, that is, pleasure or delight,...[but] strictly speaking it ought to be called utility, for it is health of mind gotten *through bitter medicine* [my italics]."[834] The crucial point

---

832   Adams, *op. cit.*, p. 148.
833   Adams, *op. cit.*, p. 148.
834   Adams, *op. cit.* 152. I do not mean to suggest that Castelvetro is the first to use a medical analogy for catharsis. Leon Golden attributes the origin to A.S. Minturno in 1559, saying:

for the moment is that we seem to have a clear example of *katharsis* as a medical metaphor, all of which additionally shows in one way the trust that the Renaissance Italians had in the authenticity of the Greek manuscript(s), for not one of them seems to question the explicitly given goal of *katharsis* (although we saw that Avicenna ignored it, that Averroes "converted" the concept to moderation, and that Valla treated it as being related to "habit"). At this stage in the historical exegesis, though, as mentioned once before, this is all perfectly natural and to be expected, because there could have been any number of reasons why Aristotle wrote *katharsis* as the goal of tragedy. Scholars coming later, with more time to consider the options in the newly available manuscripts, would presumably have been expected to discover the best reasons.

## Summary of the Italian Commentators and Additional Considerations

As we saw, the Italians often took from the ancients, and whether it was Plato, Aristotle or Horace they did not seem to care, as long as the wisdom of the Greeks could be used to advance their own agendas. Scaliger rejected *katharsis* as the goal of tragedy, not denying that Aristotle wrote the word but claiming it was unempirical. We always need to distinguish between (i) what Aristotle wrote and whether and how he justified it and (ii) whether his view is acceptable to more modern thinkers. The issue in this book is, except incidentally or in Chapter 9, not on (ii). That is, I focus not on whether Aristotle believed what we would believe, with our advances, real *or alleged*, in the arts, humanities, and sciences, but on (i).

However, it is sometimes as necessary to report what the secondary sources say, to reflect how he is generally perceived. They often determine the lens, rose-colored or not, through which many readers see Aristotle, especially since most modern readers do not read ancient Greek. If I can easily correct minor misconceptions without taking us too far off track as we go through the history with regard to the two major misconceptions that are the focus of this book, I will, and I have already done this to

---

> The first known statement of this theory [that tragedy "purges" the emotions of pity and fear] appears in 1559 in the *De Poeta* of A. S. Minturno. In this work Minturno argues that the principles of the homeopathic theory of medicine (which require for the elimination of a disease the application of a therapeutic agent similar in nature to that disease) are also applicable to mental afflictions. In his *Arte Poetica* in 1563 he explicitly connects the purgation achieved by tragedy to the medical treatment of illness in the body" (Leon Golden, "The Purgation Theory of Catharsis," *The Journal of Aesthetics and Art Criticism*, Vol. 31, No. 4, Summer, 1973, p. 473).

S. H. Butcher confirms this with more detail, anachronistically, if with a slight change of date:
> Mr. Spingarn in his interesting volume already mentioned, *Literary Criticism in the Renaissance* (New York, 1899), quotes from Minturno, *L'Arte Poetica*, p. 77 (Venice, 1564), the following passage: "As a physician eradicates, by means of poisonous medicine, the perfervid poison of disease which affects the body, so tragedy purges the mind of its impetuous perturbations by the force of these emotions beautifully expressed in verse" (Butcher, *op. cit.*, 1923, p. 247).

some extent (e.g., Gould's assertions about Aristotelian truth and its relationship to "poetry," in footnote 803). To correct another minor misconception before introducing seventeenth-century views, let us examine Orgel again. He has given a reasonably persuasive account of Averroes and the early Italian commentators and adds the following, detecting the beginning of the reaction against Aristotle on the part of many, who (to put it in my own words) find the single goal of tragedy unconvincing after the initial thrill of the discovery of Aristotle's work wears off:

> There are commentators who reject all three positions [that the *katharsis qua* purging is of (i) the identical pity and fear raised, or of (ii) the similar, generic feelings of pity and fear, or of (iii) all the emotions like pity and fear], **which sometimes involves rejecting Aristotle entirely**—it is important to stress that, for all the age's notorious devotion to the authority of the ancients, this was always an option. **J.C. Scaliger, for example, denies that catharsis can be a defining feature of tragedy, observing succinctly that it simply does not describe the effects of many tragic plots. Tasso similarly argues ... that catharsis will not account for the operation of many kinds of tragedy**, citing as examples 'those tragedies which contain the passage of good men from misery to happiness, which confirm the opinion that the people have about God's providence'—catharsis is faulted, in short, for not being applicable to medieval tragedy...[835]
>
> The best plays teach, move, and delight, he [Scaliger] says, but this quality is felt to be simply a function of their verisimilitude. And the doctrine of catharsis, the mainstay of most Renaissance theories of tragedy, he rejects out of hand... But no alternative theory is proposed, and Scaliger's genres, despite their breadth, leave little room for a critic who wishes to understand the *effects* of drama.
>
> And yet, on the whole, the most serious kind of drama was defined for most Renaissance critics precisely by its effect as described by Aristotle, **or at least by Aristotle as the Renaissance understood him**. It was generally assumed that drama was a form of rhetoric; imitation was its means, but its function was to persuade. (The principal sixteenth-century exceptions to this are found in Scaliger and Guarini, for whom imitation was not the means but the end of drama. **This is a more strictly Aristotelian line, since for Aristotle poetry was a form of logic, not rhetoric**.) Tragedy achieved its end by purging the passions of its audience through pity and terror—catharsis was the particular kind of utility produced by tragedy [his italics but my boldfacing; also, my explanation in brackets].[836]

Let us examine this passage. First, to reiterate a point from before, *katharsis* as the goal of tragedy is seen to be empirically deficient by Scaliger, which is an embarrassment for an empiricist like Aristotle. How much of Aristotle's other dramatic theory or of his reputation in general suffered by being tainted by this realization is hard to say, and, again, is something I leave to any interested specialist in that period or for any other period in which his reputation diminished accordingly. At any rate, for Orgel, some thinkers threw out at least parts of Aristotle's theory as a consequence. Ironically, given

---

835   Orgel, 2002, p. 135.
836   Orgel, 2002, p. 152 .

Chapter 7 of this book, Scaliger, Castelvetro and later authors such as Racine whom we will examine shortly, who found pleasure or enjoyment to be the end of tragedy, were perfectly Aristotelian in that respect, even though they thought they were ignoring Aristotle by rejecting his stated goal in *Dramatics* 6. Whether the tragedies also "teach" (as it should for Horace) is a different matter, and one addressed to some extent in my Chapters 4, 7 and 8, being partially supported, e.g., in *Dramatics* 4 but seemingly—and I stress the "seemingly"—denied (at least for children) in *Politics* VIII 7, subject to the caveats in my earlier chapters. However, even if this were the case for Aristotle, at best we have seen that teaching is secondary to enjoyment for him.

Now, curiously, Orgel thinks that the dismissal of *katharsis* by Scaliger and Scaliger's genres leave "little room for a critic who wishes to understand the *effects* of drama." Yet Scaliger ultimately appears to make delight at least one of the benefits of drama, even if the "moral purpose" is paramount ultimately for the poet. Hence, unless I misunderstand Orgel's cryptic comment, the topic of pleasure and its different kinds, explored in part by Plato and Aristotle themselves in various treatises, gives vast room for any critic to examine. That is, Plato and Aristotle themselves discuss pleasure and related subjects at length in, respectively, e.g., *Philebus* and the *Nicomachean Ethics* Book 7 and *Politics* VIII 3-5 especially. Thus, in no way do we need to follow Orgel on "little room" being left for the effects of drama, even if we agree with him or Scaliger on many other points, and even if we dispense with *katharsis* as the only goal of tragedy. Another interesting remark by Orgel is how Tasso argues that *katharsis* will not account for the operation of many kinds of tragedy, citing as examples "those tragedies which contain the passage of good men from misery to happiness." Ironically, we saw in my Chapter 6 that this is quite correct and supports the view (following Avicenna) that *katharsis* should be ignored. That is, we saw that for Aristotle the best tragic plots in *Dramatics* 14 end happily, so clearly Scaliger's "disastrous denouement" is not a requirement of tragedy *for Aristotle* (or apparently for Tasso). Again, though, the critical point now is that Aristotle's theory is decried because, at least in the way that Tasso understood the goal in *Dramatics* 6, it is not empirical or philosophically sound enough to account for later tragedy.

Another noteworthy part of the above quotation is the claim that drama was for some a form of rhetoric, whose function was to persuade; that imitation was the end; and that for Aristotle poetry was a form of logic. Assuming Orgel speaks not for himself but elliptically recounts the sixteenth-century attitude, we can see how those thinkers get every one of these three claims wrong insofar as the views are attributed to Aristotle (and recall Orgel's correct assertion that the theory of tragedy as "ethical rhetoric" extends back at least to Averroes or that as a form of logic it stretches back at least to Simplicius and the inclusion of the *Dramatics* in the *Organon*). Let me start with the middle claim, that imitation was the end of drama, before I advance to the claim that poetry is logic and finish with the claim about rhetoric.

The exceptions to the rhetorical camp, Scaliger and Gaurini, go too far the other way and make imitation (*mimesis*) the end.[837] This comes close insofar as *plot* is once said by Aristotle in Chapter 6, in a puzzling passage, to be the end, but *mimesis* is not the final cause (in the definition of tragedy); rather *katharsis* in the traditional view and, as we saw, intellectual delight in the rest of the *Dramatics* is. In other words, the three aspects of *mimesis* from *Dramatics* 1 that we examined in my Chapter 2 in detail—means, object, and manner—make up the material components of tragedy, but *mimesis* is not easily considered to be the *end* throughout the rest of the treatise. Consider also now the second claim that poetry is a form of logic (again, Orgel suggests this is his own view, but more likely he is recounting a view of the Italian Renaissance). However, poetry is not a "form of logic" in the way we would normally call something "a form of x." Logic is developed by Aristotle in his *Prior Analytics* and is a way of establishing valid forms of argumentation, with the syllogism being the primary structure, as a further way to determine sound arguments. (Sound arguments are those with a valid form *and* with true premises; thus, the conclusions are true, and, more importantly, true *because* of legitimate premises, not true accidentally or from luck, as it were, with at least one premise that is false).[838] Tragedy is in no way a species of logic in this way, even if logic is certainly used by the playwright, as Aristotle mentions in *Dramatics* 24 when discussing how Homer cleverly tells untruths in the right way by encouraging false inference, at 1460a19-27. Rather, again, tragedy is either a species of *poiēsis* in the Diotiman narrow sense (that is, of music-verse-dance) or in the broad sense as making or in the Gorgian sense as "language in verse," with *mimesis* a distinguishing characteristic. If "logic" is used as something ostensibly stemming from *logos* (language), then Orgel's comment, although initially puzzling, makes more sense, although still, again, one theme of this book is that tragedy does not stem from language for Aristotle.[839]

---

837 Curiously, Rashed appears now to be taking this position, as I discuss in my Post-Postscript to Chapter 6.

838 An example of an unsound argument is:
  1) All men are mortal (things).
  2) All mortal things live less than 300 years.
  3) Therefore, all men live less than 300 years.

The argument can be shown to have a valid form—All A are B; All B are C; therefore all A are C—and the conclusion is true, but the second premise is false because giant sequoias can live longer than 300 years.

839 Habib also notes that "At different times, poetry was considered to be part of logic or grammar" (*op. cit.*, p. 197). The view about grammar that was held historically is so preposterous as to not need significant discussion: Grammar for Aristotle is given in *Poetics* 20. A noun, verb or sentence is part of grammar, but saying poetry is a part of grammar is like saying poetry is part of painting because the ink for any written text has color, say, black, and color is part of painting.

Finally, concerning the third claim, about rhetoric and persuasion: One might legitimately claim that dramatists try to persuade audiences with believable fictional stories (for believability can lead to greater pleasure for Aristotle). However, this is not "persuading" in the sense that a rhetorician for him tries to persuade, namely, convincing an audience in politics or courts of law that one course of action is better than another because of the benefits or harm that will occur (cf. *Rhetoric* I 1 and 3, and especially 1358b21-29). Rather, again, drama's function for Aristotle is pleasure or enjoyment, as I demonstrated in Chapter 7, even if Aristotle sometimes discusses drama, actors, and elocution in the *Rhetoric* for various reasons. To understand other reasons behind how the belief that drama is a form of rhetoric might have arisen historically, consider the following, although I make no claims that this happened in every case and leave it to historians interested in the issue to pinpoint the exact reasons why the individual scholars of the time subsumed Aristotle's "poetical" theory under rhetoric. It is enough here to get the broad contours correct, and I assume that the scholars of the Renaissance read Plato also.

Presumably the tradition of assigning the *Dramatics* to the *Organon*—as the eighth part, after *Rhetoric*—helped determine that drama was in some significant way "rhetorical." Also, recall how we examined in Chapter 1 Plato's conceiving of the issue of drama and rhetoric in *Gorgias* 502, where *poiētikē* becomes rhetoric: Socrates asks Callicles what we would have if we stripped "musical" composition (*poiēsis*) of its music (*melos*), *rhuthmos* (dance), and meter (*metron*). Callicles agrees we would have only language (*logos*), which Socrates then identifies first—via *poiētikē*—with "public address" (*dēmēgoria*) (502c) and then, a sentence later, with "rhetorical public address" (*rhētorikē dēmēgoria*), in order to begin accusing dramatists of engaging in rhetoric in the theater (to accomplish devious political or cultural aims, presumably). Again, Aristotle starts off his own, extant treatise with "*peri poiētikēs*...," the same term, obviously, that Plato identifies ultimately with rhetoric. Moreover, in the *Rhetoric* 3.1, Aristotle also uses *harmonia*—usually translated as "harmony"—in almost the same way that we saw in Chapter 2 Plato uses the term in *Laws* II, 665a: (blending) high and low. However, Aristotle adds "intermediate" (as Plato himself also adds at *Philebus* 17d). The precise phrase is *pōs tois tonois, hoion oxeia kai bareia kai mesē*—"how the tones, that is, shrill, deep and intermediate [should be used]"[840]—which Aristotle then indicates is *harmonia*. Yet, this context does not involve music and certainly not a chorus, as only one person, the rhetorician, is speaking (and not singing), so the context is different from Plato's, which was orchestral art (as demonstrated in my Chapter 1). Nevertheless, Aristotle appears to have been borrowing and adapting slightly the idea found in Plato, and indeed this book shows that *harmonia* is a richly ambiguous word. Not taking into account the change in context, Renaissance readers probably assumed an agreement between mentor and pupil because of the superficial use of *harmonia*. The subsequent discussion in the *Rhetoric* of the impor-

---

840   1403b31, tr. W.D. Ross, *op. cit.*, 1941.

tance of delivery in speaking for both orators and actors, I gather, further encouraged the readers to believe that Aristotle thought drama was a form of rhetoric. Aristotle also uses *rhuthmos* in the *Rhetoric* at the same location in 3.1, and this is indubitably also not "rhythm" in a musical sense or a bodily ordering, but an ordering of words or syllables, or more precisely, as he says in III 8, "the numerical limitation of the form of a composition" (1408b228-9). All of this helps show that, as emphasized many times throughout this book, the context is crucial in determining what words like *harmonia kai rhuthmos* mean in the Platonic-Aristotelian corpus. The relevant point now, though, is that Aristotle uses *harmonia kai rhuthmos* in both the *Rhetoric* and the *Dramatics*. On the surface, consequently, a strong association between the two subjects, and with Plato, is created, and we have already seen that "poetry" or drama on the surface seems intended "to persuade." Thus, it should be unsurprising that some Renaissance commentators interpreted Aristotelian drama as a form of rhetoric, but only because they ignored or drastically downplayed other passages in the *Dramatics* and other texts. I discuss a number of these points in detail later and did so already in the body of this book. Let all of this suffice, then, for the Italian commentators of the Cinquecento and with the detour occasioned by examining Orgel's account.

## The 17th and Early 18th Centuries

Ben Jonson writes about Aristotle in his *Timber: Or Discoveries Made Upon Men and Matter*, published in 1641, four years after Jonson's death. He says very wisely, especially concerning the caution at the end:

> Nothing is more ridiculous than to make an author a dictator, as the schools have done Aristotle... Let Aristotle and others have their dues; but if we can make farther discoveries of truth and fitness than they, why are we envied? Let us [though] beware, while we strive to add, we do not diminish or deface; we may improve, but not augment [my clarification in brackets].[841]

Jonson's statement repeats the view of the Italian Renaissance scholars that they should try to advance the knowledge of the Greeks, but the admonition not to "deface" also helps block questioning the authenticity of the manuscripts, perhaps before anyone starts (whether there were murmurings during Jonson's time I do not know). Again, all of the manuscripts of the *Dramatics* had *katharsis*. Even if the history by the 1640's reflected more than 150 years of bafflement with the concept in the definition of tragedy stemming directly from the Greek (we can discount the Arabic commentators because they were working from a translation of a translation), still the scholars seemed confident that they might provide eventually an answer for what Aristotle intended. If not, they would "improve" while not "augmenting." In any event, according to Halliwell, the first French translation of

---

841  Ben Jonson, *Timber: Or Discoveries Made Upon Men and Matter*, edited with Introduction and Notes by Felix Schelling (Boston: Ginn & Co.) 1892, p. 66.

the *Dramatics* was produced in 1671.[842] He adds that Dacier's translation of 1692, to which I return soon, became widely circulated and "was in turn anonymously translated with its notes into English [apparently for the first time] in 1705."[843] But now, and afterward, the task of tracing the manner in which commentators interpreted Aristotle becomes even more complicated. To quote Halliwell further:

> As regards the status and influence of the *Poetics*, the Cinquecento in Italy and the seventeenth century in France can be regarded as a largely coherent period, marked by certain consistent concerns and recurring emphases. The same cannot be said of the following two centuries, during which it becomes much more difficult to pick out the interpretation of Aristotle's ideas as an identifiable cultural thread. This is in part simply because, while works specifically devoted to the *Poetics* are fewer, the range and complexity of the relevant material in this period is [sic] much greater than before, and to pick any single thread out at all becomes less realistic. But it is also because *attitudes to the* Poetics *lose much of their stability, and we need to allow for a full gamut of overlapping views and judgements, from outright rejection to attempts to make completely fresh approaches to the treatise* [my italics].[844]

There is no evidence, though, to my knowledge that the "full gamut" of views ever encompassed one which rejected the assumption that Aristotle was developing literary theory or that *katharsis* in *Dramatics* 6 was legitimate. We can see this also in part by looking at summaries from secondary sources in England and by continuing with other commentators. Tanya Pollard continues the history showing that *katharsis* continued to be interpreted in different ways:

> Fascination with tragedy's ability to alter audiences' minds and bodies was a new development in the sixteenth century, indebted especially to the emerging visibility of Aristotle's *Poetics*. In particular, critics seized on Aristotle's idea that through arousing pity and fear, tragedy could bring about the catharsis—typically translated in the period as purgation—of these emotions. Continental European critics, who influenced English writers especially through figures such as Philip Sidney, George Puttenham, and Ben Jonson, varied in their accounts of catharsis, but held to the underlying premise that effective *literature* moved both bodies and minds... *In the period's literary imagination, catharsis could be turbulent and painful, a poisonous scourge, or pleasurable, a liberating release.* In either case, the cleansing associated with successful tragedy was overwhelmingly understood as involving a forceful purgation of the emotions, embodied in tears [my italics].[845]

---

842   Halliwell, *op. cit.*, 1986, p. 303. In general, I am indebted to him for part of my post-Renaissance history of the exegesis and treatment of the *Dramatics*. Bywater, *op. cit.*, and James Hutton (*op. cit.*, 1982) also present noteworthy histories of the treatise.

843   Halliwell, *op. cit.*, 1986, p. 309. Lessing denigrates this translation by Dacier after calling him "worthy," for reasons he does not give specifically but which relate to the "German translator (Herr Curtius)" (G.E. Lessing, *Hamburg Dramaturgy,* New York: Dover Publ, 1962, pp. 107-8). One, though, nowadays still finds philologists like Tarán referring to Dacier, which presumably confirms Lessing's description as "worthy."

844   Halliwell, *op. cit.*, 1986, p. 308.

845   Tanya Pollard, "Conceiving Tragedy," in *Shakespearean Sensations: Experiencing Literature in Early Modern England,* ed. by Katharine A. Craik and Tanya Pollard (Cambridge: Cambridge Univ. Pr.) 2013, pp.

Notice, then, that it is not the period's "dramatic imagination" but rather the "literary" one. Also, in this era *katharsis* could be either a liberating release, like "purgation" was for the sixteenth-century Italians, or a "poisonous scourge." We will recall that for Averroës it helped one arrive at a good state of pity and fear (but was in effect cashed out as "moderation"), whereas here pity and fear are to be "forcefully" purged. Others continued the practice of taking Aristotle piecemeal or of interpreting him in ways that seemingly fit better their desire to make drama ethical (and perhaps attractive to the censors or political powers of the time) than to capture accurately *his* view of the matter.

Some of Castelvetro's theories, such as the unities, were accepted enthusiastically by the French Neo-Classical dramatists. As is well known, Corneille (1606–1684) and Racine (1639–1699) became intrigued with Aristotle's doctrine, the former particularly in 1660 with his *Discours,* and the latter, who also took a special interest in the Greek text itself, in the 1670s. Naturally, their success on the stage generated more interest in the *Dramatics*. For reasons we would expect, though, neither playwright appears as interested in the philosophical issues as in the immediate theoretical underpinning for dramatic or literary practice, especially regarding their own creations. They focus on topics such as "probabilities" and the effectiveness of the unities, never (to my knowledge) on whether drama is or is not independent of literature for Aristotle. What the playwrights do have to say that is of consequence for our concerns follows. As alluded to, in some ways following Scaliger, they take pleasure or delight as the aim of tragedy. Also like that Italian commentator, the playwrights proceed as evolutionary thinkers, not as ones intending to obey authentic Aristotelian doctrine in all respects (even if they follow what they perceive to be Aristotle's principles in almost all other important ways, e.g., concerning the unities of time, place and action). Regarding Corneille, and, specifically, how he accepts only parts of the *Dramatics,* Guilherme de Mendonça reports:

> What is implied by Corneille's discussion of pity and fear is a rejection of catharsis as it had been defined by neoclassicists with reference to Aristotle. "But I [Corneille] know not if [pity] can produce such [fear] or if it [the bad luck that causes their unhappiness] purges anything. *I fear Aristotle's reasoning on this particular point is but a beautiful idea, which has no effect in reality.* I am referring to those that watched the play [the *Cid*]: they can look into their own hearts, question all that they love in the theatre, to know if they were taken to that conscious fear, and if it has in any way rectified any of their passions [my italics]."[846]

Again, Aristotle's empirical weakness with regard to tragedy is asserted: The beautiful idea has "no effect in reality." Racine himself says in the preface to his tragedy *Berenice:*

---

87-8.

846   Pierre Corneille, *Trois Discours sur le Poème Dramatique* (Flammarion's 1999 annotated edition), trans. by Guilherme Abel Ferreira de Mendonça (*Acting Theory as Poetics of Drama: A Study of the Emergence of the Concept of 'Motivated Action' in Playwriting Theory,* Ph.d. Thesis, Brunel University, April 2012), p. 146. Available at: https://iconline.ipleiria.pt/bitstream/10400.8/750/1/THESIS.GuilhermeMendonca.pdf

It is not at all necessary that there would be blood and deaths in a tragedy; it suffices that the action is grand, that the actors are heroic, that the passions are excited there, and that all feel the majestic sadness there *which makes the entire pleasure of tragedy* [my translation and italics].[847]

Thus it is "majestic sadness" that colors the pleasure of tragedy, not catharsis. Yet again, the rejection of part of Aristotle's theory is empirically based and hurts Aristotle in one of the areas in which he is often most admired: his *a posteriori*, and typically scientific, approach. The ramifications of this rejection I examined to some extent, especially in Chapter 9, and discuss more, e.g., regarding Brecht. In any event, as suggested by Halliwell, the practice of taking Aristotle piecemeal when convenient continues, and with so many variations that it becomes impossible to list them here. Nevertheless, I should stress that by adapting the concept of *katharsis*, it appears that many authors leveraged Aristotle's stature to bolster their own theories, or they skirted any task of refuting one of the most influential thinkers of dramatic theory known to Western civilization, or both. Moreover, to switch back to my other alleged misconception related to literature, it is unsurprising that scholars steeped in literature and excelling at languages, both native and ancient, would focus primarily on verse and believe language is the most crucial element for Aristotelian tragedy, as I explored in Chapters 2 and 3. Let us turn, though, to a renowned dance theorist to illustrate that even apologists for dance as a theatrical art did not contest the literary claims and assumptions.

### Claude-François Menestrier (1631–1705)

King Louis XIV (1638–1715), the powerful monarch of France who was also an ardent ballet dancer, created the Royal Academy of Dance in 1661, the same year he became king and eight years *before* establishing the equivalent academy for music. Twenty-one years later, in 1682, Claude-François Menestrier wrote in *Ancient and Modern Ballets According to the Rules of the Theater* that ballet can embrace the five species of poetry: epic, tragic, lyric, satiric and elegiac.[848] He then says that, regarding the origin of dance and ballet, he will "examine the definition of Aristotle, after having given the sentiments of Plato, Athenaeus, Lucian, and Libanius."[849] Because a definition of dance *per se* by Aristotle does not exist, Menestrier appears to mean the statement in *Dramatics* 1 that dancers can represent ethos, pathos, and actions (Menestrier never cites passages). He remarks on the strophe and

---

847 « Ce n'est point une nécessité qu'il y ait du sang et des morts dans une tragédie; il suffit que l'action en soit grande, que les acteurs en soient héroïques, que les passions y soient excitées, et que tout s'y ressente de cette tristesse majestueuse qui fait tout le plaisir de la tragédie.» Available at: http://www.feedbooks.com/book/3001/b%C3%A9r%C3%A9nice

848 Claude-François Menestrier, *Des Ballets Anciens et Modernes Selon les Regles du Theatre* [*Ancient and Modern Ballets According to the Rules of the Theater*] (Paris: René Guignard) 1682, p. 4. Available at: http://books.google.fr/books?id=wqVAAAAAcAAJ

849 *Op. cit.* p. 8

antistrophe of the ancient dance, how the dancers represented at times the planets and movements of the heavens, and how the songs sung when the dancers stopped at the end of each were named then the same (strophe or antistrophe).[850]

Menestrier is at least approximately right on this last matter, and I argued that the dancing or choral form is the primary notion of *strophe* and *antistrophe*, even though the terms evolve to have purely musical and poetic meanings subsequently (as "stanza" or the equivalent), which can be seen from other sources. Two nineteenth-century classicists discuss this in translating and commenting upon the *Hecuba* of Euripides:

> Episodes [in the *Hecuba* of Euripides and often in ancient tragedy] are the dialogues which come between two choral odes, and it will be seen that they roughly divide the whole play into acts. The Doric poet Alkman gave an artistic form to the choral lyric by arranging that the chorus, while singing stasima, should execute alternately a movement to the right (STROPHE turning) and a movement to the left (ANTISTROPHE); and he composed the songs which the chorus was to sing in couples of stanzas called STROPHE and ANTISTROPHE, answering to these balanced movements. Tisias of Sicily (surnamed Stesichorus, "marshal of choruses") perfected the form of the choral lyric by adding to STROPHE and ANTISTROPHE a third part, the EPODOS, sung by the chorus while it remained stationary after the movements to right and left.[851]

The classicist T. B. L. Webster, in one of the least recognized and yet most detailed works of dance scholarship of the twentieth century, provides dozens if not hundreds of examples of how dance influenced Greek poetry and music, including meter and rhythms in our sense of the words. He explains all of this further:

> Arion [c. 615] is ... said to have 'taught' the dithyramb: the word is used in official Athenian drama records of the poet as the trainer of the chorus, and implies that Arion was not the leader of the dithyramb, like Archilochos [c. 680–645], but his dithyramb was completely choral. The Souda evidently refers to the same thing when it says that Arion first established a chorus, but this probably carries the additional implication that Arion's chorus sang in one place and was not processional. In itself there was nothing new in this. We have seen from the beginning both processional choruses and choruses which sang in one

---

850    *Op. cit.*, pp. 37-9.
851    *The Hecuba of Euripides*, a revised text with notes and an introd. by John Bond and Arthur S. Walpole (London: Macmillan & Co) 1882, pp. x-xi. Bond and Walpole also discuss the commentary tradition on Euripides, p. xi. Available at:
https://archive.org/stream/hecubaeuripides00eurigoog#page/n4/mode/2up
Roger Dunkle, a Classics professor at Brooklyn College confirms all of this:
> As is clear from their meaning, strophe and antistrophe are dance terms. These two stanzas corresponded to each other metrically. An ancient commentator on Euripides' *Hecuba* (647) says:
>> One must realize that the chorus members sang the strophe while moving to the right, the antistrophe while moving to the left, and the epode while stationary (course material, undated).

place, what we have called round dances, but it may have been new for the dithyramb, and the later dithyramb was known as a 'circular chorus' to distinguish it from the 'rectangular chorus' of drama...[852]

Stesichoros was credited with the invention of the triad form. A triad consists of a pair of strophe and antistrophe which are identical in form and an epode which has a different metrical form. After Stesichoros the form is found again in Ibykos, in most of Pindar and Bacchylides, and sometimes in tragedy. Stesichoros' triads (and those of many of his successors) were written for performance in the orchestra; they were stationary songs as distinct from processional. The ancient view, which may be old, was that the chorus circled the central altar in one direction for the strophe and in the other for the antistrophe, but were stationary for the epode: 'stationary' in this sense excluded circular movement *but does not exclude movement sideways, forwards or backwards.* In processionals there can have been no such distinction between the parts of the triad [my italics].[853]

To return to Menestrier: He then speaks of the type of dance that Plutarch, the historian and biographer of the first century CE, describes (in the *Life of Theseus*, 21) of Theseus creating at Delos.[854] Menestrier makes the crucial distinction between pure *dance* and "ballet," the latter being more complex and representational. It is what the Greeks at times called *orchēsis*. His words are:

---

852    Webster, 1970, p. 68. For those not conversant in Greek, the book will be difficult, but for dance historians a vital source of information. The wealth of metrics that he discusses and applies to the different scenarios—in not only the commonly known trimeters, anapaests, iambic pentameters and dactylic hexameters, but glyconics, telesilleans, choriambic dimeters, dactyl-epitrites, aeolics, dochmiacs, ionics, amongst many others—is awe-inspiring, and results in a greater appreciation of the technical capabilities of the ancients. My only concern is that Webster seems to believe that the dance steps were always matching the musical or verbal rhythms and meters. This "match" is often true in folk and social dance, but not always (tango being a counter-example, where the improvised movements can go with or across a melody, no matter what the meter). It is certainly not the case in fine art dance, where choreographers very quickly learn not to follow the music slavishly. Given the evidence we see throughout this book, especially in Chapters 1-2, I cannot believe that the Greek choreographers would have not played with the music, going with it at times but against it at other times to ensure the organic development of what I call "melkines" ("honeyed movements," which is to dance as melody is to music), that is, the captivating movement phrases. Conversely, if the dance steps were set first, I cannot believe the composer matched them always exactly with the word and musical rhythms. Indeed, some of Plato's complaints that we saw in Chapter 1 reflect that this lack of exact unity was happening in the New Music.

853    Webster, *op. cit.*, 1970, pp. 76-7.

854    Bernadotte Perrin pinpoints the passage explaining this, which reflects the occasionally serious and religious nature of dance in ancient Greece, as opposed to the Dionysian type that is often emphasized by historians:
> On his voyage from Crete, Theseus put in at Delos, and having sacrificed to the god and dedicated in his temple the image of Aphrodite which he had received from Ariadne, he danced with his youths a dance which they say is still performed by the Delians, being an imitation of the circling passages in the Labyrinth, and consisting of certain rhythmic involutions and evolutions. This kind of dance, as Dicaearchus tells us, is called by the Delians *The Crane* (*geranos*) (Plutarch, *Plutarch's Lives*, with an English translation by Bernadotte Perrin, Cambridge, MA: Harvard University Pr.; London: William Heinemann Ltd., 1914) p. 45.

> I call these dances "ballets" because they are not simple dances like the others, but ingenious representations, of movements of the heaven and planets, and the evolutions of the Labyrinthe, from which Theseus exited. Since then ballets were included in tragedy and comedy, and the chorus did them as we see between the acts of the tragedies of Aeschylus, Sophocles, and Euripides, and of the comedies of Aristophanes [my translation, as are other passages by Menestrier].[855]

We saw in Chapters 1 and 2 that this distinction between "simple dances" and "ballets" has an antecedent in Plato and Aristotle when in the context of orchestral art—*rhuthmos* (dance) versus *orchēsis* ("ballet")—even if the terms, like "dance" and "ballet" today, are often used interchangeably. Menestrier advises the reader further that:

> Plato spoke of the dance in general, but did not treat of ballet except in passing, and did not take care to define it but rather on occasion describes it. But Aristotle who is a philosopher, exact on all the things he treats, said in speaking of 'ballets' in the *Poetics* that they are the actions, morals, and passions that one expresses in the dances shaped by the harmonic cadences, and the movements regulate the gestures, actions, and figures. All the art of Ballets is based on this definition that it is necessary to develop... The Ballet is an imitation like the other arts, and it is what ballet has in common with them.[856]

Whether justifiably or not, Menestrier bitingly adds that "today there are lots of dances but few ballets, because the dancers like better to make beautiful steps and pretty cadences than to tax themselves to represent what should be represented in order to make decent ballets."[857]

Menestrier also explains how ballet differs from the other arts: For instance, painting only gives static representations, but ballet represents movement, which conveys the internal passions and sentiments, and he records the history of Roman pantomimes who could communicate with their gestures. Poetry and ballet have similarities and differences,[858] and Menestrier gives dozen after dozen of possible subjects based on antiquity for ballets, noting afterward that poetry can be more ingenious and can cover the weather, the night, proverbs, and so forth.[859] He states that Aristotle wrote of poetry (*poetique*), of which tragedy, ballet, opera, and comedy are four different species,[860] something, however, not found *per se* explicitly anywhere in Aristotle's corpus. However, we saw in Chapter 2 that Aristotle's theory of early drama might allow someone to extrapolate such a claim, assuming that bal-

---

855   "J'appelle ces Dances Ballets, parce qu'elles n'étoient pas de simple Dances comme les autres, mais des Representations ingenieuses, des mouvements du Ciel & des Planetes, & des Evolutions du Labyrinthe, dont Thesée sortir. On attacha depuis les Ballets à la Tragedie, & à la Comedie, & ce furent les Actes des Tragedies d'Eschile, de Sophocle, & d'Euripide, & des Comedies d'Aristophane" (Menestrier, *op. cit.*, p. 37).

856   Menestrier, *op. cit.*, pp. 40-1.

857   Menestrier, *op. cit.*, pp. 162-3.

858   *Op. cit.*, p. 45.

859   *Op. cit.*, pp. 45-56.

860   *Op. cit.*, p. 284.

let had some words (which it did in the sixteenth and seventeenth centuries) and assuming absolute precision is not required. Menestrier also claims that for Aristotle the end of tragedy was to purge the spirit of violent passions. Thus, Menestrier appropriates the standard view of the *katharsis* clause—but he strangely notes the subjects were like Merope (with a happy ending), although he mentions other tragedies by Sophocles and Euripides (Aeschylus is omitted).[861] Very interestingly, on this last point and Merope, he must refer to *Dramatics* 14, although he never specifies the chapter, nor does he point out the inconsistency with the unhappy *Oedipus* being the best plot in *Dramatics* 13. For our purposes, he begins to finish by saying that (for himself and presumably for some of the French or Europeans of his time) tragedy, comedy, "representations in music" and ballets are imitations—this is what they all have in common. Menestrier completes his discussion: Tragedy and comedy imitate actions, the first of grand personages, the other the actions of the people. Ballet imitates the nature of things and represents men *and animals* indifferently. Tragedy and comedy are for morality and instruction; ballet is for diversion and pleasure.[862]

In conclusion, Menestrier does not cite passages *per se* from the *Dramatics*; he summarizes or paraphrases Aristotle, and at the end of the book, one has the strong impression that Aristotelian tragedy is done only with language, although Menestrier never seems to commit himself one way or the other.[863] When dance enters, it comes in within discussions of ballet, and, as just noted, ballet is a species of poetry (which would be acceptable were it clear that the sense of "poetry" is a Diotiman one, not the Gorgian one, but no such senses are distinguished for him). In short, although he cites Aristotle repeatedly, he only relies on the Greek for the few passages that help support the new French notion of ballet of the seventeenth century. Absolutely no rigorous analysis is given of Aristotle's definition of tragedy and whether or how either music or dance fits into it. However, Menestrier is the first writer that I know from the Renaissance onward to make the crucial distinction between ballet and dance that he believes stems from the Greeks, a distinction that is typically ignored by ancient Greek philosophers and classicists of the last few centuries. Again, we saw how extremely important this distinction was in Chapters 1 and 2.[864]

---

861   *Op. cit.*, p. 284.

862   *Op. cit.*, pp. 290-1.

863   Some additional points he makes: Like tragedy (with beginning, middle and end), the ballet has three similar parts: the Opening (*l'Overture*), the "entrees," (*les Entrées*) and "the grand Ballet" (p. 257). Menestrier praises Lope de Vega, whom we will examine in a moment, saying that de Vega's productions are noteworthy (pp. 289-90). Ballets are done to singing, at least during part of the performance (pp. 296ff).

864   Another theorist that dance historians cite is Abbé Jean-Baptiste Dubos (1670-1742), yet in no way does he capture in my view correct Aristotelian theories concerning the matters of this book. In his *Réflexions critiques sur la poësie et sur la peinture* (*Critical Reflections on Poetry and Painting*), 3rd Vol. (Paris: Chez Pierre-Jean Mariette, 1733), he interprets Aristides Quintilianus as making this distinction between "melody" and "the making of melody" (*melopoiia*): Melody is the chant or the notes; *melopoiia* ("*la melopée*") is the art

## André Dacier (1651–1722)

Shortly after Menestrier, we obtain one of the best translations and commentaries of Aristotle of the time, by Dacier. I present his reputation first, along with his general views, before examining the precise points on the nature of tragedy as literature and on *katharsis*. To my knowledge, Dacier is the one who most closely in this period understood the importance of music, dance, and the performance of the chorus for Aristotle, and almost anticipated my views on the nature of tragedy as dramatic musical composition. Why he was thrown off, though, is captured towards the end of this history. I offer a summary first by Samuel Monk, in the Introduction to the publication that Halliwell notes, as

---

of making those notes. Then Dubos goes on to say: In the *melopée Nomique* (nome), given in the publication of civic laws, one uses high notes; in the dithyrambic *melopée*, one uses middle notes, and in the tragic *melopée* one uses the low tones (p. 56). (I remind the reader that in *Problems* 19, 919b37-920a2, Aristotle notes that the laws or nomes were first sung to be remembered but in the *Dramatics* and during Athenian times the practice is seemingly an orchestral art or at least done by soloists.)

Not only, then, does Dubos misconstrue the kind of nome that is similar to the dithyramb, thinking that it has to do still with legal pronouncements, but he arrives at a systemization of tones that to my knowledge is utterly arbitrary concerning ancient practice. At its closest, in the current context, it recalls Aristotle's statement in the *Rhetoric* that *harmonia* is of the low, middle and high tones (for a speaker), and the equivalent for Plato in *Laws* II in the context of singing: *harmonia* is the blending of low and high tones, again, as I examined in Chapter 1. Yet neither Greek assigns a whole register to one full art form, a point I discussed in Chapter 1 regarding a modern interpretation by England and Bury of Plato, which impacts our understanding of what Aristotle meant by *harmonia*. On Dubos's view, speakers in civic law would sound like sparrows chirping! Of course, what Quintilianus says can be very different from what Aristotle says, but Dubos writes as if explaining the notions applies across the ancient Greek spectrum of many centuries.

Subsequently, Dubos gives an explanation of the definition of tragedy in which Aristotle describes "sweetened language." Using explicitly the text of the Dutchman Daniel Heinsius—who was one of greatest scholars of the age and who had studied with Joseph Scaliger, the son of the Italian commentator we examined above with the same surname—Dubos says that the tragedy "excites terror and compassion, sentiments very appropriate to purge the passions" [my transl.] (p. 85). Dubos adds that "the language to please" (his translation of the *hedusmenō logō*) means the phrases "reduced and cut by measure and subjected to rhythm, which makes harmony" (p. 85). Like many, if not all commentators, he therefore removes dance from the definition of tragedy.

In a different publication, Dubos makes two additional noteworthy statements that reflect casual interpretations or personal viewpoints (*Critical Reflections on Poetry, Painting and Music*, Vol. 1, 5th ed., transl. by Thomas Nugent into English, London: John Nourse Publ., 1748). The first is "….it has been a maxim in all times, that tragedy purges the passions" (p. 354). Dubos gives no citation of Aristotle or anyone else, and clearly the ancient Athenians would not agree, as we saw, given that Callicles in the *Gorgias* correctly reports that pleasure is considered the end of tragedy for the typical person (at 502a). Second, Dubos states: "Music…men have invented, in order to add a new strength to poetry, and to render it capable of making a greater impression" (p. 360). Thus, poetry is the foundation. Anything else like music (and presumably dance) is an "addition," all of which we have seen conflicts with Plato's and Aristotle's position that *harmonia kai rhuthmos* are grounded in biology.

recounted above. These prefatory remarks capture Dacier's role at the time within French-English culture and indicates what kind of arguments were used for and against the chorus, whether it was Aristotle's or the 17th-century's conception:

> André Dacier's *Poëtique d'Aristote Traduite en François avec des Remarques* was published in Paris in 1692. His translation of Horace with critical remarks (1681–1689) had helped to establish his reputation in both France and England. Dryden, for example, borrowed from it extensively in his *Discourse Concerning the Original and Progress of Satire* (1693)... A quarter of a century later Dacier's reputation was still great enough to allow Charles Gildon to eke out the second part of his *Complete Art of Poetry* (1718) by translating long excerpts from the Preface to the "admirable" Dacier's Aristotle... A work so much esteemed was certain to be translated, and so in 1705 an English version by an anonymous translator was published...
>
> In the very year of its publication Rymer [1643–1713] read with obvious approbation Dacier's *Poëtique d'Aristote*. In the preface to *A Short View of Tragedy* (1692) he announced that "we begin to understand the Epick Poem by means of Bossu; and Tragedy by Monsieur Dacier." That Rymer admired Dacier's strict formalism is plain, but he was especially moved by the French critic's argument that the chorus is *the* essential part of true tragedy, since it is necessary both for *vraisemblance* and for moral instruction. He therefore boldly proposed that English tragic poets should henceforth use the chorus in the manner of the ancients, since it is "*the root and original, and ... certainly always the most necessary part of Tragedy.*" Moreover, he praised (as had Dacier) the example of Racine, who had introduced the chorus into the plays he had written for private performance, by the young ladies of St. Cyr—*Esther* (1689) and *Athalie* (1691)...
>
> Rymer's proposal provoked a public debate, which was begun by John Dennis, at that time an almost unknown young critic... Though Dryden avoided any extended public argument with Rymer, he obviously knew both the *Short View* and Dacier's Aristotle. In the *Parallel of Poetry and Painting* (1695), he followed Rymer's lead in equating Dacier, the critic of tragedy ("in his late excellent Translation of Aristotle and his notes upon him") with Le Bossu, the framer of "exact rules for the Epic Poem..." But he disagreed with Dacier's opinions on the chorus and explained away Racine's use of it on the sensible grounds that *Esther* had not been written for public, but for private performances which gave occasion to the young ladies of St. Cyr "of entertaining the king with vocal music, and of commending their voices." *He also suggested the practical consideration that plays with choruses would bankrupt any company of actors because it would be necessary to provide a number of costumes for the additional players and to enlarge the stage (and consequently the theater) to make room for the choral dances* [my italics].[865]

Thus, the singing and dancing choruses were dispensed with because of financial considerations and because of the suppressed premise that the ancient practice was irrelevant to modern (18th-century)

---

865  A. Dacier, *The Preface to Aristotle's Art of Poetry. With Mr. D'Acier's Notes Translated from the French* (London: Dan. Brown) 1705; The Augustan Reprint Society, Publ # 76, 1959, editor Samuel Holt Monk. Available at Project Guttenberg: http://www.gutenberg.org/cache/epub/29547/pg29547.txt (no page #'s in the reproduction)

times, not because of any consideration directly related to Aristotle. Consider now the part of the Preface by Dacier himself, paying attention to whether he attributes any of the views to Aristotle:

> From THE PREFACE: This is what, according to my Opinion, may be truly said of *Tragedy*, and the Mean we ought to keep. But to the end this may be justly said, the Parts must conform themselves entirely to the Rules of Ancient *Tragedy*, that is to say, which endeavours rather to Instruct than Please, and regard the Agreeable, as a means only to make the Profitable more taking; they must paint the Disorders of the Passions, and the inevitable Mischiefs which arise from thence. 'Twas for this the *Greek Tragedians* were so much Honour'd in their own Age, and esteemed in those which follow'd. Their Theatre was a School, where Virtue was generally better Taught, than in the Schools of their Philosophers, and at this very Day, the reading their Pieces will Inspire an Hatred to Vice, and a Love to Virtue. To Imitate them profitably, *we should re-establish the Chorus* [my italics], which establishing the *veri-Similitude* of the *Tragedy*, gives an Opportunity to set forth to the People, those particular Sentiments, you would inspire them with, and to let them know, what is Vicious or Laudable, in the Characters which are Introduc'd.[866]

On the negative side, these comments convey the "ethical rhetoric" of Averroes, not the pleasure that Callicles had said was the end of tragedy for the typical Greek or the pleasure that I showed throughout the *Dramatics* is the goal of tragedy and epic. Moreover, although Dacier says that the parts of tragedy "must conform ... entirely to the Rules of Ancient Tragedy," it is extremely doubtful that he is capturing Aristotle's view, for reasons we saw in Chapter 7 when examining the real goal of tragedy apart from catharsis. Another problem that I repeat now is that Dacier says that tragedy endeavors "rather to Instruct than Please," which contradicts Aristotle's explicit statements throughout the *Dramatics* despite the importance of mimesis with respect to learning in *Dramatics* 4. Finally, he disparages not only the schools of philosophy but implicitly, one might argue, treatises like the *Nicomachean Ethics*, and suggests that drama is in the service of ethics. Rather, on the contrary, I argued in Chapters 4, 6, 7 and 8 that, in the context of drama, (a correct) ethics is in the service of aesthetics.

On the positive side, Dacier recognizes the importance of the chorus, although whether he attributes the importance to ancient Greek practice in general or to Aristotle remains to be seen.

Then follows Dacier's translation of the *Dramatics* itself and his commentary, to which I now turn. It comes from a separate publication, Dacier's complete work in French.[867] I summarize relevant points, and translate the crucial passages, noting that his chapters always correspond to the typical chapters nowadays, except that *Dramatics* 14 gets split into two chapters, resulting in Dacier having 27 chapters, as opposed to the current 26. In these 27 chapters, we get much more authentic interpretations

---

866  *Op. cit.*, Dacier, ed. Monk, 1959.

867  André Dacier, *La Poetique d'Aristote: contenant les regles les plus exactes pour juger du poëme heroïque* [*Aristotle's Poetics: Containing the most exact rules for judging the heroic poem*] (Paris: Barbin Publ.) 1692.

Appendix:  A Brief History of the Two Misconceptions

of Aristotle's theory at times, although not always.

In Dacier's translation in Chapter 1, *poiētikēs* is given the Gorgian *Poesie*; *rhuthmos* becomes "nombre" ["number"], presumably as it was in *Rhetoric* III 8, which we saw once before; and he says dancers use "number" alone.[868]  How the latter is possible when the dancers use ordered body movement is absolutely baffling but was discussed in great detail in Chapter 3.  (We might say more sensibly that mathematicians use numbers alone, if we assume they are thinking of addition or subtraction or the like, rather than writing their calculations, because then obviously some writing apparatus is also needed.  Still "numbers" alone are not even possible in this field; operations like addition are also required.)  *Poesie* is the art of making poems for him (p. 4).  He also states that the aforementioned Heinsius claimed that the passage about dancers in Chapter 1 should be understood as "most of the dancers use *rhythmos* alone" because others danced to music or singing, which we have seen is entirely accurate and crucial for a correct understanding of *Dramatics* 1, with qualification for the exact meaning of *rhuthmos*.[869]  Dacier remarks that Aristotle does not explain in *Dramatics* 4 that Thespis was the first actor because before Thespis there was nothing but a chorus who chanted, but Dacier leaves off dance yet again.[870]  The goal or end of tragedy is essential in a perfect definition, he claims, and he begins to explain the *katharsis* phrase as a way of purging passions like compassion and terror through the means of those two emotions.[871]  Dacier continues with the *katharsis* clause, presenting the following points:

> Regard ... what is the most important [element] in the definition, and at the same time the most difficult, because all of the efforts the Commentators have made to explain it have served only to obscure it.[872]

He adds that Corneille, after much research, found, as we saw above, the inclusion of *katharsis* a "beautiful idea [on the part of Aristotle], which never had its effect in reality."  *Dacier proposes that, if we had the second lost book on comedy, where Aristotle fulfilled his promise from Politics VIII 7 to explain catharsis, the riddle would be solved, and he offers his explanation of what Aristotle's account was.*  He ignores, as I discussed in Chapter 6, why the account in comedy would *not* apply back to tragedy, given that Aristotle says at the end of *Dramatics* 26 that the account of tragedy and epic is finished.  Dacier also ignores why (as Averroes had intuited) "moderation" is not then in the definition

---

868   Dacier, *op. cit.*, 1692, p. 2.
869   Dacier, *op. cit.*, 1692, p. 10.  I do not know whether Heinsius took "*rhythmos*" to be temporal ordering, spatial ordering or spatiotemporal ordering, or better yet whether he translated it ever as "dance," although I doubt it.  Nor do I know whether he understood Menestrier's distinction between (simple or natual) dance and complex, mimetic dance.
870   Dacier, *op. cit.*, 1692, p. 46.
871   Dacier, *op. cit.*, 1692, pp. 73 & 79-83.
872   Dacier, *op. cit.*, 1692, pp. 80-3.

instead, presenting yet another medical explanation: like a cathartic medicine that purges the body and leaves it in a better state, tragedy causes not only undue pity and fear but the other bad passions to be expelled. As he concludes, "tragedy is a veritable medicine, which purges the passions, since it teaches the ambitious to moderate their ambition, the impious to fear God... But it is an agreeable medicine [harking back to Castelvetro], which only accomplishes its effect through pleasure [my comment in brackets]."[873] Why "accomplishing its effect through pleasure" rather than "through pity and fear" is not in the definition, too, then becomes also puzzling. Finally, why God and impiety enter when nothing in the Greek text comes close to such concepts can only be explained in my view by Dacier trying to sell Aristotle's dramatic theory to the religious powers of the times or because of his own religious sensibility, if any.

Subsequently, Dacier remarks on the phrase "sweetened language" in the definition of tragedy, a phrase that gets explained as *harmonia* and *rhuthmos* being added to the language.[874] Even though *rhuthmos* was oddly "number" in his translation, as noted above, he notes in his commentary—correctly, in my view—that it is music *and dance* that is added to the language. He describes the importance of the chorus and discusses the dilemma that ensues in the rest of *Dramatics* 6 because music and dance first seem necessary and then because Aristotle suggests they are not. However, Dacier resolves the dilemma—and here is where he unfortunately goes astray again, as is demonstrated in my Chapters 2 and 3—by saying that music and dance are not essential *for Aristotle* because "otherwise there would not be tragedy other than in the theater,"[875] strongly implying that merely written tragedy is legitimate in the context of the whole *Dramatics*. Again, despite Dacier recognizing the importance of the chorus, music, and dance, tragedy need ultimately only be read in his view for Aristotle.

### Lope de Vega (1562–1635) and Thomas Rymer (1643–1713)

In the late 16th to the early 18th centuries, the dramatist Lope de Vega and the drama critic Thomas Rymer, mentioned above, also came very close to Aristotle's position. However, they seem to have been only inspired by Aristotle, and they presented mostly their own conceptions of drama or, in the case of de Vega, also created performed dramas. It seems fitting, though, to at least acknowledge them in passing, given that they refer to Aristotle in significant ways.

De Vega, otherwise known as Félix Arturo Lope de Vega y Carpio, and Cervantes, slightly his elder, are ranked as the two great classical masters of Spanish literature and drama.[876] Cervantes, as some

---

873    Dacier, *op. cit.*, 1692, p. 83.
874    Dacier, *op. cit.*, 1692, p. 84.
875    Dacier, *op. cit.*, 1692, p. 86.
876    Coincidentally, both were sailors in the Spanish navy for years before, or while, becoming profession-

English-speakers realize well, wrote roughly eight plays and is known nowadays to most for *Don Quixote,* whereas it is not as well known that de Vega wrote almost 500 comedies according to his own reckoning and is reputed to have composed more than one thousand plays, along with novels, poems, and sonnets. Apparently, though, his typical "comedy," which was more an intrigue than a comic drama in our sense, was one act.[877] The crucial point here is that de Vega gives preponderance to the plot, and to the development of action and suspense on the stage, over text in his dramas. As Brender Matthews says:

> Where Lope de Vega and Shakspere [his spelling] are again alike is that they both wrote all their plays for the popular theater, apparently composing these pieces solely with a view to performance and caring nothing for any praise which might be derived from publication. Martinenche, in his study of the 'Comedia Espagnole' ... dwells on Lope's carelessness for the literary renown to be won by the printing of his dramatic poems; in his non-dramatic poems he took pride, just as Shakspere seems to have read carefully the proofs of his lyrical narratives altho he did not himself choose to publish a single one of his plays. And Moliere, it may be noted, tells us frankly that he was completely satisfied with the success of his earlier pieces on the stage, and that he had been content to leave them unprinted until his hand was forced by a pirate-publisher.[878]

The similarity of de Vega regarding textual publication to both Shakespeare and Moliere, and the priority of performance for all three dramatists, is very intriguing but one I leave aside for this book because it does not reflect their conception of Aristotle's view to my knowledge (and I have not researched the matter). My point can be made with de Vega's case alone, and it is that language for him is not as crucial as the plot or the enacted action on stage, identical to Aristotle, which I demonstrated in Chapters 2-3. Rymer follows suit, roughly speaking, at the end of the 1600s in England, asking:

> What reformation may not we expect, now that in France they see the necessity of a chorus to their tragedies? Boyer and Racine, both of the Royal Academy, have led the dance: they have tried the success in the last plays that were presented by them. The chorus was the

---

al writers, which has no bearing on the arguments in this book, but which I find fascinating and cannot help mentioning. In this regard, they followed Xenophon, who himself was a mercenary. One wonders whether the admirals trained their men to be better writers than fighters and sailors, given, for instance, the disaster of the Spanish Armada against England in 1588! (The serious reader might find this comment unnecessary, but those who know de Vega's emphasis on comedy might find it welcome relief from hundreds of pages of dry analysis.)

877   While editing the penultimate draft of this book, I discovered for the first time a play of his being performed, *El Loco por Fuerza* ("Insane by Force"), in New York City, in Spanish with electronic English sub-titles. It took one hour and forty-five minutes, so if he even wrote half of what is claimed, his output was prodigious. Suffice it to say that the various scenes were short and the plot developments fast and furious. On the one hand, I wished there were fewer sub-plots, and more character development for the main plot; on the other hand, it made me hope that his other work becomes better known to English-speaking audiences.

878   Lope de Vega, *The New Art of Writing Plays* (*Arte nuevo de hacer comedias en este tiempo*, 1609), trans. by William T. Brewster, in *Papers on Play-Making,* including an introduction by Brander Matthew (New York: Dramatic Museum of Columbia University) 1914, p. 3. Available at: https://archive.org/details/newartofwritingp00vegauoft

root and original, and is certainly almost always the necessary part, of tragedy... Aristotle tells us of two senses that must be pleased: our sight and our ears. [No citation given by Rymer.]... It matters not whether there be any plot, any characters, any sense, or a wise word from one end to the other, provided in our play we have the Senate of Rome, the Venetian Senate .... *We go to see a play acted; in tragedy is represented a memorable action...* Action is speaking to the eyes; and all Europe over, plays have been represented with great applause in a tongue unknown and *sometimes without any language at all...* Many, peradventure, of the tragical scenes in Shakespeare, cried up for the action, might do yet better without words. **Words are a sort of heavy baggage that were better out of the way**, at the push of actions, especially in his bombast circumstance... Some go to *see*, others to *hear*, a play. The poet should please both; but be sure the spectators are satisfied, whatever entertainment he give his audience [my italics & bolding].[879]

Rymer presents his own view of what a tragic play should be, even though he occasionally calls on the authority of Aristotle (along with Horace and others in pages I have not reproduced). Proof is that he denies the play need even have a plot, which is Aristotle's highest ranked necessary element, and without which, the Greek says, tragedy could not exist. Rymer thinks that plot can be part of, or also given through, the language. For Aristotle, as we saw in my Chapters 2, 3, 5 and 6, plot could—as the (the enacted) structure of actions—be given in dance or non-linguistic enactment (acting without words), which means that Rymer did not understand this point or had a different conception of plot. This is perhaps why he focuses on chorus, spectacle and the visual scenes—even while acknowledging that plays are given to great applause on the Continent with no language. In *some* ways, then, he is perfectly Aristotelian, following what Aristotle says at the end of the definition of tragedy when the Greek begins to derive the six necessary elements from the condition of enactment and spectacle, as I explained in Chapter 2. To repeat some of that explanation, Aristotle says: "*Since people acting produce the representation*, first (i) the ornament of spectacle will necessarily be a part of tragedy; and then (ii) "orchestral art" (*melopoiia*) and (iii) language (*lexis*), for these are the media in which they produce the representation [my italics]."[880]

Let us leave the exceptions, de Vega and Rymer, and return to the standard historical attitude, that language in drama was so crucial that even the dramatists, who of all people should presumably defend the importance of performance (and perhaps music and dance) in tragedy, were the ones perennially defending the view that drama was a species of language. Those writers, the playwrights or poets or authors, obviously had become the most important part of the team that created drama.

---

[879] Thomas Rymer, *A Short view of Tragedy, its Original Excellency and Corruption, with some Reflections on Shakespear and other Practitioners for the Stage* (1693), pp. 205-6 (reproduced in Barrett Harper Clark, European Theories of the Drama: *An Anthology of Dramatic Theory and Criticism from Aristotle to the Present Day, in a Series of Selected Texts, with Commentaries, Biographies, and Bibliographies*, Cincinnati: Stewart & Kidd Company, 1918).

[880] 1449b31-34, tr. Janko.

## Appendix: A Brief History of the Two Misconceptions

Actually, there is no use piling on brick upon brick when the other side of the "balancing beam"—that drama is an independent art *for Aristotle*—is not even advocated by Dacier, de Vega or Rymer, nor for anyone else in the over 600 years I have already briefly covered. We should, then, jump ahead to the 18th century, after merely recounting what was being said about *katharsis* by one last representative of the 17th century, John Milton. The author, naturally, of *Paradise Lost* and *Paradise Regained* modeled his tragic poetry at least in part on Aristotle's principles and spoke of:

> that sublime Art which in Aristotles *Poetics*, in Horace, and the Italian Commentaries of Castelvetro, Tasso, Mazzoni and others, teaches what the laws are of a true Epic Poem, what of a Dramatic, what of a Lyric, what Decorum is, which is the grand masterpiece to observe."[881]

The "Dramatic" here appears to be a style of poem or of writing, and in the rest of his life's work, when he composed the scripts of two performed masques, *Arcades* and *Comus,* there is no indication to my knowledge that he thought a performed drama or masque was independent of the language, which he unsurprisingly seems to have considered the most important element. To switch now to the second theme of this book, *katharsis*, Milton further presents it as a form of homeopathy in the preface to his poem *Samson Agonistes* (1671). In his account:

> Tragedy, as it was antiently composed, hath been ever held the gravest, moralest, and most profitable of all other poems: therefore said by Aristotle to be of power by raising pity and fear, or terror, to purge the mind of those and such like passions; that is, to temper and reduce them to just measure with a kind of delight, stirred up by reading or seeing those passions well imitated. Nor is Nature wanting in her own effects to make good his assertion; for so in physic things of melancholy hue and quality are used against melancholy, sour against sour, salt to remove salt humours.[882]

In other words, the pity and fear felt by an audience stimulate their emotions in order to calm them, turning terror into "a kind of delight." Knowingly or not, Milton has subscribed to the views of Averroes and of the 16th-century Italians: The effect is a moderation ("just measure") and homeopathy is the mechanism to explain Aristotle's frustratingly short remark about *katharsis* in the *Dramatics*. (By now the reader should realize that "short" is an understatement, given the lack of any other explanation whatsoever.) In the paragraph above, it seems as if "delight' and the kind of pleasures that tragedy could provide are *the means by which* the tempering takes place, although the passage is ambiguous and "with a kind of delight" might entail that the delight occurs concomitantly with the tempering. At any rate, to the contrary, on most traditional accounts (which I examined in depth in Chapters 4 through

---

881     *Of Education* (1644), at *The John Milton Reading Room*, Thomas H. Luxon, General Editor, Trustees of Dartmouth College at http://www.dartmouth.edu/~milton/reading_room/of_education/

882     John Milton, *Samson Agonistes,* ed. with introd. and notes by John Churton Collins (Oxford: Clarendon Press) 1883, repr. 1948; available at:
http://www.archive.org/stream/samsonagonisteseoomiltuoft/samsonagonisteseoomiltuoft_djvu.txt

7), how *katharsis* and delight are related by Aristotle in *Politics* VIII 7 clearly entails that the delight results *from* the *katharsis* of pity, fear or "frenziedness."

## Later 18th, and 19th, Century Views

I begin my examination of the later 18th-century after Rymer with a short account of the hugely influential choreographer, ballet master, and theoretician Jean-Georges Noverre, who is most responsible for the *ballet d'action*. This type of ballet essayed, intentionally or not, to capture Aristotle's emphasis on action, not only concerning tragedy but what dancers are said to represent in *Dramatics* 1 (along with ethos and pathos). *Ballet d'action* is an art form that involves action *qua* movement that was representational, notwithstanding that Noverre suggests at the end of his life that ballet could be formalist, too. Noverre cites Aristotle as an influence in his seminal *Letters on Dancing and Ballets*, but it is an interesting question whether he realized Aristotle supported the importance of dance *in tragedy* because Noverre never addresses the issue. Indeed, Noverre's general theories and the emphasis on ballet as a unified action that is lifelike are arguably much more Aristotelian than the puzzling views he attributes to Aristotle. Noverre says, for instance:

> According to Aristotle, a ballet, like poetry, of whatever style, should contain two different parts, that of quality and that of quantity... *Here, then, as you see, are ballets subordinated in some degree to the laws of poetry*; however, they differ from tragedies and comedies in that they are not subject to unity of place, time and action [my italics].[883]

I have no idea how Noverre can attribute these principles to Aristotle, notwithstanding my explanations of the *Dramatics* in which dance is a necessary element of tragedy. Noverre never cites any passages, but it is clear that he thinks he can apply principles of poetry to the dance, and thereby justify his dramatic approach. As we have seen, though, he could have achieved the same end without subordinating dance to language while still being perfectly Aristotelian. To my knowledge, he never writes about *katharsis*, and he never considers in print whether tragedy *per se* for Aristotle is poetry in the Gorgian sense or is dramatic musical performance that includes dance. Still, and this is the key point, we have another case of a dance theorist sadly "subordinating," to use his own word, dance to poetry.

I present now perhaps the most seminal work in the eighteenth century on the *Dramatics*, that of Gotthold Lessing. Lessing translated parts of the *Dramatics* and intended to write a commentary on it, but this never came to fruition, according to Victor Lange.[884] Instead, in the course of writing 104 essays and reviews of plays that themselves appeared at the Hamburg National Theater, designed to

---

883 Jean Georges Noverre, tr. Cyril Beaumont, *Letters on Dancing and Ballets* (Brooklyn, NY: Dance Horizons) 1966, p. 53.
884 Lange, ex-Chairman of the Department of Germanic Languages and Literatures at Princeton University, states this in his introduction to Lessing, *Hamburg Dramaturgy, op. cit.*, 1962, p. x.

be the "first permanent German theater devoted to the performance of serious European plays,"[885] Lessing at times presents his interpretations of Aristotle. In part this was:

> "to restore the Aristotelian ... idea of tragedy" [and to counteract not so much the] unruly anti-Aristotelians among the younger German writers but the false and irresponsible interpreters of the classical ideals who drew beliefs and precepts from the tradition of the French drama, and, in particular, from the example of Corneille... "Various French plays," he [Lessing] is ready to admit, "are most intelligent and instructive works which I think worthy of all praise—only, they are not tragedies. Their authors could not be otherwise than of high intellect, some of them take no mean rank among *poets*—only they are not *tragic poets*. Their Corneille and Racine, their Crébillon and Voltaire have little or nothing of what makes Sophocles Sophocles, Euripides Euripides, Shakespeare Shakespeare. These latter are rarely in opposition to Aristotle's demands, the former are so constantly [my italics]."[886]

Thus, the composers of tragedies were *poets*. As one continues to read Lange's Introduction, one might begin to wonder whether Lessing would be motivated to uphold the performance view that I claim truly exists in Aristotle's theory of tragedy, given Lessing's ostensible desire to support the Hamburg National Theater:

> The picture of an irresponsible and aimless theatrical life which Goethe draws in *Wilhelm Meister* is in Germany eminently true for most of the eighteenth century. At the same time a decided preoccupation with the drama *as one of the three traditional forms of literature* continued among the more academic critics. But theatre and drama existed in large measure as separate concerns. *To bring the two realms into a productive relationship was for Lessing a most urgent task*; the poet, the performer and the audience, he hoped, were to pool their resources once again, as they had often done in Greece, towards making articulate the moral and intellectual strength which the emerging age of reason demanded. **Criticism of the drama as a literary form occupies much of the Dramaturgy; the space devoted to matters of acting and stagecraft is no less extensive. It is well to remember that before Lessing there was almost no work in which the principles of theatrical presentation had been coherently set forth.** Garrick's acting was everywhere in Europe widely discussed and imitated... In France Rémond de Saint Albine had in his *Comédies* (1747) outlined a system of acting to which Lessing occasionally refers with favor. *But never before Lessing had a critic so convincingly insisted on the absolute interdependence of the poet and the speech, expression and gestures of the actor* [my italics].[887]

---

885   Lange, in Lessing, *op. cit.*, p. vii. The Theater opened in 1767 but closed in the same year, eight months later. Lessing added to the reviews, and then published them all together in 1769.

886   Lange, in Lessing, *op. cit.*, p. x. Lessing goes so far as to say about the *Poetics* in the final essays (Numbers 101-104) that "I do not however hesitate to acknowledge (even if I should therefore be laughed to scorn in these enlightened times) that I consider the work as infallible as the *Elements* of Euclid. Its foundations are as clear and definite, only certainly not as comprehensible and therefore more exposed to misconstruction" (p. 263).

887   *Op. cit.*, pp. xi ff.

Let us determine, though, whether Lessing perceives Aristotle as having the same view of "the interdependence of the poet and the speech ... and gestures of the actor." On first impression, with drama being a species of literature, the expectation is that all the other attributes of tragedy—sets, costumes, performance, and dancing—will be important for Lessing but still not as important as the script. Indeed, this expectation is soon met. In Essay 77, he claims:

> It is incontestable that Aristotle never contemplated giving a sharp logical definition of tragedy, for without limiting himself to its merely essential qualities, *he admitted several **accidental** ones that had become necessary by the customs of his day.* But when we deduct these and reduce the other distinctive features, there remains a perfectly accurate definition, namely this, that *a tragedy is a poem* which excites compassion. According to its genus it is the imitation of an action, like the epopee [epic] and comedy, but according to its species, the imitation of an action worthy of compassion. From these two definitions all the rules can be perfectly deduced and even its dramatic form may be determined [my italics, bolding and additional note in brackets].[888]

Since Lessing never cites the Greek passages *per se*, one can only assume that he means the definition of tragedy in *Dramatics* 6. Presumably, the accidental qualities for him are the ones that he omits in his own "accurate definition," namely, "music" and spectacle, which "had become necessary by the customs of his [Aristotle's] day." Yet, inexplicably Lessing even drops essential conditions such as mimesis and the "sweetened" part of "sweetened language" that are indubitably in the definition, as we saw in great detail in Chapters 2 and 3. Like his predecessors, then, but doubly disappointingly because of his professed desire to show the importance of acting and performance, these accidental qualities become mere accessories. Indeed, as he argues in Essay 81, a number of playwrights (especially the French) offer much spectacle, but, e.g., of Voltaire's *Semiramis*, "it contains pomp and decoration enough; a ghost into the bargain, and yet I know no chillier play."[889] He suggests later that, again, the script—or plot *through* the script—is most important. Moreover, stunningly Lessing does not recognize that Aristotle defines tragedy by "biological definition" and thereby presents *both* essential and necessary conditions of tragedy in *Dramatics* 6, rather than "accidental" ones, as demonstrated in my Chapters 2, 3 and 5. So much for the Lessing's "incontestable" claim.

What about Lessing's view on *katharsis*? Interestingly, the English translation is given as "purification," and Lessing summarizes his views of a number of the Essays (Numbers 77-81), pertaining to how pity and fear are the means to purification. He says: "the pity and fear excited by tragedy is to purify our pity and fear, but *only these and no other passions* [my italics]."[890] The many details of his

---

888   Lessing, *op. cit.*, p. 187. All translations of Lessing's text are by Helen Zimmern, originally published in 1890, and reproduced in the Dover edition of 1962 that I cited. That tragedy is claimed to be a poem for Aristotle is repeated in Essay 78, *op. cit.*, p. 190.
889   Essay 80, Lessing, *op. cit.* p. 201.
890   Essay 78, Lessing, *op. cit.* p. 190.

claims, and the impossibility of Aristotle being able to maintain such a view (resulting in, e.g., "pure fear," whatever that could mean when it is seemingly mixed with pity), are unnecessary to repeat here and are covered more below when I review Jacob Bernays's reaction to it. Apart from his use of "purification" rather than "purgation," the most interesting aspect of Lessing's interpretation for me, which I touched upon in Chapter 6, is his focus on whether both pity and fear are the intermediate goals to *katharsis* or whether, as Corneille thought, they could be independent, with the dramatist achieving one but not the other. All of this is in contrast to some scholars who think even today that necessarily pity and fear always occur together. This matter exercised Lessing more than any other topic in the *Dramatics*. He spends a large part of over twenty pages of *Hamburg Dramaturgy* (within pp. 175-209) grappling with the related issues, and says, e.g.:

> ... he who would exhaust *Aristotle* must prove separately— 1. How tragic pity purifies our pity. 2. How tragic fear purifies our fear. 3. How tragic pity purifies our fear. 4. How tragic fear purifies our pity...[891]

However, not one subsequent scholar to my knowledge has ever grappled with these issues, if only to argue that Lessing was mistaken about the need to explain a four-fold interaction between pity and fear. Nor has anyone to my knowledge dealt openly with the dilemma resulting from pity being purified: As I mentioned at the beginning of Chapter 6, if one has pure pity, then it hardly seems mixable with fear, because then it would be impure, just as gold mixed with nickel is not pure gold; likewise, with pure fear. Yet pity and fear are *both* required in the traditional definition of tragedy. Let this suffice for Lessing.

## Carlo Blasis (1795-1878)

I started the review of the 18th century with a ballet theoretician, Noverre, and I finish its end and the beginning of the 19th century, with another, Carlo Blasis, one of the greatest dancers, teachers, and theoreticians of the art form.[892] He is rarely known today and is under-appreciated in my view even by professional ballet teachers (which is understandable in part because he had vast erudition

---

891    *Op. cit.*, p. 193.

892    I divert attention for a few seconds to England. As Halliwell reports, we find Samuel Johnson in 1765 in his *Preface to Shakespeare* judging the Bard:
> by the essential criteria established in the sixteenth century's fusion of Aristotle and Horace... hardened by French orthodoxy of the following century: a general fidelity to "nature," approved by the traditional image of the "mirror of manners and of life"; the aspiration *of poetry* to universality or generality (Shakespeare's characters are species, not individuals); the primacy of plot in drama (Shakespeare's power lies in "the progress of his *fable*") and the necessity for unity of action [my italics] (Halliwell, *op. cit.*, 1986, pp. 309-10).

In short, Johnson judges Shakespeare with respect to poetry and fable, and, although "plot in drama" is mentioned, it is in part to emphasize that Shakespeare's power lies in his fable, all of which still prioritizes language for Johnson, whether or not Shakespeare held the same values.

and sprinkles his most famous book liberally with sayings in Latin, Italian and French, and with many examples from ancient mythology and the classics, which would make the book taxing even for literary historians who have mastered multiple languages). Blasis cares nothing about *katharsis*, essentially only saying in this regard that "the *Grand Ballet d'Action*, or serious Ballet, must be principally modelled on tragedy; but must be less gloomy, substituting more cheerful traits for the latter quality."[893]

Regarding, though, the other alleged misconception of the *Dramatics*, pertaining to literature, Blasis recounts in detail the importance of dance for the Greeks, including Plato and Socrates, and of pantomime for the Romans,[894] while omitting Aristotle *in this regard* for unknown reasons. That is, he knows Aristotle and praises him in a few places, even citing Chapter 15 correctly while noting Aristotle's precepts in not making a hero perfect and praising him as a "great philosopher ... who is almost always perfect in his conceptions."[895] However, he surprisingly never notes the adage in *Dramatics* 1 that the *corps de ballet* (and I use this in a broad sense to include soloists also) can represent ethos, pathos, and actions, which in one way is stunning given his own emphasis on pantomime and the kind of precepts that Noverre a generation before had made famous. Perhaps, though, this adage had become a platitude after Noverre (who, as we saw, followed Menestrier in this regard) and Blasis felt no need to reiterate the obvious. At any rate, Blasis believes that an author must compose a plot upon which the choreographer then structures the whole ballet, given Blasis' advice to follow the principles of drama (exposition, plot, and climax) and to read the ancient dramatic writers.[896] Probably this is from his conception, ironic as it is, that the story is fundamentally literary, not only for the reasons just given but because in an endnote, while explaining how Plato treats dance as an educational and religious necessity, he writes: "Plato says that dancing, with all its varied corporeal exercise, *draws its origin from an imitation of speech*, described by the movements and gesticulations of every limb (*Vide Plat. De Leg.*) [my italics]."[897] Blasis is probably recounting *Laws* (= "*De. Leg.*") VII 816a. Nevertheless, we also saw in Chapter 1 that Plato bases dance on the biological disposition of human beings to put order into jumps and other chaotic movements, not once but five times in *Laws* II. Thus, Plato's view seems to have changed by the time he wrote *Laws* VII. Alternatively, in the relevant passage at 816a, he focusses on more complex or representational *orchēsis* as opposed to the more natural type of dance *qua rhuthmos* that does not require training.

---

893 Carlo Blasis, *The Code of Terpsichore* (London: James Bulcock Publ, 1828, 1st ed; renamed *The Art of Dancing* for the 2nd ed., 1831) republished by Dance Horizons, Brooklyn, NY, 1976, p. 168.

894 Blasis, *op. cit.*, 1976, see espec. pp. 7-25.

895 Blasis, *op. cit.*, pp. 143 and 166-7.

896 Blasis, *op. cit.*, pp. 142-5.

897 Blasis, *op. cit.*, p. 40. He does note cite any Stephanus number that had been available since 1578, as was apparently the style for that kind of writing by non-classicists or for non-classicists *per se*.

Blasis confirms the value of pantomime and gesture, noting that the latter benefits children, savages and the unfortunate who are deprived of hearing and speaking. Gesture also allows one to communicate with those speaking different languages,[898] which is assuredly true: no matter what language one speaks—or, it might be more appropriately said in this circumstance, no matter which language one *is limited to*—one can appreciatively watch a ballet (in our modern sense, with no words). Blasis also explains the important distinction that we first saw with Menestrier above, and that hearkens back to *Dramatics* 1 (another reason to be baffled why Blasis does not cite Aristotle in this regard):

> The Romans gave the name of *pantomimes* (from the Greek *pantos*, all, and *miméomai*, to counterfeit) to those performers who expressed all kinds of things by means of gestures. The arts of Pantomime and dancing were afterwards called *saltatio*. The word *Tripudium* was also used to signify dancing. *The Greeks term both, when united, Orchestica* [my italics for the English words].[899]

Blasis adds that "pantomime is, undoubtedly, the very soul and support of the Ballet,"[900] which means that ballet is composed of dancing *per se* and gestures, the latter of which can be subdivided for him into natural and artificial.[901] For Menestrier, Blasis, us, and I submit for the ancient Greeks, it is, and was, very apropos to speak of the *corps de ballet* dancing, or the "orchestral performers" dancing, or the "company" dancing or the ballerinas performing, employing different words that all entail, suggest or explicitly state dancing, given the context. Likewise, we speak of the performers gesturing, whether or not they rhythmically do this and whether or not to music. Depending on the context, they could be merely acting or dancing for we have seen that dance, depending on how one defines it, does not always require rhythmical movement in the modern sense of "rhythmical."

This finishes my account of Blasis, who, despite his emphasis on pantomime for ballet, was one of the finest technicians of his day, turning it is said, four pirouettes à la seconde (with the raised leg ideally at 90 degrees to the side). He also began directing the ballet school at La Scala, Milan and is respon-

---

898    Blasis, *op. cit.*, pp. 111-2.

899    Blasis, *op. cit.*, p. 116. On *Orchestica* he says "See the learned dissertation of Doctor Zulatti" (p. 133). Zulatti's work and the reason why Blasis leaves off Aristotle at very opportune times for his own treatise would be a good dissertation in my opinion for a dance historian, were, e.g., Blasis's correspondence and notebooks discoverable. I know nothing of Zulatti, and guess he may be Giovanni Francesco Zulatti (1762–1805), a physician and author of the book *Della forza della Musica nelle passioni, nei costumi e dell' uso medico del Ballo* (Venice, 1787). In 2015, according to a librarian, Dr. Andrea Massimo Grassi, at La Scala, within which Blasis headed the ballet school, the tract is only in Naples, and I have not been able to travel there. Note for the 2nd edition: In 2018, the book is now available through websites, including: https://books.google.com/books/about/Della_forza_della_musica_nelle_passioni.html?id=tUNDAAAAcAAJ. It seemingly has no bearing on the issues here, although it might be of great interest to those interested in music and dance therapy and their backgrounds in ancient Greece.

900    Blasis, *op. cit.*, p. 111.

901    Blasis, *op. cit.*, pp. 114-5.

sible in large part for producing many world-famous dancers, including Enrico Cecchetti. I should emphasize, then, the continued irony of the most influential dance theorists who use Aristotle without in any way seeming to understand that dance was *necessary* for the kind of musical drama that Aristotle calls tragedy. Like Menestrier and Noverre, Blasis essentially uses Aristotle and other classicists to support his own theory of ballet as an art form. However, all of these dance theorists intuitively recognized that ballets with no language could give plots (often citing the great Roman pantomime artists), and appealed to the ancients to justify the kind of story-ballets they wished to create. As we just saw with Blasis, they also tried to apply the principles of dramatic literature to their own art form, as some film theorists did when cinema was first created. Whom better to draw from than Aristotle, and what better prestige to acquire for an art form than to rely on Aristotle, whom Blasis says "is almost always perfect in his conceptions"? In short, the *Dramatics* influenced, and still influences to some extent, ballet masters and choreographers. However, that is because of certain statements that Aristotle makes about dance that they appropriate for their balletic ends, not because those dance theorists were, or are, concerned with a part of the first misconception that I claim exists—that dance has been improperly ignored or diminished in the definition of tragedy in the *Dramatics*.[902]

## Jacob Bernays (1824-1881)

The most influential writer on the issue of *katharsis* in the *Dramatics* in the nineteenth century is Jacob Bernays, philologist and ancient Greek philosopher, whose niece Martha married Sigmund Freud. It might be worth mentioning as an aside that Freud's only non-medical course in his final years of study was apparently Aristotle's *Metaphysics*—whereas the use of *katharsis* in Freud's earlier psychological theories, and its influence in culture, is so well known as not to need stressing. Still, it might be worth emphasizing that Freud could not have been unaware of his famous uncle's contribution. Bernays' seminal treatment of *katharsis* in the *Dramatics*, along with his short discussion of the term in *Politics* VIII 7, is in "Aristotle on the Effect of Tragedy," originally published in 1857.[903] There, against Lessing, he tries to re-establish the meaning of "purgation" as a type of medical concept. I say "re-establish" because we saw from the Italian history of the sixteenth century that this was what Pazzi's translation standardly inspired. Let us quickly review Bernays' criticism of his predecessor before we continue with his own theory:

Lessing translates *katharsis* by "cleansing" [*Reinigung*]; but wherein "cleansing" consists

---

902  I demonstrate this more in Gregory Scott, "Twists and Turns: Modern Misconceptions of Peripatetic Dance Theory" (*Dance Research*, Edinburgh University Press) 2005, espec. pp. 156-8.

903  Jacob Bernays, "Aristotle on the Effect of Tragedy," reprinted in *Articles on Aristotle: Vol. 4—Psychology & Aesthetics*, ed. by J. Barnes, M. Schofield, and R. Sorabji, and transl. by Jonathan and Jennifer Barnes (London: Gerald Duckworth & Co) 1979. Originally published in *Zwei Abhandlungen über die aristotelische Theorie des Drama* (Berlin, 1880; first published Braslau, 1857).

he will "only say briefly." About this main point, however, every man—including "those up to snuff" to whom Lessing appeals about a related question—would gladly have seen a more thorough exposition and justification, all the more so since the more precise definitions of catharsis, which seemed indispensable to Aristotle himself and which he had explained in the eighth book of the *Politics* that he wanted to save for the *Poetics*, are now to be sought in vain in our *Poetics*. Now, Lessing's discussion is the following: Since, to put it briefly, *this cleansing consists in nothing other than the transformation of the passions into practical virtues*, yet with every virtue, according to our philosopher, one finds an extreme on this side and on that, between which it stands: so must tragedy, *if it is to transform our pity into a virtue, be capable of cleansing us of both extremes of pity; which is to be understood also of fear. With respect to pity, tragic pity must cleanse not only the soul of the one who feels too much pity, but also of the one who feels too little*. With respect to fear, tragic fear must cleanse not only the soul of the one who fears no misfortune at all, but also of the one who is placed in anxiety by every misfortune, even the most remote and improbable [my italics].[904]

Bernays finds all of this utterly implausible, and for good reasons.[905] I leave aside the impression that, notwithstanding differences with respect to fine points, Lessing's view reverts to Averroes's notion of tragedy as an *ethical* enterprise, with moderation as the goal (and used by Averroes as the translation for *katharsis*). As I covered in Chapters 5 and 6, rather than arguing that had Lessing been correct, "moderation" or "transforming the passions into virtues" instead of *katharsis* should properly be the goal in the definition of tragedy, Bernays argues that we should apply the discussion of *katharsis* in *Politics* VIII 7 to understand *Dramatics* 6. Rightly or wrongly, this medical understanding for Bernays excludes the notion of *katharsis* as a *moral* agent that benefits one psychologically and ethically,

---

904  Jacob Bernays, *On Catharsis: From Fundamentals of Aristotle's Lost Essay on the "Effect of Tragedy"* (1857), reproduced in *American Imago*, Vol. 61, Number 3, Fall 2004, p. 319.

905  Given my attention to Halliwell's related arguments, it is worth recording how those like Jan Helge Solbakk, a Norwegian professor of philosophy and medical ethics, construe Halliwell. Moreover, it seems as if Lessing's view on the importance but secondary status of performance has influenced Halliwell, as I demonstrate at the end of Chapter 3. Bernays' criticism is confirmed by Solbakk, who renders (unproblematically in my view, as a legitimate Greek meaning) *katharsis* as "purification" rather than as "cleansing":
> In his *Hamburgische Dramaturgie*, Lessing states that by tragic catharsis Aristotle simply meant the "metamorphosis" of strong emotions into virtue:
>> Since, to be brief, this purification consists in nothing other than the metamorphosis of the passions into virtues, and since according to our philosopher every virtue stands between two extremes, it follows that tragedy, if it is to change our pity into virtue, must be capable of purifying us of both extremes of pity; and the same is true of fear (Lessing, 1767–8/1978, p. 380).
>
> Bernays' blunt comment on this interpretation is that *it turns tragedy into a "moral house of correction which must have ready a remedy for every illegitimate display of pity and fear"* (Bernays (1857/1979, p. 155). Halliwell, on his part, finds that Lessing's interpretation is "close to the truth," based as it is on a recognition of the role of emotions in Aristotle's moral theory [my italics]. (Jan Helge Solbakk, "Catharsis and moral therapy II: An Aristotelian account," *Medicine, Health Care and Philosophy,* Springer, Europe and the United States, 2006, 9:141–153.)

in the context of a definition that should apply to all tragedies (which, again, is for him why Lessing is wrong). One correct and sufficient argument, though, that Bernays gives against Lessing, based on the end of VIII 7, is that Aristotle specifically allows—indeed, recommends—theatrical experiences that give the phenomena resulting from *katharsis*, including relief and pleasure, for mechanics, laborers and other "uncultured" individuals. The goal is to give relief and pleasure, *not* moral betterment. Why Bernays then leaves aside pleasure as the goal of theatrical experiences and focuses only on the pathological interpretation of *katharsis*, as if it has to be the goal of the whole art form is puzzling, but beyond the scope of this history. Likewise, I ignore other aspects of his article because my arguments throughout this book have already rendered those aspects irrelevant for our purposes. The crucial points for the moment from the perspective of history are as follows. As a preliminary remark, he says that:

> *katharsis* is a term transferred from the physical to the emotional sphere, and used of the sort of treatment of an oppressed person which seeks not to alter or to subjugate the oppressive element but to arouse it and to draw it out, and thus to achieve some sort of relief for the oppressed.[906]

Bernays then adds something absolutely shocking but seemingly required given his position that Aristotle refers to the *Dramatics* in the passage from VIII 7 that indicates *katharsis* is explained more *en tois peri poiētikēs*. Contrary to Dacier, however, who thought the explanation was in the lost section on comedy, Bernays states:

> In the complete *Poetics* (i.e. in the "treatise on poetry" in two books), he [Aristotle] confined his definition of tragedy within the limits required by concision and brevity... [H]e... guarded against any possibility of misunderstanding by the supplementary explanations that accompanied its individual terms.[907] For the term *katharsis*, indeed, these explanations were, *as the promissory reference in the* Politics *shows,* as abundant as the significance of the question and the unfamiliarity of the term demanded. **And the anthologist, whom we have both to thank and to blame for the extant Poetics, mercilessly cut these explanations out**; he had no care for philosophy, and he probably excised the passages for no other reason than they *were* so comprehensive and so rich in purely philosophical thought [my emphases in both italics and bolding].[908]

---

906   Bernays, *op. cit.*, 1979, Barnes transl.

907   Whether Bernays means the preliminary divisions in *Dramatics* 1-5 that form the basis of the definition or merely the explanations that follow immediately in *Dramatics* 6-7 or both, is not clear, but it is plain from the rest of his article that he means *at least* the explanations that follow immediately the definition *per se* in *Dramatics* 6.

908   Bernays, *op. cit.*, 1979, Barnes tr., p. 160. AnonC himself says:
> There's a "revised and corrected" version of Barnes' translation in A. Laird (ed.), *Oxford Readings in Ancient Literary Criticism* (Oxford 2006) [pp. 158-175]. Even in the unrevised form, it is better than Rudnytsky's unreliable version, from which the quotation...is taken."

The corrected version, though, is no different with respect to the issues of this paper, and the only noteworthy point there for our purposes is that Barnes instead calls the editor who excised the explanation of catharsis

## Appendix: A Brief History of the Two Misconceptions

In short, because of a mercilessly excising editor, we are missing the promised explanation of *katharsis* not only in *Dramatics* 6 but in all the other parts of the *Dramatics* where it should have arisen, were it really the goal of tragedy for Aristotle! Because I discussed the absurdity of Bernays' position in this regard when dealing with Halliwell's reliance on Bernays in Chapter 6, I will continue straightaway to the next point. Because this is a book and not a live performance, readers can take their time in proceeding, especially if any have to recover from stupefaction, as I did when I first read Bernays' work (although perhaps readers are inured now to his doctrine after Chapter 6 and are ready to continue immediately or are not as susceptible to stupefaction as I). In Chapters 5 and 6, I asked, or at least implied, questions such as, "If the anthologist were so merciless, why did he not excise the clause in Chapter 6 with *katharsis* also?" and "Would an anthologist not care about philosophy if he was working on a philosophical text and would he really go through each chapter of the *Dramatics* and excise all further relevant mentions of *katharsis*, where Aristotle deals with the goal of tragedy?" This suffices for Bernays for my purposes regarding *katharsis*.

I know little of Bernays's views on the nature of tragedy for Aristotle as literature or as a separate art of drama, and, to my knowledge, no one ever discusses those views nowadays or has discussed them in print over the past 100 years at least. It is hard to imagine, however, that a scholar of his stature would be ignored had he changed the whole literary tradition that I have recounted above, and so I leave aside his views on this topic. Suffice it to say here that, as evidence that he keeps the traditional view of tragedy as (at least primarily) literature, Bernays states that "tragedy *tells its story* 'in a dramatic and not a narrative form (my italics).'"[909] This is very ambiguous, as we saw in Chapter 2 when discussing *Dramatics* 3, but to my knowledge had always been taken by scholars in print before my dissertation to mean styles of writing. Also, when giving the definition of tragedy, Bernays drops dance when discussing the condition "seasoned language," and treats *rhuthmos* as mere, abstract "rhythm," before focusing on issues only related to *katharsis*: "Here by 'seasoned language' I mean that with rhythm (*rhuthmos*) and song superadded ..."[910] I assume that Bernays relied on the reason that most, if not all, previous generations of scholars had already given, namely, the remark at the end of *Dramatics* 6 wrongly suggesting on traditional translations that spectacle and thus music and performance were optional for tragedy in Aristotle's theory.

To complete the history of *katharsis* to the middle of the twentieth century from the perspective of

---

(and by implication any other instances of catharsis in the whole text) "excerptor" rather than "anthologist" (p. 168). Still, I mention all of this, with a tip of the hat to AnonC, for others who might wish to focus more deeply on Bernays.

909   Bernays, *op. cit.*, 1979, ed. Barnes, p. 161
910   Bernays, *op. cit.*, 1979, ed. Barnes, p. 161

specialists: Bernays's solution held sway for only a relatively short time in classics and ancient philosophy, although some commentators still appeal to it. Scholars had already begun criticizing it by the late 1800's, and by the mid-twentieth century it was discredited for many specialists of the *Dramatics,* when it was supplanted by "clarification" as the favored translation for many, although, again, not all. Ancient Greek specialists realized in part that "purgation" conflicted too egregiously with the rest of Aristotle's doctrines, one reason, again, being that it treated the general audience as too pathological. Another reason was that it ignored the strictures in the *Politics* that intellectual delight is the most noble end, in and of itself, of "music" and, by implication, of other theatrical experiences, and that this end is contrasted with the (less important) goal of *katharsis* as "relief/relaxation."[911] As explained in Chapter 5, "clarification" itself, too, has been shown to be extremely implausible since the 1980s, if not earlier. However, because in Chapter 5 I discussed clarification in detail, let us omit its discussion now.

My Introduction began with some commentators' different views of Coleridge vis-à-vis Aristotle, and it seems fitting now to finish my overview of the nineteenth century by stating the Englishman's own view, or at least the way literary historians now treat the relationship of the two theorists. I have cited more than enough secondary sources to confirm my claim about the two historical (mis)conceptions of the *Dramatics.* It might be helpful to cite even tertiary sources, because, to extend a theme from before, sometimes readers are influenced as much by other sources as they are by the primary ones, whom they may not read in the original language or whom they may not read because of the difference in era, even if the same language is used. All three kinds of sources spread ideas, or solidify them, across the culture. I repeat, then, another view of a specialist in the area, Malpas, concerning Coleridge but with respect to Malpas' own views, to confirm yet again how much *catharsis* and its importance has settled into the cultural consciousness despite its perplexity in this setting. According to Malpas:

> An even grander sense of the role of catharsis is given by the Romantic poet Samuel Taylor Coleridge who, acknowledging that primarily 'tragic scenes were meant to *affect* us', asserts that tragedy's real aim is to transport the mind to a sense of its possible greatness ... during the temporary oblivion of the worthless 'thing we are', and of the particular state in which each man *happens* to be, suspending our individual recollections and lulling them to sleep amidst the music of nobler thoughts. [And now Malpas seemingly presents his own view, even if he is beholden to Coleridge:] Catharsis, by evoking particular instances of pity and fear, serves to ennoble the spectator who empathises with the dignity and courage displayed by the victim in the face of her or his downfall and thereby recognises the greatness of the tragic action as a whole. Just as with real-world tragedies, the defining

---

911  As Smerdel reports, L. Spengel had relied on, for instance, *Politics* VIII 5 and intellectual delight being the end of (all forms) of music and, by implication, all art in order to refute Bernays even by the late 1800's (Smerdel, *op. cit.*, 1937, p. 39).

feature of dramatic tragedy for the Aristotelian tradition is the effect *a text* has on its audience and its formation of a sympathetic emotional bond between spectator and victim.[912]

... Tragedy, according to Aristotle, is thus at once *a moral warning* about the dangers of a particular *hamartia* [mistake], and also *a safety valve that allows excessive emotions to diffuse harmlessly* [my italics and comments in brackets].[913]

In short, then, tragedy has both a moral and medical (albeit psychological) purpose. Note that "the Aristotelian tradition" allows Malpas lots of wiggle room in making claims about Aristotle. However, he concludes by putting words into the ancient Greek's mouth that Aristotle did not voice, given what I demonstrated in Chapter 6, namely, that the supposed paradigm of Oedipus and his *hamartia* is instead only the second-best kind of play *in general*, after the kind that ends happily in *Dramatics* 14. Note also the emphasis on "psychological balancing," that is, on excessive emotions being diffused, as if one were going for a session with one's therapist. However, this may be more the view of Malpas than of Coleridge (and again, I am not so much concerned with presenting an exhaustive account of the primary or secondary sources now as with showing what gets reported at "a second remove from reality," if I may adapt Plato's complaint about art being twice removed from the Forms). Although Coleridge has an arguably more Aristotelian view, in which tragedy can "transport the mind to a sense of its possible greatness," rather than give mere *katharsis*, this also greatly extends what Aristotle actually says, as I showed in Chapter 7 when examining the clear-cut goals of tragedy once *katharsis* is properly removed. Yet even this "transporting," which probably gives a delight, is dropped in Malpas's view in favor of the view that tragedy is generally an instrument for morality and therapy—for a psychological "safety valve." In effect, we are returning full circle to a mixture of Averroes and the sixteenth-century Italians, even if neither Coleridge nor Malpas gives the same details regarding how the *katharsis* occurs through pity and fear. Malpas's view—that tragedy is a "moral warning"—also sounds like Lessing and, I might add, like some puritanical clergy, for whom not only philosophy but drama should be the handmaiden of theology if drama is even allowed in the public sphere.[914]

---

912 Malpas, *op. cit.*, 2010, pp. 181-2.

913 Malpas, *op. cit.*, p. 184.

914 I use "puritanical" quite purposefully here, given that the Puritans, similar to Justinian, banned theatrical reproductions in England from 1642 to 1660. The Parliamentary Law of September 2 says in part:
> Public Stage Plays shall cease, and be forborn, instead of which are recommended to the People of this Land the profitable and seasonable considerations of Repentance, Reconciliation, and Peace with God, which probably may produce outward Peace and Prosperity, and bring again Times of Joy and Gladness to these Nations.

We might keep all this in mind by contrast if we consider in the future the ethics of Aristotle with respect, e.g., to comic drama, because proper wit (involving laughter) is a *virtue* for him. A comparison also of the Puritans with the Taliban, fundamentalist Islamists and those of other religious persuasions in regards of performance, tragedy, and comedy might be an eye-opening project for those in religious studies.

## 20th-Century Views

In the 20th century, all of the issues about the *Dramatics* become arguably even more complex than they were in the previous four centuries, in the sense that many fine points are addressed and disputed. However, regarding fundamentals, nothing new is introduced into this debate, other than that *katharsis* means "clarification," and, to emphasize, I ruled out this possibility in Chapter 5, essentially following many other scholars. Moreover, again, any new, creative interpretation of the concept beyond purgation, purification and clarification takes us away from the assumption that Halliwell rightly emphasizes, as we saw: Aristotle uses the term in *Politics* VIII 7 in a way that the Greek reader would understand without explanation.

I therefore finish this Appendix by continuing to demonstrate that all the specialists in the twentieth century took the treatise to be about literary theory. To prove this rigorously, I would have to present the views of hundreds, if not thousands, of commentators, and thus I offer only the summaries of the most famous (almost exclusively in Anglo-American circles). Any reader is invited, as once suggested, to pull out of a dusty closet an unknown manuscript that contradicts the seemingly unanimously accepted trend, but obviously this manuscript had no impact on the tradition. Afterward, it is important to examine one last, exceptional view, namely, that the *Dramatics* is not about literary theory but more widely about aesthetics or art, before I add some additional detail on criticisms of Aristotle by, e.g., Virginia Woolf, stemming from the two misconceptions. As indicated previously, my interpretation of the *Dramatics* in Chapters 2-4 allows Aristotle to evade these criticisms entirely, and so repeating the criticisms here functions merely as reference material for readers wishing to know the historical background in greater detail.

## More on the History of the *Dramatics* as Literary Theory

The historian Habib, whom I quoted already, examines a wider range of sources than I do in at least one period and summarizes some of the points made above. However, he adds some additional, interesting developments concerning the twentieth century that bear repeating:

> The *Poetics* is usually recognized as the most influential treatise *in the history of literary criticism*... While Aristotle by the later Middle Ages had supplanted Plato as the predominant influence on philosophy and theology, Horace remained the most powerful classical influence on literary criticism. It was not until the late fifteenth century that the *Poetics* was rediscovered and disseminated through numerous translations and commentaries, beginning with a Latin translation by Giorgio Valla in 1498. The most renowned commentaries were Minturno's *De poeta* (1559), Julius Caesar Scaliger's *Poetices libri septem* (1561), and Lodovico Castelvetro's *Poetica d'Aristotele vulgarizzata e sposta*, which eventually established the predominance of Aristotelian notions *in literary criticism, especial-*

*ly as impinging on the theory and practice of drama.* These notions exerted a sustained impact on seventeenth-century French dramatists such as Pierre Corneille and on the neo-classical writers of the eighteenth century. Aristotle's influence was somewhat eclipsed in the nineteenth century when the Romantics and Symbolists turned more to Plato and Longinus. Yet critics still continued to reexamine fundamental Aristotelian notions such as *katharsis* and *hamartia* ["mistake" or "error"]. In the earlier twentieth century, the impact of Aristotle's attempt to treat poetry systemically as a distinctive sphere can be seen in Russian Formalists such as Boris Eichenbaum, in some of the New Critics, and in the systematic archetypal criticism of figures such as Northrop Frye. An interest in Aristotle was rekindled in the latter half of the twentieth century by the Chicago School of critics. His distinctive treatment of genre has been the foundation of genre theory, and his notions of plot and narrative structure continue to underlie narrative theories. Finally, his consideration of audience reaction as a crucial factor in the composition of tragedy presages much reader-response criticism [my italics as emphases].[915]

For our purposes, nothing more need be added to this account except to underscore that Habib accepts that "literary criticism" is always the category under which the *Dramatics* falls. If one wishes to find books with much more detail on the related subjects, his bibliography or a search on the Web will provide ample starting points. Obviously, then, before my view first shocked my mentors in the 1990's (and before the Ph.D. defense persuaded them), scholars and the general educated public have universally considered the *Dramatics* to be a treatise on literary theory or criticism, even if many commentators understood more correctly (but not entirely correctly) that, as Habib says, the theory was interpreted "especially as impinging on the theory and practice of drama."

Unsurprisingly, Aristotle's theories have been naturally misconstrued by those who read him only in translation. However, as we saw in Chapter 5, even all recent Greek specialists perpetuated the alleged misconception about *katharsis* until M.D. Petruševski in 1948 denied the legitimacy of the term in *Dramatics* 6. I have called those following him, including myself, the "doubters." Moreover, *all* ancient Greek specialists in the twentieth century, to my knowledge—*including the other doubters*—at least until my dissertation in 1992, continued to categorize Aristotle's *Dramatics* under literary theory or the like. Take the following examples:

D.W. Lucas writes, in the preface to his 1968 commentary and edition of the Greek text that has become an acknowledged standard for serious scholarship, that "the majority of those who take a serious interest in the *Poetics* in [Great Britain] today are teachers or students of English Literature."[916] Nor should it be surprising that Lucas himself categorizes the *Poetics* under Aristotle's works on literature.[917] Lucas's summary reflects those of the other renowned scholars of the past

---

915 Habib, *op. cit.*, 2005, pp. 60-1.
916 D. W. Lucas, *op. cit.*, p. v.
917 *Ibid.*, p. xii.

hundred years. As alluded to, S.H. Butcher, in Chapter 11 of his very influential work entitled *Poetic Universality in Greek Literature*, time and time again states or implies that Aristotle is dealing with literature.[918] Likewise, R.S. Crane assesses Aristotle's subject similarly when he says that "diction… is the underlying matter which, as significant speech, at once makes possible all the other 'parts'."[919] Crane's claim, we saw in Chapter 2, is blatantly wrong (and follows some of the sixteenth-century Italian views). Ingram Bywater, in his meticulous fashion, does not tend towards broad statements without supporting textual evidence and so only gives a clue to his overall perspective when he adds, while speaking of a problem within one of the beginning chapters: "It is clear that the four elements in a tragedy, the *muthos ethe dianoia* and *lexis* [plot, character, reasoning, and language/speech] belong to it as a work of literature, and that the music and spectacle are accessories, which attach to it only when it comes to be acted on the stage."[920] Like Bywater, Daniel de Montmollin in his *La Poetique d'Aristote* stays usually focused on precise issues, mostly philological, but in addressing the history of poetry discussed in *Dramatics* 4 and 5 he categorizes Aristotle's work as "cette histoire de la litterature."[921] G. M. A. Grube, when speaking of the basic features that distinguish tragedy in the opening chapters of the *Dramatics*, puts the matter within the framework of a "classification of kinds of literature."[922] Another writer concerned with classification, Northrop Frye, one of the preeminent Canadian scholars of literature of the twentieth century, indicates that Aristotle wants to "outline the primary categories of literature, such as drama, epic, prose fiction, and the like. This at any rate is what Aristotle assumed to be the obvious first step in criticism."[923] Furthermore, Frye adds, completely ignoring the Diotiman meaning of *poiēsis* and the absence of *any* poems in the *Dramatics*: "A theory of criticism whose principles apply to the whole of literature and account for every type of critical procedure is what I think Aristotle meant by poetics."[924] Gerald Else, in his posthumously published work, *Plato and Aristotle on Poetry*, deals almost exclusively with the *Dramatics* in his book's second half, entitled "Aristotle's Theory of Literature."[925] N. Gulley presents an article headed "Aristotle on the Purposes of Literature," in which he also discusses almost wholly the theory of the *Dramatics*

---

918 Butcher, *op. cit.*, 1923.

919 R. S. Crane, `The Concept of Plot and the Plot of *Tom Jones*', in *Critics and Criticism* (Chicago: University of Chicago Press) 1952 (2nd edition, 1954), pp. 617-8.

920 Bywater, *Aristotle on the Art of Poetry*, 1909, *op. cit.*, p. 174.

921 Daniel de Montmollin, *La Poetique d'Aristote* (Neuchatel: Imprimerie H. Messeiller) 1951, p. 36. Partially for the sake of transparency, and partially as a note of appreciation, I should acknowledge that I had the great fortune of studying with him in my doctoral program.

922 *The Greek and Roman Critics, op. cit.*, 1965, p. 71.

923 Northrop Frye, *The Anatomy of Criticism* (Princeton: Princeton Univ. Pr.) 1957, p. 13.

924 *Ibid.*, p. 14

925 Gerald Else, *Plato and Aristotle on Poetry* (Chapel Hill and London: University of North Carolina Press), ed. P. Burian, 1986. As Burian reports, p. xvii, the work is culled from, amongst other sources, the manuscript for a book that Else himself entitles *Aristotle's Doctrine of Literature*.

(and not, e.g., the *Rhetoric*).[926] Halliwell, similarly to de Montmollin, says in discussing the birth of poetry in Chapter 4 of the *Dramatics*, that "Aristotle proceeds ... to sketch a theoretical view of the natural development or evolution of the major Greek literary genres."[927] Richard Janko, whose translations I frequently use throughout this book, in part to show the traditional side for the sake of comparison and in part because he is usually an excellent translator, starts off the introduction of his translation and commentary by stating under the title "The Importance of the *Poetics*," that "Aristotle was the first person ever to write a treatise devoted to literary theory ... [and] to Aristotle belongs the credit for recognising that literature has its own set of principles, which can be discovered by careful analysis; from this recognition came the *Poetics*."[928] Likewise with George Whalley: He, along with Else and de Montmollin, spent decades of his life translating and focussing on the *Dramatics*, and emphatically treats tragedy as a form of literature on almost every page of his work.[929]

Consider, finally, what James Porter, a classicist and professor of comparative literature at the University of California, says as recently as 2010 in *The Origins of Aesthetic Thought in Ancient Greece*, and what he adds to the tradition as well. I note only three points here because anyone reading my Chapters 1 through 8 will understand where he goes astray in many other ways (notwithstanding, as discussed before, some of his informative discussion on, e.g., the eighty-line Peripatetic miniature called *On Tragedy*). First, Porter says, even while acknowledging that Aristotle "laments" in *Dramatics* 1 that there is no name for the arts of (representation in) pure language, that:

> ... one suspects, 'tragedy' is covertly doing double duty for literature in its essential and perfected form for Aristotle: for tragedy culminates the progression of literary history from epic, and it surpasses every other genre in poetic mimesis.[930]

That is, not only is tragedy a species of literature for Aristotle, but it is literature perfected, despite the requirements in *Dramatics* 6 for "music" and spectacle! Second, related to spectacle: While ignoring many of the relevant passages from the *Dramatics*, Porter claims (exactly like Oliver Taplin and Maria Grazia Bonnano, as discussed earlier) that Aristotle does not "attend to the totality of the tragic experience in all of its sensuous fullness."[931] This "fullness" pertains primarily to the performative aspects, and Porter cites Nietzsche favorably in this regard when the great classicist says, "Aristotle ... assigns spectacle (*opsis*) and song (*melos*) only to the garnishings (*hedusmata*) of tragedy—and

---

926 N. Gulley, "Aristotle on the Purposes of Literature, in *Articles on Aristotle: Vol. 4—Psychology & Aesthetics*, eds. J. Barnes, M. Schofield, and R. Sorabji (London: Duckworth Press) 1979, pp. 166ff.

927 *Op. cit.*, 1986, p. 49

928 Janko, *op. cit.* 1987, p. ix.

929 Whalley, *op. cit.*, 1997.

930 James I. Porter, *The Origins of Aesthetic Thought in Ancient Greece* (Cambridge: Cambridge Univ. Pr.) 2010, p. 96.

931 Porter, *op. cit.*, p.108.

thereby sanctions the *Lesedrama* ['drama reading']."[932] However, in Chapter 2 and 3 I demonstrated that the "garnishings" are essential conditions, which is merely one reason that Nietzsche badly misconstrued Aristotle. Third, concerning "music," Porter says, "Aristotle may mention music, but music receives no analysis in the *Poetics* whatsoever."[933] However, although this may be true if Porter has a special and restricted meaning of "analysis," such a claim ignores, for instance, *Dramatics* 12. This chapter is devoted in large part to a discussion of the chorus and includes three occurrences of *melos*, which is normally translated there as "melody" even though, as we saw, the primary meaning in ancient Greek is "limb" and even though some musicologists have also recognized that it can mean "music-dance" in ancient orchestral art. Moreover, as seen throughout this book, there is more discussion in the *Dramatics* on "music," the fifth necessary element of tragedy, than on "reasoning," which is third (before even language).[934]

This, then, completes the survey of the traditional, and even very recent, views with respect to the two misconceptions that I allege exist in the scholarship of the *Dramatics*. To rephrase: The survey provides more than ample support for my claim that until very recently the book has been always conceived to be primarily literary theory or criticism and that *katharsis* in Chapter 6 has been translated in a variety of ways and with a variety of conclusions with respect to how it ostensibly arises. Actually, there is one exception to this history, because a very few thinkers take the *Dramatics* to be about aesthetics or art theory in general, and I should address their views now, if only to dispense with them.

## The Exceptional, "Wide" Interpretation of the *Dramatics*

M. E. Hubbard and Eva Schaper argue that Aristotle gives more than just a theory of literature in the *Dramatics*, and we saw hints of this already above, with other writers.[935] They contend, rather, that

---

932    Porter, *op. cit.*, p. 102.

933    Porter, *op. cit.* p. 111.

934    Porter might reasonably reply that "reasoning" was explicitly pushed to the treatment in the *Rhetoric*, given *Dramatics* 19, but then further treatment of music was presumably left to other treatises, if even by others.

935    Malpas also extends the notion of catharsis even to non-Aristotelian tragedy, which is worth noting: The concept of 'catharsis' is complex, and has proved extremely controversial in analyses both of Aristotle's work and tragedy more generally, *but it is crucial to any definition of the genre.* For the purposes of this introduction, it might be generally understood as indicating that the experience of pity and fear in the face of some tragic catastrophe has the therapeutic effect of rebalancing or harmonising the spectator's emotions. In other words, the excess of emotion brought about by the terrible event portrayed in the text leads to a renewed balance of feeling *once there is time to reflect upon it.* Aristotle's work has influenced profoundly all subsequent understanding of tragic affect [my italics] (*op. cit.*, p. 181)

That Malpas is right about Aristotle's influence (even if, as we have seen, interpreters were wrong about what Aristotle actually could reasonably have written in some fundamental respects) is seen by what a well-known

## Appendix: A Brief History of the Two Misconceptions

he offers an aesthetic theory that is also applicable to the other arts. Hubbard says that:

> the *Poetics* envisages a variety of different interests in literature, the politician's, the poet's, the critic's: but the book is not written primarily for any of these, but rather for the philosopher. In other words, it is neither principally a defence of poetry, nor a treatise on how to write it, nor an enunciation of principles of literary criticism, though it has elements of all these; *it is first and foremost a work of aesthetic theory*, and interpretations that under-stress this fact inevitably lead to distortion [my italics].[936]

In some ways, of course, this has an element of truth. The *Dramatics* is primarily philosophy. Yet it is not a philosophy of the arts, which is what aesthetics is generally considered to be, but as we saw, mainly philosophy of drama focussing on only tragedy and comedy, with, again, epic being emphasized by Aristotle to be composed along dramatic lines and being in effect a subset of drama. Likewise, Schaper, although incidentally adding that "Aristotle gave us the first defense of creative literature," contributes also to what I call the widest interpretation of the *Dramatics* by asserting:

> The emphasis will be on the *Poetics* as a treatise on the *art of poetry, not as a treatise on poetry, or drama, or tragedy*. Aristotle has as much to say on the species of this art as on its generic nature, but what he says concerns *ars poetica* and *its* species, not poems, and plays or tragedies as objects of direct literary criticism. Of course, poems and plays figure prominently, and their discussion is exciting for the history of criticism... But this is no reason why we should read the *Poetics* as no more than a compendium for the fourth-century drama critic. Aristotle both derived his principles from *an existing literature* and applied them to it. They are principles, however, of *art* as a productive capacity which such works exemplify. *The application of them as touchstones to any thought about art is as legitimate* as is the testing of them against later evaluations of the contemporary dramatic

---

playwright, Craig Lucas, in *American Theatre* magazine, says while sounding like Lessing without the emphasis on morality (insofar as Lessing said the French only wrote plays, not tragedies):

> Modern "believability" has to a large degree driven tragedy from the stage. We now have dramas instead of tragedies—sad things, complex things, mournful things. But the point of a tragedy isn't "Oh, that's too bad—that could happen to anyone", or "Life is so complex and we hurt each other sometimes." *Tragedy is meant to invoke something much more primal—catharsis, terror and pity* [my italics]" (as reproduced in Encore Arts Programs, Seattle, Vol. 5, Issue 4, July 2001, p. 7, for the run of Lucas's *The Dying Gaul* at the Intiman Theatre).

However, Lucas never cites Aristotle *per se*, and, if he is suggesting Aristotle, he completely ignores that tragedy itself for Aristotle must also be believable, given *Poetics* 15 and other chapters. Nor does Lucas explore the oddity of suggesting that tragedy for Aristotle is not a species of drama, when the end of *Dramatics* 3 makes it very clear that tragedy and comedy are called "dramas" because of the "doing" (that is, enactment). Nevertheless, Lucas must be appealing to the Aristotelian tradition, given how he refers in the rest of the interview to ancient Greek tragedy and to, e.g., the Greek concept of *Ate*, noted to be "the mythological figure who induced rash and ruinous actions" (*op. cit.*, p. 5) and given how catharsis, pity and fear are always associated with Aristotle. None of these statements are terribly surprising given that Lucas is a modern dramatist, not a professional classicist, and I do not criticize him for his somewhat typical view but rather cite him as an example of the continuing influence of the "supposed" Aristotle.

936    M. E. Hubbard, translation of the *Poetics* included in D. Russell's *Ancient Literary Criticism* (Oxford: Oxford University Press) 1972, pp. 85-6.

and epic examples which Aristotle himself used [my italics].⁹³⁷

Again, there is at least an element of truth in this, but Schaper completely ignores *Dramatics* 25's admonition that each of the arts has its own principles. We saw in Chapters 2, 3, and 5 through 9 that, if anything, the treatise addresses the "art of *drama*," not poetry, and indeed not art in general, and that there is a danger in applying the principles indiscriminately to other art forms. If Hubbard and Schaper are understood to be saying that certain principles in the *Dramatics* (such as unity and beauty) *could* be applied in another context to art forms other than drama, with due respect for the singular nature of those art forms, then I have no objection and can only praise them for their recognition of the distinctly philosophical character of Aristotle's treatise. If, however, they are understood to be saying that the principles in the *Dramatics* are *equally* applicable to other art forms, then at least a caution and even a rebuttal is appropriate, especially given Aristotle's admonition in Chapter 25. I am far from the first to see this. Butcher nearly judged the matter correctly (except, of course, for him assuming that Aristotle is dealing with literary theory):

> Aristotle ... has not dealt with fine art in any separate treatise, he has formulated no theory of it, he has not marked the organic relation of the arts to one another. While his love of logical distinctions ... is shown even in the province of literary criticism by the care with which in the *Poetics* he maps out the subordinate divisions of his subject (the different modes of recognition, the elements of the plot, etc.), yet he nowhere classifies the various kinds of poetry; still less has he given a scientific grouping of the fine arts and exhibited their specific differences.⁹³⁸

In other words, the theory in the *Dramatics* cannot be an overarching general aesthetics unless explicit reasons are given to show how the dramatic principles are legitimately applied across boundaries.⁹³⁹ Aristotle does not supply the reasons, and whether we can provide them for him in

---

937  Eva Schaper, *Prelude to Aesthetics* (London: Unwin Hyman) 1968, pp. 57-67, 143-7. Reprinted in G. Dickie, R. Sclafani, and R. Roblin, *op. cit.*, 1989, pp. 48-9.

938  S.H. Butcher, *op. cit.*, 1923, p. 113. Butcher's book provides the Greek and English side-by-side, and an exposition of Aristotle's thought, along with many insights stemming from the Arabic mss, to augment or correct what Vahlen thought was the true archetype, A (*Parisinus*), along with the relevant explanations of those corrections. Although Butcher takes for granted many of the minor and major misconceptions addressed in this book, his work in my view is an invaluable source of the understanding of Aristotle during Butcher's day and is filled with exegetical gems. To emphasize, though, and as discussed, e.g., at the end of Chapter 6, the Greek has been perfected even more by Tarán and Gutas, *op. cit.*, and supersedes Butcher's and Rudolph Kassel's 1965 edition, which itself was the first to take into account the four branches leading back to an "archetype": A, B, the Syro-Arabic translation, and William of Moerbeke's translation.

939  Some parts of the *Rhetoric* deal with composition for the speaker and the performer. Aristotle is clearly aware of how the different arts require different considerations, and thus he would be the last to allow facile applications of rules from one art form to another. I have noted how Aristotle discusses the differences in written and performed speeches. Another example he gives which contrasts written and performed speech is this:
> The style of oratory addressed to public assemblies is really like scene-painting. The bigger the throng, the more distant is the point of view; so that, in the one and the other, high finish in detail

part, again, was discussed in Chapter 9. To add another example for illustration: Does a "tragic" film follow the principles of tragedy or of epic or of neither or both? On the one hand, it normally has a script *and* visual elements, and so would follow tragic principles. On the other hand, it can show, with flashbacks, many actions happening simultaneously, just as epic is claimed in Chapter 24 of the *Dramatics* to be able to do but which tragedy cannot do because the performance on stage constrains tragedy. Whether film, then, is more similar to tragedy than to epic seems hard to answer, and, indeed, it may be—and presumably is—the case that film has its own principles that are not to be established by orientation to another, "more central" or "more foundational" art like drama. We may, it seems, try to, and *should* avail ourselves of methods and precepts from previously analyzed arts, with suitable modification because of the different materials from which a new art is composed, but we must not allow the theory from other, older art forms to override improperly principles derived from the nature of the new media.

I conclude this section on the rarer "wide" interpretation of the *Dramatics* by presenting the irony of Butcher's applying *katharsis* not just to tragedy but art in general, notwithstanding that he explicitly and correctly, as we just saw, explains why the treatise is not about art or aesthetics in general. He states:

> But the word [*katharsis*], as taken up by Aristotle into his terminology of art, has *probably* a further meaning. It expresses not only a fact of psychology or of pathology, *but a principle of art. The original metaphor is in itself a guide to the full aesthetic significance of the term* [my italics].[940]

However, Butcher never provides any Greek passage (as he normally does) for what we have seen in this book is a completely unsupported, and I believe unsupportable, claim.

## 20th Century Criticisms of Aristotle

Let us now examine in more detail what I mentioned in the Introduction, that Aristotle has been criticized because of two views that I have amply demonstrated are not actually in his work. The first criticism pertains to how he is perceived to be at odds with modern literary theory, namely, to the position articulated in *Dramatics* 6 that plot is indispensable, with character secondary but dispensable, as I examined in Chapters 2 and 3. One example will suffice for what is often thought. In speaking of Virginia Woolf, Edna Rosenthal says:

> Woolf's rejection of plot is both historically and aesthetically motivated. If we trace her

---

is superfluous and seems better away (III 12.1414a8ff).
The same principles hold today with respect to acting on stage versus acting in front of a camera (which is usually much closer than a theatrical audience) for TV or cinema.
940 Butcher, *op. cit.*, p. 253.

own version of literary history, we see that she systematically denies plot any positive role in drama, while promoting character as an aesthetic principle in both drama and fiction. Beginning with Greek tragedy, she notes that "nobody can fail to remember the plot of the *Antigone,* because what happens is so closely bound up with the emotions of the actors that we remember the people and the plot at one and the same time" (*Notes on an Elizabethan Play*, 1.56).

> When it comes to Elizabethan drama, plot is bitterly attacked as the enemy of character... For Woolf, it is not plot that delivers aesthetic affect but character, for where character is missing, there is no pathos. The attack on "plot" strikes a new pitch when Woolf turns to neoclassical drama ... [and] ... The final toppling of plot and shift in critical emphasis to character occurs with the Romantic reaction against French neoclassical drama (based, as Lessing had argued, on a misconception of Aristotle's *Poetics*)...[941]

In short, with Woolf and anyone else sympathetic to her views on literature, character is the primary element, and plot is either secondary or insignificant. As a consequence, if indirectly, Aristotle becomes irrelevant, or less relevant, to modern literature and even to drama, notwithstanding that he recognizes a sub-type of tragedy called "tragedy of character" in *Dramatics* 18.

Ironically, regarding movement rather than text, not only classicists in general but recent famous dance theoreticians over the last hundred years have wholly missed how fully Aristotle supports both performance and especially their art form, typically the "poor cousin of the arts."[942] For example, I discussed Taplin's views, along with Halliwell's attempted rebuttal of them, at the end of Chapter 3. Some influential modern dance theorists continued in the twentieth century to focus on mimeticism, as did Menestrier, Noverre, and Blasis but now as grounds for *criticizing* Aristotle and as inadvertent grounds for maintaining, and even hardening, the literary view of the *Dramatics*. For example, a major dance theorist, André Levinson, superficially recognizes in a seminal article Aristotle's words on dance in *Dramatics* 1 but rails against the Northern Greek for thereby subsuming dance under mimetic representation.[943] Levinson claims that Aristotle *requires* dance to convey a story and does not allow dance to be merely formalistic, a position of Levinson's that I have refuted already in print.[944] Levinson's (unsubstantiated) complaint is not an issue of treating tragedy as a form of literature or as lyrical poetry directly, as much as the complaint is an indirect consequence of that view. Levinson

---

941     Edna Rosenthal, *Aristotle and Modernism: Aesthetic Affinities of T.S. Eliot, Wallace Stevens and Virginia Woolf* (Eastbourne, U.K. and Portland, OR: Sussex Academic Press) 2008, pp. 84-5.

942     For why aestheticians have tended to neglect dance, and why at least in terms of intellectual cachet it is the "poor cousin of the arts," and even leaving aside how, e.g., in terms of government funding it often gets short shrift relative to the static visual arts, literature, theater, music and now cinema, see Francis Sparshott, *op. cit.*, 1982.

943     André Levinson, *The Idea of the Dance: From Aristotle to Mallarmé,* 1927, in Roger Copeland and Marshall Cohen, eds., *What is Dance?* (Oxford: Oxford University Press) 1983, pp. 47-54.

944     Scott, *op. cit.*, "Twists and Turns," 2005.

believes that because the treatise is about poetry or drama as literature, the qualities of mimesis are wrapped up with story-telling, with dance getting further wrapped up in the story-telling and mimesis, like a small Fabergé egg within two larger ones. A correct reading of Aristotle, however, reveals that although he probably prefers dance that represents emotions or actions, he definitely accepts the value of "merely formalistic" variants, analogous to the value he admits one can get from the formalistic visual art he mentions in *Dramatics* 4 and 6, when one cannot understand any mimetic representation (1448b17-19; 1450b1-3). Perhaps more importantly, like all other dance critics, Levinson entirely misses that *harmonia kai rhuthmos* for Aristotle mean, as we saw in Chapters 2 through 4, "music and dance." The standard translation as "harmony/melody and rhythm" allowed, of course, Western aesthetics to omit dance from much of Aristotle's artistic theory and to leave an abstract musical phenomenon in its place. This further allowed tragedy to be thought more easily as a kind of (lyric) poetry for Aristotle rather than a fully performed theatrical practice that requires choral bodily movement, although we saw how even music was always demoted to optional status for tragedy by commentators.

Let us now switch back to *katharsis* in the 20th century and notice how its role as the purpose of tragedy has been the basis of criticisms, or rejections, of Aristotle's views, all the while reinforcing the impression that Aristotle wrote the word in the definition of tragedy. Some ancient Greek specialists in the early part of the 20th century followed Bernays concerning the meaning of the term. Some still follow him, not accepting the criticisms leveled against the translation as "purgation" but never addressing the contradictions and inconsistencies laid out in my Chapters 5 and 6. Others reject his view but continue to think katharsis is legitimate, although needing a correct interpretation. Additional others, whom I discuss now, as a result of Aristotle's specifying katharsis as the goal of tragedy chose not to be Aristotelian, to greater or lesser degree. For instance, as mentioned previously, Brecht purposefully wrote non-Aristotelian drama, resulting at least in part from the seemingly perceived role of *katharsis* for the Northern Greek. As Brecht writes:

> Written in the style of the didactic pieces, but requiring actors, *Die Mutter* is a piece of anti-metaphysical, materialistic, non-Aristotelian drama. *This makes nothing like such a free use as does the Aristotelian of the passive empathy of the spectator; it also relates differently to certain psychological effects, such as catharsis.* Just as it refrains from handing its hero over to the world as if it were his inescapable fate, so it would not dream of handing the spectator over to an inspiring theatrical experience. *Anxious to teach the spectator a quite definite practical attitude, directed towards changing the world*, it must begin by making him adopt in the theatre a quite different attitude from what he is used to [my italics].[945]

---

[945] Bertolt Brecht, tr. John Willett, *Brecht on Theatre: The Development of an Aesthetic* (Frankfurt: Suhrkamp Verla) 1957, 32nd printing, 2001, p. 57. Recall that authors like Scaliger and Corneille long before rejected catharsis as the goal of tragedy because it did not fit the facts.

Because, as mentioned, I am not evaluating competing aesthetic theories in this book, I will not assess Brecht's purpose of teaching the spectator a practical attitude using "didactic pieces," which strongly sounds like propaganda or theater as education. The question is how he took Aristotle's drama and the notion of *katharsis*, and whether this caused an unfavorable reaction on his part. The answer is that however Brecht took it he clearly rejected it. Another rejection of traditional Aristotelian *katharsis*, however the word gets unpacked in English, or, in this case, Portuguese, comes from South America, by the internationally recognized Brazilian drama theorist, Augusto Boal, who was educated at Columbia University in New York but kidnapped and tortured by the military regime in 1971 after becoming a cultural activist upon his return to Rio de Janeiro. As he says:

> Aristotle declares the independence *of poetry* (lyric, epic *and dramatic*) in relation to politics. What I propose to do in this work is to show that, in spite of that, Aristotle constructs the first, extremely powerful poetic-political system for intimidation of the spectator, for elimination of the "bad" or illegal tendencies of the audience. This system is, to this day, fully utilized not only in conventional theater, but in the TV soap operas and in Western films as well: movies, theater, and television united, through a common basis in Aristotelian poetics, for repression of the masses…
>
> … *Tragedy, in all its qualitative and quantitative aspects, exists as a function of the effect it seeks, catharsis. All the unities of tragedy are structured around this concept. It is the center, the essence, the purpose of the tragic system.* Unfortunately, it is also the most controversial concept. Catharsis is correction: what does it correct? Catharsis is purification: what does it purify?
>
> … We have also seen that nature tends toward certain ends, and when nature fails, art and science intervene to correct it. We can conclude, therefore, that when man fails in his actions—in his virtuous behavior as he searches for happiness through the maximum virtue, which is obedience to the laws—the art of tragedy intervenes to correct that failure. How? Through purification, catharsis, through purgation of the extraneous, undesirable element which prevents the character from achieving his ends.[946]

Leaving aside that virtue and happiness are part of Aristotle's ethics, not his politics (which is the rubric of "obedience to the laws"), and leaving aside that we examined the importance of different kinds of "theatrical music" in Aristotle's *Politics*, which involves the government recognizing the value of all classes of citizens in the state, Boal's statement in some ways is very perceptive. For instance, Boal grasps the way that Aristotle might teleologically structure or subordinate the unities with respect to any final end (being, naturally, in Boal's view *katharsis*). Boal's interpretation intrigues for other reasons. One of them I addressed indirectly in Chapter 9, when I discussed the danger of extending the dramatic theory of the *Dramatics* to other, even very closely related art forms like literature, trag-

---

[946] Augusto Boal, *Theatre of the Oppressed* (New York: Theatre Communications Group, Inc.) 1985, 6th printing 2001, orig. publ. as *Teatro de Oprimido*, 1974, and in English by Urizen Books, 1979) pp. xiv, 27 and 32. It is enlightening to note that the first chapter of his book is entitled "Aristotle's Coercive System of Tragedy."

ic film, or, what may amount to the same as tragic film in this context, "soap operas," to use Boal's own example. As should be clear from our discussion, however, of *Dramatics* 15 that focused on character, Aristotle's primary consideration is that the protagonists be as good as possible (only when necessary to the plot are evil characters allowed). Aristotle does not have the repressive purposes that Boal ascribes to him, and Boal should not be taking Aristotle to be somehow complicit in the kind of oppression used by the military in Brazil, perhaps viciously employing dramas if "charmingly" and subtly to justify authoritarianism. Just as a car can be used for many purposes, as determined by the driver, be it taking a child to the hospital or escaping with stolen money from a bank, without being at fault (rather, any fault belongs to the driver), likewise drama can be used for many purposes. However, any particular use of drama is not Aristotle's doing, and the pleasure given will depend on both the work and the audience's values, which are covered in the *Nicomachean Ethics* and the *Politics*. First, the *Ethics* has a strong emphasis on justice. Second, if the play is authoritarian or totalitarian (whether fascist, communist or corrupt capitalist), and the audience rational and politically fair, they will detest it. If the play treats left-wing revolution sympathetically and the audience is extremely right wing, they will also naturally feel no pleasure. Aristotle only gives, e.g., the conditions according to which a dramatist or artistic director puts together the various elements for tragedy as defined in the *Dramatics*, and he clearly says that the play should represent good men. Anyone understanding Aristotle's ethical and political views—and what he means by "good men"—would realize his ethical theory could not have justified, and will never justify, oppression by Brazilian-type militaries of the 1970's. At any rate, Boal believes *katharsis* is crucial to tragedy in the *Dramatics*—"*Tragedy, in all its qualitative and quantitative aspects, exists as a function of the effect it seeks, catharsis*"—and this is the most critical point in this slice of history for us.

Except for a few reactionaries like Brecht and Boal, very few modern scholars to my knowledge have rejected explicitly the importance and role of *katharsis* in tragedy, especially in "the Aristotelian tradition," whatever that means at times and whether in literature or drama. Perhaps they have been daunted by the formidable task of arguing against not only an influential mind such as Aristotle's but the massive weight of over 450 years of tradition built on his theoretical foundations. Certainly, only starting with M.D. Petruševski in 1948 did someone deny in print the authenticity of *katharsis* in *Dramatics* 6. Besides, a continued cursory review of very current literary theory finds scholars again offering alternatives—as did Scaliger, Corneille, and Racine—or evading whether *katharsis* should have a role, or of adapting *katharsis* to their own ends, giving it a new meaning. In other words, it becomes difficult to determine whether other modern authors reject Aristotelian artistic theory *because* of *katharsis*, although some come close or do so with qualification or do so without in any way seeming to understand clearly what the term means for Aristotle. One final example from literary studies brings us up to date (given that the views of specialists of ancient philosophy, who are often unknown by the general literary community, were already discussed separately in Unit 3 and mentioned already just above). Naomi Rood states:

> Certain scholars (Vyacheslav Ivanov, Komarovich) apply to Dostoevsky's works the ancient (Aristotelian) term "catharsis" (purification). If this term is understood in a very broad sense, then one can agree with it (*without catharsis in the broad sense there is no art at all* [my italics]). But tragic catharsis (in the Aristotelian sense) is not applicable to Dostoevsky.[947]

The implication is that trying to understand Dostoevsky through the prism of Aristotelian theory, with *katharsis* as the goal, will lead to failure or disappointment. I leave aside the extremely dubious claim that "without catharsis in the broad sense there is no art at all," because in over twenty years of working in, and teaching, the philosophy of art, I have never read a professional aesthetician who claimed *katharsis* was a necessary condition for *all* art, although *some specialists of Aristotle* come close to it or even advance the position, as we saw above with respect to Butcher.[948]

## Summary of the First Misconception: Literature versus Drama

Starting with the Arabic scholars (if not the Alexandrians), language for Aristotle is the most crucial aspect of tragedy. That is, *poiētēs* always gets used in the Gorgian sense, as one who primarily creates in versified language (with "imitation" as the distinguishing characteristic); likewise, with the cognate terms. If my reports on the most famous commentators spanning 1000 years are representative of all, this assumption had never been questioned until my work in the 1990's. Perhaps because authors, and especially scholars, were educated and probably because the authors were generally of the higher classes, in doing historical exegesis of a text in an ancient, foreign language they were always more focused on language, including poetry, at which they were skilled, than on any other aspect of drama as the Greeks practiced it. The oppressive Justinian had stopped drama in the sixth century (and, as an aside, I should mention that readers unfamiliar with his brutality should take with the proverbial grain, if not spoonful, of salt the typical white-washed reputation that has come down to

---

947  Naomi Rood, "Mediating the Distance: Prophecy and Alterity in Greek Tragedy and Dostoevsky's *Crime and Punishment*," in *Russian Literature and the Classics*, ed. by Peter Barta, David Larmour, and Paul Allen Miller (New York and Abingdon: Routledge) 2013, p. 40.

948  A second example is given by Lynn Anne Adam, *Kathy Adcer and The Hysterical Sublime: The Movements of Technological Martyrdom, Grotesque Perversity, and Post-Freudian Aesthetics* (Ph.D. dissertation, Univ. of Alberta, Edmonton, 2001), p. 131. She says:
> In novels such as Genet's *Our Lady of the Flowers*, there is not an evident air of tragic circumstance that could bring about a moral restitution, and therefore, Aristotle's model can no longer provide a morally capable catharsis for the reader.

What does a "morally capable catharsis" even mean? Howsoever she explains it in the rest of her dissertation (if she does), the passage shows the need to address catharsis if only to reject it.

us historically). Performers and musicians were generally from the lower classes and not even given proper burial grounds in medieval and early Renaissance times, by which point the conceptual framework of the *Dramatics* had been set. The performers seemed to have regained full stature only about the time of Lessing. Again, without any ancient or early Byzantine commentary on the treatise, the conceptual framework was usually taken for granted, as it was by myself when I first read the *Dramatics* as an undergraduate student and well into my graduate years. Since everyone, and all translations, spoke of the treatise as being about poetry and literature, it had to be the case that Aristotle thought the same. Indeed, to question this assumption never even occurred to me for years, and it was only because I have a background in the philosophy of dance that I noticed oddities in the interpretations, especially with respect to *rhuthmos*, that led to my reappraisal of the texts and then to doubt regarding the legitimacy of *katharsis* in *Dramatics* 6, occasionally to sneering denunciations by fellow specialists even before they read my arguments. Moreover, authors had the most, or complete, control of the Renaissance and post-Renaissance plays. Like the composer in opera nowadays or the director of a film, playwrights were the most influential team member insofar as a play was to be staged (and insofar as tragedy was just a written piece of literature, as it was for Chaeremon, the issues I am raising never even surfaced). Other aspects like spectacle, if very attractive in their own rights, were considered by all to be ancillary. De Vega and Rymer came close to seeing the view that I argue is more Aristotelian, although they never applied it to the *Dramatics per se*, and Dacier also in his commentary presented a few of the views I follow. Happily, my views were formed independently of these three historical figures, virtually unknown today in Anglo-American aesthetics, and it was a delight to discover subsequently that they had some of the same intuitions.

In short: Not a single author before me even considered the question in a surviving publication whether tragedy (or drama in general) could be a different art form apart from literature *per se* for Aristotle if only to reject that challenge. This is a slightly different question from whether performance is a necessary or important addition to the ostensibly most important element, language, as I demonstrated in Chapter 3. In other words, no one questioned whether *poiēsis* should be used in a Diotiman rather than a Gorgian sense. We saw that Julius Caesar Scaliger published in 1561, without giving the reasons in his discussion which we examined, that the dialogue in which Diotima appears, the *Symposium*, is "monstrous" and not worth reading. Certainly, all or almost all commentators of the *Dramatics* recognized the importance of music as an accessory and at most a handful even recognized the importance of dance for Aristotle, but none considered those elements *necessary* to tragedy. To reiterate, this is not a guarantee that some writer did not stand aside from the crowd, but given all the other historical evidence, the burden of proof is surely on anyone who disagrees with me to prove the point and publish the obscure work. In any event, as remarked, that writer had no impact on the whole tradition.

## Summary of the Second Misconception: Catharsis in *Dramatics* 6

I noted that the Syriac translation had additional words in the *katharsis* clause, diverging from the Greek manuscripts we have. I then showed how Avicenna dropped *katharsis*, as if he had no reasonable belief it could be authentic or as if he could not understand it. Averroes followed the Syriac but interpreted *katharsis* as "moderation," which indeed could convey Aristotle's ethical views, but which is impossible as the Greek meaning of the word in that particular location (*Dramatics* 6) or any other location. William of Moerbeke rendered the term as *purgatio* in his faithful translation but with no commentary his two manuscript copies were completely ignored during the late Middle Ages, in favor of the approximately twenty-three copies stemming from Averroes. Averroes's nature of tragedy as "ethical rhetoric" remained influential and was even combined for some time with the Italian commentaries stemming directly from the Greek manuscripts in the Cinquecento. Valla, in 1498, has in his Latin version for the *katharsis* clause "completing through pity and fear the purgation of such *habits* [my italics, =*disciplinae*]," perhaps not being sure about the *mathēmatōn* ("learnings") that I am guessing he saw in manuscript A in lieu of the *pathēmatōn* ("emotions") of manuscript B.[949] Following Pazzi, who published the Greek along with the Latin, Robortello and Castelvetro used "purgation," and many other Italians subsequently also treated it as a quasi-medical term, specifically for moral psychotherapy pertaining to the emotions, whatever "moral psychotherapy" really means. Scaliger ignored catharsis, claiming Aristotle was wrong and the notion unempirical, but did not question whether or not Aristotle himself had written the term.

Corneille and Racine followed Scaliger in their own ways. Milton and other English scholars, among still others, followed those who accepted purgation as the end of tragedy, although, depending on the writer, different details may have been given as to how the psychological mechanism with respect to pity and fear resulted. Lessing used "purification" or "cleansing," but in order also to arrive at a psycho-ethical goal. Bernays refuted that view, but only by returning to purgation and by jumping from the frying pan back into the fire. In a stunning fashion that has not received enough criticism, he also claimed that an "excerptor" stripped out on purpose the explanation of *katharsis* in the *Dramatics*, the explanation that had been promised by *Politics* VIII 7. "Clarificationists" then advocated the next set of solutions during the twentieth century. We examined these solutions in Chapter 5, and saw that the advocates took little advantage of the reading of *mathēmatōn* ("learnings") in manuscript A, from which all other—approximately thirty—copies of that branch of the *Dramatics* derive, two other copies with *pathēmatōn* being the very damaged B and the Syriac. These solutions based on "clarification" were rejected, however, by some scholars right from the outset. Those scholars

---

[949] The differences of the manuscripts are discussed in Chapters 5-6.

pinpointed the contradictions that still ensue on that reading with well-accepted Aristotelian texts, both internal and external to the *Dramatics*, even before I entered the fray. In the very early 21st century, and during the beginning of this book, no universally favored solution existed. When some proposed new ways of looking at *katharsis*, the immediate rejoinder was given by no less than Halliwell himself. Notwithstanding that he offers his own solution, he claims correctly in arguing against one of the "doubters" that Aristotle assumes the readers of *Politics* VIII 7 know the basic meaning of *katharsis* (which would be a well understood one in ancient Greece). Thus, to repeat the ramification that Halliwell inadvertently but ultimately supports, *katharsis* has to have an ordinary meaning that the Greeks knew, and should be limited to purification, purgation or clarification or perhaps to an admixture of those concepts.

A willingness to give still other new meanings despite Halliwell's prudent implicit warning can be seen much more now, in the following. It is one of the most up-to-date views on the issue. I return full circle to the Arabic culture that knows the West, in part in homage to al-Fārābī's, Avicenna's and Averroes's admiration of Aristotle. Adnan K. Abdulla, a professor of English and Arabic literature at the University of Sharjah, United Arab Emirates, also summarizes the history above but adds additional insights, especially with recent developments:

> There are three commonly acceptable historical interpretations of catharsis: purgation, purification, and clarification. The first and second interpretations specifically refer to emotions; the third, clarification, refers to intellectual understanding. All three interpretations try to explain the effects of tragedy on its spectators: that is, what happens to us when we apprehend what happens to the hero or protagonist. *By extension, the problem can be stated in the following way: what are the effects of art on its readers, and how do these effects come about?* The attempt to answer these questions and the narrower question of what catharsis means turn out to be attempts to define the nature and value *of literature. Since accounting for the meaning of catharsis involves the broader question of the value of art, the continuing debate on such an important and pervasive subject accounts for the variety of existing discussions about catharsis.*
>
> Catharsis is such a complex phenomenon that no one has ever presented a single, definitive statement about what it means, or how it works. Each writer captures only a part of it; *each looks at catharsis from his particular point of view, and, by extension, explains it (or, for that matter, the function of literature) from his own ideological or epistemological premises.* If such premises are susceptible to changing values, mores, and systems of thought, then it is legitimate to claim that ideas about the meaning and function of catharsis indicate changes in theories and practices of human epistemology, thought, and political systems. Such a hypothesis explains not only why so many thinkers have shown an interest in catharsis, but also the curious fact that *the meaning of catharsis changes with author, age, and historical moment.* In the Renaissance, catharsis often had heavy moral connotations; in the Augustan age, catharsis was usually thought to be a function of verisimilitude; in the Romantic period, catharsis frequently described the suffering of the poet; in the twentieth century, which is characterized by a multiplicity of critical thought,

catharsis has a multiplicity of meanings. *Each school of thought manages to wrench out an aspect of catharsis that is appropriate to its own critical focuses or premises.* It is no mere coincidence that catharsis, in the last twenty years or so, has acquired an important element: communication. The communicative element of catharsis reflects a basic change, which in turn reflects technological advances in a society that necessitates a new justification for literature, its role in our lives, and its function. *Catharsis as communication is a product of our concern with communication,* an idea that fits in snugly with the cultural, technological, and scientific climate of the second half of the twentieth century [my italics throughout].[950]

The new historical developments and the relativism portrayed by Abdulla—namely, that every age develops a notion of *katharsis* that is suitable to it—are both a tribute to Aristotle's influence even to the present day but also a dismaying misrepresentation, insofar as Aristotle may be thought to be responsible for any or all applications of the term. Aristotle tended to use words exactly, even while granting and often explaining that a single word can have different meanings, examples of which we have seen throughout this book. It would be remarkable had he meant *katharsis* to mean something as varied as the list of meanings given above (beyond purgation, purification or clarification). In other words, granting Abdulla his general points, the question remains: How many of these various "definitions" are to be found in Aristotle's theories, whether in the *Dramatics* or any other text (even in the biological and lost ones)? I answered that question partially in Units 2 and 3, and it is still open concerning the explanation that Aristotle promised in *Politics* VIII 7. As Dacier, W.D. Ross, I, and now Rashed have suggested—following Proclus and Iamblichus, to a large extent—that explanation seemingly occurred within Aristotle's mature aesthetics in the context of comedy and, in my view, *at best* only secondarily or incidentally regarding tragedy. Future research in this area is required, even after all of these centuries. Fortunately, if my major conclusions hold, upcoming results need not be refracted through an exegetical lens both darkly rose-colored and fractured because of the two fundamental misconceptions. Thus, those results might involve findings more analogous to the ending of *Cresphontes, Oklahoma!,* or *The Road to Mecca* than to *Oedipus* or *West Side Story*, compelling and worthy as those last two dramatic musical compositions are.

---

[950] Adnan K. Abdulla, *Catharsis in Literature* (Bloomington: Indiana Univ. Press) 1985, pp. 3-4.

# Bibliography

**Aristotle**

**<u>Greek text (and commentary)</u>**

*Aristotle's Ars Poetica,* ed. Rudolph Kassel (Oxford: Clarendon Press) 1966.

*Aristotle: Poetics,* Greek text with commentary, D.W. Lucas (Oxford: Clarendon Press) 1968. Reprinted (Oxford: Clarendon Press) 1988.

Tarán, Leonardo and Dimitri Gutas. *Aristotle Poetics: Editio Maior of the Greek Text with Historical Introduction and Philological Commentaries* (Brill: Leiden and Boston) 2012.

**<u>Translations or commentaries (in alphabetical order)</u>**

*Poetics.* Transl. by Ingram Bywater, *The Complete Works of Aristotle,* ed. Jonathan Barnes, Vol. 2 (Princeton: Princeton Univ. Press) 1984.

*Aristote: La Poetique,* trans. and comm. R. Dupont-Roc and J. Lallot (Paris: Éditions du Seuil) 1980.

*Aristotle's Poetics: A Translation and Commentary for Students of Literature,* trans. Leon Golden and O.B. Hardison (Tallahassee, FL: University Press of Florida) 1981.

*Aristotle's Poetics,* trans. Humphrey House (London: Rupert Hart-Davis) 1964.

*Poetics,* partial trans. and commentary by M. Hubbard in *Ancient Literary Criticism,* eds. D.A. Russell and M. Winterbottom, *op. cit.*, 1972.

*Aristotle's Poetics,* trans. James Hutton (New York: W.W. Norton & Co.) 1982.

*The Poetics of Aristotle,* trans. D. S. Margoliouth (London: Hodder and Stoughton) 1922.

*La Poetique d'Aristote: Texte Primitif et Additions Ultérieures,* trans. and comm. by Daniel de Montmollin (Neuchâtel: Henri Messeiller) 1951.

*Poetics,* trans. K. Telford (Chicago: Chicago University Press) 1961.

Twining, Thomas. *Aristotle's Treatise* on *Poetry, Translated with Notes* (New York: Viking Press) 1972. Originally published London, 1789.

Whalley, George. *Aristotle's Poetics: Translation and with a Commentary by George Whalley,* ed. by John Baxter and Patrick Atherton (Canada: McGill-Queen's University Press) 1997.

Other translations of, or commentaries on, the *Poetics* by authors with additional works, as detailed below*:*
    ---. A. Dacier (see *op. cit.*)

---. G. Else (see *op. cit.*)
---. M. Heath (see *op. cit.*)
---. R. Janko (see *op. cit.*)

Translations of other works by Aristotle*:*
    ---. *Politics,* trans. R. Kraut (Oxford: Clarendon Press) 1997.
    ---. *Posterior Analytics,* trans. G. R. G. Mure (Digireads.com) 2006. Originally published in *The Works of Aristotle,* Vol. 1 (Oxford: Clarendon Press) 1928.
    ---. *Problemata,* in *The Works of Aristotle,* Vol. II, tr. by E. F. Forster, under the editorship of W. D. Ross (Oxford: Clarendon Press) 1930.

*The Basic Works of Aristotle,* ed. R. McKeon (New York: Random House) 1941.
    ---. *Metaphysics,* trans. W. D. Ross.

*The Complete Works of Aristotle,* ed. Jonathan Barnes, 2 vols. (Princeton: Princeton University Press) 1984.
    ---. *On Interpretation,* tr. J. L. Ackrill.
    ---. *Politics,* trans. Benjamin Jowett.
    ---. *Topics,* trans. W. A. Pickard-Cambridge.
    ---. *Nicomachean Ethics,* trans. W. D. Ross, revised by J. O. Urmson.
    ---. *Rhetoric,* trans. W. Rhys Roberts.

*Aristotle in 23 Volumes* (Cambridge: Harvard University Press; London: William Heinemann Ltd.) 1944.
    ---. Vol. 21 *(Politics),* trans. H. Rackham.
    ---. Vol. 22 *(Rhetoric),* trans. J. H. Freese.
    ---. Vol. 23 *(Poetics),* trans. W. H. Fyfe.

## Other Works

Abdulla, Adnan K. *Catharsis in Literature* (Bloomington: Indiana University Press) 1985.

Adam, Lynn Anne. *Kathy Adcer and the Hysterical Sublime: The Movements Of Technological Martyrdom, Grotesque Perversity, and Post-Freudian Aesthetics* (Ph.D. dissertation, University of Alberta, Edmonton) 2001.

al-Fārābī, *The Enumeration of the Sciences,* see Tarán and Gutas, *op. cit.*
    ---. *Canons of the Arts of the Poets,* see Tarán and Gutas, *op. cit.*

Anagnostopoulos, Georgios, ed. *A Companion to Aristotle (*Hoboken/Oxford: Wiley-Blackwell Publishing) 2009.

Aquinas, Thomas. *Commentary on the Posterior Analytics by Aristotle,* trans. by F. R. Larcher, (Albany, N.Y: Magi Books) 1970.

Aristophanes, *The Frogs* (London: Penguin Books) tr. by David Barrett, 1964.

# Bibliography

Aristoxenus, *Fragmenta Parisina,* Cod. bibl. imp. Par. 3027.
   ---. *Elementa Rhymthica* (see Marchetti)

Athenaeus. *The Learned Banqueters,* ed. and trans. S. D. Olson (Cambridge: Harvard University Press) 2011.
   *The Deipnosophists, or Banquet of the Learned of Athenaeus,* ed. C. D. Yonge (London: Henry G. Bohn, Covent Garden) 1854.

Auger, Danièle. *Artémidore et le théâtre* (Nanterre: Presses universitaires de Paris Ouest/Open Edition Books), 2012; as published on the Internet on 6/30/2016:
   http://books.openedition.org/pupo/3260?lang=en

Barker, Andrew. *Greek Musical Writings: Volume 1, The Musician and His Art* (Cambridge: Cambridge University Press) 1984.

Barnes, Brooks. "To Lure Young, Movie Theaters Shake, Smell and Spritz," *NY Times,* 11/29/2014.

Barnes, Jonathan and Miriam Griffin, eds. *Philosophia Togata II: Plato and Aristotle in Rome.* (Oxford: Clarendon Press) 1997.
   ---. See under "Aristotle" for translations.

Battin, Margaret Pabst. "Aristotle's Definition of Tragedy in the *Poetics,*" Pts. 1–2, *Journal of Aesthetics and Art Criticism,* 33 (Hoboken/Oxford: Wiley-Blackwell Publishing) 1975. 155–170 and 293–302.

Belfiore, Elizabeth. "The Elements of Tragedy" in *A Companion to Aristotle,* ed. Georgios Anagnostopoulos, *op. cit.,* 2009. 628-42.
   ---. "Pleasure, Tragedy and Aristotelian Psychology," *Classical Quarterly,* Vol. 35, Issue 2 (Cambridge: Cambridge University Press) 1985. 349-61.
   ---. *Tragic Pleasures: Aristotle on Plot and Emotion* (Princeton: Princeton University Press) 1992.

Bennett, K. C. "The Purging of Catharsis," *British Journal of Aesthetics,* 21/3 (Oxford: Oxford University Press) 1981. 204-13.

Benveniste, Emile. *Problems in General Linguistics* (Miami: Univ. of Miami Press) 1971; original French version, *Problèmes de linguistique gènérale (*Paris: Editions Gallimard) 1966.

Bernays, Jacob. "Aristotle on the Effect of Tragedy," trans. by Jonathan and Jennifer Barnes. Reprinted in *Articles on Aristotle: Vol. 4—Psychology & Aesthetics,* eds. J. Barnes, M. Schofield, and R. Sorabji: 154-165 (London: Duckworth) 1979. Originally published as *Zwei Abhandlungen über die aristotelische Theorie des Drama* (Braslau) 1857; reprinted Berlin, 1880.
   ---. *On Catharsis: From Fundamentals of Aristotle's Lost Essay on the "Effect of Tragedy"* (1857). Reproduced in *American Imago,* Vol. 61, No. 3, Fall (Baltimore, MD: The John Hopkins University Press) 2004. 319-341.

Blasis, Carlo. *The Code of Terpsichore* (New York: Dance Horizons) 1976. Originally published (London: James Bulcock Publishing) 1828; Renamed *The Art of Dancing*, 2nd ed. (London: James Bulcock Publishing) 1831.

Blocker, Déborah. « Elucider et équivoquer: Francesco Robortello (ré)invente la catharsis », in *Stratégies de l'équivoque, numéro dirigé par J.-P. Cavaillé, Cahiers du Centre de Recherches Historiques*, 33 (2004). 109-140.

Boal, Augusto. "Aristotle's Coercive System of Tragedy," *Theatre of the Oppressed* (New York: Theatre Communications Group, Inc.) 1985. 6th printing 2001. Originally published as *Teatro del Oprimido*, 1974.

Boggess, William F. "Hermannus Alemannus and Catharsis in the Mediaeval Latin *Poetics*," *Classical World*, Feb. 1969. 212-214.

Bongiorno, Andrew. *Castelvetro on the Art of Poetry*: An Abridged Translation of L. Castelvetro's *Poetica d'Aristotele Vulgarizzata et Sposta* (Binghamton, NY: Medieval & Renaissance Texts & Studies) 1984.

Boym, Svetlana. *Another Freedom: The Alternative History of an Idea* (Chicago: University of Chicago Press) 2012.

Boys-Stones, George. "Subject Reviews," *Greece & Rome*, Vol. 52, No. 1, *The Classical Association*, www.classicalassociation.org

Brantley, Ben. "Bearing Witness to Pain of Fate," *New York Times*, 11/13/2015.

Brecht, Bertolt. *Brecht on Theatre: The Development of an Aesthetic*, trans. John Willett (Frankfurt: Suhrkamp Verla) 1957. 32nd printing, 2001.

Brisson, Luc. *Plato the Myth Maker*, ed. and trans. Gerard Naddaf (Chicago: University of Chicago Press) 1999.

Brunius, Teddy. "Catharsis," in *Dictionary of the History of Ideas,* 4 vols., ed. Philip P. Wiener (New York: Charles Scribner's Sons) 1973.

Butcher, S.H. *Aristotle's Theory of Poetry and Fine Art* (London: Macmillan and Co. Ltd.) 1st ed. 1895, reprinted 1923.

Butterworth, Charles and Ahmad Haridi. *Averroes' Middle Commentary on Aristotle's Poetics*, (Princeton: Princeton University Press) 1986.
---. *Averroes' Middle Commentary on Aristotle's Poetics* (South Bend, Indiana: St. Augustine's Press) 2000.

Calame, Claude. *Choruses of Young Women in Ancient Greece: Their Morphology, Religious Role, and Social Function*, trans. Derek Collins and Janice Orion (Oxford: Rowman & Littlefield

Publishing) 2001.

Cavanagh, Dermot, ed., with Alan Gillis, Michelle Keown, James Loxley and Randall Stevenson. *The Edinburgh Introduction to Studying English Literature* (Edinburgh: Edinburgh University Press) 2010.

Cieply, Michael. "U.S. Box Office Heroes Proving Mortal in China," *NY Times*, 4/ 28/2013.

Clark, Barrett Harper. *European Theories of the Drama: An Anthology of Dramatic Theory and Criticism from Aristotle to the Present Day, in a Series of Selected Texts, with Commentaries, Biographies, and Bibliographies* (Cincinnati: Stewart & Kidd Company) 1918.

Cohen, Leah Hager. "What to Watch," *NY Times, Sunday Book Review*, 6/1/2008.

Collingwood, R.G. *The Principles of Art* in *Aesthetics: A Critical Anthology,* eds. George Dickie and Richard Sclafani (New York: St. Martin's Press) 1977. 94-123.

Connelly, Joan Breton. *The Parthenon Enigma* (New York: Alfred A. Knopf) 2014.
---. "Parthenon and *Parthenoi*: A Mythological Interpretation of the Parthenon Frieze," *American Journal of Archaeology* 100 (1996). 53-80.

Cooper, Lane. *An Aristotelian Theory of Comedy, with an Adaptation of the Poetics, and a Translation of the Tractatus Coisilianus* (New York: Harcourt Brace) 1922.

Corneille, Pierre. *Trois Discours sur le Poème Dramatique,* trans. Guilherme Abel Ferreira de Mendonça in *Acting Theory as Poetics of Drama: A Study of the Emergence of the Concept of 'Motivated Action' in Playwriting Theory* (Ph.D. dissertation, Brunel University) April 2012.

Crane, R.S. "The Concept of Plot and the Plot of *Tom Jones*," in *Critics and Criticism* (Chicago: University of Chicago Press) 1952; 2nd edition, 1954. 616-648.

Csapo, Eric. "The Politics of the New Music," *Music and the Muses: The Culture of 'Mousikē' in the Classical Athenian City*, eds. Penelope Murray and Peter Wilson (Oxford: Oxford University Press) 2004. 207-248.
---. "General Introduction" in *The Origins of Theater in Ancient Greece and Beyond: From Ritual to Drama*, eds. Eric Csapo and Margaret Miller (Cambridge: Cambridge University Press) 2008. 1-40.
---. and William J. Slater, *The Context of the Ancient Drama* (Ann Arbor, MI: University of Michigan Press) 1995.
---. "The Earliest Phase of 'Comic' Choral Entertainments in Athens: The Dionysian Pompe and the 'Birth' of Comedy," in *Fragmente einer Geschichte der griechischen Komödie/Fragmentary History of Greek Comedy*, Stylianos Chronopoulos and Christian Orth, eds., *Studia Comica* 5 (Heidelberg: Verlag Antike) 2015. 66-108.

Curran, Angela. *Routledge Philosophy Guidebook to Aristotle and the Poetics* (New York: Routledge) 2016.

Dacier, André. *La Poétique d'Aristote: contenant les regles les plus exactes pour juger du poëme heroïque* [*Aristotle's Poetics: Containing the most exact rules for judging the heroic poem*] (Paris: Barbin Publ) 1692.
---. *The Preface to Aristotle's Art of Poetry. With Mr. D'Acier's Notes Translated from the French* (London: Dan. Brown), 1705. The Augustan Reprint Society, Publ. # 76, 1959, editor Samuel Holt Monk.

Dahiyat, Ismail M. *Avicenna's Commentary on the Poetics of Aristotle* (Leiden: Brill) 1974.

Destrée, Pierre. "La Purgation des Interprétations: Conditions et Enjeux de la Catharsis Poétique chez Aristote," *Littérature et Thérapeutique des Passions. La Catharsis en Question*, ed. J.-C. Darmon (Paris: Hermann) 2011. 13-35.
---. and Fritz-Gregor Herrmann, eds. *Plato and the Poets* (Leiden & Boston: Brill) 2011.

Dickie, George, Richard Sclafani, and Ronald Roblin, eds. *Aesthetics: A Critical Anthology*, 2nd ed. (New York: St. Martin's Press) 1989.

Dodds, Eric R. *The Greeks and the Irrational* (Berkeley: University of California Press) 1951.

Donini, Pierluigi. *La Tragedia e la Vita. Saggi Sulla* Poetica *di Aristotele* (Alessandria: Edizioni dell'Orso) 2004.
---. "La Tragedia, Senza la Catarsi," *Phronesis* (Leiden: Brill Publishers) 1998. 26-41.

Dubos, Abbé Jean-Baptiste. *Réflexions critiques sur la poësie et sur la peinture* (*Critical Reflections on Poetry and Painting*) 3rd Vol. (Paris: Chez Pierre-Jean Mariette) 1733.
---. *Critical Reflections on Poetry, Painting and Music*, Vol. 1, 5th ed., trans. by Thomas Nugent into English (London: John Nourse Publ.) 1748.

During, I. *Aristotle in the Ancient Biographical Tradition* (Goteborg: Goteborg Universitets Arsskrift) 63/2, 1957.

Eldridge, Richard. "How Can Tragedy Matter for Us," *The Journal of Aesthetics and Art Criticism*, Vol. 52, 3, Summer (Hoboken/Oxford: Wiley-Blackwell Publishing) 1994. 287-298.

Eliot, T.S. "The Perfect Critic," *The Sacred Wood: Essays on Poetry and Criticism* (London: Methuen and Co.) 1961.

Emmanuel, Maurice. *The Antique Greek Dance*, trans. by Harriet Jean Beauley (New York: John Lane Company; London: John Lane, The Bodley Head); orig. publ. in 1895 in French (publisher not listed).

Else, Gerald. *The Argument* (Cambridge: Harvard University Press) 1963; first publ. 1957.
---. "'Imitation' in the Fifth Century," *Classical Philology* Vol. 53, #2, Univ. of Chicago Press, 1958. 73-90.
---. *Aristotle's Poetics* (Ann Arbor: University of Michigan Press) 1967.
---. *Plato and Aristotle on Poetry*. Ed. P. Burian (Chapel Hill and London: University of North

Carolina Press) 1986.

England, E.B. *The Laws of Plato: The Text Edited with Introduction, Notes, etc.* (Manchester: The University Press; New York: Longmans, Green & Co.) 1921.

Euripides. *The Hecuba of Euripides*, a revised text with notes and an introd. by John Bond and Arthur S. Walpole (London: Macmillan & Co) 1882.

Fendt, Gene. "The Others In/Of Aristotle's *Poetics*," *Journal of Philosophical Research*, Vol. 22 (Charlottesville, VA: Philosophy Documentation Center) 1997.
---. "Resolution, Catharsis, Culture: *As You Like It*," *Philosophy and Literature* 19 (Baltimore, MD: The John Hopkins University Press) 1995. 248-260.

Ferri, Rolando. "Review of 'J.H. Hordern, *Sophron's Mimes. Text, Translation, and Commentary*,'" *Bryn Mawr Classical Review* 08.02 (Bryn Mawr: Bryn Mawr College/University of Pennsylvania) 2005.

Feyerabend, Paul. *The Tyranny of Science* (Cambridge, MA: Polity Press) 2011. First published in Italian as *Ambiguitá e armonia: lezioni trentine* (Gius: Laterza e Figli) 1996.

Fitton, J.W. "Greek Dance," *Classical Quarterly*, New Series, Vol. 23, No. 2, 1973. 254-274.

Ford, Andrew. "The Purpose of Aristotle's *Poetics*," *Classical Philology* 110, Vol. 1 (2015). 1-21.

Freire, António. "A Catarse Tragica em Aristoteles," *Euphrosyne*, 3 (Lisbon, Portugal: Universidade de Lisboa/ Centro de Estudos Clássicos) 1969.

Friesen, Joanna. "Aristotle's Dramatic Theories Applied to Dance Criticism," *New Directions in Dance,* ed. Diana Taplin (Toronto: Pergamon Press) 1979. 13-23.

Gallop, David. "Animals in the *Poetics*" in *Oxford Studies in Ancient Philosophy*, Vol. VIII (Oxford: Clarendon Press) 1990. 145-171.

Golden, Leon. *Aristotle on Tragic and Comic Mimesis*. American Philological Association: American Classical Studies, 29 (Atlanta: Scholars Press) 1992. ['*Tragic Mimesis*' in Chapters 5-6]
---. "The Purgation Theory of Catharsis," *The Journal of Aesthetics and Art Criticism*, Vol. 31, No. 4, Summer, 1973. 473-479.

Goldschmidt, Victor. *Questions Platoniciennes* (Paris: J. Vrin) 1970.

Gould, Rebecca. "The *Poetics* from Athens to al-Andalus: Ibn Rushd's Grounds for Comparison," *Modern Philology*, 112.1 (2014). 1-24.

"Greek Dance Pandect Project: The World of Greek Dance," as given online: http://www.dance-pandect.gr/pds_portal_en/index.php?option=com_content&view=article&id=56&Itemid=58

Griffith, Mark. *Greek Satyr Play: Five Studies* (Berkeley: California Classical Studies) 2015.

---. "Cretan Harmonies and Universal Morals: Early Music and Migration of Wisdom in Plato's Laws," in *Performance and Culture in Plato's Laws*, ed. A-E. Peponi, *op. cit.* 15-66.

--. "Is Korybantic Performance a (Lyric) Genre?", in M. Foster, L. V. Kurke, and N. Weiss, eds, *The Genres of Archaic and Classical Greek Poetry* (forthcoming, Leiden, Brill 2019).

Grube, George. *The Greek and Roman Critics* (Toronto: Hackett Publishing) 1965.

Gudeman, Alfred. *Aristoteles: Peri Poietikes* (Berlin: Walter de Gruyter) 1934.

Gulley, N. "Aristotle on the Purposes of Literature, in *Articles on Aristotle: Vol. 4—Psychology & Aesthetics*, eds. J. Barnes, M. Schofield, and R. Sorabji (London: Duckworth Press) 1979.

Habib, M.A.R. *A History of Literary Criticism: From Plato to the Present* (Hoboken/Oxford: Wiley-Blackwell Publishing) 2005.

Haigh, A.E. *The Tragic Drama of the Greeks* (New York: Dover Public.) 1968. Originally published (Oxford: Clarendon Press) 1896.

Hall, Edith. *Greek Tragedy: Suffering under the Sun* (Oxford: Oxford University Press) 2010.

Halliwell, Stephen. *The Aesthetics of Mimesis: Ancient Texts and Modern Problems* (Princeton: Princeton University Press) 2002.

---. *Aristotle's Poetics* (Chapel Hill: University of North Carolina Press) 1986.

---. *The Poetics of Aristotle: translation and commentary* (Chapel Hill: University of North Carolina Press) 1987.

---. "Aristotelianism and anti-Aristotelianism in Attitudes to Theatre," *Attitudes to Theatre from Plato to Milton*, ed. Elena Theodorakopoulos, Nottingham Classical Literature Studies, Vol. 7 (Bari: Levante Editori) 2003. 57-75.

---. *Between Ecstasy and Truth: Interpretations of Greek Poetics from Homer to Longinus* (Oxford: Oxford University Press) 2011.

---. *Greek Laughter: A Study of Cultural Psychology from Homer to Early Christianity* (Cambridge: Cambridge University Press) 2008.

---. "La Psychologie Morale de la Catharsis: un Essai de Reconstruction," *Les Etudes Philosophiques*, Number 64 (Paris: Presses Universitaires de France) 2003-4. 419-517.

Hammond, N.G.L., and H.H. Scullard, eds."Music.9. Instruments" in *Oxford Classical Dictionary*, 2nd ed. (Oxford: Oxford University Press) 1978.

Hardison, Jr., O.B. *Poetics and Praxis, Understanding and Imagination: The Collected Essays of O.B. Hardison, Jr.*, ed. by Arthur Kinney (Athens: Univ. of Georgia Press) 1997.

Harrison, Jane E. *Prolegomena to the Study of Greek Religion* (Princeton: Princeton University Press) 1922.

Heath, Malcolm. *Aristotle Poetics* (London: Penguin Books) 1996.

---. "Aristotle *On Poets*: A Critical Evaluation of Richard Janko's Edition of the Fragments," *Studia Humaniora Tartuensia*, vol. 14.A.1 (2013), ISSN 1406-6203, available online at http://sht.ut.ee.

Herington, John. *Poetry into Drama: Early Tragedy and the Greek Poetic Tradition*, Sather Classical Lectures, Vol. 49 (Berkeley: University of California Press) 1985.

Herodotus, *The Histories*, with an English translation by A. D. Godley (Cambridge: Harvard University Press) 1920.

Herrmann, Fritz-Gregor. "Poetry in Plato's *Gorgias*," in *Plato and the Poets*, ed. by Pierre Destrée and Fritz-Gregor Herrmann, *op. cit.*, 2011. 21-40.

Hesychius Alexandrinus. *Lexicon*. Ed. Moritz Schmidt (Sumptibus Hermanni Dufftii: Libraria Maukiana) 1867.

Hofstadter, Albert and Richard Kuhns, eds. *Philosophies of Art and Beauty: Selected Readings in Aesthetics from Plato to Heidegger* (Chicago: The University of Chicago Press) 1964.

Holden, Stephen. *The Piano Teacher*: Film Review "Kinky and Cruel Goings-On in the Conservatory," *NY Times*, 3/29/2002.

Hordern, J.H. *Sophron's Mimes. Text, Translation, and Commentary* (Oxford: Oxford University Press) 2004.

Istros, *Tragicorum Graecorum Fragmenta*, Vol. 4, *Life of Sophocles*.

Jaeger, Werner. *Aristotle: Fundamentals of the History of his Development*, trans. Richard Robinson, 2nd ed. (Oxford: Oxford University Press) 1948. Originally published as *Aristoteles: Grundlegungeiner Geschichte seiner Entwicklung* (Berlin: Ostern) 1923.

Janko, Richard. *Aristotle on Comedy: Towards a Reconstruction of Poetics II* (London: George Duckworth & Co. Ltd.) 1984. ['Comedy' in Ch 5]
---. *Aristotle: Poetics, with the Tractatus Coisilianus, Reconstruction of Poetics II, and the Fragments of the On Poets* (Indianapolis: Hackett Publishing Company) 1987.
---. *Philodemus: the Aesthetic Works. Vol. I/3: Philodemus, On Poems Books 3–4, with the Fragments of Aristotle, On Poets* (Oxford: Oxford University Press) 2011.
---. Philodemus *On Poems* and Aristotle's *On Poets* ['Philodemus' in Ch 5] *Cronache ercolanesi*, 21 (1991). 5-64.
---. "A Fragment of Aristotle's Poetics from Porphyry, concerning Synonymy," *The Classical Quarterly*, Vol. 32, No. 2 (1982). 323-326.
---. "Book Reviews," book review of Tarán and Gutas, *op. cit.*, in *Classical Philology* 108 (2013), 252–7. Also at: http://www-personal.umich.edu/~rjanko/review%20Gutas%20&%20Tar%E1n.pdf as of May 1, 2018.

Javitch, Daniel. "The Assimilation of Aristotle's *Poetics* in sixteenth-century Italy," *The Cambridge*

*History of Literary Criticism: Volume 3, The Renaissance*, edited by George Alexander Kennedy, Glyn P. Norton (Cambridge: Cambridge Univ. Pr.) 1999. 53-65.

Jonson, Ben. *Timber: Or Discoveries Made Upon Men and Matter.* Edited with Introduction and Notes by Felix Schelling (Boston: Ginn & Co.) 1892.

Kakutani, Michiko. "His Weirdness Attracts Types Even More Weird," *New York Times*, 8/8/2000.

Kenny, Sir Anthony. *Aristotle POETICS* (Oxford: Oxford University Press, 2013).

Kitto, H. D. F. "Catharsis" in *The Classical Tradition*, ed. L. Wallach (Ithaca: Cornell University Press) 1966. 133-47.

Koller, Hermann. *Mimesis in der Antike* (Berne: Francke Publishing) 1954.

Kosman, Aryeh. "Acting: Drama as the Mimesis of Praxis," in *Essays on Aristotle's* Poetics, ed. A. O. Rorty (Princeton: Princeton University Press) 1992. 51-72.

Kowalzig, Barbara. "Broken Rhythms in Plato's *Laws*," in Anastasia-Erasmia Peponi, *op. cit.*, 2013. 171-211.

Kraut, Richard. *Aristotle Politics: Books VII and VIII* (Oxford: Clarendon Press) 1998

Kurke, Leslie. "Imagining Chorality: Wonder, Plato's Puppets, and Moving Statues," in Anastasia-Erasmia Peponi, *op. cit.*, 2013. 123-170.

Laertius, Diogenes. *Lives of the Eminent Philosophers*, trans. R.D. Hicks., 2nd ed. (Cambridge: Harvard University Press) 1972. Originally published 1925.

Landels, John. *Music in Ancient Greece and Rome* (London/New York: Routledge) 1999.

Lawler, Lillian. *The Dance in Ancient Greece* (Middletown, CT: Wesleyan University Press) 1964.
---. *The Dance of the Ancient Greek Theatre* (Iowa City: University of Iowa Press) 1964.

Lear, Jonathan. "Katharsis," *Phronesis*, 33/3 (Leiden: Brill Publishers) 1988. Reprinted in *Essays on Aristotle's* Poetics, ed. A. O. Rorty (Princeton: Princeton University Press) 1992. 315-340.

Lessing, G.E. *Hamburg Dramaturgy,* trans. Helen Zimmern (New York: Dover Publ.) 1962.

Levinson, André. *The Idea of the Dance: From Aristotle to Mallarmé*, Theatre Arts Monthly, 1927. Republished in *What is Dance?: Readings in Theory and Criticism,* eds. Roger Copeland and Marshall Cohen (Oxford: Oxford University Press) 1983. 47-55.

Liddell, Henry George and Robert Scott. *Greek-English Lexicon,* 1968 impression; first ed. 1889.
---. Revised and augmented throughout by Sir Henry Stuart Jones with the assistance of Roderick McKenzie (Oxford: Clarendon Press) 1940.

Lloyd-Jones, Hugh. "Problems of Early Greek Tragedy: Pratinas, Phrynichus, the Gyges Fragment," as given at:
http://interclassica.um.es/var/plain/storage/original/application/70832cffe7f36dafc1ab-7b4e2ca99cfb.pdf
Published subsequently as "Problems in Early Geek Tragedy. Pratinas and Phrynichos" in *Greek Epic, Lyric and Tragedy: The Academic Papers of Sir Hugh Lloyd-Jones* (Oxford: Oxford University Pr) 1990. 225-237.

Lobel, E., *The Greek Manuscripts of Aristotle's* Poetics (Oxford: Oxford University Press) 1933.

Lucas, Craig. "The Dying Gaul," Encore Arts Programs, Seattle, Vol. 5, Issue 4, July 2001.

Lucian. "On Dance," in *Lucian: Volume V,* Loeb Classical Library 302, trans. by A. M. Harmon (Cambridge: Harvard Univ Pr) 1936.

Maas, Martha and Jane Snyder. *Stringed Instruments of Ancient Greece (*New Haven: Yale University Press) 1989.

Mallette, Karla. "Beyond Mimesis: Aristotle's *Poetics* in the Medieval Mediterranean," *Theories and Methodologies*, PMLA 124 (2009). 583-91.

Malpas, Simon. "Tragedy", in *op. cit.,* Cavanagh, 2010. 180-88.

Marchetti, Christopher C. *Aristoxenus "Elements of Rhythm": Text, translation, and commentary with a translation and commentary on POxy 2687* (Ph.D. dissertation, Rutgers University, NJ) 2009.

Marx, William. "La Véritable Catharsis Aristotélicienne. Pour une Lecture Philologique et Physiologique de la *Poétique, " Poétique* 166 (Paris: Editions du Seuil) 2011.

Mathiesen, Thomas J. *Apollo's Lyre: Greek Music and Music Theory in Antiquity and the Middle Ages* (Lincoln, NE/London: University of Nebraska Press) 1999.
---. *Aristides Quintilianus, On Music—in Three Books,* Book 1, 13 (New Haven: Yale University Press) 1983.

Matthew, Brender. "Introduction" to *The New Art of Writing Plays (Arte Nuevo de Hacer Comedias en Este Tiempo*, 1609) by Lope de Vega, trans. William T. Brewster in *Papers on Play-Making III: The Law of the Drama,* ed. Ferdinand Brunetiere (New York: The Dramatic Museum of Columbia University) 1914.

McCoy, Marina. *Wounded Heroes: Vulnerability as a Virtue in Greek Tragedy and Philosophy* (Oxford: Oxford University Press) 2013.

McKirahan, Richard. "The Place of the *Posterior Analytics* in Aristotle's Thought, with Particular Reference to the *Poetics," Apeiron* 43/2-3 (Austin, TX: University of Texas) 2010. 75-104.

McOsker, Michael. Book review of Tarán and Gutas, *op. cit., Bryn Mawr Classical Review* 2012.11.26, also found at http://bmcr.brynmawr.edu/2012/2012-11-26.html.

Menestrier, Claude-François. *Des Ballets Anciens et Modernes Selon les Regles du Theatre (Ancient and Modern Ballets According to the Rules of the Theater)* (Paris: René Guignard) 1682.

Meyer, Susan Sauvé. "Pessimism and Postponement: Comments on André Laks 'Postponing the *Laws*'," unpublished conference presentation, Princeton University Colloquium, Dec. 1996.
---. *Plato Laws I and II, Translated with a Commentary* (Oxford: Clarendon Press) 2015.
---. "Legislation as a Tragedy: On Plato's Laws VII, 817B-D," *Plato and the Poets*, ed. by Pierre Destrée and Fritz-Gregor Herrmann, *op. cit.,* 2011. 387-402.
---. "Plato on the Evaluation of Images," as noted in "Scholarship, Research and Creative Work at Bryn Mawr College" (presented at the conference titled *Plato on the Evaluation of Images*, October 2013, Bryn Mawr College and February 2014, Louvain, Belgium): http://repository.brynmawr.edu/plato/

Milton, John. *Of Education* (1644), *The John Milton Reading Room,* Thomas H. Luxon, General Editor (Trustees of Dartmouth College) at:
http://www.dartmouth.edu/~milton/reading_room/of_education/
---. *Samson Agonistes,* ed. with introd. and notes by John Churton Collins (Oxford: Clarendon Press) 1883; repr. 1948.

Monroe, James T. "The Tune or the Words? (Singing Hispano-Arabic Strophic Poetry)," *Al-Qanṭara* (*Revista de Estudios* Árabes) Vol. VIII, 1987. 265-317.
---. "Prolegomena to the Study of Ibn Quzmān: The Poet as Jongleur," *The Hispanic Ballad Today: History, Comparativism, Critical Bibliography,* Eds. Samuel G. Armistead, Antonio Sánchez-Romeralo, and Diego Catalán (Madrid: Cátedra-Seminario Menéndez Pidal and Gredos) 1979, Vol. 3. 77-129.

Moore, Timothy J. *Music in Roman Comedy* (Cambridge: Cambridge University Press) 2012.

Morrow, Glenn. *Plato's Cretan City: A Historical Interpretation of the* Laws (Princeton: Princeton University Press) 1960; 2nd ed. 1993.

Mountford, J. F. "Introduction" to *The Greek Aulos: A Study of its Mechanism and of its Relation to the Modal System of Ancient Greek Music* by Kathleen Schlesinger (London: Methuen & Co) 1939.

Mullen, William. *Choreia: Pindar and Dance* (Princeton: Princeton University Press) 1982.

Munteanu, Dana Lacourse. *Tragic Pathos: Pity and Fear in Greek Philosophy and Tragedy* (Cambridge: Cambridge University Press) 2012.

Natali, Carlo. *Aristotle: His Life and School*, ed. by D.S. Hutchinson (Princeton: Princeton University Press) 2013.

Nagy, Gregory. *Poetry as Performance,* published online in 2009 by the Center for Hellenic Studies: http://chs.harvard.edu/CHS/article/display/5581 (orig. publ. by Cambridge Univ. Pr., 1996).

---. *Pindar's Homer: The Lyric Possession of an Epic Past* (Baltimore: The John Hopkins University Press) 1990. Accessed online, October 2015, at: http://chs.harvard.edu/CHS/article/display/5262

---. "A poetics of sisterly affect in the Brothers Song and in other songs of Sappho." Published online 2015.09.8; printed version forthcoming in *The Newest Sappho (P. Obbink and P. GC Inv. 105, frs. 1-5)*, edited by Anton Bierl and André Lardinois (Leiden: Brill) 2015": http://chs.harvard.edu/CHS/article/display/5983

---. "Genre, Occasion, and Choral Mimesis Revisited—with special reference to the 'newest Sappho'," *Classical Inquiries: Studies on the Ancient World from Center for Hellenic Studies*. Published online 2015.10.1 at http://classical-inquiries.chs.harvard.edu/genre-occasion-and-choral-mimesis-revisited-with-special-reference-to-the-newest-sappho/

---. "Epic." In *The Oxford Handbook of Philosophy and Literature*, ed. Richard Eldridge (Oxford: Oxford University Press) 2009. 19-44. Republished online, 2010, at http://chs.harvard.edu/CHS/article/display/3627

---. "Aristotle's *Poetics*, translation and commentary in progress, Part 1," *Classical Inquiries*, dated 2015.11.15 online, and viewed 2015.12.31: http://classical-inquiries.chs.harvard.edu/aristotles-poetics-translation-and-commentary-in-progress-part-1/

National Endowment for the Arts. "Fact Sheet, Spring 2013," Spring 2013. Viewable online at: http://www.nasaa-arts.org/Research/Grant-Making/NEAFactSheetSpring2013.pdf

Nehamas, Alexander. "Pity and Fear in the *Rhetoric* and the *Dramatics,*" in *Essays on Aristotle's Poetics*, ed. A. O. Rorty (Princeton: Princeton University Press) 1992. 291-314.

Notomi, Noburu. "Image-Making in *Republic* X and the *Sophist*," in *Plato and the Poets*, ed. by P. Destrée and F. Herrmann, *op. cit.*, 2011. 299-326.

Noverre, Jean Georges. *Letters on Dancing and Ballets,* trans. Cyril Beaumont (New York: Dance Horizons) 1966. Originally published Stuttgart, 1760.

Nussbaum, M. "Tragedy and Self-Sufficiency," in *Essays on Aristotle's* Poetics, ed. A. O. Rorty (Princeton: Princeton University Press) 1992. 261-90.

Nuttall, A. D. *Why Does Tragedy Give Pleasure?* (Oxford: Oxford University Press) 1996.

Oates, Joyce Carol. "Confronting Head On the Face of the Afflicted," *New York Times*, 2/19/1995.

Oberg, Alcestis. "Maybe 'Big Wedding' Will Wake Up Hollywood Big Wigs," *USA Today,* 9/12/2002.

Olson, Elder. *Aristotle's Poetics and English Literature* (Chicago: University of Chicago Press) 1965.

"Opera," *The International Cyclopedia of Music and Musicians,* Vol. 2, 11th ed., ed. Oscar Thompson (New York: Dodd, Mead & Co.) 1985.

Orgel, Stephen. *The Authentic Shakespeare, and Other Problems of the Early Modern Stage* (New York/London: Routledge) 2002.

Otte, Heinrich. *Kennt Aristoteles die sogenannte tragische Katharsis?* (Berlin: Weidmann) 1912.

Owens, Joseph. *The Doctrine of Being in the Aristotelian Metaphysics* (Toronto: Pontifical Institute of Medieval Studies) 3rd ed., 1978; first publ. 1951.

Pakaluk, Michael. "Review of 'David Sedley, ed., *Oxford Studies in Ancient Philosophy* (Oxford: Oxford University Press) Volume XXV, Winter 2003,'" in *Bryn Mawr Classical Review* 06.18 (Bryn Mawr: Bryn Mawr College/University of Pennsylvania) 2006.

Pappas, Nickolas. "Aristotle," in *Routledge Companion to Aesthetics*, 2nd and 3rd editions, eds. Berys Gaut and Dominic McIver Lopes (New York: Routledge) 2005 and 2013.
---. *The Philosopher's New Clothes: The Theaetetus, the Academy, and Philosophy's Turn against Fashion* (Oxford: Routledge) 2015.

Patterson, Richard. "The Platonic Art of Comedy and Tragedy," *Philosophy and Literature* 6. (Baltimore, MD: The John Hopkins University Press) (1-2):76-93. 1982.

Peponi, Anastasia-Erasmia. "*Choreia* and Aesthetics in the *Homeric Hymn to Apollo*: The Performance of the Delian Maidens (Lines 156–64)," *Classical Antiquity*, Vol. 28, No. 1 (Berkeley: University of California Press) 2009.
---. *Performance and Culture in Plato's Laws*, ed. Anastasia-Erasmia Peponi (Cambridge: Cambridge University Press) 2013.
---. "Aristotle's Definition of Tragedy," in *Choreutika: Performing and Theorising Dance in Ancient Greece*, ed. Laura Gianvittorio, 215-43 (Pisa/Roma: Fabrizio Serra Editore) 2017.

Perrotta, Tom. "Fall from Grace," *New York Times Book Review*, 5/10/2015.

Petruševski, M. D. "La Définition de la Tragédie Chez Aristote et la Catharsis," *L'Annuaire de la Faculté de Philosophie de l'Université de Skopje*, 1 (Skopje, Macedonia) 1948.
---. "Pathēmatōn Katharsin ou bien Pragmatōn Systasin?," *Ziva antika/Antiquite vivante* (Skopje: Societe d'etudes classiques Ziva Antika) 1954.

Plato. *The Republic*, Vol. 1 and 2, trans. Paul Shorey. Loeb Classical Library (Cambridge: Harvard University Press) 1956.

Plato. *The Laws of Plato,* trans. A. E. Taylor (London and New York: Dent & Sons Ltd.) 1934.

*Platonis Opera* (Greek text), ed. John Burnet (Oxford: Oxford University Press) 1903.

Plato. *The Collected Dialogues of Plato*, eds. E. Hamilton and H. Cairns (Princeton: Princeton University Press) 1961. 11th printing 1982.
---. *Ion*, trans. Lane Cooper.
---. *Philebus,* trans. R. Hackforth.

*Plato in Twelve Volumes.* Vol. 9 (Cambridge: Harvard University Press; London: William Heinemann Ltd.) 1966.
   ---. *Ion,* trans. W. R. M. Lamb.
   ---. *Laws,* Vols. 10 & 11, trans. R. G. Bury.
   ---. *Symposium,* trans. Harold N. Fowler.

*Plato in Twelve Volumes.* Vol. 12 (Cambridge: Harvard University Press; London: William Heinemann Ltd.) 1921.
   ---. *Sophist,* trans. Harold N. Fowler.

*Plato: The Complete Works,* Ed. John Cooper, Assoc. Ed., D.S. Hutchinson (Indianapolis and Cambridge: Hackett Publishing Co.) 1997.
   ---. *Laws,* trans. Trevor J. Saunders.
   ---. *The Republic*, trans. George Grube and C.D.C. Reeve.

Plutarch. *Plutarch's Lives*, with an English translation by Bernadotte Perrin (Cambridge, MA: Harvard University Press; London: William Heinemann Ltd.) 1914.

Pocock, Gordon. *Corneille and Racine: Problems of Tragic Form* (Cambridge: Cambridge University Press) 1973.

Podlecki, Anthony J. "Reviews," *The American Journal of Philology*, Vol. 91, No. 2, Apr. 1970. 253-255. Online at: http://www.jstor.org/stable/293056?seq=1#page_scan_tab_contents

Pollard, Tonya. "Conceiving Tragedy," in *Shakespearean Sensations: Experiencing Literature in Early Modern England,* eds. Katharine A. Craik and Tanya Pollard, 85-100 (Cambridge: Cambridge University Press) 2013.

Porter, James I. *The Origins of Aesthetic Thought in Ancient Greece* (Cambridge: Cambridge University Press) 2010.

Prudhommeau, Germaine. *La Danse Grecque Antique: Tome I et II* (Paris: Editions du Centre National de la Recherche Scientifique) 1965.

Racine, Jean. "Preface" to *Berenice.* 1670. Republished (Oxford: Oxford University Press) 1915.

Rand, Ayn. *The Romantic Manifesto: A Philosophy of Literature* (New York: New American Library) 1975 rev. ed., first publ. 1971.

Rashed, Marwan. "*Katharsis versus mimèsis*: simulation des émotions et définition aristotélicienne de la tragédie," *Littérature*, Vol. 182, No. 2, 2016. 60-77.

Rohter, Larry. "Romania's Overlooked New Wave," *New York Times,* 12/18/2013, reprinted as "My Mother the Metaphor," 2/9/2014.

*Romeo and Juliet.* DVD. Directed by L. Armstram and Leonid Lavrovsky (Russia: Mosfilm) 1955.

Rood, Naomi. "Mediating the Distance: Prophecy and Alterity in Greek Tragedy and Dostoevsky's *Crime and Punishment*," *Russian Literature and the Classics*, eds. Peter Barta, David Larmour, and Paul Allen Miller, 35-58 (New York and Oxford: Routledge) 2013.

Rorty, A. O., ed. *Essays on Aristotle's* Poetics (Princeton: Princeton University Press) 1992.

Rosenthal, Edna. *Aristotle and Modernism: Aesthetic Affinities of T.S. Eliot, Wallace Stevens and Virginia Woolf* (Sussex, England and Portland, OR: Sussex Academic Press) 2008.

Ross, W.D. *Aristotle: A complete exposition of his works & thought* (New York: Meridian Books, Inc.) 1959.

Russell, D.A. and Winterbottom, M., eds. *Ancient Literary Criticism* (Oxford: Oxford University Press) 1972.

Rymer, Thomas. "A Short View of Tragedy, its Original Excellency and Corruption, with Some Reflections on Shakespear and Other Practitioners for the Stage (1693)," in *European Theories of the Drama: An Anthology of Dramatic Theory and Criticism from Aristotle to the Present Day, in a Series of Selected Texts, with Commentaries, Biographies, and Bibliographies*, ed. Barrett Harper Clark (Cincinnati: Stewart & Kidd Company) 1918.

Sachs, Joe. "Tragic Pleasure," *The St. John's Review*, Vol. XLIII, #1, 1995. 21-38.

Sadic, Stanley, ed. *New Grove Dictionary of Musical Instruments*, 3 Vols. (London: Macmillan Publishers Limited) 1985.

Sandbach, F. H. *Aristotle and the Stoics*, Cambridge Philological Society, Suppl. 10 (Cambridge: Philological Society) 1985.

Sansone, David. *Greek Drama and the Invention of Rhetoric* (West Sussex: John Wiley & Sons) 2012.

Scaliger, Julius Caesar. *Poetica* (1561), in *Select Translations from Scaliger's Poetics*. Transl. F.M. Padelford. (New Haven: Yale University Press) 1905, as found in Hazard Adams, ed., *Critical Theory since Plato*, 136-143 (New York: Harcourt Brace Jovanovich, Inc.) 1971.

Schaper, Eva. *Prelude to Aesthetics* (London: Unwin Hyman) 1968. Excerpt reprinted in G. Dickie, R. Sclafani, and R. Roblin, *op. cit.*, 1989. 48-56.

Scheff, T.J. *Catharsis in Healing, Ritual, and Drama* (Berkeley: University of California Press) 1979.

Schironi, Francesca. "Theory into Practice: Aristotelian Principles in Aristarchean Philology," *Classical Philology* 104 (2009). 279–316.

Schlesinger, Kathleen. *The Greek Aulos: A Study of its Mechanism and of its Relation to the Modal System of Ancient Greek Music* (London: Methuen & Co.) 1939.

Schollmeier, Paul. "Purgation of Pitiableness and Fearfulness," *Hermes: Zeitschr. für klassische Philologie,* Vol. 122, 1994. 289-299.

---. "Aristotle on Comedy," *International Philosophical Inquiry,* Vol. 40, Num. 3-4, Spring-Summer 2016. 146-162.

Scott, Gregory. "Banes and Carroll on Defining Dance," *Dance Research Journal* (Cambridge: Cambridge University Press) 29/1, Spring 1997. 7-22.

---. "The *Poetics* of Performance: The Necessity of Performance, Spectacle, Music, and Dance in Aristotelian Tragedy," *Performance and Authenticity in the Arts (Cambridge Series on Philosophy and the Arts)* eds. Salim Kemal and Ivan Gaskell (Cambridge: Cambridge University Press) 1999. 15-48.

---. "Purging the *Poetics*," *Oxford Studies in Ancient Philosophy,* Vol. 25, 2003 (Oxford: Oxford University Press). 233-264.

---. "Twists and Turns: Modern Misconceptions of Peripatetic Dance Theory," *Dance Research: The Journal of the Society for Dance Research,* Vol. 23, No. 2, 2005 (Edinburgh: Edinburgh University Press). 153-172.

---. *Unearthing Aristotle's Dramatics: Why There is No Theory of Literature in the Poetics* (Ph.D. dissertation, University of Toronto) 1992.

---. *Aristotle's Favorite Tragedy: Oedipus or Cresphontes?* (New York: CreateSpace/Amazon) 2016; 2nd edition (New York: ExistencePS Press) 2018.

Seidensticker, Bernd. "Dithyramb, Comedy, and Satyr-Play," *A Companion to Greek Tragedy,* ed. Justina Gregory (Blackwell: Oxford) 2005. 38-54.

Sidnell, Michael J., ed. with D.J. Conacher, Barbara Kerslake, Pia Kleber, C.J. McDonough, and Damiano Pietropaolo. *Sources of Dramatic Theory 1: Plato to Congreve* (Cambridge: Cambridge Univ. Press) 1991.

Smith, Adam. "*Of the Nature of that Imitation which takes place in what are called The Imitative Arts/Of the Affinity between Music, Dancing, and Poetry,*" from *Essays on Philosophical Subjects, Glasgow Edition of the Works and Correspondence of Adam Smith* [1795] Vol. III, eds. W. P. D. Wightman and J. C. Bryce (Indianapolis: Liberty Fund) 1982.

Smith, Dinitia. "Critic at the Mercy of His Own Kind," *New York Times,* 5/24/2003.

Smerdel, Anton. *Aristotelova Katarsa* (Skopje: Južna Srbija) 1937.

Solbakk, Jan Helge. "Catharsis and Moral Therapy II: An Aristotelian Account," *Medicine, Health Care and Philosophy* (New York: Springer Publishing) 2006. 9:141–153.

Somville, Pierre. *Essai sur la Poétique d'Aristote* (Paris: Librairie Philosophique J. Vrin) 1975.

---. Translation of the *Poetics*, in R. Bodéüs, ed., *Aristote, Oeuvres. Éthiques, Politique, Rhétorique, Poétique, Métaphysique. Bibliothèque de la Pléiade.* Paris: Gallimard, 2014, pp. 1500-1518.

Sorabji, Richard. *Emotion and Peace of Mind: From Stoic Agitation to Christian Temptation* (Oxford: Oxford University Press) 2000.

Sörbom, Göran. *Mimesis and Art, Studies in the Origin and Early Development of an Aesthetic Vocabulary* (Uppsala: Svenska Bokförlaget Bonniers) 1966.

Sparshott, Francis. "On the Question: 'Why do Philosophers Neglect the Aesthetics of the Dance?'" *Dance Research Journal* 15, No. 1, Fall 1982 (Cambridge: Cambridge University Press). 5-30.
---. "The Riddle of Catharsis," *Centre and Labyrinth: Essays in Honour of Northrop Frye*, eds. Eleanor Cook *et al* (Toronto: University of Toronto Press) 1983. 14-37.
---. *Off the Ground : First Steps to a Philosophical Consideraton of the Dance* (Princeton: Princeton University Press) 1988.

Struck, Peter T. "Sophron," Classics Dictionary of the University of Pennsylvania; see online at: http://www.classics.upenn.edu/myth/php/tools/dictionary.php?regexp=SOPHRON&method=standard

Sultan, Nancy. "Kithara," Perseus Encyclopedia. See online at:
http://www.perseus.tufts.edu/hopper/text?doc=Perseus%3Atext%3A1999.04.0004%3Aalphabetic+letter%3DK%3Aentry+group%3D1%3Aentry%3Dkithara

Telford, K. *Aristotle's Poetics* (Chicago: Gateway) 1961.

Tkatsch, J. *Die arabische Übersetzung der Poetik des Aristoteles und die Grundlage der Kritik des griechischen Textes*, 2 vols. (Vienna: Wien und Leipzig) 1928 and 1932.

Vatry, M. l'Abbé. "Dissertation sur la récitation des Tragédies anciennes," in *Mémoires de Littérature*, 8th book (Paris: L'Imprimerie Royal) 1733.

Vega, Lope de. *The New Art of Writing Plays* (*Arte nuevo de hacer comedias en este tiempo*, 1609), trans. William T. Brewster, in *Papers on Play-Making, op. cit.*, Brander Matthew.

Veloso, Cláudio William. "Aristotle's *Poetics* without *Katharsis*, Fear, or Pity," *Oxford Studies in Ancient Philosophy* Vol. 33, 2007 (Oxford: Oxford University Press). 255-84.
---. *Pourquoi la Poétique d'Aristote? DIAGOGE* (Paris: Vrin) August 2018 ("*Pourquoi*").
---. *Aristóteles Mimético* (São Paulo: Discurso Editorial/FAPESP) 2004.
---. "La valeur de l'objet de *mimeisthai* et ses enjeux," *Littérature*, Vol. 182, No. 2, 2016. 53-59.

Watson, Walter. *The Lost Second Book of Aristotle's Poetics* (Chicago: University of Chicago Press) 2012.

Webster, T. B. L. *The Greek Chorus* (London: Methuen & Co.) 1970.

Weinberg, Bernard. "Robortello on the *Poetics*," in *Critics and Criticism: Ancient and Modern*, ed. R. S. Crane, 319-348 (Chicago: Univ. of Chicago Pr.) 1952.
---. "Castelvetro's Theory of Poetics," in *Critics and Criticism: Ancient and Modern*, ed. R. S. Crane, 349-37 (Chicago: Univ. of Chicago Pr.) 1952.

West, M.L. *Ancient Greek Music* (Oxford: Oxford University Press) 1992.

White, S.A. "Aristotle's Favorite Tragedies," *Essays on Aristotle's* Poetics, ed. A. O. Rorty, 221-40 (Princeton: Princeton University Press) 1992.

Wilson, Peter. "Costing the Dionysia," *Performance, Iconography, Reception: Studies in Honour of Oliver Taplin,* eds. Martin Revermann and Peter Wilson (Oxford: Oxford University Press) 2008.

Woodard, R. D., ed. *The Cambridge Companion to Greek Mythology* (Cambridge: Cambridge University Press) 2007.

Woodruff, Paul. "Aristotle on Mimesis," *Essays on Aristotle's* Poetics, ed. A. O. Rorty, 73-95 (Princeton: Princeton University Press) 1992.
---. "Aristotle's *Poetics*: The Aim of Tragedy," *A Companion to Aristotle*, ed. Georgios Anagnostopoulos, *op. cit.*, 2009. 612-27.
---. *The Necessity of Theater: The Art of Watching and Being Watched* (Oxford: Oxford University Press) 2008.
---. "The Paradox of Comedy," *Philosophical Topics*, Vol. 25, #1, Spring 1997 (Fayetteville, AR: University of Arkansas Press) 1997. 319-35.
---. "Rousseau, Molière, and the Ethics of Laughter," *Philosophy and Literature*, Vol. 1, # 3 (Baltimore, MD: The John Hopkins University Press) 1977. 325-36.
---. *Antigone: Translated with Introduction and Notes* (Indianapolis/Cambridge: Hackett Publishing Company) 2001.

Xenophon, *Xenophontis opera omnia* (Oxford: Clarendon Press) vol. 2, 2$^{nd}$ ed. 1921, repr. 1971; transl. by E. C. Marchant and O. J. Todd, *Xenophon in Seven Volumes*, 4 (Cambridge, MA: Harvard University Press) 1979.

*Aristotle on Dramatic Musical Composition*

# Index

## Symbols

2-1-3 pattern 155, 158

## A

Abdulla 601
absolute necessity 153
Abū Bishr Mattā 13, 528
Abū-Bišr Mattā ibn-Yūnus 530
academic blinkers 156
Achilles 402
Achilles chasing Hector 509
acted the role of 251
action 153, 268
actions 268
actor of rhythmical tragic dance 307
Aegisthus 418
Aeschylus 68, 250, 252, 253
aesthetical pleasures 476
*agalmatopoios* 117
Agathon 260, 442
agathos 432
*agōn* 162
*agōnian* 298
*aisthēsin* 72, 73
Ajax 424
*akrasia* 476
Alcaeus 115
Aldine printing 542
*alēthinas* 311
Alexandrians 525, 598
al-Jurjānī 539
Alkaios 108
Alkman 50, 562
alleviate 476
amazement 427
amazingness 509
Amphiaraus 229
amusement/relaxation 295
Anakreons 174
Anaximander 514
Andronicus 433
Andron of Catane 175
animals' sounds 120
annual competition 298
annual theatrical festivals 341
Antheus 260
anthologist 582
anti-Aristotelianism 286
Antiatticist 526

Antidosis 297
Antigeneides 175, 176
*Antigone* 17, 415, 418, 419, 420, 462, 594
anti-metaphysical 595
*antistrophe* 37, 562, 563
apart from the *melos* and *rhuthmos* 304
Apellicon 446
Apellicon of Teos 366, 433
*aphosiōsis* 494
*apokathairomen* 496
*aporia* 299
Aquinas 540
Arabic scholars 598
Arcades 573
Arcadian education 109
Archaic 123
archetype 445
Archilochos 562
Archilochus 68, 191
Argives 17
Ariadne 563
Arion 562
Arion of Methymna 191
Aristarchus 462
Aristarchus of Samothrace 525
Aristides Quintilianus 68
Aristophanes 31, 57, 68, 150, 253, 264
Aristotelian aesthetics 501
Aristotelian comedy 500
Aristotle's classicism 517
Aristotle's empirical method 517
Aristotle's library 366, 408
Aristoxenus 28, 37, 65, 66, 67, 71, 84, 515
arrangement of ... incidents 353
arts 470
assemblage-of-three-elements 436
Athalie 567
Athena 17
Athenaeus 33, 50, 56, 57, 129, 131, 201, 408
Athenians raiding Sardis 141
Athenian Stranger 55
athetesis 386
athletics 52
Attalid kings 366
Auger 308
Augustan age 601
Augustus 308
*aulos* 170
*aulos*-type instruments 180
*Ausdruck(sform)* 251
autonomous 508
*autoschediasmatōn* 181
Avicenna 4
*azjāl* 535

## B

Bacchae 130
bacchants 111
Bacchic dance 26
Bacchic frenzy 335
Bacchic rite 327, 489
Bacchylides 563
Bacon 542
Bal 1
ballerinas 119
*ballet d'action* 574
banish pictures 486
banning indecent speeches 488
Barbaro 542
*barbaros* 514
bare language 259
Barker 29, 32, 42
Barnes 408
Bathyllus and Pylades 308
Battin 354
Baxter 2
beer 447
beliefs 538
believability 512
Bentham 511
Benveniste 101
*Berenice* 560
Bernays 407, 580
best plays 554
best plots 411
*bētarmones* 83
better citizens 486
bi-focal 497
biological definition 394
biological division 140
biped animal 416
*Birth Pangs of Semele* 175
black-and-white outline 462
Blasis 509, 577
Blocker 547
Boal 19, 596
bodily excellence 95
Boggess 537, 541
Bonnano 286, 589
boorishness 486
Brazilian-type militaries 597
Brecht 1, 2, 19, 595, 596, 597, 596
Brechtians 511
Briand 89, 107, 108, 326, 520
Brisson 29, 34
Broadway musicals 505
*Brothers Song* 116
Brunius 354

buffoonery 486
bull sound 252
bull-voiced 250
Bury 63
Butcher 588
Butterworth 534
butt of jokes 485
Bywater 438, 588
Byzantine 7, 446

## C

Cadmus 130
Calame 174
Callicles 38, 125, 403, 471
candle-makers 549
Carcinus 229
Carli 394
Cassandra 151
Castelvetro 460
catharsis as communication 602
catharsis in comedy 499
Cechetti 580
Centaur 221
Cervantes 570
Chaeremon 150, 221, 509
*chainé* turns 119
Chalcidian 488
changing senses of *rhuthmos* 93
chant 465
chapter breaks 291
characteristic of virtue 474
cheironomein 248
Chicago School of critics 587
*Children of Paradise* 307
choice 486
choir-master 62
choral composition 109
choral dances 567
choral songs of Aeschylus 171
*Choregi* 129
*choreia* 23, 37, 42, 110
choreographers 26
choristry 23, 37
*chorodidaskalous* 62
*choros* 74
choruses of satyrs with lyres 174
chorus leader 133
*chrōma* 118, 331
*chudēn* 462
Cicero 132, 544, 550
*Cid* 560
cinema 508
Cinesias 76

*Cinquecento* 559, 600
Cintio 543
circular chorus 563
clarification 352, 359, 360, 584
Classical period 174
classification 218
cleansing 580
Clinias 55, 91, 96
*Clouds* 31
Cohen 89
Coleridge 1, 2, 584, 585
Collingwood 263, 514
colours 258
*Comédies* 575
comedy 406, 484, 499
comic or "musical" *katharsis* 501
*Commentary on the Posterior Analytics* 542
commonality in tragedy and comedy 498
common function 364
competitions 466
composer 61
Comus 573
Connelly 16
*consideratio* 538
consonant 194
*Constitution of the Athenians* 466
contemplation 483
contrivance 512
Cooper 500
Cordova 533
Corneille 425, 560, 569
*corps de ballet* 145, 170
Corybantian worshippers 111
Corybantism 327, 489
Corybants 111
Crane 563, 588
Cratinus 448
*Crébillon* 575
Creon 17, 415, 418
Creon's elder son 17
*Cresphontes* 3, 418, 419
Cretan Harmonies 179
Cretans 97
Crete 563
Croatian 380
Croce 83
Csapo 30, 69, 174, 175
*Curetes* 130
Cyclops 443

D

Dacier 406, 421
Daedalus reproduction 253

Dahiyat 527
Damon 56, 57
dance 69
dancers' counts 75
dances 56
Dance Studies Association 89
dancing in accompaniment to spoken words 123
dancing on points 122
*Darstellung* 251
Darwin 514
Deburau 307
defining by division 139, 356
defining the individual 160
definition 138
definition of man 454
Delian girls 252
Delians 563
delightful 462
delight in mimesis 261
delivery 150
*Della forza della Musica* 579
Delos 563
Demetrius 129
Demetrius of Byzantium 129
Democritus 28, 68, 103
Demodocus 140
*Demoi* 175
de Montmollin 433, 451, 588
Demosthenes 252
Dennis 567
deontology 511
Destrée 382, 483
*deus ex machina* 163, 511
*diagōgēn* 321
*dianoia* 152
*diastēmata* 103
Dicaearchus 563
Dickens 149
Dickie 1
*Dictyulci* 443
didactic pieces 596
*diēgēmatikous* 208
*Die Mutter* 595
Dinos painter 122
Diogenes Laertius 369, 491
Dionysian chorus 49
Dionysodotos the Lakonian 50
Dionysus 55
Diotima 6, 23, 116
disastrous denouement 550
*disciplinae* 544, 600
*Discours* 560
discovery of the correctness of a belief 537
dithyramb 298

dithyrambs 215, 340
divergences of character 177
Dodds 328, 383
Dolon 252
Dorian mode 57
Doric poet 562
Dostoevsky 598
double metonymy 50
double-oboe 170
double-structure 418, 463
doubters 587, 601
drama as a literary form 575
dramatic incidents 152
dramatic musical creator 230
dramatic performances in the Arab world 536
dramatic speeches 381
*dramatikous* 206
*Dramaturgy* 575
Dryden 567
Dubos 565
*dunamis* 212, 385, 389, 510
*dys* 46

# E

eared owl 181
early classical 123
Early Classical period 174
early poets 58
*Edonoi* 250, 252
effect of tragedy 166
efficient cause 11, 141
Egyptian 180
Egyptians 88
Eichenbaum 587
*eikonopoios* 117
*ekdedomenois logois* 492
Eleatic Stranger 336
*Elements of Rhythm* 66
Elias 398
Eliot 1, 2, 594, 608, 618
Elizabethan drama 594
Else 250, 251, 451, 588
embellished speech 138
*emmelia* 39, 123
Empedocles 221, 225
emulation 255
*Encomium of Helen* 115
England 42, 63
*enharmonic* 39
enjoyment 467
*enthousiasmos* 324, 339
*enthousiastikais* 324
*enthousiastikas* 301, 302

enthrall 461
enthusiasm 300
*enthusiasmos* 339
*en tois peri poiētikēs* 368
Epameinondas 58
epic 206
epic poetry recited 466
epic rhapsode 465
Epicureanism 511
Epidauras 465
*epieikês* 462
*epieikēs* 430
epode 563
*epodos* 562
*epopoios* 117
equip a chorus 133
*ergon* 271, 438, 439
esoteric 492
essential conditions 138, 153, 399
*Esther* 567
ethical rhetoric 540, 542
*ēthikōtatais* 324
*Etymologicum Magnum* 373, 449
*eudaimonia* 483
*euharmoston* 60
eulogy 534
*eumelē* 292
*euphraneien* 462
Eupolis 175
*eurhuthmon* 60, 292
Euripides 247, 420, 443, 511
evil representations 488
exceptions to the rule 414
excerptor 583
exciting 491
exegetical philosophical responsibility 453
exegetical responsibility 452, 453
exoteric 492
*exō tou dramatos* 513
expiation 494
expression 251, 262
Expressionism 263
extraordinary suffering 423

# F

*Fall of Miletus* 422
fantastic image-making 256
Farnell 26
Father of Early Modern Medicine 527
fear 489
feet 195
Fendt 467, 509
Ferrara 543

Feyerabend 411
figures 67, 258
final cause 362
Final Cause 353
first philosophy 513
first rigorous chronological study 491
fitting together 29
Fitton 26, 57, 85, 113, 195, 251
focussing 589
Fokine 119
Ford 141
foreign cults 328
formal cause 7, 138
form of logic 555
form (*rhuthmos*) of atoms 102
forms of the mouth 194
*Formwerdung des Seelischen* 251
fortune to misfortune 417
four kinds of tragedy 422
four subspecies of tragedy 376
four sub-types 450
four sub-types of epic 465
four sub-types of tragedy 378
fourteen surviving tragedies 441
four types of tragedy 214
fractious babies 489
François vase 174
Freire 354
French neoclassical drama 594
frenziedness 339, 471, 489
Freud 580
friendliness 533
Friesen 89
*Frogs* 57, 505
Frye 587, 588
function 271
function (*ergon*) of tragedy 437
function of art 468
function of literature 601
function of tragedy 438

G

Garrick 575
Garrick's acting 575
*gelotopoioi* 252
general aesthetics 514
*geranos* 563
German theater 574
gesture 579
gestured dance 170
Gildon 567
*Giselle* 508, 509
give expression (to) 251

gladdening 462
goal of tragedy 459
goat 373, 449
gods 512
Goethe 575
Golden 553
Gonzalez 481
good dance 60
good judge of art 118
good tune 60
Gordian knot 547
Gorgian sense 523, 598, 599
Gorgian sense of poetry 535
Gorgias 6, 38, 53, 54, 403, 471
*Gorgias* 501e-502c 125
Gorgias combating earnestness with jests 493
Gould 539
*Grand Ballet d'Action* 578
Grassi 579
*Greek Laughter* 498
*Greek Satyr Play* 206, 163
Griffith 112, 327, 179, 328, 497, 163
Grube 588
Guarini 554
Gudeman 353, 380, 500
Guild of Artists of Dionysos 109
Gulley 588
*gumnastikē* 52
Gutas 530
gymnastics 52
*gymnopaidiai* 50

H

Habib 586
*hadēs* 465
*hadete* 465
Hall 442
Halliwell 285, 382, 476, 491, 498, 589
*hamartia* 418
Hamburg Dramaturgy 577
Hamburg National Theater 574, 575
hand-gestures 248
happiness 514
Hardison 538, 541
*harmonia* 23, 28, 32, 35, 199
Harmonia 28
*harmonia kai rhuthmos* 25
*harmonian* 58
harmony 23, 32
*harmony-steppers* 83
Harrison 447
H'Doubler 56
healing 328

Hector 402
*Hecuba* 562
*hēdonē* 463, 464
*hēdonēn* 468
*hēdusmenō logō* 138
Heinsius 566, 569
*Helen* 442
*hen* 46
*hendiadys* 53
Herculaneum 526
Hermannus Alemannus 13, 540
Herman the German 540
Herodotus 191
*heterophōnian* 61
Hill 56
hillside Dionysiac cult 328
history 551
*History of Animals* 140
Hofstadter 1
homeopathy 573
Homer 150, 264
Homeric Problems 434, 525
*homoiōmata* 258, 300, 311
honeyed movements 563
Horace 527, 540, 550, 551, 577
Horatian principles 482
*horon tēs ousias* 353
Hubbard 590
humanist 512
human sacrifice 17
hunting scene 253
*hupokeitai* 410
*hupokrisis* 287, 307
*hupokritai* 162
*hupomimnēskontos kai egeirontos* 73
*huporchēmata* 113
Hutchinson 298, 325, 326
Hutton 182
*Hymn to Apollo* 251, 308
*hypokritikē* 246
*hyporchēmata* 56
hypothesizing 410
hypothetical necessity 153, 161, 270
hypothetical structures of action 288

I

iambic 254
Iambic 485
Iamblichus 327, 405, 496
Ibn Quzmān 535
Ibn Rushd [Averroes] 539
identity 255
image-making 255, 257

imitation 255
imitation in metrical language 183
imitation of animate beings 253
imitations 258
impersonated 251
impersonation 255
improvisations 181
Indian classical dance 193
inebriated 448
infallible philosopher 317
inordinate pity 475
instruments 256
intellectual delight 511
intellectual enjoyment 295, 352, 379
*Ion* 442, 465
Ionic-Attic orbit 254
Ion of Chios 68
*Iphigenia* 17, 418
*Iphigenia in Tauris* 442
Isḥāq ibn Hunain 529
Isocrates 297
Istros 163
Ivanov 598

J

Jaeger 370
Janko 144, 397, 589
Javitch 527
jests 368
Jocasta 419
Johnson 577
*Jongleur* 536
Jonson 558
Justinian 526

K

*kalon* 60
*kamptô* 76
Kant 511
*kathairei* 496
*katharmous poleos* 382
*katharseōs* 321
*katharsis* 499
*katharsis pathēmatōn* 381
*khayr al-shi' rakdhabuhu* 539
*khoros* 108
*kineisthai* 41
*kinēseōs* 23, 33
*kinēsin* 178
*kinēsin kinountai* 178
*kinēsis* 33, 44, 165
*kinesis sōmatikē* 146
*Kinesthai* 44

*Kinētikon* 314
*King Lear* 259
*Kitharas* 170
*kitharistēn* 61
Kleolas of Thebes 175
Koller 250, 252, 264
Komarovich 598
*komast* 175
*kōmōdopoiois* 117
*koruphaios* 133
Korybantic 112
Korybantic performance 112
Korybantism 489
*koryphaios* 175
*kouphizesthai* 476
Kowalzig 69
Kraut 297, 298, 329
*Kresphontes* 418
*krokotos* 175
Kuhns 1
Kurke 54

L

Laban 82
Labyrinth 563
Labyrinthe 564
Lacedaemonians 97
lamenting heroes 473
lament of Odysseus 473
laments 473
lampoons 485
Landau 536
Landels 75
Lange 574
*L'Arte Poetica* 553
Lawler 29, 58, 69, 74, 373, 449
lead dancers 58
learnings 600
Le Bossu 567
*lēkuthion apōlesen* 79, 80
Lesbos 444
*Lesedrama* 590
*Les Enfants du Paradis* 307
Lessing 574, 575
Levinson 594
*lexeōs geloias* 190
*lexis* 40
Libanius 524
Liburnian cloak 253
*Life of Theseus* 563
limb 67, 68
literature 223, 594
literature perfected 589

Lobel 451
*logois psilois* 221
*logos* 40
*logous psilous* 120
Lombardi 543
Longinus 587
lost his bottle of oil 79
Louis the XIV 56
love song 535
Lucan 549
Lucas 149, 587
Lucas, Craig 591
Lucian 58, 307, 308
ludicrous 493
Lumière brothers 508
*lupeîsthai* 476
lyric poetry 113
lyric poets 111

M

Macedonian text 367
machine 162
Maenads 26
Maggi 543
Magnesia 173
magnitude 394
Mallette 3, 540
*mallon* 463
Malpas 3, 584, 590
manners of mimesis 149
Marceau 307
Marchetti 66
Margites 206
Margoliouth 25
Martinenche 571
Marx 381
masque 573
material cause 7
*mathēmatōn* 13, 377, 544, 600
*mathēmatōn katharsin* 354, 360
Mathiesen 31, 89
Matthews 571
McCoy 402
McOsker 530
McPherson 56
means of mimesis 144
measure of justice 102
*Medea* 419
medicine 322
Megareus 17
*megethos* 394
*melē* 61
melic poetry 108, 111

melkines 563
*melōdian* 61
*melopoiia* 106, 157, 268
*melopoiian* 153
*melopoioi* 111
*melopoios* 117
*melos* 43, 68, 89, 105, 106
Melos 110
*melpesthai* 59
*melpō* 106
Melpomene 157
*merē* 219
metaphor 247
metaphorical 254
metaphorical account of the origin of mimesis 254
metaphysical 513
*metarruthmizesthai* 102
metonymy 50, 53
*metra* 23
*metron* 105, 125, 197
*metrōn* 203
Meyer 28, 44, 54, 61
*mian* 396
*miaron* 392, 448
*miaros* 392
Michelangelo 551
*micron muthos* 201
Middlebrow 497
Middle Commentary 534
Mill 511
Milton 573
mime 253
*mimeisthai* 251, 252, 253, 257
*mimēma* 251, 253
mimes 221
mimesis 257, 263
*mimēsis* 251
mimesis as processive word 257
miming 253
*mimoi* 250
*mimos* 254
*mīmos* 251, 252, 253
Minoan 180
Minturno 553
M is a *mimema* of O 256
misfortune to fortune 417, 444
Mitrevski 367
mixed pleasure and pain 363
Mixed styles 475
Mnasitheus 165
Mnasitheus of Opus 145
moderate pity and fear 384
moderate villain 427
moderation 537, 548

modern hermeneutical methods 380
modern serious musical theater 510
modern "straight" plays 506
Moliere 571
*molpē* 113
monastery at Ikalto 144
Monk 566
Monroe 535
monstrous 464, 549
monuments 131
Moore 29
moral betterment 582
moral satisfaction 427
moral warning 585
Morrow 44, 54, 74
Morse code 193
most fundamental aspect of mimesis 250
motion 23
*mousikē* 6, 23, 26, 87, 110
*mousikēs* 58
movement sideways, forwards or backwards 563
moves 39
Munch 263
Munteanu 425, 464
Muses 118
music-dance 89, 157
music therapy 327
*muthos* 239, 272
*muwashshahāt* 535
Myronides 175, 176
Mythic statements 538

## N

Nagy 108, 115, 207, 210
Naples 579
narration 277
narrative 208
Natali 408, 488
natural causes of *poiētikēs* 189
natural recognition 420
Nauplios 175
necessary 153
necessary and sufficient conditions 361
necessary conditions 138
Nehamas 472
neoclassical drama 594
Neoplatonists 370
Nestorian patriarch of Baghdad 144
*Net Fishers* 443
New Comedy 505
New Critics 587
New Music 30, 64, 175, 563
Nietzsche 23, 589

*nombre* 569
nomes 39, 215, 303
non-Aristotelian drama 595
nonny-noes 33, 305
*Notes on an Elizabethan Play* 594
Notomi 6, 115
novel 223
Noverre 574
number 569
numerical limitation 192

O

*ōdais* 33, 42
*ōdas* 56
*ōdē* 110
Odyssey 83, 140
Oedipus 3
*oidē* 85, 447
Olympiodorus 369, 398
Olympus 300, 301
*On Dance* 308
one revolution of the sun 395
*On Interpretation* 182
*On "Musical" Composers* 491
*On Poets* 369, 401, 492
*On Poietic Art* 205
*On The Mysteries* 496
*On Tragedy* 175
*opsis* 213, 389
*Oration* 397
*Orbecche* 543
*orcheisthai* 74
*orchēseis* 56
*orchēsesin* 42
*orchēsin* 34, 97
*orchēsis* 38, 110, 516
*orchestes* 58
*orchesthai* 7
*Orchestica* 579
*orchēstōn* 170
orchestra-dancers 145
orchestral art 153, 203, 268
Orchestral art 47
*orchoumena* 35, 36, 41
ordered body movement 84
ordered temporality 51
*Oresteia* 443
Orestes 10, 418, 442
*Organon* 529
*orgiastikon* 491
origins of mimesis 254
Otte 381
outside the play 513

Owens 416
owl 261

P

Padua 543
*paians* 50
*paideia* 96
*paidia* 96
*paidotribikē* 297
pain and pleasure 498
*paizontōn orchēsin* 95
Pakaluk 381, 383
*palaestra* 57
*palē* 34
paleography 445
Panathenaia 331, 466
Panathenaic 16
pan-pipes 173
pantomime 307, 579
pantomime dance 515
pantomimes 579
pantomimic dancing 307
Pappas 133, 443, 447
*parabēnai ta tettara* 58
paradigmatic 42
paradigmatic axis 42
*Paradise Lost* 573
*paradosis* 451
*parakechrōsmena* 331
*Parisinus Arabus* 2346 530
*Parisinus Graecus* 13
Parliamentary Law of September 2 585
Parthenon 16
partial censorship 488
parts 219
*pathēmatōn* 13, 355, 366, 377, 381, 600
*pathēmatōn katharsin* 353, 365
Pauson 258, 310
Pazzi 543, 600
Peisistratos 180
Pentheus 123
Peponi 59, 179
*peranousa* 366
perfect *melos* 106
Peripatetic miniature 175
Peripatetic miniature called *On Tragedy* 589
*peri poiēmatōn* 129
*peri poiētōn* in three books 492
Perrin 563
Persae 39
Persian polymath 527
Persian shah 'Abbās I 144
Persian war 141

persuading 557
Petruševski 5, 351, 353, 381, 500, 587
Petruševskian 435
*Phaedrus* 141, 381
*pharmakeias* 322
*Philebos* 67
*Philebus* 44, 363, 497
Philip 252
Phillis the Delian 176
Philocleon 130
Philoctetes 372
Philodemus 370
Philoxenos 109
Philoxenus 175, 176, 336, 373, 449
*phobos* 489
*Phoenissae* 192
*phōnais* 41
*phōnas* 41
Phrygian 335, 491
Phrynichus 192, 422
Phrynis 175
*phthoggois* 61
*phusiologon* 221, 225
*Physics* 256
piety 533
Pindar 26, 130, 209, 252, 563
Pinter 203
pipe-playing 178
Platonic dichotomy 140
Plato's condemnation of poetry 141
play 97, 259
playful dancing 95
pleasure 463, 464, 467, 468, 471, 478
pleasure [arising] from pity and terror 478
*pleistē* 260
plot 214
plot in a literary sense 224
Plutarch 50, 366, 408, 563
Pocock 425
Podlecki 255
poet 130
poetry in English 205
*poiēsis* 8, 23, 26, 115
*poiēsis* in the Gorgian sense 526
*poiēsis* in the Platonic-Diotiman sense 523
*poiētai* 23
*poiētēs* 6, 11
*poiētikēs* 6, 336
*poiētou* 61
Poliziano 542
polluted 392
Pollux 58
Polybios 109
*polychordia* 30

Polygnotus 258, 310
Polyneices 17
polyphony 30
*polyphthongos* 30
Pompeii 442
Porphyry 526
Porter 175, 589
Poseideon 17
Posidonius 408
posture 59
potential 212
potentially performable 270
practical advice for poets 141
*pragmatōn rhēseis* 381
*pragmatōn sustasin* 353, 366
*praktikais* 324
*prattontas* 268
Prauscello 37
*praxeis* 268
*praxeos* 153, 268, 399
*praxeos mimesis* 438
predominant element 239
preliminary *diaeresis* of tragedy 138
Priam 402
primacy in the metaphysical sense 242
primary 241
Principle of Oral Addition 385
*Prior Analytics* 556
*Problems* 33, 39, 192
*Problems XIX* 33
Proclus 369, 406, 494
*prohairesis* 486
prologue 397
Pronomos 174, 175
*proorchesteres* 58
proper laughter 486
proper pleasure 438, 511
*prophorikos* 544
prosodist 530
prosody 195
*proton* 241
Prudhommeau 75
*psuchagōgei* 461
psyche 514
public address 125
published works 492
purgation 351
purification 351, 494, 581
purificatory rites 10
purified 496
Puritans 585
Puttenham 559
Pyrrhic 34
*Pythic Nomos* 106

## Q

quality 219
quantitative 219
Quintilian 550
Quintilianus 106
*Qur'ān* 534

## R

Racine 560, 567
Randazzo 79
random 462
Rashed 387, 453, 454
rectangular chorus 563
reducible to literature 285
*reductio ad absurdum* 239
reed-songs and lyre-songs 207
refutation 382
regular pattern 75
*Reinigung* 580
relevant pity and fear 417
relief 443
Rémond de Saint Albine 575
repetition 255
replica 253
re-present 264
reproduce the form 102
reproduction 255
respectable 432
*Return of Hephaistos* 174
rhapsodes 207
*rhapsōdia* 246
*rhein* 101
*rhēmasi* 40, 114
*rhēseis* 272, 435
*Rhesus* 252
*Rhetores graeci* 543
rhetoric 557
*Rhetoric* 494, 493, 249
rhetorical public address 125
*rhētorikē dēmēgoria* 125, 557
*rhipsauxheni* 26
*rhusmos* 68
*rhuthmizein ta paidika* 102
*rhuthmon* 58
*rhuthmos* 23, 34, 67, 101, 110
*rhuthmos* (dance) versus *orchēsis* ("ballet") 564
rhymist 530
rhythm 23, 66
rhythmical schemes 88
rhythmized objects 84
*rhythmizomena* 37, 68
*rhythmus* 515
Riccardianus 13

Richards 307
Ripe Archaic 123, 174
*riqah* 533
Robbin 39
Robert 307
Roblin 1
Robortello 543
Romantic period 601
Romantics 587
Rood 598
Rosenthal 593
Ross 406
round-dance 74
rule-based ethics 511
Russell 524
Russian Formalists 587
Rymer 567

## S

*Sack of Troy* 425
sacred rites 491
safety valve 585
Saint Albine 575
*saltatio* 579
*Samson Agonistes* 573
Sappho 108, 109
Saracens 540
Sardis 141
satire 534
satyr "act" 445
satyric 254
satyric dance 33
satyric poetry 201
satyr play 253, 373, 443, 449
satyr plays 16
satyrs 173
Scaliger 417, 506, 566
scary masks 422
scene-painting 164
Schaper 590
*schēmata* 58, 258, 298
*schēmatizomenōn rhuthmōn* 145, 170
*schēmatōn* 165
Schiele 263
Schironi 462, 524
Schlesinger 29
Schollmeier 418, 498
scientific knowledge 141
Sclafani 1
Scylla 33, 178
second Aristotle 527
secondary or tertiary goal 470
Seidensticker 443

*Semiramis* 576
serious Ballet 578
*Seven Generals against Thebes* 176
Shakespeare 571, 577
shameful things 496
Sheff 247
shocking 392, 419
showmanship 47
Sicily 253
*sicinnis* 33
Sidnell 545
Sidney 559
significant by convention 182
sign languages 193
signs 304
signs, of character 258
silly language 190
simple dances 564
Simplicius 526
simulation 255
sing and dance in a chorus 59
singers (victorious) at the Panathenaia 174
single 396
single speaking orator 192
Sisyphus 413, 425, 427
six conditions of tragedy 506
*skeuopoios* 117
Skopje 367
*Skylla* 175
Slater 524
Smerdel 5, 367, 380, 381, 500, 584
Smith 515
soap operas 596
Society of Dance History Scholars 89, 520
Socrates 58
Solbakk 581
solo and choral poetry 108
solo nome 109
solo performer-musician 107
*sōmasi* 41
Somville 145, 170, 455
song-and-dance 113
song-dance 109
song of the goat 447
song of the spelt 447
songs 56
*Sophist* 256, 264
Sophocles 150, 264, 420
Sophron 221, 224
Sorabji 430, 498
Sörbom 254
Sorbonne 453
Sosibios 50
Sosistratus 165

Spanish Armada 571
Sparshott 86, 383
Spartans 97
spectacle 532
spectacle 213, 389
spectators of *iambi* or of comedy 485
spelt 447
Spengel 584
Speusippus 443
*sphodra* 412
spirit of Aristotelian theory 510
spondees 196
*spoudaias* 399
*spoudaios* 430
Stagira 488
*stasimōteron* 314
state expense 332
statue of a river god 551
Stephanus number 578
Stesichoros 563
Strabo 366, 408
straight plays 511
strange bedfellows 429
*strophe* 37, 562, 563
St. Zenon's monastery 144
subject of the speech 273
sub-type of tragedy 411
sub-types 449
sub-types of tragedy 501
*Suidas Lexicon* 123
Sulla 408
Sultan 173
*sunalgeîn* 476
*sustasin pragmatōn* 381
*Swan Lake* 463
syllogism 556
Symbolists 587
*Symposium* 23, 28
synaesthetical 326
synecdoche 52
synonyms 41, 247, 526
syntagmatic 42
syntagmatic axis 42
Syriac 13
Syriac translation 600
*syristês* 173


T

tables and diagrams 433
Taplin 286, 589
*taqwā* 533

Tarán 12, 229
*technes* 470, 493
technical skill 486
*teleias* 393
*teleion melos* 106
teleologist 417
Telephus 164
Telestes 176
*telos* 435
temporality 51
temporal ordering 93
tendency to laughter 406
ten distinct genres 209
tetralogy 495
tetralogy structure 443
Thaletas 50
Thamyris 175
Theaetetus 133, 257
*The Art of Dramatic Musical Composition* 232
the art of the Muses 110
Théâtre des Funambules 307
theatre of the individual mind 289
theatrical orchestral art 333
theatrical performing arts 263
*theatrikēn mousikēn* 333
Thebes 17, 58
*The Capture of Miletus* 192
*The Crane* 563
*The Dying Gaul* 591
Themistius 397, 398
Theodorus 488
Theognis 68
theological 513
Theophrastus 175
*theoria* 483
the particular manner of flowing 103
*The Principles of Art* 263
therapeutic 491
*Thesaurus Linguae Graecae* 28
Theseus 174, 563
Thespis 397, 398
Thessalians 58
*The Theory of Moral Sentiments* 515
*The Trojan Women* 418
thoroughly villainous 413
thousand miles long 394
three types of chorus 55
Thucydides 68
*tibia* 176
vexed 425, 427
virtue 497
virtue ethics 511
virtue of wit 497
virtuosi 39, 303

Time or Measure 515
Timotheos 109
Timotheus 39, 336
Timotheus' piper 175
Timothy I 144
tin ear 523
Tiresias 130
*to eidolon eidōlopoiikē* 256
Toledo 540
tonal composition 31
*ton elenchon lekteon* 382
*Topics* 454, 455
total *dunamis* 438, 439
*Tractatus* 493
*Tractatus Coisilianus* 143, 407, 484, 495
tragedy 447
tragedy of character 423
tragedy of suffering 423, 438
tragic dance 308
tragic plot-types in general 417
*tragikē kinesis* 308
*tragikēs enrhuthmou kinēseōs hupokritēs* 308
*tragōidia* 431, 435, 447, 449, 497, 501, 507
*tragos* 373, 447, 448
trance 328
tri-focal 497
*Tripudium* 579
trivial plots 201
trochaic 254
trochaic tetrameter 254
troubadours 535
tumult 76
tuneless words 120
twenty-seven chapters 568
Tyrannion 433, 434
*tyrbé* 76

U

Ulanova 509
unaccompanied words 221
unhappy outcome 506
unities of time, place and action 551
University of Zagreb 380
Unmoved Mover 512
unspecified genus 274
utilitarianism 511
utilitarian notion of purgation 460

V

Vahlen 438, 592
valid forms of argumentation 556
Valla 542, 600
Veloso 250, 255, 259, 379, 470

virtuous 430
*Vita Ambrosiana* 209
Vives 543
Vodopija 379
Voltaire 575, 576
von Laban 82
vowel 194

# W

Wagner 75
*Wasps* 130
weak will 476
*Wealth of Nations* 515
Webster 50, 108, 109, 122, 131, 174, 562, 563
Weinberg 460, 544
well-educated man 60
West 173
Whalley 2, 158, 451
White 429
white boots 163
wholeness 393
Wilamowitz 380
*Wilhelm Meister* 575
William of Moerbeke 13, 540
wine 92, 485
wolfskin 252
Woodruff 194, 250, 262, 418, 438, 499
Woolf 593
wrestling 34
wrestling school 57

# X

Xenarchus 221
Xenophon 34, 58, 68

# Y

Yahyā ibn 'Adī 530
young ladies of St. Cyr 567

# Z

Zeus 299
Zeuxis 310
Zulatti 579

# ABOUT THE AUTHOR

After working in the ballet field professionally, Gregory Scott finished his doctoral dissertation, *Unearthing Aristotle's Dramatics: Why There is No Theory of Literature in the Poetics*, under Francis Sparshott at the University of Toronto, while also studying there under one of the esteemed 20th-century scholars of the *Poetics*, Daniel de Montmollin. Other mentors were Joseph Owens (Aristotle's *Metaphysics*) and Brad Inwood (Pre-Socratics). Scott then taught for four years as a full-time philosopher at universities in the U.S. and Canada. Afterwards, he simultaneously engaged in a post-doctoral fellowship under Sarah (Waterlow) Broadie at Princeton University (Philosophy) while directing the doctoral program in dance education at New York University (NYU).

Scott's publications include "The *Poetics* of Performance: The Necessity of Performance, Spectacle, Music, and Dance in Aristotelian Tragedy" (Cambridge University Press, 1999). His "Purging the *Poetics*" (*Oxford Studies in Ancient Philosophy*, 2003) has generated substantial debate on both sides of the Atlantic, with some internationally known specialists considering him on the basis of this article alone to have solved finally the problem of catharsis in Aristotle's definition of tragedy (the article is reprinted here as Chapter 5). He has also published on the philosophy of dance in journals such as *Dance Research Journal*, including "Twists and Turns: Modern Misconceptions of Peripatetic Dance Theory" (*Dance Research*, Edinburgh University Press, 2005). His *Aristotle's Favorite Tragedy: Oedipus or Cresphontes?* was published in 2016 and its 2nd edition appeared in 2018.

Scott has taught occasionally since 1995 in Humanities at NYU (SPS) and is finishing a book entitled *Aristotle's "Not to Fear" Proof for the Necessary Eternality of the Universe without the Unmoved Mover* (anticipated publication 2019-20). He can be reached at: gls62@columbia.edu.

www.ingramcontent.com/pod-product-compliance
Lightning Source LLC
Chambersburg PA
CBHW080847020526
44118CB00037B/2267